The Making of the Crofting Community

For Evelyn

THE MAKING OF THE
CROFTING COMMUNITY

James Hunter

JOHN DONALD PUBLISHERS LTD
EDINBURGH

The Publisher acknowledges the
financial assistance of the Scottish
Arts Council in the publication
of this volume.

ISBN 0 85976 014 6

Printed and bound in Great Britain by Morrison & Gibb Ltd., London and Edinburgh

Is an-aoibhinn dhuibh-se a tha 'cur tighe ri tigh, agus a' cur achaidh ri achadh, gus na bi àit ann, agus gu-n gabh sibh comhuidh air leth ann am meadhon na tìre!

Woe unto them that join house to house, that lay field to field, till there be no place, that they may be placed alone in the midst of the earth!

Isaiah.

I cannot bear evidence to the distress of my people without bearing evidence to the oppression and high-handedness of the landlord and his factor.

Angus Stewart, crofter, Braes, 8 May 1883.

The first man who, having enclosed a piece of ground, bethought himself of saying 'This is mine', and found people simple enough to believe him, was the real founder of civil society. From how many crimes, wars, and murders, from how many horrors and misfortunes might not any one have saved mankind, by pulling up the stakes, or filling up the ditch, and crying to his fellows:'Beware of listening to this imposter; you are undone if you once forget that the fruits of the earth belong to all, and the earth itself to nobody',

J.J. Rousseau, *A Discourse on the Origin of Inequality.*

PLACE NAMES

IN the course of the period examined in this book many Highland place names have undergone frequent changes of spelling. In order to obviate confusion, therefore, all place names are given the spellings found on modern Ordnance Survey maps.

Acknowledgements

I SHOULD like to express my gratitude to the many people who helped make this book possible. Dr. William Ferguson and Dr. John Bannerman gave me valuable assistance and good advice. Mr. Donald J. Withrington encouraged and assisted the project from the outset. Mr. Kenneth J. Logue directed me to sources I should not otherwise have discovered. The staffs of the Scottish Record Office, the National Library of Scotland, Edinburgh and Aberdeen University Libraries and the Public Libraries of Inverness and Stornoway were unfailingly helpful. The editors of the *Oban Times* and *Stornoway Gazette* gave me access to the files of their newspapers. Dame Flora MacLeod of MacLeod kindly allowed me to inspect the records of the Dunvegan estate. The Department of Agriculture and Fisheries for Scotland permitted me to consult parts of their Crofting Files that would otherwise have remained closed to me. Professor Derick S. Thomson kindly allowed me to make use of his translation of the poem *Spiorad a' Charthannais*. My thanks are due to Mrs. Alison Sandeson who drew the maps which appear in this book and to Mrs. Helen Perren who typed the greater part of it. I have benefited greatly from the work of past and present historians of the Highlands. And I am indebted to the many people in north-west Scotland who have discussed crofting matters with me at what must sometimes have seemed to them inordinate length. It is to them, to my own family and to my Highland upbringing that I owe my approach to the Highland past. Above all, I am grateful to my wife. She has lived with this project for a long time. But her enthusiasm for it has never wavered. To her, with love, this book is dedicated.

J.H.

Abbreviations

AHR	Agricultural History Review.
Ann. Rep.	Annual Report.
BoAS	Board of Agriculture for Scotland.
C.	Correspondence relating to the measures adopted for the relief of distress in Ireland and Scotland, 1846-47.
CBM	Central Board of Management of the Fund for the Relief of the Destitute Inhabitants of the Highlands of Scotland.
CDB	Congested Districts Board.
C.F.	Crofting Files.
Clan.P.	Clanranald Papers.
Croft. Comm.	Crofters Commission.
D.F.C.	Report of the Royal Commission on the Highlands and Islands (Deer Forest Commission), 1895; with minutes of evidence.
DNB	Dictionary of National Biography.
DoAS	Department of Agriculture for Scotland.
EHR	Economic History Review.
f.	folio.
f.n.	footnote.
HIDB	Highlands and Islands Development Board.
HIES	Highlands and Islands Emigration Society.
HLLRA	Highland Land Law Reform Asssociation.
J.M.N. Rep.	Report to the Board of Supervision by Sir John MacNeill on the Western Highlands and Islands, 1851.
MacD.P.	Lord MacDonald Papers.
MacL.P.	MacLeod of Dunvegan Papers.
Nap. Rep.	Report of the Commissioners of Inquiry into the Condition of the Crofters and Cottars in the Highlands and Islands of Scotland (Napier Report), 1884.
N.C.	Napier Commission. (Minutes of evidence to the above.)
NSA	New Statistical Account.
OSA	Old Statistical Account.
P.	Papers. (As in Ivory P.)
Pol. Rep.	Police Report.
P.P.	Parliamentary Papers.
Q.	Question. (In evidence to royal commissions, etc.)
Sea.P.	Seaforth Papers.
SGM	Scottish Geographical Magazine.
SHR	Scottish Historical Review.
SHS	Scottish History Society.

S.O.	Scottish Office.
SRO	Scottish Record Office.
SSPCK	Scottish Society for the Propagation of Christian Knowledge.
TGSI	Transactions of the Gaelic Society of Inverness.
THASS	Transactions of the Highland and Agricultural Society of Scotland.
Trans.	Transactions.
TRHS	Transactions of the Royal Historical Society.

Contents

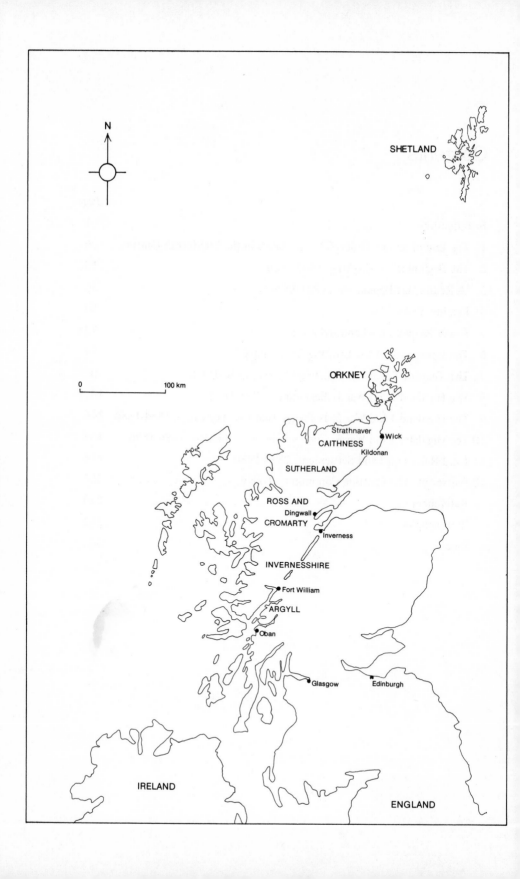

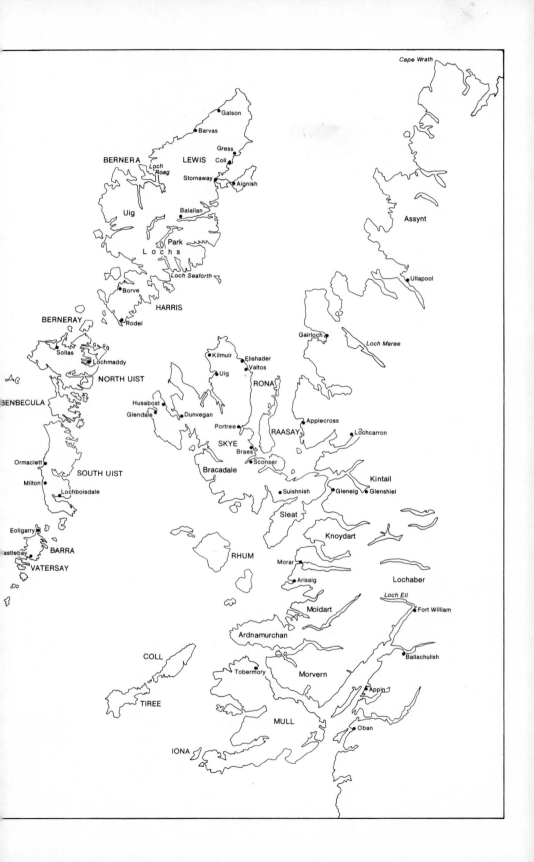

Introduction

THERE are today in the north-west Highlands and islands of Scotland some 10,000 crofters. (1) A few hundred live on the west coast of the mainland and in Mull; the remainder in Skye, Tiree and the Outer Hebrides, islands where crofters and their families constitute the greater part of the population and where crofting townships — typically consisting of straggling groups of variously designed houses surrounded by long narrow fields — are the predominant form of human settlement on the land. As in other parts of Europe's fragmented north-western fringe the land itself is poor and could not, one might justifiably think, be more unsuited to its task of maintaining a smallholding population. From the bare rocky hills of Skye and Harris to the undulating peat bogs of Lewis or the loch-bespattered surface of North Uist the dominating impression is one of infertility. Only in a few areas — in the Sleat peninsula in Skye and in some unusually sheltered parts of the mainland, for example — are there any trees worthy of the name. Elsewhere in the region, especially in the islands, there are almost none — the uniformly brown heathy landscape being broken only by a few relatively fertile straths, by the raised beaches that occasionally provide small low plateaus of gravelly soil between the hills and the sea, and by the swathes of green machair land that delineate the Hebrides' outermost rim. All these sites, particularly the machairs — natural grasslands which rest on the shell sands thrown up by the Atlantic and which occur spasmodically in Lewis, more widely in Harris and more extensively still in the Uists and Tiree — are the natural *foci* of crofting settlement; and the crofts that occupy them are conspicuously more productive than those consisting of a few acres of sour shallow soil reclaimed, over many generations, from the peat. But nowhere in the region is the crofter's lot an easy one. The most fertile croft cannot escape the frequent rain and gales that are a consequence of the north-west Highlands' proximity to the Atlantic depressions that track incessantly north-eastwards between Scotland and Iceland; and of all the numerous uncertainties of the crofter's condition, therefore, none is more permanent than the weather. In this book the natural hazards of geography and climate figure only occasionally — when a harvest does not ripen because of an unusually wet summer or is destroyed by an exceptionally severe autumnal gale; or when crofters are confronted with the task of winning holdings from previously uncultivated moorland. But the difficulties inherent in the Highlands' geographical position and circumstances are a constant backdrop to crofting history, and they should never be overlooked. That they are relatively unemphasized in this account is not because they are judged unimportant but because crofters have always considered the hardships that are the unavoidable consequences of their natural environment to be more bearable than those that have resulted from human action. The excessive and ostentatious comfort of a privileged few; their oppressive and unjust conduct: these have always seemed less tolerable than the vagaries of the climate and the general scarcity of resources. And

1

it is for that reason that this book deals more with the exploitation of man by man than with the unalterable conditions which have long defied men's efforts to create a prosperous agriculture in the Highlands.

Numerically insignificant and geographically distant from the centres of British industry, trade and political power, crofters exercise no great influence on the country as a whole. Nor have they done so in the past. Crofters and their families are, however, a distinctive social group. They possess their own culture, speak their own language and generally live their lives in a way long since abandoned in the rest of Britain. The uniqueness of the crofting way of life — itself a reason for studying the crofting past — has long been apparent. At one time it tended to provoke in outsiders a desire to sweep crofters and crofting into the dustbin of history and to remake the Highlands in the image of the southern British countryside. Today, principally because of the steady erosion of the nineteenth century belief in the self-evident virtue of 'progress', a quite opposite reaction is more common. In 1954, for example, a royal commission concluded that the crofting system deserved to be maintained if only for the reason that it supportee 'a free and independent way of life which in a civilization predominantly urban and industrial in character is worth preserving for its own intrinsic quality'. (2) And in the last twenty years that opinion has gained a growing number of adherents, a development accompanied by a radical revision of the crofter's popular image. To the nineteenth century advocate of industry and empire the crofter was an idle feckless fellow whose difficulties were largely of his own making — 'the natural fruits' of his own 'indolence and ignorance' , as one writer put it. (3) In the increasingly congested and polluted environment of urban Britain in the 1970s, on the other hand, the crofter is frequently idealised, his way of life romanticised, and the region in which he lives depicted as a placid pastoral haven in an ever more frantic world.

The Highlands of the tourist brochure and the holiday cottage are not, however, the Highlands of the crofter. The crofter has never been immune from the pressures generated by capitalist civilization. Indeed he has suffered from them more than most. And today, as the effects of a rapidly expanding tourist trade are supplemented by the consequences of oil-related industrilisation, such pressures are stronger than ever. The crofting tenant is no longer threatened with starvation when his crops fail or when the herring shoals do not materialise. And when his land is expropriated the process is more subtle and less violent than it once was. But the uncertainties of the crofter's day to day existence are nonetheless real and worrying. He has still to work hard for a meagre return. His holding is almost invariably small; his land often poor; his financial resources far from ample. His life, the crofter would agree, has its compensations. That is why he does not abandon it. But his independence is often more apparent than real, while such freedom as he does enjoy is purchased at a price which few of his urban admirers would be willing to pay. The crofter is consequently entitled to respect, not as a quaint anachronism who lives closer to Nature's bosom than the rest of us, but as one of that large majority of mankind which, in the face of immense difficulties, still wins a part of its living by its own efforts from the land.

Like that of peasant cultivators the world over, the crofter's way of life is more easily described than defined. The Napier Commission, that small body of men charged in 1883 with the task of conducting the first official enquiry into crofting conditions, tackled the problem by stating that the term crofter referred to 'a small tenant of land with or without a lease, who finds in the cultivation of his holding a material portion of his occupation, earnings, and sustenance, and who pays rent directly to the proprietor'. (4) Legislation passed since 1883 has modified the crofter's tenurial status, but as a delimitation of his social and economic position the Napier Commission's definition has yet to be bettered. The crofter, it makes clear, is the tenant of an individual holding. The returns from that holding usually meet only a part of his needs and consequently have to be supplemented in some way if he and his family are to attain an adequate standard of living. And he rents his land from a landlord and not from a superior tenant.

The second of these points — that the crofter is not a subsistence agriculturalist but a man who, while retaining his stake in the land, has always had to have an occupation ancillary to that of farming his holding — will be returned to again and again in this book. For present purposes, however, the first and last of these three statements about the crofter's essential characteristics are of most significance; for they show the crofter to be a relatively modern phenomenon. Until the end of the eighteenth century smallholdings occupied by single tenants paying rent to a land-owner had no place in the Highland scheme of things; (5) and the origins of the crofting system are consequently to be found not in the middle ages, as is often loosely supposed, but in the period which also witnessed the appearance of the cotton mill and the steam engine.

Apart from a brief glance at eighteenth century occurrences, this book is concerned, therefore, with the development of crofting and of crofting life from its beginnings around 1800 until 1930 when, with the virtual completion of the Board of Agriculture's land settlement programme, the modern pattern of crofting settlement was finally delineated. What follows is not, however, a history of the crofting counties as that expression has been understood since the passing of the first Crofters Act in 1886. Within the larger region the Gaelic areas are separated from the northern isles and much of Caithness by important historical and geographical differences. These have led not only to obvious cultural divergences but also to the physical structure of crofting in the Gaelic west being quite dissimilar to that prevailing in the three northern counties or, for that matter, in the eastern Highlands and in south and mid-Argyll. (6) Thus the heartland of the crofting community is and always has been the islands from Mull and Tiree to Lewis, and the west and north coasts of the mainland from Ardnamurchan to the borders of Caithness. In this district, the last bastion of Scottish Gaelic and the culture associated with it, is to be found the greater part of all the land held under crofting tenure. When the crofting community is mentioned it is usually the people of this area who are referred to. And it is their history that is recounted in what follows.

The 'making' of the title refers to the social, economic, cultural and political influences and events that have made the crofting community what it is. And the phrase 'crofting community' has itself been preferred to any obvious alternative because it is in common usage and because it comprehends all the people whose history is to be investigated:

the cottars or landless people, once numerous now few, as well as crofters in the strict sense of occupiers of holdings. Like any other group or class in society, however, the crofting community cannot be studied in isolation. One of the greatest of modern social historians contends that the phenomenon of social class occurs only 'when some men, as a result of common experiences ... feel and articulate the identity of their interests as between themselves and as against other men whose interests are different from, and usually opposed to, theirs' (7) — thus implying that the development of any social class can be understood only if its relations with other social classes are taken into account. And it is for this reason that Highland landlords and their policies loom large in the following pages. Their part is a considerable one not because this is their history but because in the western Highlands and islands during the period under consideration landlords constituted the ruling class. They brought crofting into existence. They decided which areas should be occupied by crofters and which should not. And most important of all, the emergence of a feeling of community among crofters was itself a consequence of their recognition of the fact that their interests and those of their landlords were mutually irreconcilable.

Because the conflict between those who owned the land and those who lived and worked upon it is a major theme of this study its approach to modern Highland history is necessarily different from that adopted in most recent books and articles on the subject. The majority of these — and there have been a lot of them — have been written by economic historians in an attempt to analyse and explain the modernisation of the Highland economy in the hundred years after Culloden. And most of them have been based on the surviving records of Highland estate managements. (8) The consequence has been that while old simplifications about Highland history have been replaced by scrupulously documented accounts of the way in which the modern economic structure of the region was established, the people upon whom estate managements imposed their policies have been almost completely neglected. In the present century, for instance, there has been only one serious attempt to evaluate the impact of economic change on the Gaelic consciousness — and that by a Gaelic poet, Sorley MacLean, rather than by an historian. (9)

This situation is in marked contrast to that prevailing in the nineteenth century when, with the exception of the self-justifying tomes produced by one or two landowners and estate managers, (10) accounts of what was then the contemporary history of the Highlands were usually written from a professedly popular standpoint. Such accounts were mostly propaganda pieces, written by radical critics of Highland landlordism when hunger and eviction were stark realities or when crofters were engaged in open conflict with their landlords. (11) As propaganda they were brilliantly successful. As history, however, they seem less than adequate to most modern historians simply because they were written by men who were totally committed to one side in the class struggle between crofters and proprietors. Recent writers have consequently tended to dismiss the works of their radically minded predecessors as the product of what one economic historian has called 'social prejudice'; (12) and their interpretation of Highland history is usually examined only to be refuted. Books which argue the crofting population's case — and which argue it forcefully, lucidly and sympathetically — have been published. It is arguable, however, that the modern authors who stand closest to the radical tradition of the nineteenth century (13) have, by the very strength of their commitment to it, done it a disservice. Their published histories, for example, are largely made up of refurbished versions of their precursors' books and pamphlets. Thus abstracted from their historical context, the older works are deprived of purpose and effect, their message is distorted and their undoubted weaknesses highlighted — facts that have made it easy for authors whose sympathies lie with Highland landlords to damn the few recent writers who have adopted an explicitly pro-crofter stance as, for instance, 'popular historians ... interested chiefly in the propagandist or sensational aspects' of the Highland past. (14)

In this book neither of these approaches to the older historical tradition is adopted. It is freely admitted that the popular view of Highland history is, as has been said on more than one occasion, (15) invariably prejudiced, frequently emotional and sometimes inaccurate. That view is not rejected, however. Instead, a serious attempt is made to understand it and to explain why the crofter's conception of his own past — as preserved in the nineteenth century books and pamphlets already referred to, in Gaelic poetry, in press and police reports of Highland Land League meetings and not least in the collective memory of the crofting community itself — is so radically different from the typical historian's portrayal of it. Such an explanation can be arrived at only by putting the crofter at the centre of his own history; and in essence, therefore, this book is an attempt to write the modern history of the Gaelic Highlands from the crofting community's point of view. The recent historians of the region may question the validity of this perspective and the soundness of the conclusions to which it leads. But if it illuminates crofters' attitudes to their own past, the writing of this account of it will not have been in vain.

1. The End of an Old Order: The Highlands in the Eighteenth Century

IN the world of the eighteenth century, Britain was recognisably unique. In the tumultuous events of the 1640s it had experienced the first great social and political revolution of modern times. A hundred years later it was embarking on the equally significant economic revolution that was to make it the world's first industrial nation. And though its political life was still dominated by a landed oligarchy, Britain's rulers, unlike many of their continental counterparts, were not feudal aristocrats; nor was their king an absolute monarch. In Scotland, admittedly, feudal jurisdictions persisted until the 1740s — an indication, if one was needed, that its earlier history had been very different from that of the larger, wealthier and more populous kingdom south of the Tweed. But in Scotland as in England the monarchic principles of prior centuries had never recovered from the assaults made upon them in the era of Cromwell and the Covenant. And it was as the heirs of the previous century's anti-absolutist revolutions that the Whig magnates of eighteenth century Britain held power. While still given to assessing their personal prestige and influence in terms of acreages owned, Britain's political élite were distinctly unfeudal in outlook. They measured their country's greatness in terms of its trade and commerce and in their quest for control of global markets they did not hesitate to wage war in India, in America and on the oceans of the world.

The society which supported the beginnings of imperialism was itself increasingly orientated towards the accumulation of wealth. Towns and cities were being built on the proceeds of the slave trade, the tobacco trade and a dozen other forms of commercial enterprise. By the century's end the construction of other cities was to be financed with fortunes created by that world-shattering invention, the factory. Nor was capitalism's advance confined to the rapidly expanding urban centres. The countryside too was being reorganised on commercial lines. As his fields were expropriated and his commons enclosed in the interests of an economically efficient agriculture, the peasant was vanishing from the land. And the land itself was being irrevocably altered as 'improving' landlords laid out fields and farms, planted woods and hedges; in short, brought the modern rural landscape into existence.

Beginning in England, these developments soon spread or were carried to other parts of the British Isles. In Ireland the last of the old Celtic society's semi-independent enclaves were overrun during the opening years of the seventeenth century. Thereafter the country was drawn inextricably into England's imperial ambit and its land parcelled out among English landlords. Politically merged with England since 1707 Scotland, for its part, was — by the middle of the eighteenth century if not before — clearly following the example set by its southern neighbour. Having at last gained unrestricted access to England's overseas empire, Glasgow's merchants were showing themselves to be every bit as enterprising and as successful as their counterparts in Liverpool or Bristol; while the lairds and farmers of the Lothians were embarking on the task of emulating and in the end surpassing the achievements of more southerly 'improvers'. (1)

By the 1740s, then, the modernisation of British society was everywhere proceeding apace; everywhere, that is, except in the Highlands of Scotland. There an older way of life persisted: a way of life whose social forms were based not on ties of economic dependency as was increasingly the case in the south, but on the much older bonds of kinship. (2) In the Highlands the descent group, defined genealogically and institutionalised as the tribe or clan, was the focus of all social, economic and cultural activity — a clan, as was noted at the time, being

> a set of men bearing the same surname and believing themselves to be related the one to the other and descended from the same common stock. In each clan there are several subaltern tribes ... but all agree in owing allegiance to the Supreme Chief of the clan or kindred and look upon it to be their duty to support him at all adventures. (3)

In the eighteenth century kin-based societies of the type thus described had long since vanished from the rest of western Europe and in attempting to enlighten his southern colleagues as to the true nature of Highland society Duncan Forbes of Culloden, author of that statement and one of the British government's principal representatives in the Scotland of the 1740s, had to contend with a conceptual gulf of considerable dimensions.

Even before Duncan Forbes penned his analysis of clanship, however, there were signs that the gulf between the Highlands and the rest of Britain might soon be bridged. Commercial interchange between the two societies was expanding at an unprecedented rate, its most important component being the export of cattle from the Highlands to the south. A part of Highland life since at least the sixteenth century, the cattle trade grew rapidly after 1700, largely because of the increased demand generated by the steadily developing southern economy. (4) Nor were southern influences on the Highlands confined to those associated with trade. Long addicted to dabbling in the politics of lowland Scotland, not to mention those of England and of Ireland, the higher ranks of Highland society were well accustomed to moving in two cultural universes: that of the Gaelic Highlands on the one hand and that of southern Britain and the rest of western Europe on the other. This tendency to be involved in southern as well as Highland affairs was particularly characteristic of the chiefs who constituted the apex of the traditional power structure. In the early eightennth century, depending on whether they favoured the Whigs or the Jacobites, many chiefs were as at home in Edinburgh or Paris as they were in the Highlands, and French or English rolled off their tongues as easily as — perhaps more easily than — Gaelic. While away from his clan, moreover, the typical chief — conscious since childhood of his immensely aristocratic status in the Highland society whence he came — felt obliged to emulate, or even surpass, the life style of the courtiers and nobles with whom he mingled. And it was at this point that the eighteenth century chief's two roles came into irreconcilable conflict with one another. As a southern socialite he needed more and more money. As a tribal patriarch he could do very little to raise it.

That is not to say, of course, that he did not make the attempt — the criticisms made of a late seventeenth century MacLeod of Dunvegan by Roderick Morrison, a blind Gaelic bard and harper, telling their own story:

> Théid seachd trusail air dhàil
> air each crudhach as gàirmhor srann;
> diallaid làsdail fo'n tòin;
> 's mór gum b'fheairrd' e srian òir 'na cheann...
> Cóig ginidhean òir –
> gun téid siod ann an cord d'an aid;
> urad eil' oirre féin...
> Théid luach mairt no nas mò
> 'm paidhear stocainn de'n t-seòrsa 's fearr,
> is cha chunntar an corr...
> Thig e mach as a' bhùth
> leis an fhasan as ùr bho'n Fhraing,
> 's an t-aodach gasda bha 'n dé
> m'a phearsa le spéis nach gann
> théid a shadadh an cùil...

Expenditure on such a scale had its inevitable outcome:

> An uair a thilleas e rìs
> a dh'amharc a thìre féin,
> 'n déis na mìltean chur suas,
> gun tig sgrìob air an tuath mu spréidh,
> gus an togar na mairt
> 'n déidh an ciùradh 's an reic air féill:
> siod na fiachan ag at,
> gus am fiarach ri mhac 'na dhéidh. (5)

In the seventeenth century, it must be said, such behaviour was unusual and indeed there is some evidence that Morrison's *Oran do Mhac Leòid Dhùn Bheagain*, from which these lines are quoted, did something to curb the extravagances of other chiefs. (6) The effects of *An Clarsair Dall*'s strictures were neither widespread nor lasting, however, and after 1700 the ostentatious extravagance and the commercial outlook which he had so bitterly condemned became increasingly prevalent.

Thus the Camerons of Locheil involved themselves in the West Indies trade; (7) while in Skye in the 1730s Sir Alexander MacDonald of Sleat and Norman MacLeod of Dunvegan sold some of their own clansmen into slavery. (8) In its cynical disregard of the bonds and obligations of kinship that episode was indeed 'a grim foretaste of the clearances'. (9) But still more indicative of what was to come were the contemporary developments on the Campbell lands in Argyll. There in the late seventeenth and early eighteenth centuries the Duke of Argyll's need for increased revenues was partially met by a drastic reorganisation of the tenurial relationships prevailing on his clan lands in mainland Argyll and on Mull and Tiree. The object of the reform was the production of higher money rents and the assumption on which it was based was that 'land should produce a revenue ... like any other capital asset and that it should therefore be allocated, not as a token of kinship, as a reward for allegiance or as a means of maintaining a following, but in response to the operation of competitive bidding'. (10) As R.H. Tawney once remarked of a similar shift in aristocratic attitudes to and beliefs about land in sixteenth century England,

It is easy to underrate the significance of this change, yet it is, in a sense, more fundamental than any other; for it marks the transition from the ... conception of land as the basis of political functions and obligations, to the modern view of it as an income yielding investment. Landholding tends, in short, to become commercialised. (11)

The commercialisation of the agricultural structure in response to chieftains' financial necessitousness — an undertaking in which the Campbells were eventually joined by every other leading family in the region — is the great fact of eighteenth century Highland history. From it all else follows. But it was not something that could be achieved within the context of traditional Highland society. Even the Dukes of Argyll had to temper the dictates of commercialised estate management with those of military security; (12) while chiefs who lacked the Campbell's extra-Highland power base were quite unable to interfere with existing tenurial arrangements to any significant extent. The reason was simple. Until 1746 the Highlands lay outside the effective limits of British jurisdiction; and the law and order which were necessary preconditions for the commercial and industrial developments occurring in the south were consequently absent. In England or lowland Scotland 'the turbulent days' when 'lords had ridden out at the head of their retainers to convince a bad neighbour with bows and bills; and a numerous tenantry had been more important than a high pecuniary return from the soil', (13) had long since passed away. In the Highlands, however, a chief's status and even his life still depended on the number of armed men he could command — a truth encapsulated in MacDonnell of Keppoch's famous remark that his rent-roll consisted of five hundred fighting men, (14) and one that was reflected in the traditional agrarian system.

The essential feature of that system was that it depended on land being laid out to ensure the continued existence of the clan as a socially unified and militarily effective organisation, considerations of agricultural efficiency being of decidedly secondary importance. Most of a clan's territorial possessions were consequently held by tacksmen, an essentially military caste for whom courage and prowess in war were the ultimate virtues. Tacksmen were generally kinsmen of the chief to whom they paid only a nominal rent for their farms — on the understanding that their principal role was to provide him with skilled soldiers rather than with cash. Inordinately conscious of their status as the *daoine uaisle* or gentlemen of the clan, most tacksmen did not deign to soil their hands with the day to day tasks of farming, a role assigned to the subtenants to whom the tacksmen sublet the greater potion of their farms or to the cottars and mailers who, as the subtenants of subtenants, constituted the lower orders of the clan. (15)

The traditional landholding system thus supported a formidably efficient military machine which was bound together by a chain of command and kinship stretching from the chief through his lieutenants, the tacksmen, to the subtenants and cottars whose function and duty it was to make the apparently undisciplined but undeniably devastating charges which were the basis of Highland warfare. Burdened with such an intricate array of tenures and subtenures the land was clearly incapable, however, of yielding its full agricultural potential and though the clan could scarcely be bettered as an instrument of war its rent-producing capacity was extremely limited. Nor could that capacity be easily increased. The bonds of kinship and mutual obligation on which the clan was based effectively precluded the introduction of impersonal money relationships and it was consequently obvious to even the most casual of eighteenth century observers that if a clan's lands were to produce a worthwhile rental for its chief the multiple gradations of the traditional society would have to be swept away and the land let directly to men who were willing and able to work it efficiently and to pay a realistic money rent for the privilege of so doing. This in fact was the aim of the Campbell reforms already referred to. No chief, however, could effect such a revolution without alienating the tacksmen upon whom, in the unsettled conditions prevailing in the region, his own survival depended. In the Highlands, therefore, a chief's conduct had to conform, at least approximately, to the standards of the traditional society rather than to those prevailing in the commercial world in which he spent a growing amount of his time and to which he was increasingly attracted. As far as his clansmen were concerned he could transgress the southern moral code and the Scottish or British government's laws with impunity; but he could not introduce the apparatus of southern landlordism. To have done so would have been to invite his own downfall. It was a predicament resolved only by the forcible incorporation of the Highlands into the social and political system of Great Britain.

The eventual subjugation of the Highlands was perhaps inevitable. The problem of how to pacify the region was one that had taxed successive Scottish governments long before any administration in London was called upon to tackle it. And in the last analysis it was most improbable that two societies as unlike each other as that of the Gaelic Highlands and that of the rest of Britain could coexist in close proximity for any length of time. That Highlanders were left largely to their own devices for so long was to some extent a consequence of their homeland's relative remoteness. More fundamentally, however, it was a consequence of the nature of the southern economy's demands on the Highlands. In the seventeenth and eighteenth centuries, as in more modern times, traditional societies which were felt to stand in the way of English or British interests were habitually destroyed. In Ireland, for example, a Celtic society very similar to that of the Highlands was ruthlessly obliterated; and the Indian peoples of the eastern part of North America were wiped out in the same way. In both cases, however, the motive was principally that of clearing the way for colonisation; and where such a motive was absent British commercial interests were quite content to leave traditional societies alone — as long that is as they produced the required goods. (16)

The Highlands, although part of Scotland and, after 1707, of Britain, were remote and infertile. They consequently offered little to attract the coloniser; (17) while the British economy's main requirement from the area, black cattle, could demonstrably be obtained without incurring the trouble and expense of effectively subordinating the cattle rearers to British rule. Despite the absence of a simple economic motivation for such a development, however, the early eighteenth century was characterised by a steadily growing British military presence in the Highlands. The reasons had little to do with black cattle. They derived from essentially political and strategic considerations which turned on the fact that the Highlands were the last great reservoir of Jacobitism in the British Isles.

Why Highlanders should have been so devoted to the cause of the exiled Stuart monarchy is a complex question which has never been satisfactorily answered, least of all by the hosts of romantic writers who have dwelt so lovingly on every detail of Highland Jacobitism. (18) What is clear, however, is that a government of capitalist aristocrats — which habitually acted in the interests of an increasingly powerful mercantile class and which was for that reason engaged in a protracted struggle with France for control of world markets — was unlikely to tolerate the indefinite existence within its frontiers of a stronghold of an older way of life which could and did serve as a convenient springboard for Jacobite and French attempts to renew in Britain the debilitating civil conflicts of the seventeenth century. Successive Jacobite risings were consequently followed by ever more determined efforts to suppress Highland Jacobitism, the final stages of the process being initiated by the amazing successes achieved by that small Highland army which in a few short months in 1745 conquered Scotland and marched to within 127 miles of London. Decidedly shaken by these events the British government determined to destroy the traditional society of the Highlands, thus ensuring that Highlanders could never again challenge Britain's imperial might. The outcome was Culloden and the bloody and brutal repression which followed it.

The significance of Culloden was not that it was a catastrophic defeat for Highland arms. There had been such defeats before and at the time most Highland Jacobites considered Culloden to be little more than a singularly unfortunate prelude to a future renewal of hostilities. (19) What distinguished Culloden from previous reverses, however, was the fact that it was merely an overture to a massive assault on the social and political institutions of clanship. In 1746 and in the years that followed clansmen — Jacobite and non-Jacobite — were disarmed finally and completely, the wearing of the Highland dress was prohibited, and the chiefs' judicial powers over their clans were abolished — developments that were accompanied by a determined attempt to modernise the Highland economy and to integrate the region and its people into a civilization from which they had hitherto kept aloof. (20)

The immediate effect of these events was to accelerate and enforce the modernising tendencies already at work in the Highlands. The destruction of the clan as a paramilitary organisation and the establishment of law and order as these things were understood in the south meant that chiefs had no further need for the military services of their clansmen. It also meant that chiefs were divested of their traditional trappings and that their social status consequently depended more than ever on the amount of cash at their disposal. As a contemporary Highlander put it, 'The number and bravery of their followers no longer supports their grandeur; the number and weight of their Guineas only are put in the scale'. (21) After 1746, therefore, the incentive to exploit land commercially became stronger than ever before. And as a result of the government's post-Culloden policies, the obstacles which the traditional society had put in the way of such exploitation were removed.

As the need for commercial profitability became the dominant influence in estate management, Highland chiefs or landlords as they now were fell into an easy and inevitable alliance with the commercial and industrial capitalism of the south; easy because southern society enabled them to gratify their aristocratic tastes and aspirations; inevitable because in the south were to be found rapidly expanding markets for their produce. At first Highland landlords made desultory attempts to promote indigenous economic development. (22) But in the face of natural difficulties and southern competition native Highland industry was doomed to unprofitability, and industrial ventures consequently failed or were abandoned as their promoters increasingly concentrated on the export of the raw materials needed by the urban and industrial south.

In the second half of the eighteenth century, therefore, the old semi-independence of the Highland economy was transformed into an essentially neocolonial subordination to the requirements of the developing industries of England and lowland Scotland. (23) At first black cattle, the Highlands' traditional export, continued to be virtually the only saleable product of Highland estates.(24) But in the fifty years after 1760 the place of cattle was more and more effectively challenged by two new commodities: wool and kelp. The large scale production of both these materials required a massive transformation of the Highlands' traditional agrarian system; and it was in the course of the consequent changes that crofting, as we know it today on the north-western seaboard and in the Hebrides, came into existence.

In 1773, only twenty-seven years after Culloden, Dr Samuel Johnson came to the Highlands hoping to discover 'a People of peculiar appearance and a system of antequated life'. He found, to his evident chagrin, that he had come too late:

> There was perhaps never any change of national manners so quick, so great, and so general as that which has operated in the Highlands by the late conquest and the subsequent laws ... The clans retain little now of their original character. Their ferocity of temper is softened, their military ardour is extinguished, their dignity of independence is depressed, their contempt for government subdued, and their reverence for their chiefs abated. (25)

Nearly a century later, Johnson's judgment that the events of the 1740s had destroyed clanship for ever was echoed by the Court of Session, the fount of Scottish legal wisdom:

> When all military character, all feudal subordination, all heritable jurisdiction, all independent authority of chiefs are extracted from what used to be called a clan, nothing remains of its essential character and peculiar features. (26)

Although such statements about the demise of clanship are not altogether unfounded, the nature of the historical changes involved in the traditional society's collapse was undoubtedly more complex than was realised by Dr. Johnson or by the Scottish judiciary of the 1860s. The institutional forms of a society with a continuous history of at least a thousand years were, it is true, destroyed simply by passing and enforcing laws that abolished them. The mental attitudes and beliefs engendered by the Highlands' traditional social system could not be so easily erased, however, and the economic transformations outlined above consequently precipitated a crisis of cultural adaption that has left its mark on a great deal of the subsequent history of the Highlands.

Principally because they had been gradually absorbing southern ways and attitudes for many years before 1746, Highland chiefs took to their new roles with alacrity. And the British government was therefore able to pursue its policy of modernising the Highlands, not by expropriating the Gaelic aristocracy as had been done in Ireland, but by winning the upper rank of the old order to its side. Only the relatively small number of chiefs who had played an active part in the last Jacobite rebellion were exiled or executed — and even their lands were returned to their families in 1784. The remainder were left in undisturbed possession of estates of which they were now considered to be the outright owners. All concept of the kindred's interest in the land was consequently cast aside, while the encouragement thus given to former chiefs to become landlords on the southern model virtually shattered the already weakening paternal affection which the traditional chief had felt for his clan.

By the eighteenth century's end any lingering traces of a patriarchal outlook had been strictly subordinated to the pursuit of profit, (27) and Highland 'chieftains' were firmly set on the road to becoming the landed and anglicized gentlemen that they have ever since remained. And in subjecting the dictates of kinship to those of financial expediency the Highlands' ruling class did not, contemporaries agreed, experience any undue difficulty:

> The more necessitous, or the less generous, set the example; and one gradually followed another, till at length all scruple seems to be removed, and the proprietors in the Highlands have no more hesitation than in any other part of the country in turning their estates to the best advantage. (28)

That was written in 1805. As early as 1750, however, a government agent had noted that some Highland lairds had already 'screwed their Rents to an extravagant Height', (29) and during the next twenty years the 'rage of raising rents', commented on by a traveller in Lochaber in 1764, (30) spread throughout the Highlands. But while the most remarkable feature of the chiefs' response to the commercial order was thus the ease with which they adapted to it, the reaction of the lower strata of the traditional society was significantly different.

First to feel the full force of the wind of change were the tacksmen whom chiefs *cum* landlords not unnaturally wished to transform into the businesslike farmers who were the mainstay of estate economies in the south. Most tacksmen, however, were unwilling or unable to make the requisite adjustment. Tied to the traditions of their caste they were usually more concerned to keep up a host of unproductive dependents and retainers than to cultivate habits of industry and thrift. As the military side of clanship passed into history the tacksmen consequently became the bogeymen of the 'improvers', hopeless reactionaries whom landlords increasingly thought of as expensive and not altogether desirable luxuries on their estates. (31) Tacksmen's traditional tenancies were therefore ended and their lands offered to the highest bidders; developments which tacksmen — who had long considered their lands to be almost as much the inheritance of their families as of the chief from whom they held them (32) — greeted with an incredulity which rapidly turned into resentment. And as a Highland traveller observed in the 1770s, 'Resentment drove many to seek a retreat beyond the Atlantic'. (33)

The extraordinarily complete emigration or migration of the tacksmen is still represented as a catastrophe which deprived the Highlands of its nascent middle class and the region's small tenants of their natural leadership (34) — despite the fact that popular sayings, like

> Is don an gabhalach
> Ach don an donuis
> Anns an ath-ghabhalach, (35)

indicate that the tacksmen's social inferiors were not greatly saddened by their departure. The real significance of the tacksmen's decision to take themselves off to America, however, is not that it left the clans' lower orders without leaders but that it provides a measure of the literally awesome problem of adjustment which ordinary Highlanders faced. If the tacksmen, men who were usually well educated and knew something of life outside the Highlands, could not adapt to the situation created by the establishment of commercial landlordism, how could the much less well equipped commons of the clans make the still greater adjustments required of them?

The answer was simple. They could not. Left to fend for themselves in a strange and hostile environment in which the land of the kindred could be sold for cash and the people who lived on the land treated as an element in a calculation of profit and loss by men 'grown so niggardly', as a Hebridean poet remarked in the 1760s, that they 'would geld a louse if it would rise in value a farthing', the small tenantry of the north-west Highlands could take refuge only in a profound sense of betrayal:

> Dh' fhalbh na ceannardan mileant'
> Dh' an robh sannt air an fhìrinn,
> Dh' an robh geall air an dìlsean
>   Agus cuing air an nàmhaid ...
>
> Seallaibh mun cuairt duibh
> Is faicibh na h-uaislean
> Gun iochd annt' ri truaghain,
>   Gun suairceas ri dàimhich;
> 'S ann a tha iad am barail
> Nach buin sibh do'n talamh,
> 'S ged dh'fhàg iad sibh falamh
>   Chan fhaic iad mar chall e;
> Chaill iad an sealladh
> Air gach reachd agus gealladh
> Bha eadar na fearaibh
>   Thug am fearann-s' o 'n nàmhaid ... (36)

The waning of chieftainly prestige, a development amply testified to by these un-surprisingly bitter verses, was also remarked on by the increasingly numerous travellers in the Highlands. The chiefs, Johnson noted in the 1770s, had 'already lost much of their influence; and as they gradually degenerate from patriarchal rulers to rapacious landlords, they will divest themselves of the little that remains'. (37) The accuracy of the Doctor's gloomy predictions was inexorably borne out by events until, by the turn of the century, it was possible for another visitor to the region to observe — with some surprise — that Highland landlords, 'instead of being almost adored', were 'in general despised'. (38) By about 1800, therefore, the tenantry of the Highlands had already begun to discard, albeit reluctantly, the duties and obligations imposed on them by their sense of clanship. In the next few years, as those of them who did not follow the tacksmen to America were converted into crofters, the need for such a coming to terms with the realities of the Highland situation was to become still more pressing. But the emergence of the modern crofting community from the dispirited and demoralised commons of the clans was destined to be a slow as well as an intensely painful process.

2. The Beginnings of Crofting, 1800-1820

Na Caoraich Mora or big sheep, as Highlanders called southern graziers' Blackface and Cheviot stocks in order to distinguish them from their own smaller and wirier breeds, were introduced into Perthshire from the lowlands in the 1760s. By 1800 they had largely replaced black cattle as the main agricultural product of those parts of the Highlands that lie to the south of the Great Glen. And in the years around the turn of the century, a time of soaring wool prices, the white tide swept on northwards and westwards into Inverness-shire, Ross-shire, Sutherland, and the Hebrides. (1) 'In this as in every other instance of political economy,' remarked James Loch who, as the Sutherland family's estate manager and business adviser, knew all there was to know about the coming of the big sheep,

> the interests of the individual and the prosperity of the state went hand in hand. And the demand for the raw material of wool by the English manufacturers enabled the Highland proprietor to let his lands for quadruple the amount they ever before produced to him. (2)

Even Karl Marx, who was as bitter in his condemnations of capitalism as Loch was exultant in its praises, and who saw in the events associated with the introduction of sheep farming into the Highlands a particularly vicious manifestation of the general process of making 'the soil part and parcel of capital', (3) could scarcely have coined a more forceful expression of the connection between Highland 'improvement', as its promulgators liked to call it, and southern industrialisation. Industrial demand for wool and the need for ever larger quantities of mutton to help feed the burgeoning populations of southern towns: these made the commercial exploitation of the Highlands' pastoral resources almost as welcome to southern industrialists as to Highland landowners. And it was for this reason, as the English poet Robert Southey remarked during his tour of the Highlands in 1819, that the political economists of the time had 'no hesitation concerning the fitness of the end in view, and little scruple as to the means'. (4)

The means, of course, were the clearances; and with them the beginnings of crofting are inectricably bound up. According to Marx and to Donald MacLeod the Sutherland stonemason who was another of Highland landlordism's early critics, the displacement of whole populations by a few sheep farmers and their shepherds amounted to nothing less than 'reckless terrorism', (5) Crofters were to take the same view. Their landlords, however, considered the clearances to be a necessary precondition to the establishment of an economically efficient agricultural system in the Highlands, and with regard to sheep farming they were probably correct. As one of their apologists remarked at the time:

> Sheep cannot be cultivated to a profit unless in large flocks... Small capitalists cannot thence manage them; and thus arises the necessity of large sheep farms. (6)

The great increase in wealth and production brought about by the arrival of *na caoraich mora* consequently created no opportunities for the small tenants who constituted the bulk of the Highlands' population. (7) Lacking the capital and expertise of the south country graziers who dominated Highland sheep farming from the start, the original land-holders were ousted and dispossessed. Their landlords made no attempt to remove them from their estates, however. An obstacle in the sheep farmers' way they might have been, but they retained their usefulness; for without the participation in it of the region's small tenantry, the kelp industry of the north-west Highlands and Hebrides — an even more profitable enterprise than sheep rearing itself — could not have functioned for a single day.

Kelp, an alkaline seaweed extract then used in the manufacture of soap and glass, was first made in Scotland in the 1720s. At that time the industry was con-fined to the Forth estuary and the Orkneys; but in the 1740s it spread to the western isles and by the mid-1760s was firmly established in all the Hebrides and on parts of the north-western coast of the mainland. (8) Until the 1760s, when the average price of kelp first exceeded £2 a ton, landlords were generally unaware of the industry's growth potential and of its possible value to themselves. Most of the early profits from Hebridean kelp were consequently pocketed by a few enterprising tacksmen and by a small band of independent entrepreneurs, most of them Irish-men. (9) The landlords' state of innocence was of short duration, however. Increasing industrial demand for kelp pushed its price steadily upwards. By the 1790s, when imports of Spanish barilla — kelp's main rival as a source of industrial alkali — were cut off by French military action, the average price was in the region of £10 a ton, and even that figure was transiently doubled in the 1800s. (10) Production was accordingly stepped up. Profits rose markedly. And landlords, making up for their initial dilatoriness, stepped in and took over the industry, establishing legal rights to the seaweed on which it was based and taking control of all its productive and marketing sequences from the cutting of the ware to the unloading of the kelp on the Liverpool and Glasgow waterfronts. (11)

In the opening years of the nineteenth century between 15,000 and 20,000 tons of kelp were annually exported from the Hebrides. (12) The profits accruing to the islands' owners were estimated to be in the neighbourhood of £70,000 a year, (13) the accuracy of the estimate being testified to by the size of individual proprietor's takings. Between 1807 and 1809, for example, Clanranald's annual average income from kelp sales was £9,454, a figure which compared very favourably with his land rental of £5,297. (14) The kelp made on Clanranald's South Uist estate was admittedly among the best and most valuable in the Hebrides. (15) But even those landlords whose properties were somewhat less favoured by natural circumstances had little cause for complaint. The kelp produced on Lord MacDonald's North Uist estate was reckoned to be worth 'nearly double' the island's land rent, (16) and its sale accounted for the greater part of Lord MacDonald's reputed kelping income of £20,000 a year. (17) Lewis kelp was calculated to be worth £3,500 a year after expenses — and that was a notably conservative estimate made by the trustees of the island's proprietor, MacKenzie of Seaforth, some years after the height of the boom. (18) MacNeill of Barra and the Duke of Argyll — who had considerable kelp-ing interests in Tiree — benefited proportionately; (19) and although equally immense gains were quite beyond the reach of landlords whose properties were situated on Mull, Skye, or the mainland, areas where seaweed was in less abundant supply, there was scarcely an estate in the north-west Highlands where kelp was not an important source of revenue.

The vast profits which thus accrued to the region's landowners were secured, in the last analysis, by a labour force consisting of as many as 10,000 families (20) whose members — men, women and children alike — cut, gathered, dried and incinerated the seaweed during the Highland kelping season which began in April or May and continued into August. The seaweeds harvested were principally the deep sea tangle thrown up on the Outer Hebrides' west coasts, and the knobbled, black and bladder wracks which cover the rocky shores that are to be found all around the north-west coast of the mainland as well as in the Inner Hebrides and on the eastern seaboard of Lewis, Harris and the Uists. The growing weed — which made much finer kelp than that cast up by the Atlantic — had to be cut from the tidal sounds or rocky islets where it grew most profusely by kelpers whose work places were often an island's breadth away from their homes. Once cut it was dried in the sun and wind — a process calculated to occupy no more than three of the warm sunny days which commonly occur in the north-west Highlands in early summer. The dried weed was carried in carts and creels to the kilns, long low constructions of stone built handily on a nearby beach and filled with peat. The peat was fired and the seaweed spread on top. It was then carefully reduced to ashes, the alkaline residue or kelp accumulating at the kiln's base as a glowing molten mass which cooled into the brittle, bluish material that was eventually shipped to the glass and soap works of England and lowland Scotland. (21)

Kelping was clearly an arduous occupation. One traveller commented that compared to the kelpers' way of life 'the state of our negroes is paradise'. (22) Other observers agreed. Kelpers' working conditions, wrote one of them, were much worse than those of southern factory hands (23) — and that, in the early years of industrialisation, was no facile comparison:

> If one figures to himself a man, and one or more of his children, engaged from morning to night in cutting, drying, and otherwise preparing the sea weeds, at a distance of many miles from his home, or in a remote island; often for hours together wet to his knees and elbows; living upon oatmeal and water with occasionally fish, limpets, and crabs; sleeping on the damp floor of a wretched hut; and with no other fuel than twigs or heath; he will perceive that this manufacture is none of the most agreeable. (24)

Hardships like these would have been rendered more tolerable by adequate remuneration. But kelpers' returns were extremely meagre; amounting to only a tiny fraction of the gross proceeds of kelp sales.

That the kelper made comparatively little money from his labours was not his fault. Kelping was an ideal trade for a small tenant to engage in. The process of production was simple, requiring only a few elementary tools: sickles to cut the ware and the long iron pokers known as 'clatts' which were used to stir the burning seaweed in the kilns. As a result of their own remoteness from southern markets and their landlords' determination to gain control of the industry, however, kelpers were quickly reduced to the status of wage labourers whose earnings bore little relation to the selling price of the material they produced. (25) Varying slightly from one area to another, kelpers' wages generally stood between £1 and £3 a ton, a figure little affected by the rapid rise in kelp prices in the fifteen years after 1790. Even when the finished product was selling at up to £20 a ton Hebridean kelpers were receiving only £2 a ton on average; (26) while their landlords' total expenses — which included shipping charges as well as wages — were calculated to amount to about £3.12s. on each ton of kelp produced. (27) The difference between that and the selling price was pure profit.

That landlords were able to reduce their kelpers' share of the proceeds to such an abysmally low level was the consequence of a well devised and cruelly efficient system of exploitation which turned on the fact that the kelper's connection with the land was deliberately maintained by his employer who was also his landlord. (28) Because the kelper remained an agricultural tenant who lived on the land and continued to raise cattle and grow crops upon it, the proprietor was able to draw on his labour during the kelping season and leave him to his own — unpaid — devices for the rest of the year. And as the provider of the land without which the kelper could not survive, the landlord was able to establish a degree of control over his work force which was quite unmatched by even the most tyrannical factory owner. The first step was to raise rents to a level which, as a Benbecula crofter was to put it, was quite unrelated to the land's 'intrinsic value'. (29) Unable to pay their new rents from the proceeds of their agricultural production alone, small tenants were forced into kelping in order to earn the necessary cash. The proprietor consequently recovered a considerable part of his kelping wage bill in the guise of a land rental; and because he controlled the industry's raw material and was the sole buyer of the kelp produced on his estate he was able to direct his tenants to work where and when he liked and to fix their wages at the level he found most convenient — as low as was consistent with their survival.

The one essential prerequisite for the effective enforcement of this method of labour control was that the Highlands' traditional landholding system be reformed in a way that would bring every one of the region's small tenants into a direct tenurial relationship with their landlords. By the eighteenth century's end, it was true, the number of small tenants who paid rent to a landed proprietor rather than to a superior tenant was larger than it had ever been in the past — largely because of the departure of many of the tacksmen who had formerly dominated the agrarian system. Highland farms, however, were still laid out on traditional lines, a typical farm being held in common by the families who were its joint tenants. The latter paid rent to a landlord rather than to the tacksman who had once stood between them and their chief; but they still sublet a considerable part of their holding to a miscellaneous collection of cottars and servants whose plots were held in return for stipulated amounts of labour on the joint farm. Because this system's communal features as well as its array of subtenurial relationships presented a serious obstacle to landlords who were seeking to manipulate rents and landholding in such a way as to provide themselves with large and docile labour forces, there was by the 1790s a growing movement in favour of abolishing the traditional agricultural structure and replacing it by a system composed of single holdings occupied by individual tenants — a method of landholding that was at once pleasing to 'improvers' and amenable to the type of manipulation on which a profitable kelp industry depended.

In the years around 1800, therefore, a steadily growing number of landlords began to drastically reorganise their estates. Old tenures were ended and the scattered strips or rigs of arable land which were the basis of the joint farming economy were divided into separate holdings, each occupied by a single tenant or crofter. In the Outer Hebrides the crofting system which was thus created was conceived of as an adjunct to the kelp industry. On the mainland and in those parts of Mull and Skye where its appearance coincided with the handing over of vast tracts of territory to sheep farmers, crofting was seen as a convenient and potentially profitable means of disposing of a displaced population — fishing taking the place of kelping in the areas where the latter industry was not widely available. As fishermen, and still more as kelpers, crofters were thus of vital importance to their landlords. And as was demonstrated by the events surrounding the passing of the Passenger Act of 1803, Highland proprietors were prepared to go to almost any lengths to retain their tenantries on their estates.

In 1799 Lord MacDonald's extensive estates in Skye and North Uist were surveyed with a view to their modernisation and the consequent procurement of a substantial increase in their owner's revenue from them. The traditional runrig system, 'a careless and slovenly' mode of management the surveyor called it, was to be swept away as were a number of small and chaotically laid out joint farms which the surveyor thought to be understocked with animals and overstocked with people and which, he added, 'never can be so profitable to the tenants or afford such a high rent to the landlord as large farms'. (30) The more extensive farms thus to be established were to be let to tenants recruited outside the Highlands — and hopefully in possession of more money and greater agricultural knowledge than the farms' original occupants. On most of the new farms, it was envisaged, cattle rearing would continue, at least for the moment. But some of them — and this was a portentous development — were to be stocked with sheep, Lord MacDonald having 'no objection ... to try one or two sheep farms on a proper scale'. (31) The future of the large number of people who would obviously be displaced by these changes was clearly mapped out. Each family would be settled on a single lot or croft by the seashore. (32) And there, as kelpers and fishermen as well as agriculturalists, they would make a very significant contribution to the estate economy:

The soil is not only to be tilled but from the surrounding ocean and its rocky shore immense sums may be drawn, equal at least, if not passing, the produce of the soil. As these funds are inexhaustible, the greater the number of hands employed, so much more will be the amount of produce arising from their labour. (33)

The newly established crofters, it was realised, might not willingly take to a life of kelping and fishing. They were therefore to be forced into it by the simple expedient of ensuring that none of the new holdings could provide its tenant with an agricultural return large enough to afford an adequate living for himself and his family. Crofts were thus to be laid out in places where they did 'not interfere with, or mar, the laying out of better farms' and on boggy and rocky land in 'the least profitable parts of the estate'. (34)

In Skye, therefore, the mass of the people were to be settled on the coast and the interior holdings handed over to large farmers. In North Uist, however, a somewhat different mode of proceeding was to be adopted. Instead of being transferred to incoming graziers as in Skye, the island's runrig farms were themselves to be divided into crofts 'for the encouragement of people who carry on the business of making kelp, which is the first object of the landlord here'. (35) In North Uist, Lord MacDonald's surveyor observed — in order to explain his otherwise inexplicable departure from the bigger-means-better philosophy of agricultural 'improvement' — kelp was the 'staple' product and 'encouraging a number of inhabitants to settle or remain ... is the sure means of keeping up the advantages and revenue to be derived from the manufacture of that article'. (36) And to the owner of any kelping estate, that would have been a readily comprehensible argument. 'As you inform that small tenants can afford to pay more rent for farms in Tiree than gentlemen farmers,' the Duke of Argyll wrote to his chamberlain in that island in 1799, 'this determines me to let the farms to small tenants which have been and are at present possessed by tacksmen ....' (37) The implication was clear: there was more money in kelp than in farming. Previous plans for agricultural improvement were accordingly abandoned and an immediate start made on dividing the island's farms into crofts. (38) By 1806 four fifths of Tiree was occupied by crofters; and on the Argyll estates in Mull — where the same principles were applied — almost all the coastal farms had been made available for crofting settlement . (39)

The major problem confronting the men in charge of such innovations was the innate conservatism of the people most affected by them. To persuade a peasantry to abandon an age-old method of cultivation is seldom easy; and the task of establishing the crofting system was no exception — not least because of a widespread and justifiable suspicion that the proposed change would not be for the better. A Harris crofter was subsequently to recall that he had 'seen a woman weeping at being separated from her neighbours by the division of the crofts'; (40) and in parts of Skye the abolition of runrig was said to be widely lamented even eighty years after its occurrence. (41) It is scarcely surprising, therefore, that the author of the 'improvements' on the MacDonald estates should have remarked in 1799 that the tenantry's 'adherence to inveterate opinions and old uncorrected customs operates powerfully against improvements or even alterations'. Among the existing joint farms' tenants and subtenants there was no marked disposition to become crofters. There was, on the contrary, a feeling that it might be better to leave the estate rather than acquiesce in the proposed changes. (42) And as the full implications of the envisaged reform became apparent that feeling deepened into a profound conviction.

The tenantry of North Uist, reported Lord MacDonald's chamberlain in that island in the spring of 1801, were 'equally averse to settle in situations for villages or to take moor crofts for improvement'. They would, he added ominously, 'much rather try their chance in other countries'. (43) A similar antipathy towards the intended reforms was evident in Skye where Lord MacDonald and his agents were bombarded with petitions requesting their abandonment. (44) The estate authorities were determined to proceed as planned, however; and in 1801 alone they ordered no fewer than 267 of Lord MacDonald's Skye tenants to quit their possessions. (45) Not unnaturally, removals on such a scale aroused bitter resentment. Tenants at Uig refused point blank to leave their farms. (46) And as the date fixed for the completion of the new arrangements — Whitsun 1803 — approached, it became clear that the popular dislike of the new order was about to be translated into mass emigration to America. (47) By April 1803 about two thirds of the tenants of Strath and Sleat, two of the parishes on Lord MacDonald's Skye estate, had made or had begun to make preparations to emigrate to America; and some parts of the property, it appeared, would be completely evacuated. (48)

The initial reaction of Lord MacDonald and his advisers to their tenants' declared intention of taking themselves off to the other side of the Atlantic was to put it down to the activities of the emigration agents who were undeniably active in the Highlands in the early years of the nineteenth century. These 'worthless itinerant men', it was argued, were spreading 'false hopes' among the people and thus deluding them into deserting their native land. Lord MacDonald's chamberlains in Skye and North Uist were accordingly instructed to make it known that his lordship viewed with extreme disapprobation the activities of individuals who were 'encouraging the depopulation of the country'. (49) Unfortunately for the estate management, however, the fact that their tenants were only too ready to respond to emigration agents' portrayal of America as a land where people 'were not troubled with land-lords and factors', (50) had less to do with these gentlemen's undoubted propaganda skills than with their audiences' utter disillusionment with conditions at home.

That the current rearrangement of his estates was at the root of his tenantry's evident desire to be off to America was admitted in 1803 by Lord MacDonald himself. But the strength of their resolve he professed himself at a loss to understand. His people, he wrote, had been 'invariably treated with kindness'. The proposed increase in his Skye rental — it was to go up from £5,550 in 1799 to £9,690 in 1803 — he considered moderate. As for those of his tenants 'whom it was necessary to remove', the establishment of crofting townships within easy reach of kelp shores and fishing grounds 'secured to them the means of living comfortably in their own country'. Bewildered by what he clearly thought of as his small tenants' disloyalty Lord MacDonald may have been; but he had no intention of risking the depopulation of his estate and the consequent annihilation of his enormous income from kelp. The implementation of the controversial reforms, he decided, should be delayed until 1804. (51) That postponement, made known in April 1803, had the desired effect. Most of the prospective emigrants elected to remain at home for another year, (52) no doubt convinced — like Lord MacDonald's factor who thought it 'beneath the dignity' of his employer 'to yield to a few restless, infatuated people' (53) — that they had won a notable victory. But as he must have known when he made it, Lord MacDonald's concession was a sham. Within two months of its announcement emigration from the Highlands was virtually outlawed by Act of Parliament.

The years immediately before and after 1800 were prosperous ones for British agriculture. Economic growth was proceeding at a rapid rate and because the practically incessant wars with revolutionary and Napoleonic France had the effect of reducing the level of imports from continental Europe there was a marked rise in the price of practically every kind of domestic product. Not the least affected commodity was wool, the price of which reached hitherto unprecedented levels in the nineteenth century's opening years. (54) The consequence was that those

Highland landlords who had not already turned their estates over to sheep farmers faced almost irresistible pressures to do so; for the profits to be made from sheep farming were almost as spectacular as those to be made from kelp, principally because the boom in wool prices was accompanied by a flurry of speculative interest in the sheep rearing potential of the north-west Highlands' vast tracts of hill pasture. Throughout this area 'The competition for farms became excessive, and rents were given which were often extravagant'. (55) Enormous expanses of land were made available to southern graziers. And because the need to provide winter grazings for the latters' sheep stocks rendered it 'compulsory to take from petty agriculture the ... tracts which are adapted to this purpose ... it became imperative on the proprietors to eject' the small tenants or subtenants who had hitherto occupied them. (56) 'Wherever it takes place,' a contemporary political economist observed about the introduction of sheep farming on to an estate, 'if the country has any inhabitants at all, they must, to a trifle, be expelled.' (57)

And expelled they were: from those parts of Lord MacDonald's Skye estate that were put under sheep at this time and from the many other places where landlords enforced a similar change in land use. Parts of Mull were let to sheep farmers in the first year of the nineteenth century, (58) as were parts of the estate belonging to MacLean of Ardgour. (59) Large scale sheep farming began on Cameron of Locheil's estate at about the same time with the consequent removal of scores, perhaps hundreds, of tacksmen, tenants and subtenants, especially from Glen Dessary and the area around Loch Arkaig. (60) 'Families who had not been disturbed for four or five hundred years are turned out of house and home and their possessions given to the highest bidder,' wrote the son of one of Locheil's tacksmen. 'So much for Highland attachment between chief and clans.' (61) Throughout the north-west Highlands there were similar developments. In Morvern 'the method of uniting farms' was 'gaining ground in proportion to the avidity for high rents and the rage for sheep stocks'. (62) In Glenelg by the 1790s 'one man often rents a farm where formerly many families lived comfortably'. (63) In Glenshiel and Kintail black cattle were replaced by sheep and farms taken over by incomers. (64) In Lochbroom 'the engrossing of farms for sheep walks' began in the eighteenth century's last decade; (65) and on the Sutherland estate the first steps towards the establishment of a sheep farming economy were taken in 1799. (66)

The popular response to these developments was the same as that encountered by Lord MacDonald in Skye and North Uist: emigration. Towards the end of 1801, for example, MacDonell of Glengarry surveyed his estate 'with the view', as he put it, 'of ascertaining the real value of it, and thus from known data to be enabled to fix the ... price at which it would be reasonable I should let it to my numerous Tenants and Dependants'. The 'price' having been determined with reference to prevailing market circumstances, it not unsurprisingly exceeded Glengarry's current rental by a considerable sum; and he attempted to forestall the consequent discontent by making an 'offer to my old tenants of remaining upon their lands at ... Ten per Cent below the amount of offers from Strangers'. His 'handsome sacrifice' proved insufficient, however, and in March 1802 he 'was very much surprised to learn that the Tenants for whose comfort and encouragement I had proposed to make the above sacrifice, in general wished to surrender their leases, and that they had all with very few exceptions signed engagements to go to America'. (67)

About Glengarry's experience there was little that was unique. In the 1790s emigration from the Highlands had been curtailed by the war with France. As soon as the Peace of Amiens was signed, however, it 'began to revive', as the gentlemen of the Highland Society observed, 'with a spirit more universal than at any former period'. (68) In 1801 about 830 people emigrated from the Highlands. In 1802 at least eleven ships carrying some 3,300 passengers were known to have sailed from the Hebrides and from the west coast north of Fort William. Other ships were believed to have sailed undetected and from preparations in progress in the spring of 1803 it was estimated that up to 20,000 people were likely to leave that year for America. Entire districts, it appeared, were in imminent danger of being completely denuded of their population. 150 of the 153 families resident on one small estate were said to be preparing to emigrate. On another larger property, the whole population of about 2,000 was reported to be contemplating a similar course. (69)

This unprecedented exodus was greeted with evident alarm by Highland landlords and by the Highland Society of Edinburgh, a body which they dominated. So seriously did they view the situation that in July 1801 a special meeting of the Society was called to consider the phenomenon of emigration and a committee under the chairmanship of an Edinburgh lawyer, Colin MacKenzie, appointed to investigate it. (70) Like Lord MacDonald, the committee inclined to the view that emigration agents were principally to blame for the Highland tenantry's departure. Their skill in 'the arts of deceit and imposition', it was claimed, enabled these nefarious characters to dupe 'the ignorant and unwary' into adopting a course that was clearly not in their best interests. (71) Even the Highland Society, however, felt bound to admit that a contributory cause of emigration was 'the removal of many of the tenants from their farms in consequence of a conviction on the part of the proprietors that they would be better cultivated and managed and pay better rents when let in large divisions'. (72) And that conclusion was affirmed by many less biased observers. The most important single cause of emigration, according to Alexander Irvine, a Highland clergyman who, in 1802, published an *Inquiry into its Causes and Effects,* was the rapid pace of 'improvement' in the north-west. Whether rearrangements were intended to facilitate the production of kelp, as was usually the case in the islands, or to pave the way for the introduction of sheep farming, as was invariably the case on the mainland, the consequences were the same:

> This plan of improvement has put the whole Highlands into commotion. They who are deprived of their possessions ... feel a reluctance in settling anywhere else, conceive a disgust at their country, and therefore prefer leaving it ... and the connection once broken they care not where they go. (73)

Other ministers and other pamphleteers agreed. (74) And when Thomas Telford came to the Highlands in 1803 to conduct an official enquiry into emigration, his investigations left him in no doubt that its 'most powerful' single cause was the conversion of large tracts of territory into sheep farms. (75)

That Irvine and Telford were substantially correct in their diagnoses is indisputable. (76) The emigrations from the estates of Lord MacDonald and Glengarry had their counterparts on all the other properties then being subjected to drastic reorganisations of one kind or another. Locheil's 'improvements' were accompanied by the departure to Canada of over 600 of his tenants. There they considered themselves 'better off to be out of the reach of such unnatural tyranny', (77) a feeling that was probably shared by emigrants from Ardgour, Knoydart, Glenelg, Coll, Tiree, Applecross, North Uist, and all the other places where — as the Marchioness of Sutherland's factor remarked in 1803 — 'the people ... held out a threat of Emigration for accomplishing their purposes'. (78)

To Highland proprietors it was inconceivable that their tenants' 'purposes' should be allowed to prevail over their own. A few of them perhaps retained a trace of their ancestors' desire to be surrounded by a numerous tenantry; (79) while others among them shared the widespread concern about the probable effect on Britain's defence capabilities of the departure to America of the Highlands' large reserves of military manpower. An anachronistic paternalism and an anxiety for the nation's security were reinforced, however, by solid financial interests. None of the Highlands' landed magnates wanted to lose the chance of availing themselves of the profits to be made from raising and recruiting Highland regiments. (80) And those west coast and Hebridean proprietors who drew large revenues from kelp had no intention of depriving themselves of these revenues by tamely aquiescing in the decampment of the people who provided them.

It is utterly unsurprising therefore that the Earl of Selkirk — one of Canada's foremost colonisers and the principal advocate of Highland emigration in the years around 1800 — should have found that the most determined and vociferous opposition to his schemes emanated from the kelping proprietors. (81) The reasons are plain to see. Not only did kelping require a labour force so vast as to rule out the possibility of seasonal migrations of workers to the kelp estates; it was, as was pointed out by Robert Brown, an agent for Clanranald and — not insignificantly — the author of the most influential critique of Selkirk's arguments in favour of Highland emigration, 'a dirty and disagreeable employment and must, if the present race of people were to leave the country, be given up altogether'. Brown's aim was not to limit emigration but to stop it completely; for it was in the proprietors' interest, he pointed out with more truth than tact, to have as many tenants as possible in order to keep up production and keep down wages. (82)

The government was consequently called upon to act. In March 1802 Glengarry gave it as his considered opinion that 'if the Government or the Legislature do not speedily interpose, the Highlands will be *depopulated*'; (83) while the Highland Society's committee — faithfully reflecting the proprietors' prejudices — was convinced from the beginning that emigration ought to be curtailed by legislation. The committee's chairman consequently took great pains to bring its findings and recommendations to the attention of Henry Dundas and any other influential politician who was prepared to listen. And each of the three reports produced by the committee between January 1802 and March 1803 reflected its members' concern about the 'rapidly progressive increase of the evil' by demanding in ever more strident tones that measures designed to put an end to emigration be immediately enacted. (84) Having attracted the support of Charles Hope, the lord advocate, the committee's campaign culminated in Telford's officially sponsored 'survey of the coasts and central Highlands of Scotland' in the autumn of 1802. Telford's brief was to simultaneously enquire into the possibility of improving Highland communications and 'the causes of emigration and the means of preventing it'. (85) His investigations demonstrated that emigration from the region was undoubtedly increasing and that the upward trend was likely to be maintained. The House of Commons select committee to which his report was referred accordingly recommended prompt legislation. A Bill was drawn up by Charles Hope and, having passed through parliament without the slightest difficulty, it became law as the Passenger Vessels Act of June 1803. (86)

In campaigning for legislation, Hope and the Highland Society's committee had made a great deal of the sufferings endured by emigrants on the unregulated passenger vessels which then plied the Atlantic. And according to Hope's public pronouncements on the subject his Act was an obviously humanitarian measure which, with disinterested zeal, laid down a series of regulations designed to limit the number of passengers carried on any one vessel and to ensure the provision of adequate supplies of food, water and medicine. (87) As Hope admitted in a letter he wrote in 1804, however, the Passenger Act had another, less ostensibly humanitarian, purpose'

I had the the chief hand in preparing and carrying thro' Parliament an Act which was professedly calculated merely to regulate the equipment and victualling of Ships carrying Passengers to America, but which certainly was intended, both by myself and the other gentlemen of the Committee appointed to enquire into the Situation in the Highlands, indirectly to prevent the effects of that pernicious Spirit of discontent against their own Country, and rage for emigrating to America, which had been raised among the people ... by the Agents of Lord Selkirk and others, aided, no doubt, in some few cases, by the impolitic conduct of the landholders, in attempting changes and improvements too rapidly. (88)

The desired curtailment of emigration was achieved simply because even the most token compliance with the Act's provisions entailed an increase in costs large enough to put the price of an Atlantic crossing beyond the reach of most ordinary Highlanders. Before June 1803 the cost of a passage from north-west Scotland to Nova Scotia, the destination of many Highland emigrants, had been about £3.10s. or £4. After that date it rose to around £10 or more. (89)

As far as most Highlanders were concerned, therefore, the immediate effect of the Act was to deprive them of the opportunity of emigrating, and thus of their most efficacious means of demonstrating their opposition to their landlords' policies. Proprietors and their agents, on the other hand, welcomed the Act with unconcealed delight — Lord MacDonald's Skye chamberlain reporting that 'the emigration is entirely stopped now from the Act of Parliament which puts it out of the poor people's power to pay the increase of freight'; (90) and the Duke of Argyll noting 'that the means of removing to America have been rendered more difficult by the operation of the late Act'. (91) But for those of Lord MacDonald's tenants who had made up their minds to emigrate the Act was an unmitigated disaster. Having sold their stock and having refused to accept the new holdings intended for them they were left, as Lord MacDonald's chamberlain noted with a hint of malicious satisfaction, 'without any situation at all'. (92) Fortunately for them, however, the unusually high cattle prices of that year (93) enabled them to scrape together the necessary fares. And in October 1803 about a hundred families left Sleat for North Carolina, the adults paying £12.12s. each for the passage. 'Their having done so,' Lord MacDonald's chamberlain ruefully remarked, 'shows that no expense ... if they are able to pay it will deter them from their wandering schemes.'

Emigration, he reported in 1804 and 1805, remained as popular as ever. People who had gone to America in 1803 had sent 'very encouraging letters' to their friends at home and a large number of the remaining small tenants or crofters — as many of them now were — were consequently 'determined to follow them as soon as an opportunity offers'. Such an opportunity in fact occurred in 1804 when recruiting agents for a Canadian Fencible regiment visited parts of the Highlands and islands. Volunteers and their families were offered free passages to Canada and promised that land would be made available to them on their discharge. The regiments' recruiting sergeants were astonished by the number of men who enlisted and Charles Hope, who was still keeping a wary eye on the region's affairs, received 'complaints ... from all parts of the Highlands of the mischief the recruiting agents were spreading among the people ... Thousands, instead of hundreds, were eager to enlist'. (95)

Such opportunities were necessarily rare, however. And as Hope, the Highland Society and Highland landlords had intended, emigration from the Highlands became less and less possible in the years after the passing of the Passenger Vessels Act. Small tenants who had not left before June 1803 had mostly to reconcile themselves to staying at home and making the best of the new agrarian system. It was in an attempt to make the latter course more attractive that the government, acting on Telford's recommendations, began the construction of the Caledonian Canal and a network of new Highland roads. (96) The employment thus provided proved a mere palliative, however; for the crofting system then being brought into existence in the north-west Highlands and Hebrides suffered from an economic malaise that was too deep-seated to be affected by such superficial applications of government assistance. (97)

With emigration less of a problem, the years after 1803 were marked by a steady extension of the crofting system. The miserable, overcrowded townships which constituted the most characteristic feature of the agrarian system which prevailed on the north-west coast of the Scottish mainland for most of the nineteenth century were established during this period — and settled by people who had been cleared from inland straths and glens in order to make way for sheep. Once established on their coastal crofts, the inhabitants of these townships were expected by their landlords to become fishermen or kelpers as well as crofters. Although kelping was less widely available on the mainland than in the islands there were high hopes of developing the fishing industry; and mainland crofters were consequently compelled to participate in it by a method identical to that used to force their Hebridean counterparts to become kelpers: individual crofts were made deliberately small and their rents fixed at a level that was quite unrelated to their agricultural potential. (98) No longer able to emigrate and in desperate need of a plot of ground on which to build some sort of house or hovel and a patch of land on which to grow potatoes, evicted tenants had no choice but to accept crofts on their landlords' terms. 'These poor people, unable to go to America, are glad to get any sort of plot and hut,' noted

MacKenzie of Coul in 1813. Many landlords, he added, 'took advantage of their
necessities and tied them down to perform services, to work at fixed prices when
called upon, and to turn up a certain space of waste ground annually'. (99) In this
way, according to John MacCulloch – a geologist who spent a lot of time in the
Highlands around 1820 and who was very much in favour of agricultural improvement as practised by his friends the Highland landlords – arable acreages were
increased and rentals raised. 'To these advantages,' he went on, 'I need scarcely add
the clearing out of the pasture farms which the small tenants had encumbered, and
the power thus given to the proprietors to occupy them in an advantageous manner.' (100)

From the north coast of Sutherland to the Sound of Mull the pattern was
the same. On the Reay estate in north-west Sutherland clearances began in the nineteenth century's first decade and continued until about 1820. The interior was let
as 'seven great sheep farms' and the population settled on the coast. (101) Elsewhere
in Sutherland the clearances executed for the Sutherland family by James Loch,
Patrick Sellar and their assistants were, and still are, notorious; (102) although the
tendency of most accounts to concentrate on the events surrounding the most brutal
episodes – notably *bliadhna na losgaidh,* the year of the burning, in Kildonan (103) –
has obscured the fact that the evictions affected not just a few localities but almost
the whole of a very large county. Even in the 1880s old men could still give the
names of forty-eight cleared settlements in the parish of Assynt alone, (104) and
the implicit contention that the removals were on an unprecedented scale is supported
by a large volume of contemporary evidence.

'Lord and Lady Stafford,' wrote Patrick Sellar in 1815

> were pleased *humanely,* to order a new arrangement of this Country. That the
> interior should be possessed by Cheviot Shepherds and the people brought down
> to the coast and placed there in lotts under the size of three arable acres, sufficient
> for the maintenance of an industrious family, but pinched enough to cause them
> turn their attention to the fishing. I presume to say that the proprietors *humanely*
> ordered this arrangement, because, it surely was a most benevolent action, to put
> these barbarous hordes into a position where they could better Associate together,
> apply to industry, educate their children, and advance in civilization. (105)

It was, thought James Loch, 'A policy well calculated to ... increase the happiness
of the individuals who were the objects of the change (and) to benefit those to
whom these extensive but hitherto unproductive possessions belonged'. (106) That
the Sutherland family benefited is undoubted. That their tenantry did so is a considerably more debatable proposition. The net effect of what Loch liked to call 'the
Sutherland improvements' was to crowd the county's population on to coastal holdings 'of a size to induce every man to engage actively in the prosecution of the
herring fishery', (107) and therefore too small to afford their occupants an adequate
subsistence. This was the case even on good land. On poorer soils the crofters'
plight was even more unenviable – and in many instances the terrain involved was
quite unsuited to settlement. (108) In Farr, on Sutherland's north coast, for example,
tenants evicted from Strathnaver were 'thickly settled along the sea coast of the
parish – in some instances about thirty lotters occupying the land formerly in the
possession of twelve, and some of them placed on ground which had been formerly
uncultivated'. And around the Kyle of Tongue land which had been 'occupied by

a few' was 'divided among many', thus becoming 'totally inadequate for the main-tenance of all'. (109) Sutherland crofters, said Loch to his critics, would easily maintain themselves by fishing and growing potatoes. (110) Unfortunately for his reputation — and much more unfortunately for the people whom he had compelled to become crofters — the one was to prove as precarious a resource as the other.

Developments in Sutherland had their parallels on more southerly estates. In Wester Ross the introduction of sheep farming led to the establishment of hope-lessly congested crofting townships on the coast. Here too the fishing industry was thought to be the panacea for all ills. (111) And here Dr. John MacCulloch discovered that the consequences of agricultural improvement were not universally beneficial. In a miserable hovel on the shore of Loch Carron he found 'a poor woman cooking some shell fish over a peat fire, attended by two children'; while on the bare mud floor, 'scarcely covered by a wretched supply of blankets, lay the husband, sick of a fever'. Apart from the blankets and the cooking pot the hut was completely un-furnished. 'We found on enquiry,' MacCulloch added,

> that having been ejected from their farm and having no other resource, they had been suffered by a neighbouring farmer to build their hut from his woods, and to graze their only cow upon his waste; and thus, with the assistance of shell fish which they caught at low water, and some casual labour, they had contrived to live through the portion of the summer which was past. How the winter was to be surmounted it was both too easy and too painful to imagine. (112)

All along the west coast, evicted tenants and subtenants faced similar predicaments. In Glenshiel the establishment of a sheep-farming economy was accompanied by the removal of most of the population to coastal crofts where, as the parish minister put it in the 1830s, they were 'dependent for subsistence on the laborious and un-certain pursuit of the herring fishing'. (113) Those people who did not emigrate from Glenelg at the beginning of the century were herded into ramshackle town-ships on the Sound of Sleat. (114) MacLean of Ardgour and Cameron of Locheil provided crofts for displaced tenants on the shores of Loch Eil and Loch Linnhe. (115) And in Morvern the interior was depopulated and new and squalid townships established on the Sound of Mull. (116)

In the islands too the number of crofts and crofters was rapidly increasing. On Lord MacDonald's Skye estate, for example, the traditional runrig system had been largely swept away by 1811; and as was the case on the mainland the crofts which took its place were invariably small and confined to coastal districts, while the interior pastures on which small tenants had long grazed their cattle were occupied by large farmers. (117) In 1806, the emigration crisis safely behind him, Lord MacDonald had announced his intention 'to introduce some respectable and substantial tenants to his estate from the south country'. (118) And since the latter were of course sheep farmers their arrival necessitated further removals of tenants and subtenants. 'It is no doubt a very hard case to remove a herd of this description,' commented Lord MacDonald's factor

> but on the other hand it is impossible that a proprietor can receive the same rent ... if the tenant is to be burdened with a set of needy cottars ... and were a portion of the grazing to be set aside for their accommodation, such an arrangement

would be detrimental to the farm and prevent its being let to the same advantage. (119)

Evictions accordingly went ahead. And in the 1830s the minister of Sleat, one of the parishes on the MacDonald estate, was to remark that one of the most striking developments to have occurred in the district since the turn of the century was to be found in the fact that 'lands which were then possessed by labouring tenants are now converted to sheep farms'. (120)

The inauguration of the new order was not always accomplished without difficulty, however, In 1811 MacLeod of Dunvegan embarked on a series of reforms which included a sharp increase in rents, the introduction of sheep farming, and the establishment of several crofting townships — the latter to be situated in close proximity to some of the best kelp shores on the Dunvegan estate. (121) One of MacLeod's more substantial tenants, unwilling to pay his new rent, threatened to emigrate and to contribute to the costs of as many small tenants as wished to accompany him. 'The common people,' reported MacLeod's factor, 'flocked to his standard.' And it was only after a great deal of energy had been expended by his estate management that the majority of the intending emigrants were induced to remain on MacLeod's property. (122)

1811 was also marked by rumours of impending emigrations from MacKenzie of Seaforth's estates in Lewis and Wester Ross. Because it would entail a loss of income from kelp the prospect of a popular exodus from Lewis was particularly worrying to Seaforth's agents. (123) And although their anxiety proved groundless the reasons for it would have been appreciated by the managers of any kelping property, not least by the men in charge of Clanranald's estates in Benbecula and South Uist. Their eagerness to expand kelp production and profits by establishing the crofting system on the estate was equalled only by their apprehension that 'such an innovation' could not be affected 'without the risk of stirring up a spirit of emigration, or any other unpleasant consequence'. And when it finally began in the summer of 1816, the allocation of crofts was confined in the first instance to Benbecula — 'from the circumstance,' as the factor reported, 'of an emigration going on in the adjoining island of Barra' which, he feared, 'might extend to South Uist should he attempt to introduce too generally a change to which the inhabitants, from attachment to old habits are very averse'. (124)

At the beginning of the nineteenth century crofting was virtually unknown in the area with which it is now most associated — being confined to a few parts of Mull and western Inverness-shire. (125) Twenty years later, however, 'the ancient system of runrig' had 'almost expired' and the crofting system was in existence all along the west and north coasts and in the larger islands. (126) MacDonald, MacLeod, Clanranald, Locheil, Sutherland: all of them, along with many lesser landowners, had by the end of the nineteenth century's second decade settled the coastal fringes of their estates with crofters, large numbers of whom had been evicted from older farms which were by that time under sheep. And even in Lewis, the remotest of all the Hebrides, the division of runrig farms into crofts was recommended in 1800 and commenced about ten years later. (127)

Kildonan and Geirinish in South Uist; Barrapoll, Kenovay, Scarinish, Balemartine, and Crossapoll in Tiree: these and many other crofting townships were established simply by dividing the arable lands of an already existing joint farm into individual holdings. (128) In many places in Sutherland, Skye, Lewis, Harris and elsewhere, however, townships were laid out on land which had been previously uncultivated. (12 A township established on waste was obviously at a special disadvantage, and their differing origins are partly responsible for the wide range of township types which are still to be found. (130) But all crofting townships had, and still have, important common characteristics which generally outweigh the differences between individual settlements: a nucleus of arable land made up of a number of separate smallholdings and surrounded by a tract of hill pasture varying considerably in quality and extent, known as the outrun or rough grazing, and held in common by all the township's tenants — that particular legacy from the old tenurial system to the new being less due to design than to the fact that, given the number of crofters to be accommodated and the transfer of large tracts of hill pasture to sheep farmers, the principle of division could not be applied to it. (131)

Although the crofting system established in the north-west Highlands and islands was to experience many vicissitudes during the next hundred years its fundamental features remained, and still remain, unchanged. At a time when the agricultural revolution was being consolidated in the Scottish lowlands and a modernised agricultural structure was being established even in the southern and eastern Highlands, therefore, agricultural improvement — as it was understood in the south — made little impact on the north-west. (132) Its only major achievement was the sweeping away of runrig. And whatever the demerits of the old agrarian system, it could not be claimed that the method of landholding which replaced it was any more efficient in an agricultural sense. Mainland proprietors, anxious to put as many acres as possible under sheep and to force small tenants to assist in developing the fishing industry, encouraged the proliferation of minute holdings as a means to these ends; while landlords with extensive kelping interests eagerly subdivided their estates in order to maximise their profits from kelp. Throughout north-west Scotland, therefore, the requirements of an effective arable agriculture were strictly subordinated to landlords' desire to make money by whatever means came to hand.

As a means of creating a virtually unlimited supply of cheap labour, however, the crofting system was an undoubted and immediate success. In the 1840s a Hebridean factor remarked that 'the kelp trade produced the population' that was an essential precondition of its profitability; (133) and demographic statistics bear out the general accuracy of his claim. The population explosion of the late eighteenth and early nineteenth centuries was not confined to the Highlands and its causes, there as elsewhere, are still a matter for debate. But it is no coincidence that while the population of northern and north-western counties as a whole rose by 48 per cent between 1755 and 1831, that of the Outer Isles — the principal kelping area and the district where crofting was most widely established in the early nineteenth century — rose by 139 per cent in the same period. On being further broken down, these figures are still more revealing. Thus the population of Harris, an island where not a great deal of kelp was made, rose by 98 per cent during the period in question. But that of North Uist where kelping was much more important rose by 141 per cent; while that of South Uist, most productive of all the kelp islands, increased by no less than 211 per cent. (134) This immense expansion, as was pointed out in the 1830s, was partly due to the fact that 'the kelp manufacture was ... so profitable to the landlords that they encouraged the people to remain on their estates' (135) — not least by denying them the opportunity to emigrate. Much more decisive, however, was the contribution made to population growth by the establishment of the crofting system itself.

Land was the be all and end all of the small tenant's existence, and in the kelp islands in the early years of the nineteenth century more land than ever before was made available to him. The disadvantages and limitations of subtenancy; the restraints imposed by joint tenancy and the communal management of arable land: these were suddenly and completely removed. The crofter was the sole tenant of his croft and, because the beginnings of crofting coincided with the commencement of the potato's long reign as the ordinary Highlander's staple crop and diet, (136) he needed considerably less land on which to grow the food previously provided by cereal crops of one kind or another. And to be self-sufficient in food was, in any case, less imperative than it once had been; for high cattle prices and the proliferation of opportunities to earn money as a kelper, or as a labourer on canal and road construction projects, made it fairly easy for the crofter to buy the food that his plot of land could not produce. (137) Directly or indirectly, every one of these developments was related to the introduction of crofting; and every one of them tended to remove restraints on early marriage. With land and money more freely available than ever before early marriages became the rule and because potatoes with a little fish and milk are a healthy, if excessively monotonous diet, more children from these marriages survived. As contemporaries observed, therefore, crofting and population growth went hand in hand. (138)

Because crofts were originally designed in such a way as to make it impossible for their occupants to be self-sufficient agriculturalists the subdivision of arable land into miniscule units was an integral feature of the crofting system from the moment of its conception; and it was one that simultaneously accelerated, and was accelerated by, the population explosion. Originally encouraged by proprietors who were all too ready to rate profits from kelp more highly than the agricultural wellbeing of their estates or tenantries, subdivision soon acquired a momentum of its own and became, as landlords eventually discovered, virtually unstoppable. In conjunction with the development of the kelp industry and other sources of non-agricultural earnings it meant, as Clanranald's factor pointed out in the early 1820s, that the population soon expanded to a level 'much beyond what the land can maintain'. (139) In Tiree, for example, five of the farms which the Duke of Argyll had converted into crofting townships in order to cash in on the kelp boom were occupied by no less than 1080 people. (140) And there were similar occurrences throughout the Hebrides. For proprietors to thus encourage, in fact compel, an essentially agricultural people to become dependent for their livelihood on non-agricultural pursuits — whether kelping or fishing — was a recipe for ultimate catastrophe. And as if that were not bad enough, the kelp industry, by its very nature, resulted in the neglect and consequent stagnation of the crofting economy's agricultural base.

The agricultural effects of kelping, contemporary writers agreed, were uniformly bad. In the perceptive analysis of Hebridean agriculture which he published in 1811, James MacDonald noted that

> On kelp estates the land is almost entirely sacrificed to that manufacture and is at best, with regard to its agriculture, in a stationary condition ... In this state of agriculture the land is considered as of no further value than merely to accommodate the kelp manufacturers with some milk, a few carcases of lean sheep, horses, or cattle, and a wretched crop of barley, black oats, and potatoes. Turnips and all other green crops demanding attention in summer, are (excepting potatoes) quite out of the question. (141)

Seaweed, traditionally used to manure the land, was everywhere reserved for incineration. In the 1790s the minister of Harris pointed out that arable land had already 'degenerated much through want of the manure formerly afforded by the shores'; (142) while James MacDonald calculated that in the first decade of the nineteenth century Hebridean land was being deprived of no less than nine tenths of the fertiliser it had once received. (143) This particular consequence of the kelp industry was raised as an objection to it in Skye in the 1770s. (144) But as the kelp boom developed it was completely lost sight of. And in their scramble for profits landlords went out of their way to ensure that every scrap of seaweed found its way to the kilns. In 1816, for example, Seaforth's factor in Lewis was instructed to 'take the most effectual means of punishing any person or persons who may be concerned in cutting, using, or destroying the ware'. (145) And the most efficacious punishment was of course eviction.

The agriculturally debilitating consequences of such a regime were seriously aggravated by the fact that in the summer months, when their fields were most in need of attention, all the small tenants' energies had to be devoted to the making of their landlord's kelp — a situation so obviously fraught with dangers for the future of Hebridean agriculture that it caused at least one estate management a qualm of conscience. As long as kelp was a major source of revenue, observed Clanranald's trustees in 1815, 'it is impossible that the tenants can give that attention to the production of the land which to secure a decent return is indispensably necessary'. At the time of year when they 'ought to be labouring and sowing their ground', the tenantry were 'almost uniformly called off, and that in the best weather too', to the kelp shores. That his tenants were 'continually distracted' in this way was the reason, his trustees believed, for the exceedingly low level of agricultural production on Clanranald's estate. But though they regretted the existence of such a state of affairs they could see no alternative to it. The kelp had to be made. (146)

The kelp boom, although it provided capital which could have been applied to such ends and proved that massive agrarian reorganisation was not inherently impossible, thus removed any pecuniary incentive that landlords might have had to establish an effective arable agriculture on their estates. The Duke of Argyll's abandonment of his plans for agricultural improvements on Tiree and his subsequent adoption of policies which were to make that island one of the most congested and poverty-stricken of all the Hebrides was typical of the times. (147) Throughout the north-west Highlands and islands landlords subordinated the dictates of good estate management to those deriving from their desire to make quick and easy profits; for unlike the landed proprietors of England and lowland Scotland most Highland landlords had no interest in their estates or tenantries other than as sources of ready cash. Of that state of affairs contemporary writers were highly critical — James MacDonald, for example, complaining bitterly about 'the non-residence of many of the proprietors who drain the poor Hebrides of their wealth and, too often residing in other parts of the empire, pay little attention to the improvement of their estates'. (148) But such strictures had little effect. 'What Hebridean proprietor lives on his estate that can live elsewhere?' asked Seaforth in 1823. (149) And none did so. By the 1830s there was no resident proprietor in any of the Outer Isles while of the 195 owners of land in the north-west Highlands and Hebrides as a whole, only 46 lived fairly permanently on their estates. (150)

Having adopted the *mores* of a capitalist society in the eighteenth century, Highland landlords had wittingly and willingly embarked on a policy of substituting a commercial rent economy for the familial economy of traditional Highland society. In the process they had opened the way for an individualistic scramble for land reinforced by a population explosion and by their own manipulation of the agrarian system as an adjunct to their kelp, sheep and fishing interests. The consequences for the crofting tenants whom landlords had brought into existence was that their holdings were too small, their rents too high, and their security almost non-existent. Crofters profited to some extent from the favourable circumstances of the period around the turn of the century. Their gains, however, were an inconsiderable fraction of those accruing to their landlords; and after 1820 their economic position deteriorated markedly. That deterioration was in essence due to altered market circumstances — themselves the consequence of the British economy's having entered a period of intermittent crisis which lasted until the 1840s. But crofters were made pitifully vulnerable to the effects of economic change by the fact that the ownership of the land on which they lived had remained the monopoly of a small group of men whose pursuit of easy profits had reduced their tenants to the status of kelping labourers or unsuccessful fishermen. And after 1820 the crofting population's vulnerability and insecurity were tragically underlined, not only by the increasing frequency of seasons of hunger and distress, but by the fact that as fishing proved a broken reed and as the profit indicator swung away from kelp and cattle towards sheep — with the implication that landlords' interests lay in the removal of what had become, as far as they were concerned, a surplus and useless population — crofters were quite unable to prevent the clearances and deportations which ensued.

5. A Redundant Population; 1821-1844

AS long as kelping was a profitable enterprise crofters were highly esteemed by their landlords and the development of the crofting system was generally considered an integral and important part of estate management. The possibility that the fishing industry might become an equally remunerative undertaking also entered into proprietors' calculations — especially those of the Sutherland family. But because the majority of crofters were kelpers rather than fishermen and because the long held vision of an indigenous Highland fishing industry never materialised, it was on their role as kelpers that most crofters' usefulness to their landlords depended. And by the 1820s the kelp industry was in serious trouble.

The turning point in the fortunes of the Hebrides' staple commodity occurred at the end of the nineteenth century's first decade. In 1810 and 1811 prices of certain grades of kelp fell to around £10 a ton. By 1815 this figure represented the average price of even the best kelp. (1) And although the position was by no means disastrous there were indications that it could quickly become so, a particularly ominous portent of future events occurring in 1813 when Newcastle glass manufacturers asked the government to abolish import duties on Norwegian kelp. (2) The kelp proprietors responded by meeting in Edinburgh and agreeing to put their own case before the government. (3) The Highland interest prevailed — but only temporarily. In 1818 renewed rumours of an impending reduction in duties — this time affecting imports of Mediterranean barilla — produced another crisis meeting and renewed representations to the government. Among the Highland proprietors' ranks there were now perceptible tremors of panic. To lower tariffs on kelp, they informed the administration in London, would be to ruin them: 'Many persons have purchased their estates relying on the permanency of kelp, and others have lent money on the security of the annual returns arising from it.' (4) Such was undeniably the case. Even at the height of the wartime boom occasional fears had been expressed that kelp prices, 'supposing a time of peace', might fall as a result of foreign competition. (5) But most proprietors and their financiers for that matter — seem to have been blithely unaware of the intrinsically vulnerable nature of the industry. Estates were organised as if the kelp boom was bound to continue indefinitely. And enormous amounts of money were lent to proprietors on the same unfounded assumption. (6) What was not realized was that the industry's profitability was largely a creation of wartime circumstances, and that its days were therefore numbered.

Glass and soap manufacturers — some of whom were soon to be pressing for the abolition of the Corn Laws, most eminent of all the monuments to the power of Britain's landed interest — saw no point in maintaining artificially high duties on foreign alkali in order to keep Highland landlords in the style to which they had become accustomed. Having failed in 1813 and 1818 to persuade the government to reduce the relevant tariffs they merely intensified their campaign and, as chemical processes for the manufacture of alkali from salt were perfected, they added the abolition of the salt tax to their list of demands. 'Chemistry,' observed MacKenzie of Seaforth in one of his more perceptive moments, 'is the true enemy of kelp and we can only last as long as its advance to perfection is going on.' (7) As something of a liberal in his politics he should also have been aware of the threat to kelp from middle class industrialists whose advance to political influence was proceeding with a rapidity at least equal to that of the progress of science, and whose demands north-west Scotland's proprietors — lacking the numbers and influence of the southern magnates whose rents came from corn rather than kelp — were unable to resist successfully. In the early 1820s import duties on barilla were lowered drastic- ally; that measure being accompanied by a simultaneous reduction in the salt tax and followed by its complete abolition in 1825. (8)

The effects were immediately apparent. The average price of kelp at Liverpool, the main selling centre, fell from £9. 4s. 11d. a ton in 1823 to £6. 16s. 10d. in 1826, £4. 11s. 5d. in 1827, and finally to £3. 13s. 4d. in 1828. (9) As these figures demonstrate, it was in 1827 that the situation became really critical. In June that year a considerable part of the previous crop was still on hand in Liverpool, (10) and as the year advanced the bottom fell completely out of the market. By December 1827 the best grades of kelp — which had been selling for £6 or £7 a ton in August — were fetching less than £3 as a result of the market having been flooded with cheaply manufactured alkali. (11) That month the kelp proprietors and their agents met in Edinburgh in an atmosphere of considerable gloom. (12) The kelp industry, they resolved, 'has declined and is rapidly declining', a conclusion borne out by their analysis of kelp prices. In the ten years after 1817 the price of prime kelp had fallen by two thirds and by 1827 the industry had ceased to be a profitable undertaking on many north-west Highland and Hebridean properties. (13) In the hypothetical case of an estate on which 600 tons of kelp were made each year — i.e. one in the middle range of kelp properties — it was calculated that the profits from kelp would have fallen from an annual average of £2,535 in the years between 1817 and 1826 (much less than would have been fetched between 1800 and 1810, but enough to make the industry worthwhile) to £695 in 1827 and to only £180 in 1828. (14)

In steadily increasing desperation the kelp proprietors cast around for ways to revive the industry's flagging fortunes. A reduction in its costs was an obvious expedient. But shipping charges were more or less immutable. Kelpers' wages had never been allowed to rise above a bare subsistence level. And substantial economies thus proved impossible to effect. At the instigation of Clanranald and Lord MacDonald, who had most to lose from the industry's collapse, various experiments aimed at raising kelp's alkaline content and thus its value were carried out in the Uists. All of them, however, proved fruitless (15) — as did appeals for government assistance; the latter being based on the argument that 'the distress or rather ruin' confronting the kelp proprietors was 'plainly, undeniably, incontrovertibly owing to ... the repeal ... of taxes such as those on salt and barilla'. (16)

A more unusual and more ruthless solution to the problem was devised by MacNeill of Barra. Between 1830 and 1833 he built an alkali works on his island estate in order to process his kelp on the spot, thus eliminating transport and agency costs. The project was naturally an expensive one ; and like other Hebridean proprietors MacNeill was very short of capital. To raise the necessary funds he divided every croft in Barra in two, charged the same rent for a half croft as had formerly been paid for a whole croft, and thus doubled the apparent value of the property. About 500 of MacNeill's crofting tenants emigrated rather than fall into line with their landlord's plans, their places being taken by several hundred people from elsewhere in the Hebrides, people whom, it was said, 'the other proprietors were anxious to get rid of'. Such reckless subdivision did nothing to increase MacNeill's real rental, however; and a chemical works on a remote island could not, in the nature of things, compete effectively with factories in England and southern Scotland. Within a few years of the project's commencement MacNeill was bankrupt and Barra's vastly increased population of some 2,300 were unemployed and quite unable to pay the inflated rents demanded of them. On the estate being sold to an Aberdeenshire laird, Gordon of Cluny, in 1841, therefore, MacNeill's creditors seized almost all the cattle on the island in lieu of rent. (17) Gordon thus inherited a demoralised, poverty-stricken population, most of whom he transported to Canada ten years later. (18)

MacNeill's activities were unique, however; and on most estates kelping was allowed to go into decline in the later 1820s. By the 1840s it had ceased altogether on large stretches of coastline, being effectively prosecuted only on the better shores of the larger Hebridean properties. (19) That kelping survived at all was partly due to a continuing, though much reduced, demand for high quality kelp — needed at first for the manufacture of fine glass and later as a source of iodine. (20) More fundamentally it was a consequence of the fact that the agrarian structure of Hebridean estates had become so inextricably involved with the kelp industry that kelping could not be abandoned without precipitating a complete collapse of landlordly finances. (21) Clanranald's South Uist factor summed up the consequent dilemma as follows:

> If the kelp is given up the small tenants cannot continue to pay the present rents, because the work they got enabled them to pay for portions of ground so small that they could pay nothing from the produce. (22)

Crofting townships, he pointed out, had been laid out with a view to their rents being paid from kelpers' wages, and as long as the kelping population remained on the estate some sort of employment would have to be provided or rents would not be paid at all. As kelping ceased on the less productive shores, therefore, large numbers of crofting tenants, many of them labouring instead of paying rent, were employed to drain bogs, build roads, seed sand dunes and otherwise improve Clanranald's estate, 'to the great benefit of the property and at very little real expense to the landlord, a considerable sum of arrears having thus been recovered which must otherwise have been totally lost'. (23) But works of this kind were necessarily temporary; and as the 1820s advanced and kelp became more and more obviously doomed to decline more radical solutions were sought.

The need to solve the problems created by the kelp industry's sudden collapse was made more pressing by the effects of the equally unexpected agricultural depression which followed the ending of the Napoleonic wars. (24) 'During the war,' it was remarked in a report on Lord MacDonald's estates drawn up in 1829, 'prices assumed almost an unnatural height. Since the commencement of the peace they have year after year gradually declined.' (25) It was a sombre but broadly accurate assessment;

though in the first instance at least the fall in prices was rapid rather than gradual. In 1816, for example, low cattle prices were already causing considerable alarm in Skye. Less cattle than usual were being exported from the island and small tenants on the MacDonald estate and, for that matter, on every other property in the west Highlands and islands were consequently in a 'lamentable and ... calamitous state'. (26)

The decline in cattle prices, which was not reversed until the 1850s, (27) was particularly serious for crofting tenants. Even on kelp estates where rents were paid largely from wages the steadily expanding returns from cattle sales had helped the crofter to meet the ever rising rent imposed by his landlord and to buy the meal he needed to eke out the scanty produce of his meagre holding. (28) 'Had the prices continued as high as formerly,' Clanranald's factor noted in 1823, 'it is likely that no great sum of arrears would have been lost.' But in the Uists, as in Lewis where 'the constant partial payment of the rents' became a serious problem at about the same time, the post-1815 depression was marked by accumulating arrears and by increasingly frequent seasons of hunger and distress. (29) And a broadly similar pattern of events could be discerned throughout the region.

During the kelp boom and the period of high agricultural prices which had accompanied the wars with France, Highland landlords had been at the crest of a wave of prosperity. The rental of the MacLeod estate in Skye rose from £2,296 in 1800 to £7,374 in 1811; (30) while that of Lord MacDonald's estate on the same island rose from £5,550 in 1799 to about £14,000 in 1811. (31) Other proprietors benefited proportionately. (32) The sensible response to the post-war depression would thus have been to reduce rentals in line with the fall in agricultural commodity prices. And this in fact was done in the sheep farming sector of the economy where tenants were substantial businessmen ready to pull out at the first hint of trouble. (33) Crofters' ties with the land were of a quite different order, however, There was no way in which they could induce landlords to lower rents; and landlords themselves, accustomed to a life style and expenditure pattern secured by some twenty years of exorbitant income, were reluctant to cut their coats according to the available cloth. 'It is impossible I can forego the present rent without extreme inconvenience to my affairs,' wrote Lord MacDonald in 1817, (34) expressing the prevalent attitude which was that rentals should be kept at or near levels more appropriate to the preceding period of prosperity than to the circumstances of the years after 1815. (35)

But though rentals remained nominally high, the inescapable realities of agricultural depression made them increasingly fictitious. 'All rentals since 1814 have been a mere joke,' remarked Seaforth in 1823. (36) And other observers agreed that because of the proprietors' unwillingness to come to terms with the facts of economic life the rents of Highland and Hebridean estates were 'considerably higher than the tenants can afford to pay'. (37) Arrears inevitably continued to accumulate, for as Seaforth observed with some asperity, only those with first hand experience of it could appreciate 'the difficulty of getting rents from a Highland estate in bad times'. (38) Short of confiscating his cattle — a course which was recognisably disastrous for the future (39) — or evicting him, a scarcely practicable proposition in a situation in which every tenant might be in the same predicament, the landlord had simply to accept the crofter's excuses and allow his backlog of rent to mount up. (40) Allowances of some sort had thus of necessity to be made. And these usually took the form of annual abatements of rent. In Skye and Mull in the ten years after 1816, for example, abatements of crofting rent varying in size from 10% to 25% were commonplace. (41) These reductions were of an essentially temporary character, however; and they were never large enough to cover the deficiency in crofters' incomes. The inevitable outcome was that crofting tenants were plunged into a morass of perpetual debt. (42) The psychological consequences of inexorably increasing indebtedness were profound. 'When a tenant is sensible he owes his landlord more than he is able to pay,' observed Clanranald's factor in 1823, 'he becomes quite desperate and ceases to make any effort.' (43) The causes of crofters' desperation, however, derived more from the exigencies of their tenurial position than from any innately personal characteristic. Many of them were well aware that in the new economic situation sheep were more profitable than their traditional stocks of black cattle. But while entire estates could be, and often were, turned over to sheep farmers, crofters were quite unable to effect such a change within their own small confines simply because they lacked the necessary capital. Where crofters did acquire a few sheep they were invariably the cheapest on the market and were therefore 'of the worst description possible'. (44) And even if a crofter knew how to improve his land or increase his agricultural production, there was no point in his so doing, for the consequent increment in his income would at once be appropriated by the factor and set against his arrears in the rent ledger. (45) Apathy and hopelessness inevitably ensued. 'We have seen whole tracts of country on the north-western coast,' commented Hugh Miller,

> in which the rents of five whole years hung in one hopeless millstone of debt around the necks of the inhabitants. What wonder if, in such circumstances, the industrial energies of the Celt should be miserably overlaid. (46)

The same was true of the islands. And in such circumstances there grew up the myth of the ingrained idleness of the crofter, a myth that was to persist for many years to come. (47)

Although all Highland estates experienced serious difficulties in the second quarter of the nineteenth century, the impact of the economic crisis was greatest on the properties where kelp had been of most importance. Several Hebridean landlords went to the wall during this period, among them MacKenzie of Seaforth, MacLeod of Harris, Clanranald, MacNeill of Barra, and MacLeod of Raasay. Thus, within the space of about fifteen years, the whole of the Long Island, with the exception of North Uist, not sold by Lord MacDonald until 1855, passed out of the hands of its traditional owners. (48) Several mainland properties changed hands at about the same time. (49) Since the seventeenth century the great families of the Hebrides had spent vast sums on maintaining what they thought of as their rightful place in southern society; and the loss of their income from kelp merely demolished familial finances that had long been tottering. The effects of the kelp industry's collapse on its labour force were considerably more complicated.

Where kelping ceased completely the consequent loss of wages was a serious blow. On the Dunvegan estate, by no means a major kelp property, about £400 a year was lost to crofters in this way. (50) And even on estates where, for reasons mentioned above, kelping was not entirely abandoned or was replaced by some other form of labour, increasing arrears tended to ensure that the kelper received no actual cash in return for work done, his wages merely being credited against the amount of rent he owed his landlord. (51) This was bad enough. But the major consequence of the kelp industry's sudden decline was more profound and more serious — at least as far as crofters were concerned. Originally conceived of by the proprietors who created it as little more than an adjunct to the virtually insatiable labour requirements of a kelping economy, the crofting system and crofters themselves ceased to be of any use to landlords at the moment in the 1820s when kelp became unprofitable. Crofters and their families became a burden, a 'redundant population' who occupied potentially profitable land for which they were increasingly unable to pay an economic rent. The inevitable consequence was that landlords' desire to maintain, indeed increase, the population of their estates was transformed within the space of a very few years into an equally ardent determination to get rid of as many crofting tenants as possible.

On Clanranald's estates in South Uist and Benbecula the initial response to the kelp industry's troubles was, as already mentioned, to provide alternative employment for crofters who were left without work. But by 1827 — the year in which it became manifestly apparent that kelp prices would never recover — the estate management resolved that it was 'absolutely necessary to arrange Clanranald's ... estates so as to draw a revenue from the lands altogether independent of kelp', the most obvious and attractive course, seeing that sheep farming was now much more profitable than the traditional cattle husbandry, being the 'parcelling out of the estate' into sheep farms. (52) While financially alluring, such a policy was of course 'incompatible with the residence of the tenantry'; and the solution, according to Duncan Shaw — factor on the estate and a man who only eleven years before had been at great pains to keep up kelp production by preventing emigration (53) — was to ship 'at least 3,000 people to America'. (54)

Since Shaw's scheme involved ridding South Uist and Benbecula of almost half their population it was clearly not unambitious. (55) And as such it appealed to Clanranald's trustees. Obviously, wrote one of the latter gentlemen, large numbers of people would have to be removed, for no landowner who had decided to introduce sheep farming on to his property could afford to 'keep a swarm of lazy, idle tenants' for a term beyond his pleasure'. All over the Highlands, he pointed out, there were 'hundreds of instances of whole parishes and districts ... being depopulated to make room for sheep'. And he could see no good reason why a similar change should not take place in the Outer Isles. (56)

The shift from kelp to sheep having thus been accepted in principle, only one problem remained: Clanranald's funds were so depleted as to make it impossible for him to pay for emigration on the scale envisaged, while their growing poverty made it unlikely that his small tenants would be able to meet the cost of their own transportation. Government assistance was accordingly sought. (57) The Colonial Department, however, was inconveniently sceptical of the theory that the interests of Clanranald's estate and the Canadian colonies coincided, and neither the estate authorities' appeals nor the petitions from people who had 'received warning to quit their little possessions' (58) succeeded in eliciting a favourable response. Duncan Shaw, with the trustees' and proprietor's approval, modified his plans accordingly.

Since the best kelp produced on the estate was made by tenants in Benbecula he

decided to leave things as they were in that island 'while the kelp is at all worth manufacturing'. The northern part of South Uist was to be similarly unaffected and the 600
or so people who occupied its several settlements — including the townships of Balgarv
Liniquie, Kilaulay and Ardivachar — left to get on with the task of manufacturing as
much marketable kelp as possible. In the central portion of South Uist, however, the
kelp industry had become completely unprofitable and small tenants superfluous.
Four of the district's townships, notably Geirinish and Drimore, were still in the
nominal possession of tacksmen but were in fact occupied by large numbers of subtenants. The tacksmen, Shaw recommended, should be removed along with their
subtenants and the tenants of the crofting townships of Grogarry and Stilligarry. The
380 people thus evicted would be accompanied by another 400 who were to be
cleared from Howbeg, Snishival, Peninerine and Stoneybridge, and by the 150 occupants of Kildonan, a township lotted between 1816 and 1818 in order to make room
for the kelpers who had then been more important to Clanranald than any sheep
farmer. Kildonan was to be added to the farm of Milton whose tenant had taken
possession at Whitsun 1827 and was willing to give a good rent for the displaced
crofters' holdings. A similar accommodation was to take place in the southern part
of the island where the farm of Askernish had been let to a sheep farmer in 1826.
The township of Daliburgh which marched with Askernish would, Shaw concluded,
make 'a most desirable addition to it', as would the hill grazings held by the small
tenants of Kilpheder. (59)

The inconvenience of evicting about a thousand people, Shaw believed, would
be offset by the several advantages which would accrue to the proprietor from the
adoption of his plan. Because they would not 'emigrate to so small an island without
being certain of having a great return for their capital', South Uist sheep farmers' rents
would not at first be much higher than the aggregate rents of the crofters they would
displace. But their rents could be raised substantially when their initial leases lapsed
and they would, unlike those of the crofters, be 'well and punctually paid'. As a
result of the proposed changes, therefore, 'Clanranald would have a well paid money
rent and a certain income independent of kelp. His lands would be well cultivated
and properly managed.' And he would retain on his estate a population which, his
factor thought, would be 'more than sufficient' to work these kelp shores that were
to be kept in production. (60)

Although not executed exactly as planned, (61) Shaw's recommendations provided
the guide lines of estate policy in South Uist and Benbecula for the next few years.
Geirinish, Drimore, Ormaclett, Peninerine, Kildonan and several other townships
were cleared and let as, or added to, sheep farms in the late 1820s and early 1830s (62)
— the rearrangements being accompanied by considerable emigrations. (63) But it
was not until the islands had been bought by a proprietor wealthy enough to finance
the wholesale transhipment of his tenantry to Canada that the main objectives of
the factor's plan were finally and fully realised. (64)

The remorseless logic of Duncan Shaw's arguments was universally applicable and
developments on Clanranald's estate thus had their parallels throughout the islands.
By the 1830s crofters were everywhere on the defensive as they were found to be
'less advantageous to the proprietors than farmers occupying the same tracts of

ground'. (65) People who could afford to emigrate did so; and by 1828 there were reports of considerable emigrations from the Hebrides, 'hundreds' leaving that summer alone. (66) Between 1826 and 1827 about 1,300 people left Skye for the North American colonies. In 1828 over 600 people left North Uist for the same destination. And there were extensive emigrations from Barra at about the same time. (67) On the mainland there were similar occurrences — further extensions of the sheep farming system bringing about the emigration of about 1,000 people from Wester Ross and western parts of Inverness-shire in 1823 and 1824 alone. (68)

Although the word 'alarming' was applied to them by some commentators, (69) there was a vital difference between the emigrations of the 1820s and 1830s and those which had occurred before 1803. Nothing was done to stop them and they were, on the contrary, 'encouraged very much' by proprietors. (70) Throughout Britain the post-war depression had made emigration much more popular than hitherto — to 'shovel out paupers' or, in other words, transport the unemployed to the colonies was an obvious solution to the unemployment problem, and one to which Highland landlords were far from averse. (71) Landowners who would formerly have been riven with anxiety at the slightest hint of an emigration which might have deprived them of their kelpers were now convinced that their only hope of financial salvation lay in removing crofting tenants from the land and consolidating their recently created holdings into sheep farms — a policy strikingly similar to that being pursued in Ireland where the collapse of cereal prices after 1815 had produced a widespread tendency to switch from arable to pastoral farming, the consequent evictions and consolidations being facilitated by legislative action and by state-sponsored emigrations. (72)

The latter, which began in 1822, attracted the attention of at least one Highland proprietor, MacKenzie of Seaforth who, in correspondence with the chancellor of the exchequer, suggested that a similar scheme be launched in the Highlands. (73) But Seaforth was well in advance of his fellow proprietors who, as he remarked with more than a hint of bitterness, were unwilling to allow, let alone encourage, emigration as long as their tenants' kelping activities were worth anything at all. In a prophetic letter which he wrote in 1823, however, Seaforth recorded his conviction that Hebridean landlords would sooner or later have to provide

> for their wretched tenantry either by giving them the means of other employment or of emigrating ere it is too late. And convinced I am that before five years have expired this they will be driven to under increased difficulties, and then without even the semblance of benevolent and human feeling towards the starving mass of whom in the interval they will make use, so their applications will lose their power and sordid motives will be too justly laid to their charge. (74)

That prediction was quickly and amply vindicated. In 1826 and 1827, the years during which kelp prices finally fell through the floor, those who could afford to emigrate were the fortunate few, while landlords who could afford to sponsor emigration were even rarer. The Colonial Department consequently received scores of petitions from the Hebrides and the north-west coast of the Scottish mainland, many of them signed by tenants who had 'suffered from the introduction of sheep into these parts', and all of them asking for assisted passages to Canada. By that time, however, no assisted passages were to be had and each appeal for aid was turned down. (75)

Something was achieved, however. In 1827 the restrictions imposed on emigration by the Passenger Act of 1803 were completely removed, (76) a development which Highland proprietors greeted with a delight (77) that was perhaps a little unbecoming in men who had, for allegedly humanitarian reasons, been instrumental in putting the Act on the statute book in the first place. All the wiles of the once despised and castigated emigration agents were now employed on the proprietors' behalf with results that were, from the landlords' point of view, encouraging:

> Thig iad ugainn, carach, seòlta,
> Gus ar mealladh far ar n-eòlais;
> Molaidh iad dhuinn Manitòba,
> Dùthaich fhuar gun ghual, gun mhòine. (78)

The trouble with this type of emigration, as Seaforth's factor remarked in 1827, was that it tended to attract 'the best and most active tenants' - that is, those with most initiative and most money — while 'the poor and weak' were left behind in even worse circumstances than before. (79) To most estate managements, however, any emigration seemed better than none and everything possible was done to encourage it. (80)

By the end of the 1820s, therefore, 'informed' opinion — which meant the opinion of landlords, factors, sheep farmers, Established Church clergymen and anyone else of higher social standing than crofters — had concluded that over-population was the root cause of the social and economic problems confronting the north-west Highlands and islands. (81) Quickly elevated to the status of a received truth, that doctrine held sway in landowning and government circles for the rest of the nineteenth century, one of the first signs of its appearance — apart from landlords' sudden discovery of the benefits of emigration — being a sudden change in attitudes to the subdivision of crofters' holdings. Blithely encouraged during the kelp boom, subdivision was, from the 1820s onwards, regarded by estate managements as a virtually criminal act which, by making provision for young couples, helped to perpetuate the growth of a population whose economic usefulness was at an end. As Clanranald's factor remarked in 1827, subdivision was difficult to eliminate: 'Marriages cannot be prevented and, of course, parents will not see their children starve'. (82) But plenty of proprietors were willing to make the attempt. On the MacDonald estates in 1831, for example, it was decreed that any man who married 'without holding lands directly from Lord MacDon — that is, before he had inherited the family croft — would be 'forthwith removed from the property'. (83) A similar policy was in force in Coll. (84) And the managers of Sir James Riddell's Ardnamurchan estate thought that one obvious 'remedy for over-population' was 'to purge the rent roll, and punish every delinquent or doubtful character by immediate ejection furth of the Estate'. (85) Such regulations were inherently difficult to enforce, however, and it was generally agreed that the simplest, most effective and most profitable way of dealing with an overpopulated estate was to remove its small tenants and put their lands under sheep — an attitude encapsulated in the evidence given to a parliamentary committee by the factor of John Hay MacKenzie's estate at Coigach, Wester Ross. Asked: 'If Mr. MacKenzie's estate were cleared of the surplus population, what steps would or could be taken to prevent a recurrence of the evil?' he replied: 'To immediately let the land as sheep farms', a proceeding which would not only ensure the property's continued depopulation but would also result in its owner receiving an 'undoubtedly ... better rental'. (86) Coigach crofters were in fact left in undisturbed occupation of their holdings until the 1850s. (87) Crofters elsewhere were not so fortunate.

Among north-west Highland and Hebridean landlords, all of whose finances were showing signs of strain by the 1820s, none was more impecunious than Stewart MacKenzie of Seaforth, a Galloway laird who had acquired his Highland estates and territorial designation by marrying the late Lord Seaforth's daughter and heir. (88) To wed a Highland heiress was not, in the economic circumstances of 1817, the year that the marriage took place, the way to make a fortune, however. And by 1819 Seaforth was convinced that the only way to reverse the decline in his income from his newly acquired properties was to convert them into sheep farms. The Canadian colonies, he believed, were the natural receptacle for the people who would be displaced by incoming sheep farmers, and to an influential friend of his in London he accordingly addressed an urgent enquiry as to whether the government would be willing to subsidise the envisaged transportation:

> If it becomes necessary for me, as I fear it will, to carry through the measure of dispossessing a population overgrown and daily becoming more burdensome to pave the way for the grand improvement of the introduction of mutton in lieu of man, the numbers almost appal me and will astonish you when I add that 5,000 souls and upwards I calculate may be spared ... to render the change complete. (89)

These figures included a number of tenants from the Seaforth estates on the mainland. But it was in the development of the large and remote island of Lewis, of which he was the sole owner, that Seaforth was particularly interested. And by the autumn of 1820 the essential features of a plan for its transformation had been committed to paper.

Because no officially subsidised passages were forthcoming, (90) the major obstacle in the way of the successful establishment of a sheep farming economy in Lewis was 'the population and how it is to be disposed of'. The solution arrived at was to set up large numbers of crofting townships, 'the whole northern part of the island' being thought 'suitable for this plan'. As was usual in such cases, the division of traditional farms into crofts was intended to increase the number of people living on a given area of land, the essence of Seaforth's scheme being that

> Whatever grounds are from their nature and situation peculiarly fitted for sheep pasture must be so arranged that the present occupiers may be removed to allotments which are for that purpose to be laid out for them. (91)

The places most obviously 'fitted' for sheep rearing were the parishes of Uig and Lochs which occupy the southern portion of Lewis and where the low-lying moors that characterise the northern part of the island rise up to meet the hills of Harris. That this area was 'best adapted for sheep' was pointed out to Lord Seaforth in 1800. (92) And in 1819 the newly established tenant of most of north-west Harris, a sheep farmer named Alexander MacRae, (93) was casting increasingly envious eyes across Loch Resort to the hills of Uig, a district that was, and is, particularly well suited to sheep farming. (94) If the Lewis side of the loch were to be 'planted with sheep', wrote MacRae to Seaforth, he would be delighted to become its tenant. But because the lands in question were held by a motley collection of small tenants and subtenants with whose neighbourhood he 'would gladly dispense' he would be happy to see Uig 'laid out for sheep, whoever stocks it'. (95) MacRae's wish was granted by his being made tenant of the Uig farm of Scaliscro. (96) His success in no way mellowed his attitude to the parish's original occupants, however; for in 1833 he was writing to Seaforth to complain of the depredations committed on his land and stock by the small tenants of a nearby holding. Anxious 'to get rid of so troublesome and dis-agreeable neighbours', he offered, if they were removed, to take the tenancy of their lands at a rent at least equivalent to that already being received by the estate. (97)

Although MacRae's request demonstrates the ease with which evictions could be arranged, the fact that he had to make it shows that Seaforth's plans had not gone as smoothly as he had originally hoped. In the spring of 1823, ten years before MacRae penned the letter which sealed the fate of his unfortunate neighbours, Seaforth had intended to remove up to 1,000 people from Uig and Lochs and settle them in crofting townships in the northern parishes of Stornoway and Barvas. The 'violent change' implied by evictions on such a scale alarmed Seaforth's trustees, however. His finances, they pointed out, were in a parlous state – that, after all, was why they had been appointed to take charge of them – and he had not the means to properly establish so many crofts, let alone equip their occupants with the boats and gear they would need if they were to participate effectively in the fishing industry, on whose prospects Seaforth pinned wildly exaggerated hopes. (98) Lack of capital was in fact the fatal flaw in all Seaforth's plans. But it was a flaw whose existence he could not perceive or was unwilling to admit. Although forced to accept his trustees' advice he continued to be possessed of an urge to take what he termed 'decisive steps' in Lewis. (99) Unable to afford the grandiloquent, Sutherland-type clearances which he had initially planned, he therefore settled for a more gradual chipping away at existing tenurial arrangements. But 'decisive' or not, his measures left a marked imprint on crofting society in Lewis.

Even before 1823 a group of Skye farmers had been given a lease of the farm of Park in the eastern part of the parish of Lochs; (100) and in the following twenty or so years the farm was steadily extended until it occupied the greater part of the extensive and hilly peninsula from which it derived its name. In the 1820s and 1830s, a royal commission was informed in 1883, about twenty-eight settlements were cleared and their lands added to Park farm. In the process, said an old man who had witnessed his own father's eviction from one of these holdings, over a hundred families were removed – some to nearby townships in Barvas or in the neighbourhood of Stornoway. (101) Contemporary evidence bears out the general accuracy of these claims. Evictions from Park began in the early 1820s. (102) And in 1826 some of the peninsula's former occupants were being settled on new crofts at Balallan and Leurbost – the 'crofts' in many instances consisting of roughly pegged out plots on those townships' common grazings, a method of settlement which began the process by which the number of tenants in Balallan grew from 26 at the beginning of the nineteenth century to 104 in 1888. (103) The 1830s brought renewed evictions. Eishken, Orosay, Shiltenish and Lemreway, all in the Park peninsula, were cleared between 1833 and 1841, their tenants, of whom there were at least sixty, being sent to Crossbost, Tong and Tolsta where tacks and joint farms were lotted to make room for them. (104)

In 1823 Seaforth had remarked that tenants to be evicted from Park 'must and ought to be content with whatever land we can give them', (105) the implication being that the setting up of a soundly based crofting system was one of the least of his concerns. In accordance with these instructions little attempt was made to provide the new crofters with adequate or even fertile holdings, several townships being situated on land that had never been previously settled or cultivated. One of these was Aird Tunga, the Aird of Tong, a settlement which was established on some waste land about three miles north of Stornoway and into which some of Park's former occupants were moved in 1827. (106) In the following spring Alexander Craig, who managed Seaforth's estate at Brahan on the mainland, had occasion to visit Lewis and to satisfy his curiosity about the recent developments on the island he went to inspect the new township at Aird Tunga. What he found appalled him:

> Until I saw the actual situation of the new lotters on the Aird of Tong I had no idea of the great hardships and privations that the poor people endure who are forced into new allotments without matters being previously arranged for their moving. The situation of the new lotters on the Aird of Tong at this moment beggars all description. It is worse than anything I ever saw in Donegal where I always considered human wretchedness to have reached its very acme.

In a treeless island like Lewis, Craig went on, timber was almost unobtainable and evicted tenants had therefore to transport the rafters of their old houses to the sites set aside for their new homes. While being dismantled and carried northwards, however, many of the timbers — which were often old and rotten to begin with — had been irreparably broken. And the consequence was that many of the new houses — if ramshackle erections of stone and turf could be graced with such a title — were inadequately roofed. Being too poor to buy new rafters, there was little the crofters could do to remedy their situation. But it was a fact, according to Craig, that Seaforth could have provided his crofting tenants with all the timber they needed for a fraction of the legal expenses incurred in evicting them from their original holdings. And if the houses were bad, Craig concluded, their surroundings were worse. There was no track, far less a road, to the new settlement and its occupants had 'literally to step to their knees in mud the moment they quit their thresholds'. (107)

Craig's protests, like those of the less articulate Lewismen who demonstrated their opposition to the new order by committing 'great depredations' among the sheep stock in Park, (108) seem to have had no effect on Seaforth's policies. All over the southern part of Lewis in the 1820s and 1830s, sheep farming was being consolidated and extended, for sheep farmers, as Seaforth's factor remarked, 'could be got as fast as the lands could be cleared for them'. (109) In 1826, for example, Duncan Stewart who had been manager of Park farm before becoming factor to MacLeod of Harris — on whose estate he had at once provided himself with a sheep farm (110) — expressed a desire to rent some grazings on the eastern shore of Loch Seaforth, an area adjoining his lands on the Harris side of the march. His offer was accepted and the tenants of Aird an Troim 'duly warned' to remove. (111)

Events in Uig took a similar course. The western part of that parish, especially the area around Loch Roag, had been the main kelping centre in Lewis, (112) and the industry's collapse no doubt strengthened the estate management's professed resolve to have the district 'put into large tracts of pasture'. (113) Clearances began in the 1820s and continued into the following decade, the evicted tenants being moved northwards or accommodated in newly lotted townships on Uig's Atlantic coast. (114) Deprived of their inland pastures, (115) the tenants of these townships were in an unenviable and, it transpired, an insecure position. One of the coastal settlements, Mealista, was soon seen to be suitable for conversion into a sheep farm; (1 and in 1836 a good offer was made for its tenancy. Seaforth's factor accordingly proposed to move Mealista's sixteen families to townships in Ness, in the northern part of the island. (117) That scheme having foundered — most probably on the expense involved — six of the tenants cleared from Mealista were crammed into the nearby — and already congested — township of Brenish. The rest, as an Uig crofter subsequently remarked, were 'hounded away' to America. (118)

'It must be admitted,' declared an official report of 1837, 'that few cases could arise to which the remedy of emigration on a great scale would appear more appropriate than to that of the Hebrides.' (119) And aided by the government's subsequent decision to make official funds available to meet the expenses of emigration from the Highlands to the Australian colonies, (120) other proprietors showed no more hesitation than Seaforth or Clanranald in switching from kelp to wool and therefore from crofting to sheep farming — the process beginning as early as 1826 when MacLean of Coll arranged to have about 300 people shipped from his Rhum estate to Canada. MacLean spent £5 14s. on each adult emigrant's passage. (121) But the investment from his point of view — if not from that of the islands' occupants who were noticeably reluctant 'to leave the land of their ancestors' — was an eminently sound one. Rhum's original rental was about £300. Cleared and let as a single sheep farm, it brought in £800 a year to its proprietor. (122)

Economic imperatives were everywhere seen to be the same. 'The fall in the value of kelp,' observed Lord MacDonald's North Uist factor in 1839,

> renders ... a change in the management of the North Uist estate necessary. The tenants have hitherto been accustomed to pay for the greater part of their rents by their labour as kelpers. Kelp is not now a productive manufacture. The population of the estate is greater than the land, the kelp being abandoned, can maintain. The allotments of land held by the small tenants are so small that they cannot maintain their families and pay the proprietor the rents which the lands are worth if let in larger tenements. It becomes necessary, therefore, that a number of small tenants be removed; [and] that that part of the estate calculated for grazings be let as grazings. (12

The former policy of doing everything possible to facilitate the proliferation of smallholdings on North Uist (124) was accordingly abandoned. Between 1838 and 1843 Lord MacDonald helped around 1300 people to emigrate from the island, (125) their departure being marked by the conversion of considerable tracts of land into sheep farms. (126)

In Harris, where widespread removals began in the 1820s, there were similar developments. Several clearances were instituted by MacLeod of Harris' factor, Duncan Stewart, in order to extend his own sheep farming interests. (127) Another beneficiary was Alexander MacRae who, like Stewart, also had a hand in Seaforth's clearances in Lewis. (128) About thirteen settlements situated on the Atlantic coast between West Loch Tarbert and Kinlochresort were cleared to make way for MacRae's

North Harris sheep farm, and their former occupants moved to the island's east coast. (129) Initiated on MacLeod's instructions, these transformations were continued in the 1830s by the island's new proprietor, the Earl of Dunmore. By 1837, according to Dunmore's factor, the population had 'in a great measure been removed from the west coast of Harris and other arrangements [were] in contemplation by which what remains of the population [were] very likely soon to be removed'. (130) The nature of the contemplated 'arrangements' became clear in 1838 when the tenant of one of Dunmore's sheep farms refused to renew his lease unless the township of Borve, the largest remaining settlement on the west coast, was added to his lands. About fifty families were accordingly evicted, (131) thus completing the process by which 'the most fertile farms possessed by small tenants' were 'depopulated and converted into extensive sheep walks'. (132)

In the 1820s and 1830s, therefore, the relatively fertile machair lands on the Atlantic coast of Harris were completely cleared and the evicted population settled on the island's bare and rocky east coast, a district where, as a Harris crofter bitterly remarked, 'beasts could not live'. (133) There, in the hollows between the rocks, they constructed the lazybeds or *feannagan* which alone could provide a depth of soil sufficient to raise a scanty crop of potatoes. 'Nothing,' Sir Frank Fraser-Darling has written,

can be more moving to the sensitive observer of Hebridean life than these lazybeds of the Bays district of Harris. Some are no bigger than a dining table, and possibly the same height from the rock, carefully built up with turves carried there in creels by the women and girls. One of these tiny lazybeds will yield a sheaf of oats or a bucket of potatoes, a harvest no man should despise. (134)

Such harvests could not support a population used to living on the good arable lands of the west, however, and many people, 'reduced to extreme distress by being crowded into places incapable of affording them subsistence', were forced to emigrate. (135) Between 600 and 800 emigrants sailed from Harris in 1828 alone, and they were followed by a further 600 in the early 1840s. (136)

Across the Minch in Skye, meanwhile, the clearances which had begun in the nineteenth century's first and second decades went ahead with renewed rigour in the 1820s and 1830s. 'The small tenants have paid wretchedly ill,' wrote MacLeod of Dunvegan's factor in his report on the Martinmas rent collection of 1833, 'and since kelp must be given up they will be worse and worse every year unless some other plan is fallen upon to employ them.' (137) Unable to think of any plan that could be as profitable to MacLeod as the extension of sheep farming, he suggested emigration as the best solution to the problem; (138) the emigration to be facilitated of course by evictions. The latter, in fact, were already occurring on a fairly massive scale as vast tracts of the Dunvegan estate, especially the parts of it contained by the parish of Bracadale, were put under sheep. (139) Bracadale's population in 1821 was 2,103. Ten years later it was 1,769; (140) and the decrease, according to the parish minister, was 'solely to be ascribed to the system of farming which has for some time been adopted, viz., throwing a number of farms into one large tack for sheep grazing and dispossessing and setting adrift the small tenants'. (141) The number of tenants 'set adrift' in this way can be gauged from the fact that in 1826 no fewer than 229 people from Bracadale, all of whom had received notices of eviction from the MacLeod estate management, applied for assisted passages to Canada, their applications being accompanied by similar requests from the neighbouring parish of Duirinish (142) where, by 1841, over 3,000 acres had been converted from arable to pasture. (143)

Sheep farmers not unnaturally welcomed these developments. Of the 384 people on his farm, complained one of MacLeod's principal tenants, only his shepherds were of any use to him. 'The other people' he found 'really an encumbrance'. (144) The presence of the 'poor families' who were 'domiciled in all parts' of another Bracadale farm meant that 'the quietness of the flocks is always subject to disturbance and their safety also put in jeopardy'. And if only 'the people, or the greater part of them could be got rid of', the farm's rent could at once be raised. (145) The farm was accordingly cleared, and along with small tenants evicted from other farms in the vicinity, a number of its former occupants were sent to Glendale where MacLeod hoped to establish a fishing station. (146) As was usual with such schemes, the fishing station proved a failure. But in order to force the district's crofters to participate in his planned development of the Minch herring fisheries, MacLeod deliberately overcrowded Glendale — employing techniques previously used to coerce Sutherland's crofting population into taking an active part in equally illusionary enterprises. In the townships of Upper and Lower Milovaig, for example, MacLeod subdivided existing crofts in an attempt to ensure that their occupants could not avoid becoming fishermen. (147) In this way, although he did not realise it at the time, he sowed the seeds of the grievances that underlay the eventually triumphant crofters' revolt which began in Glendale in 1882. (148)

At the beginning of the 1840s that revolt was far in the future, and crofters' immediate prospects were almost as bleak as they could be. A comment made about Applecross summed up the plight of crofters everywhere:

Of the working class, the ordinary means of subsistence is renting a small croft for about £5, the free produce of which may be £3 per annum, in addition to which they follow the herring fishing, the returns from which are very precarious and sometimes a dead loss. (149)

Deliberately created by landlords who could not bring themselves to remove it even when it had served its exploitative purpose, that yawning chasm between income and rent was, in the second quarter of the nineteenth century, the crucial fact of crofting life. It made saving impossible. It crippled and stifled all initiative and enterprise. Combined with the omnipresent threat of eviction, it ensured the absence of any kind of security. And in conjunction with the smallness of holdings, the other major consequence of landlords' former need to manoeuvre their small tenants into a position of utter dependence and subservience, it pushed crofters into a virtually complete reliance on one lowly crop: the potato. That root, wrote the minister of Morvern, was the crofting population's staff of life:

Indeed there are many, it is feared, much in the predicament of a little boy of the parish, who, on being asked on a certain occasion of what his three daily meals consisted, gave the same unvarying answer — 'Mashed potatoes'; and on being further asked by his too inquisitive inquirer, 'What else?' replied, with great artlessness, but with evident surprise, 'A spoon!' (150)

This almost unrelieved dependence upon a single and inherently vulnerable crop constituted the greatest of all crofters' insecurities. And the poverty stricken Highland emigrants who were a feature of life in the Canada of the early 1840s (151) were soon to be joined by very many more of their compatriots — driven there by threat of starvation and by clearances which were more brutal and more sweeping than any that had yet occurred.

4. Famine, 1845-1850

FAMINE and scarcity were not novel occurrences in the Highlands. In the later eighteenth century the region was estimated to suffer from food shortages in one year out of every three, (1) and there are records of several periods of acute distress. In the spring of 1772, for example, the starving people of Skye were living on the carcasses of cattle which had themselves died of hunger; and other islands were similarly affected. (2) Storms and crop failures brought renewed hunger in the autumn of 1782. And on that occasion a serious famine was averted only by the British government's decision to send more than £17,000 worth of food to the Highlands. Most of the official aid consisted of peasemeal, of which the British army – in consequence of the ending of the American war of independence – had a large surplus. And 1783 was accordingly remembered in the Highlands as *bliadhna na peasrach,* the peasemeal year. (3)

Such scarcities, however, were essentially transient phenomena – the consequence of one bad harvest; inevitable, though nonetheless tragic, concomitants of a system of subsistence agriculture. The famine which began in 1846 was of a different order of catastrophe. A human tragedy on a scale unparalleled in modern Scottish history, it was unprecedented in severity and duration. It was also the culmination of thirty years of growing hardship and despair. (4) In every year since 1815, the government was informed in 1847, there had been 'a gradual deterioration in the position of the people', and each decade had 'shown them more impoverished and less able to meet a season of distress'. (5)

The causes of crofters' declining fortunes are clear enough: the economic effects of the kelp industry's collapse and the prolonged fall in cattle prices were aggravated by the loss of two other sources of income as a result of the effective suppression of illicit distillation and the completion of the canal and road construction programme which had begun in 1803. (6) The consequent fall in crofters' earnings was temporaril offset by a seasonal migration of their sons and daughters to the lowlands where they helped to bring in the harvest. But in the 1830s and 1840s even that employment became precarious – harvest work having become the virtual monopoly of Irish labourers enabled by the inauguration of steamer services to come across from Ireland more quickly and more cheaply than Highlanders could make their way southwards, and consequently willing to work for lower wages than their Highland counterparts. (7

The loss of alternative sources of income made crofters more dependent upon the land. The land, however, was becoming more and more congested and less and less able to support the people who lived on it, a development that was partly due to the inexorable pressure of population – for though growing less rapidly than during the kelp boom the north-west Highlands' population continued to expand, except in areas such as Mull where clearances were more than usually widespread and urban receptacles for displaced tenants relatively close. (8) More people meant more subdivision of holdings that had been too small to begin with, as did the overcrowding that resulted from proprietors putting whole districts under sheep. In 1847, for example, it was calculated that some 6,000 of the 16,000 arable acres in Skye were held by thirty sheep farmers. Almost all this area had been converted from tillage to pasture, while the remaining 10,000 acres were expected to support over 4,000 families. (9) Of course, they could not; and in this situation — which was to worsen before it improved (10) — is to be found one cause of crofters' growing poverty and proneness to hunger. (11)

Despite the population explosion of the late eighteenth and early nineteenth centuries, therefore, the Highland famine of the 1840s is inexplicable in terms of the sheer weight of numbers alone. The experience of the islands during the kelp boom and of Ulster during the Irish famine (12) showed that large smallholding populations, and even rampant subdivision, were not in themselves disastrous — as long as money incomes held up and the greater part of the land was in the smallholders' hands. The famine was thus an economic rather than a biological catastrophe; and as such its origins lay in the virtual evaporation of crofters' cash earnings and the growing tendency to take their land away from them and give it to sheep farmers — developments which gave an unprecedented importance to crofters' diminishing plots and their universally predominant crop, the potato.

According to that early Highland chronicler, Martin Martin, potatoes were part of the 'common diet' of the people of Skye as long ago as the 1680s. (13) From other accounts, however, it seems likely that they did not achieve any widespread acceptance in the Highlands until the mid-eighteenth century, a common tradition being that they were introduced into South Uist by Clanranald in 1743. There, as elsewhere, they were by no means popular. 'You made us plant these worthless things,' the people of South Uist are said to have told Clanranald, 'but, Virgin Mary, will you make us eat them!' (14) Be that as it may, there is no doubt that the potato made rapid progress in the Highlands during the second half of the eighteenth century. (15) Tolerant of lime deficiency and responding well to manuring with seaweed, it was clearly suited to the region and by the turn of the century was to be found in every part of it. (16) Because it was the only crop which could support so large a population on what one observer called 'such miserable patches of land', (17) the rise of the kelp industry and the consequent development of the crofting system consolidated the potato's position. By 1811 potatoes were calculated to provide the typical Hebridean crofter with no less than four fifths of his food, (18) a ratio that was only slightly higher than that prevailing on the north-west coast of the mainland and one that in no way diminished during the 1820s and 1830s. (19)

A population used to living on meat, fish, or even bread, can in times of scarcity have recourse to humbler foodstuffs. But as was remarked by one of the officials charged with the task of alleviating famine in Ireland and the Highlands in the 1840s,

> those who are habitually and entirely fed on potatoes live upon the extreme verge of human subsistence, and when they are deprived of their accustomed food there is nothing cheaper to which they can resort. They have already reached the lowest point of the descending scale, and there is nothing beyond but starvation and beggary. (20)

By the 1840s, then, the agrarian structure of north-west Scotland was — as was observed by Norman MacLeod, a Church of Scotland minister who knew the area well – 'in a very hollow and rotten state'. (21) The potato was its only prop and if it were to give way the whole fabric of crofting life would inevitably disintegrate. As early as the spring of 1817, indeed, there had been indications of the nature of the cataclysm that was likely to ensue.

In that disastrous year the economically detrimental effects of a bad harvest in 1816 and a complete failure of the coastal herring fishing were added to the consequences of a significant fall in cattle prices. And because thousands of Highlanders were returning from wartime military service, greater than usual demands were made upon less than usual amounts of money and food. Only one outcome was possible: as a hard winter gave way to a cold, inclement spring it became apparent that many people in the Highlands, and especially in the Outer Isles, were on the verge of starvation. Hebridean proprietors accordingly appealed to the government for assistance (– their pleas evoking a remarkably prompt and generous response. Seaforth was sent 2,500 quarters of grain and Clanranald 2,000 quarters; while MacLeod of Harris and MacNeill of Barra got 800 and 600 quarters respectively. Such munificence they found somewhat embarrassing – especially when asked to foot the bill. And MacKenz of Seaforth's share of over £6,000, though eventually halved in deference to his well founded pleas of approaching poverty, became for several years a matter of no little contention between him and the government. (23)

But if proprietors became indebted to government, tenants became indebted to landlords; for though the latter distributed the supplies they received they did not do so gratuitously. On Lord MacDonald's Skye estate, for example, the price was fixed at the grossly inflated level of two guineas a boll, payable at Whitsun 1818. (24) Unwilling to add a further large debt to their already accumulating arrears of rent, crofters were naturally reluctant to accept their landlord's 'assistance'. Even when 'actually starving', Lord MacDonald's factor reported, they 'always underestimate the quantity they actually need when aware they have to pay high for it'. (25) And as was demonstrated in the 1830s, when crofters' financial position was much worse than it had been in the years immediately after the Napoleonic wars, (26) Lord MacDonald's estate managers were past masters at collecting debts of this kind. In 1837, to alleviate the effects of a particularly bad winter, Lord MacDonald supplied his crofting tenants with seed oats valued at £1,303. Only £81 remained outstanding two years later. (27)

When kelping was all important such outlays were regarded as investments, the return from which was an adequately fed labour force and a good kelp crop, and the expenses of which could in any case be deducted from the kelpers' wages. (28) As a Benbecula crofter subsequently remarked, therefore, 'there were stores of meal and no destitution in the country while the kelp was going on'. (29) In the 1820s and 1830s, however, grants of meal to crofters brought no bonuses in the shape of increased kelp profits – and not all estate managers were as good at collecting debts as were those employed by Lord MacDonald. Landlords became correspondingly less enthusiastic about assisting their crofters; (30) and the latter were increasingly left to fend for themselves.

The outcome, made the more unavoidable by crofters' deteriorating finances, was that seasons of hardship and scarcity became steadily more frequent. A chronic shortage of meal and of the cash needed to buy it made potatoes quite literally

irreplaceable. And every summer there was provided — in the weeks or months
between the exhausting of the old potatoes and the digging of the new ones — a
miniature rehearsal of what would occur in the event of the staple crop being lost:
the shores were ransacked for shellfish; while nettles, brambles and any other vaguely
edible plants were uprooted, stewed and eaten. (31) In one year, 1836, the potato
crop did fail fairly extensively and only governmental and charitable assistance prevented a calamity. The following year brought a good harvest, however, and the
1836 crisis soon passed. (32) That which began ten years later was not so temporary;
nor were its effects so easily alleviated.

Although its origins remain obscure, potato blight is now known to be caused by a
fungus, *phytophthora infestans,* to which the potatoes of the 1840s had absolutely
no natural resistance. Still the most serious plant pestilence in the northern hemi-
sphere, blight spreads with astonishing rapidity. Given appropriate weather conditions —
notably warmth, moisture and light winds — the spores formed on a single potato
plant can infect many thousands of other plants in a matter of days, or even hours.
To people who had no scientific understanding of its causes, blight was a mysterious
and terrifying scourge. And as anyone who has experienced one of the region's typically mild, damp summers will readily appreciate, the western Highlands and islands
provided for *phytophthora infestans* an environment that was little short of ideal. (33)
The first major outbreak of blight in Europe occurred in the summer of 1845.
But though the fungus was fairly widespread in southern Scotland that year, most
of the north and the Highlands escaped its devastations. Only in Islay and mid-Argyll
were serious losses reported. (34) Elsewhere in the region the crop was healthy and
abundant — a state of affairs which enabled some enterprising crofters and proprietors
to take advantage of the high prices that resulted from scarcities in other parts of the
British Isles. No less than 15,410 barrels of potatoes were sent south from Tobermory;
and on the Mull estates belonging to the Duke of Argyll and Campbell of Kilpatrick
at least £3,158 was received from sales of grain and potatoes to southern dealers —
a sum which exceeded the rental by more than £550. (35)

    The Highlands, then, were more than usually well prepared for the winter. Nor
did the New Year bring any immediate change in their fortunes. The spring of 1846
was mild and pleasant, the early summer warm and dry with the promise of another
good harvest. (36) In July, however, it began to rain and with the wet weather came
the blight. It appeared in Skye in the middle of the month and within a few weeks
the whole region was affected. (37) In June the all important potato crop had been
unusually well advanced. In July and August, it was devastated: 'In course of a week,
frequently in course of a single night or day, fields and patches of this vegetable,
looking fair and flourishing, were blasted and withered and found to be unfit for
human food.' (38) Towards the end of August the *Inverness Courier* sent one of its
reporters to Skye, Knoydart, Lochalsh and Kintail. His despatches make depressing
reading: 'In all that extensive district he had scarcely seen one field which was not
affected — some to a great extent, and others presenting a most melancholy appearance as they were enveloped in one mass of decay.' (39) And from all the scorched
and blackened plots and lazybeds there emanated a 'foetid and offensive smell which
poisoned the air' — the obnoxious, inescapable stench of rotting potatoes. (40)

No area escaped the blight. But losses were greatest in the islands — Skye, where less than a fifth of the average crop was harvested being fairly typical. (41) On the mainland the failure of the crop was not quite so universal, but local variations in the blight's incidence and severity were more pronounced. In Glenelg nine tenths of the usual crop was destroyed. In Ullapool less than half the potatoes were affected. On Sutherland's west coast the potatoes failed more or less completely, while on the north coast the loss was comparatively trifling. (42) The existence of a few favoured localities did not, however, significantly modify the general picture. As the official report put it: 'The failure is all but universal and complete, the partial exemptions being too inconsiderable to cause any sensible diminution of the tragedy.' (43) And by the end of 1846, it was estimated, at least three-quarters of the entire crofting population of the north-west Highlands and Hebrides were completely without food. (44

The first hint of the coming calamity occurred in Harris in the early summer. The previous year's potatoes having proved inedible when lifted from their storage pits, the island's population were forced to subsist on a diet of shellfish and sand eels. (45) In July and August, as the old potatoes were finished and the new crop blighted, a similar situation began to arise in every part of the region. Norman MacLeod visited the islands in August and frequently 'met and conversed with poor people returning from the potato fields, accompanied by their famished children, with empty baskets, and unable to collect what would afford them one meal'. (46) Mull, from which grain and potatoes had been exported twelve months before, was by the end of September completely dependent on imported meal. (47) In Kilmuir, Skye, those crofters lucky enough to occupy larger than average holdings were still managing to eke out their scanty crops of oats. But people with little land, or no land at all, were by October 'reduced to a state of abject famine, and live for the most part on seaweed and scanty supplies of shellfish'. (48)

Crofters were no strangers to scarcity. But its onset in September and October was unprecedented. 'We frequently had bad Springs.' wrote one Skye minister towards the end of 1846, 'but this is a Winter of Starvation.' (49) And it was a winter which set in early and proved cold and stormy with frequent gales and snowstorms. (50) To the incessant cold and hunger — intolerable enough in themselves — were added sickness and disease. Typhus and cholera broke out in several places. The shellfish scavenged from the beaches produced dysentery when eaten. And even when a little meal was added to such a diet it remained, in the absence of potatoes, seriously deficient in Vitamin C. The inevitable outcome was that scurvy reappeared in districts where it had been unknown for more than a century. (51)

To quantify human suffering is impossible and probably undesirable. All that can be done to give some idea of the appalling conditions endured by crofters and their families in the winter of 1846-47 is to quote from a single — but by no means untypical report — made by a member of a Free Church deputation which visited the Skye parish of Strath on Christmas Day, 1846:

We found the condition of very many of them miserable in the extreme, and every day, as they said, getting worse. Their houses — or rather their hovels — and persons the very pictures of destitution and hopeless suffering. A low typhus fever prevails here in several families who seemed to be left to their fate by their neighbours. (52) In one most deplorable case, the whole of the family of seven persons had been laid down, not quite at the same time, in this fever. The eldest of the children, a son about nineteen years of age, had died just when his mother was beginning to get on foot. No one would enter the house with the coffin for the son's remains. It was left at the outside of the door, and the enfeebled parent and a little girl, the only other member of the family on foot, were obliged to drag the body to the door and put it into the coffin there, whence it was carried by the neighbours with fear and alarm to its last resting place. When I entered the wretched house ... I found the father lying on the floor on a wisp of dirty straw, his bedclothes, or rather rags of blanket, as black nearly as soot, his face and hands of the same colour, never having been washed since he was laid down; and the whole aspect of the man, with his hollow features and sunken eyes, and his situation altogether was such as I had never beheld before. In a miserable closet, beyond the kitchen where the father lay, I found the rest of the family, four daughters from about eleven years of age to seventeen, all crammed into one small bed, two at one end and two at the other. The rags of blanket covering them worse, if possible, than those on the father; their faces and persons equally dirty, the two youngest having no night clothes of any kind. One of these poor girls was very ill and was not likely to recover. The others had the fever more mildly, but had not yet been so long in it. The effluvia and stench in this place, and indeed in every part of the miserable dwelling, were such that I felt I could not remain long without great risk of infection, as there was no means of ventilation whatever, and not even of light. The poor woman said she had got a stone or two of meal, she said she did not know from whom, which had barely served to make gruel for the unfortunate patients. The family had no means whatever of their own. (53)

In the midst of such a disaster there was relatively little that people could do to help themselves. 'The flocks of the large sheep-owners,' the minister of Duirinish in Skye had written some years before the coming of the blight, 'are annually thinned by those who feel the pinching of famine.' In 1846 and in subsequent years the thinning was particularly drastic; (54) while some North Uist crofters' plan to take forcible possession of 'a certain portion of wheat' was thwarted only by the efforts of the local Free Church minister. (55) Such windfalls as were gathered in were supplemented with shellfish and other makeshift substitutes for potatoes and with the meal which crofters bought with such savings as they possessed. All these alternative sources of food were inherently limited, however; while the obvious substitute for the potato — fish — was largely unobtainable because of the way in which the fishing industry had developed, or failed to develop, since the days when James Loch and his fellow 'improvers' had envisaged the wholesale transformation of agricultural tenants into fishermen.

Because of their low incomes and high rents crofters had been quite unable to accumulate the capital needed to purchase the relatively sophisticated boats and gear required for deep sea fishing. The lion's share of the profits made in west coast waters went, therefore, to the better equipped and more highly skilled fishermen from the east coast of Scotland. And crofters were left with little but the summer herring fishing in the sea lochs, an essentially precarious resource which 'served only to eke out the insufficient subsistence derivable from the soil'. (56) Although 'ostensibly a fishing population' therefore, crofters were — as the government's 1846 enquiries revealed — 'so poorly skilled and so ill provided with means that ... they [did] not possess the ability to pursue the occupation with effect'. This, rather than any innate Celtic indolence, it was concluded, lay behind their otherwise incomprehensible neglect of 'the stores apparently within their reach'. (57)

Apart from emigration — the cost of which was usually beyond their unaided resources (58) — the only other course open to the crofting population was to move south in search of employment, a procedure whose unpopularity was usually put down to the ingrained laziness of the Highlander. The real reasons for crofters' reluctance to move to the lowlands — even temporarily — were the language difficulty the risk of falling ill far away from home, the obstacles in the way of making adequate provision for a distant family, and not least what one observer called 'The tenacity of their attachment to their native soil'. (59) But despite the prevalence of such feelings, seasonal migration was by no means unknown. (60) And in 1846 it was undertaken on an unprecedented scale, with crofters themselves joining the younger members of their families in the trek to the lowlands where — aided by the labour demand generated by the current railway construction boom — not a few of them succeeded in obtaining employment. (61)

Like stealing sheep or collecting shellfish, however, this type of migration could only alleviate, or delay the onset of, the distress which the blight had made inevitable. Only outside assistance could avert catastrophe and for the necessary help the Highland people could look to only three agencies: the government, their landlords, and private charity.

As the dimensions of the Highland calamity became apparent during the summer of 1846, the government were made aware of it in a variety of ways. At the end of July the Marquis of Lorne wrote to Sir George Grey, Home Secretary in Lord John Russell's administration to ask if, in the event of the potato harvest being lost, the government would 'extend to Scotland the advantage they have given to Ireland under the same affliction'. (62) Three weeks later, reporting the crop's 'total failure', the Marquis informed Grey that 'a very unusual calamity' seemed likely to occur in the Highlands if steps were not at once taken to forestall it. (63) And similar warnings of catastrophe and appeals for aid were soon pouring into the Home Office. The principal proprietors and farmers of Skye met in Portree on 18th August and resolved to ask for government aid. (64) Sir James Riddell wrote to Grey from Ardnamurchan on the 24th and requested immediate government intervention. A public meeting at Glenelg passed resolutions to the same effect. (65) And the Free Synod of Argyll, meeting at Campbeltown on 3rd September and noting the existence of 'extreme destitution' in the area under its jurisdiction, decided 'to make immediate representations of these present and threatened sufferings of the people to the Government ... praying that means may be devised by the Government for administering relief to the suffering poor'. (66)

On receipt of these communications and of a letter from the lord advocate — the executive's chief spokesman in Scotland — warning about the possible occurrence of a 'great, general, and urgent ... calamity' in the Highlands, (67) the government acted with commendable alacrity. The delays and vacillations which had characterised their policy in Ireland — where the potatoes had first failed in 1845 — were not repeated in the case of the Highlands, largely because the machinery for dealing with distress was already in existence. Responsibility for the prevention of famine in north-west Scotland as well as in Ireland was handed over to the Treasury and specifically to that department's powerful Assistant Secretary, Sir Charles Trevelyan, already 'the director and virtual dictator of Irish relief'. (68) By 2nd September Trevelyan had decided that one of his subordinates should at once be despatched to conduct an enquiry into the Highland situation and, if necessary, take charge of famine relief operations in the region. And within a few days the task was formally allocated to Sir Edward Pine Coffin. (69)

Almost at the end of a public service career which had begun during the Peninsular War and which had taken him to corners of the globe as far apart as Mexico and China, Coffin — in spite of his inauspicious name — was a kindly, painstaking man of marked ability. (70) Since January 1846 he had been in charge of famine relief in the remote and impoverished south-west of Ireland, an experience which had earned him a knighthood and given him an understanding — unmatched among government officials — of the problems of the underdeveloped Celtic fringe of the British Isles. This understanding he was to put to good use in the Highlands. Most men in mid-nineteenth century public life — and Coffin's coldly efficient superior, Sir Charles Trevelyan, was as good an example as any — were, in their attempts to deal with the Irish and Highland famines and their consequences, unable or unwilling to rise above the economic conventions and perspectives of their time. To that rule, Coffin was the outstanding exception.

Pausing in Edinburgh to confer with Sir John MacNeill — the official charged with the administration of the poor law in Scotland — and with the agents of several Highland landowners, Coffin reached Oban in mid-September and immediately began a four week voyage of investigation along the north-west coast and among the islands. His findings confirmed the worst reports already received: the crofting population undoubtedly stood in need of immediate and massive assistance — assistance which would not, as the government had originally hoped, be provided by Highland landlords. (71) Landowners' obligations to their tenants, 'if not very frequently acknowledged', were not, it was true, denied. But while professing 'an inclination to provide for the wants of their dependants', most Highland proprietors declared 'an utter inability to effect it from their own resources'. The validity of such excuses was of no great importance. True or false, wrote Coffin, 'they serve to show that the moral obligation supposed to attach to the landowners cannot be relied on to secure the people from destitution'. (72) In accord with Irish precedent, it was consequently decided to establish two meal depots in the area — one at Tobermory, the other at Portree — for even if Highland landlords could be cajoled into buying provisions, local 'commercial enterprise', as Coffin discovered, was 'hardly to be trusted for a regular and sufficient supply'. (73) In mid-October, therefore, work began on fitting out two naval frigates as depot ships while three Admiralty mills and two private mills commenced 'grinding night and day' to provide the necessary meal. (74)

Such a gross interference with the cherished principles of *laissez-faire* could not be lightly undertaken, however. Instructions were accordingly given that no meal was to be issued from the depots until 'all available resources ... from the produce of the late harvest or otherwise' had been exhausted; (75) and that nothing was to be done which could in any way be construed as impeding the natural development of local commerce. There was thus to be no question of a gratuitous distribution of meal — a 'fair price' was to be charged. That, however, was easier said than done; and the determination of the fair price became one of Coffin's constant preoccupations. (76)

Highland meal prices were those of a few small dealers, completely unable to cope with the massive demand engendered by the famine and exacting exorbitant rates from those fortunate enough to be able to compete for their scanty stocks. In Tobermory, for example, oatmeal which sold for around 16s. a boll in normal years was fetching 26s. a boll by November. (77) To have adopted such prices, wrote Coffin, 'would have been either to tantalize the hungry with the sight of food which they were unable to purchase, or to convert a professedly beneficient measure into one of usurious profit'. (78) To deliberately undersell the local dealers, on the other hand, would have been to destroy their trade (79) — a step which no Victorian government could countenance.

Although the dilemma was partially resolved by adopting a rate based on the current Liverpool and Glasgow prices, 'with a proper addition for the expense of conveyance, etc.', (80) Coffin — in short supply of everything except letters from London — continued to find the Treasury's instructions about prices 'the hardest to reconcile with the humane consideration due to the objects of relief'. (81) Because Liverpool and Glasgow meal prices were invariably higher than those prevailing in Dundee and Aberdeen where many local merchants obtained supplies, these hardy entrepreneurs made extravagant profits simply by charging the same as the government depots. (82) And as winter set in the whole problem of prices was seriously aggravated by the general scarcity that resulted from shortages of grain in the rest of Britain and Europe. (83) By the New Year Coffin felt such 'great alarm at the continuing advance of prices' that he dared to question the soundness of Treasury policy: 'At such rates as we ought to charge ... it is impossible for men to maintain their families above the level of starvation on the ordinary wages of labour'. (84) Trevelyan, however, was adamant. 'We cannot,' he insisted with all the fervour of a devout free trader, 'force up the wages of labour, or force down the prices of provisions without disorganising society.' (85)

In the autumn of 1846, these bureaucratic wrangles lay in the future. The depot ships did not arrive at their stations until December. (86) And throughout October and November, therefore — as the few remaining potatoes were consumed and the beaches cleared of shellfish — the only people in a position to provide assistance to their starving tenantries were Highland landlords themselves. Not unappreciative of the latter's financial difficulties, the government instructed Coffin to draw their attention to the Drainage Act — a recently passed measure which was intended to help solve the Irish crisis by providing official funds for estate improvement and, therefore, for the employment of the destitute. Highland proprietors, it was hoped, would follow their Irish counterparts' example, take advantage of the Act's provisions, and employ large numbers of crofters as ditchers on their estates. (87) To this plan, as Coffin discovered, landlords were unwilling to conform. Most of them did not even apply for a loan until around the New Year; and this, coupled with various technical difficulties, completely nullified the Drainage Act's potential impact on the immediate crisis. (88) In the short term, therefore, such aid as the crofting population received came from their landlords' unaided resources — and especially from those of the few proprietors who rose to the exigencies of the occasion.

In a circular which he issued in December 1846 MacLeod of Dunvegan acknowledge his 'duty to see that there was a sufficiency of good wholesome food in the country' and promised that no exertion would be spared on his part to prevent starvation and alleviate distress. (89) This pledge, MacLeod faithfully kept. For the rest of the winter almost all the able-bodied men on the Dunvegan estate were provided with regular employment. (90) And by the early spring of 1847 MacLeod was feeding about 8,000 people – his own tenantry as well as many people from the estates of neighbouring, and less generous, proprietors. (91) The average weekly cost of his endeavours was between £225 and £300. (92) But he would rather, he wrote, face ruin than let his people starve (93) – a sentiment which was unique in the Highlands of the 1840s.

MacLeod's dedication to his tenants was unequalled. But the second Duke of Sutherland, disregarding James Loch's advice to leave his tenants' sufferings to be alleviated by the mechanisms of supply and demand, (94) spent £18,000 on famine relief, most of it on the provision of meal and seed for the overcrowded crofting townships on the west coast. (95) In terms of sheer expenditure, however, the lead was easily taken by Sir James Matheson who had bought the Lewis estate from the finally bankrupt Seaforths in 1844. Matheson's Lewis improvement programme – which he had begun in 1845 and which involved drainage schemes, road construction works and a variety of other measures – was stepped up to deal with the crisis caused by the blight, and by 1850 Lewis' new owner had spent some £329,000 on his island. Only a tiny proportion of that vast sum found its way into crofters' pockets. But the employment generated by it undoubtedly helped to protect Lewis from the worst of the famine. (96)

The proprietors of one or two smaller west Highland estates played similar, if less grandiose, roles. Lord Lovat, for example, did a lot to help his tenants in North Morar; (97) while MacLean of Ardgour's estate, according to Coffin, was 'quite a model of good management' – the proprietor showing his crofting tenants how to cultivate peas, carrots, cabbages and other substitutes for potatoes, as well as providing them with the food they needed to get through the worst of the winter. (98) The success attending MacLean's efforts, wrote one observer, constituted 'an unanswerable reply to those who are always exclaiming against the inveterate indolence and incorrigible obstinacy of the Highlanders'. (99) To blame the famine on its victims' shortcomings remained, however, a convenient excuse for doing nothing about it and the endeavours of the few humanitarian landlords who did exist were, from the beginning, quite exceptional.

Always reluctant to call landowners' motives into question, Trevelyan suggested that 'the backwardness of some of the proprietors in their preparations for meeting the crisis was, in some cases, owing to their not being sufficiently alive to the grave and extensive character of the emergency'. (100) But even Trevelyan did not doubt that Highland landlords' lack of urgency was a fact. Many proprietors – expecting the government to provide aid on a massive scale, and optimistically ignoring its repeated declarations that no 'general system of relief' would be set up (101) – did nothing at all, in the hope of forcing the administration's hand. That their expectations were unfounded was a truth that dawned only very slowly; and more than one landlord's representative travelled to Sir Edward Coffin's Oban headquarters in the hope of eliciting a promise of financial support. 'With regard to assistance to proprietors,' reported MacLaine of Lochbuie's factor after one such interview in

January 1847, 'he says he has but one answer: take money under the Drainage Act. From Government nothing else is to be got.' (102)

Originally conceived of as an Irish measure, the Drainage Act was not altogether suited to Highland conditions. The drainage schemes instituted under its provisions on several Highland estates did little permanent good; (103) while as far as crofters were concerned its effects were positively detrimental. Where drains were dug it was not crofters' holdings that benefited, and in accordance with their usual custom, those proprietors who borrowed government money in order to finance improvements passed the financial burden on to their crofting tenants. Even forty years after the famine, crofters in Skye, Tiree and other areas were still paying 'drainage money' over and above their rents. (104)

Drainage schemes, however ineffective, would have been better than nothing. But as one of their more prominent critics remarked at the time, the famine 'appears rather to have paralysed than aroused the possessors of the soil'. (105) On the majority of Highland estates, crofters and their families were left to their own devices — Coffin consequently confessing himself 'deeply grieved and disappointed' by the landowners' evident indisposition to take steps to alleviate their tenants' sufferings. 'It is a mistake.' he told Trevelyan at the beginning of 1847, 'to suppose that all the proprietors are yet doing what we consider their duty.' (106) And among the most negligent he included Gordon of Cluny, the recent purchaser of Barra, South Uist and Benbecula.

Reports of a critical situation in these islands began to reach Coffin in December. And in January he sent one of his subordinates, a Captain Pole, to discover the true position. Gordon, Pole wrote, had provided some employment on road works on the islands in the early part of the summer of 1846. But in August, despite the advent of the blight, these projects had been abandoned and the tenants working on them dismissed. Informed by his factor that at least 8,000 bolls of meal would be required to prevent widespread destitution, Gordon — who lived in Aberdeenshire — had made arrangements to send 900 bolls. In January none of these had yet arrived, and Pole found 'greater wretchedness and privation' on Gordon's estate than on any of the other Highland or Hebridean properties which it had been his 'painful duty' to inspect. (107) So desperate, for example, was the plight of the inhabitants of Eriskay, a small island lying between Barra and South Uist, that even the herbs and grasses growing on the island were divided into plots, each one of which was allocated to a crofter and his family — an action which was to lead Eriskay's people to recall the famine with the words: 'Bhiodh 'ad a' roinn a' bhloinigein an uair sin'. (108) And in Barra where Pole found 'few families with any food at all' the situation was equally ghastly. Everything that could be eaten — including the seed corn needed for the spring sowing — had been eaten; and the island's population were subsisting on a debilitating diet of shellfish. Dysentery, typhoid and cholera were even more widespread than elsewhere in the region. (109) And although most of the many deaths in the north-west Highlands and islands that winter were officially attributed to disease, rather than to the hunger which had made the disease so prevalent, there not surprisingly occurred in Barra the only two deaths which even the poor law authorities were forced to put down to starvation. (110)

Horrified by his discoveries, Pole found it 'an awful reflection ... that at this moment the wealthy heritor [proprietor] of this island is not employing the poor

population'. If Gordon did not at once take action, he believed, 'scenes will occur
in South Uist, Barra, and Benbecula, which would be disgraceful to his name, and
injurious to the reputation of Great Britain'. (111) Sharing these opinions, Coffin
at once addressed a fiery letter to Gordon, threatening 'to interpose in favour of
the sufferers ... leaving to Parliament to decide whether or not you should be
legally responsible for the pecuniary consequences of this just and necessary intervention'. (112) This step had the desired effect. Road works were restarted and
Gordon's tenants supplied with quantities of meal which, even if they did not come
up to Coffin's stringent expectations, were considerably in excess of the amounts
which Gordon had originally planned to despatch. (113)

The predicament of crofters in Barra and South Uist was paralleled by that of
small tenants on many other properties in the islands and on the mainland. In
January 1847, for example, Sheriff-Substitute Fraser of Fort William was despatched
to report upon the situation in western Inverness-shire and Wester Ross. And in
every part of that large district he found 'a considerable population ... bordering on
starvation'. (114) One of the places visited by Fraser was Glenelg, bought in 1837
by Baillie of Dochfour. Already the owner of an extensive estate at the eastern end
of Loch Ness, Baillie, like his factor, was an absentee. The one had not been in
Glenelg for several years. The other came only to collect the rent. (115) Because of
its sheltered situation and relatively good soil, Glenelg is one of the most fertile
parishes in the north-west Highlands. In the nineteenth century's opening years,
however, the greater part of the parish — including the previously cultivated straths
of Glenmore and Glenbeg — were put under sheep and the bulk of the population
removed to a few ramshackle and grossly overcrowded townships on the coast. (116)
'Such a collection of wretched, filthy, smoky, unglazed, and in every respect com-
fortless hovels, I have never seen, even in Ireland,' remarked one visitor to the area. (117)
And in Glenelg, perhaps more than anywhere else, the famine thus served to point
to the tragically ironic consequence of the clearances: 'fertile land lying waste at one
end of a glen and people starving at the other'. (118)

On Lord Cranstoun's Arisaig estate, where no less than four fifths of the entire
population were in need of assistance, the position was equally bleak, Cranstoun and
his factor having no more interest in the property than their Glenelg counterparts:
'The one lifts the rent and the other carries it off and consumes it; and this comprehends the whole of the relation between landlord and tenant in Arisaig.' (119)
Baillie had at least provided his crofting tenants with a little meal before abandoning
them to the government. (120) But Cranstoun did not make even this gesture, complete catastrophe being averted only by the heroic efforts of Arisaig's principal
tenant, MacDonald of Glenaladale, and the local priest, Father William MacIntosh. (121)

Examples of proprietorial apathy could be multiplied endlessly — from the Ross-
shire laird who expressed his regrets about his tenants' virtual starvation but added
that he could do nothing to save them 'till a more convenient season', (122) to the
Inverness-shire landowner who kept all the meal on his estate locked up in a store
which, as one official bitterly remarked, 'might as well be in China'. (123) The
Hebrides were particularly unfortunate. In Mull, wrote Tobermory's Sheriff, the
proprietors' conduct was 'with a few honourable exceptions... extremely remiss
and impolitic'. (124) And in Skye, reported Major Haliday — the officer in charge

of the government's Portree meal depot — 'MacLeod of MacLeod is the only thoroughly active and good landlord of the larger class and Mr. MacLennan of Lyndall of the smaller.' (125) Of Skye's other landowners, Haliday singled out Lord MacDonald for particular censure. Confronted with a destitute population of about 14,000 he had agreed to employ 400 of them on a government-funded drainage project — which he had abandoned within a few weeks of its commencement (126) As for his tenantry in North Uist — they were most assisted by the shipwreck of a vessel that chanced to be laden with £15,000 worth of flour and other provisions. (127)

Official attempts to coerce reluctant landlords into buying supplies for their tenants met with little success. Lord MacDonald's factor, for example, bought a considerable quantity of meal in Liverpool. On pausing to consider, however, he decided that he could not transport it to Skye 'without being forced to sell it at a great loss'. The meal was consequently resold; and since prices were steadily rising the MacDonald estate management made 'a handsome profit' on the transaction. (128) The upshot, as Major Haliday remarked with more than a hint of bitterness, was that Lord MacDonald's crofters had to come to Portree 'every week, often distances of thirty or forty miles from the extreme points of the island, to procure the food which he or his factor would not import for them'. (129)

And because of proprietors' general and evident lack of enthusiasm for the role which the government had optimistically assigned to them, the pattern of events on Lord MacDonald's estate was repeated throughout the north-west: the original ruling that the meal depots' wares be sold only to landlords — to be redistributed by them in the form of wages to crofters employed on drainage projects — being of necessity revoked, and the meal sold directly to its consumers. In townships, and occasionally in groups of townships, crofters therefore clubbed together and spent their meagre savings on the minimum quantities of meal that the depot regulations allowed them to buy. Long, tedious and sometimes dangerous journeys had to be made to Portree and Tobermory from districts separated from these places by many miles of bad roads and rough seas. And at the end of it all, crofters had bought £24,000 worth of government meal — as against the £12,000 worth purchased by their landlords. (130) Although Coffin's assertion that his measures had in many instances 'saved the people from inevitable starvation' (131) is consequently unchallengeable, the cost to the crofting population was immense; and the inevitable outcome of intolerable hunger and the expenditure it necessitated was that the spring of 1847 found crofters without sufficient seed and without the cash to buy it.

Seed potatoes had been destroyed by the blight. Stocks of seed oats — urgently required because of the obvious risk of renewed potato failures — were generally low and in some carea, such as Barra, the Uists and Arisaig, non-existent, for the simple reason that they had had to be eaten during the winter. (132) The government refused to supply the necessary seed on the somewhat dubious grounds that to do so would be to subsidise the landlords.(133) And Coffin's immediate priority became the task of persuading proprietors to make good the deficiency. (134) Despite the government's offer to cover transport costs, however, Highland landlords were no more eager to supply their crofters with seed than they had been to provide them with meal. Lord MacDonald, for example, refused to sell seed corn to his tenants except at prices 'which their present necessities deprive them of the power of taking advantage of'. (135) And suspecting that grants made to their impoverished tenantries would never be recovered, many other proprietors adopted a similar stance, (136) with the result, as MacLeod of Dunvegan's sister pointed out at the time, that 'Many a crofter had the misery of seeing his land lie fallow'. (137) By the spring, in fact, even MacLeod was becoming dispirited. Engaged 'in discouraging the cultivation of land for which the crofters [were] unable of themselves to buy seed', (138) he was, he wrote, 'getting very low about it all' and wished himself 'away from this scene of wretchedness'. (139) And although Coffin's exhortations, supplemented by some charitable funds from the south, did something to encourage him and several other proprietors to further exertions, the spring sowing was neither as large nor as early as it should have been. (140)

In view of the magnitude of crofters' troubles and the generally lackadaisical attitude of their landlords, it was perhaps fortunate that the government was not left to shoulder all the responsibility for famine relief in the Highlands. First to come to its aid was the Free Church whose Argyll Synod began to collect funds and distribute food in September and October 1846. (141) In November, with the appointment of a Free Church Destitution Committee, the Argyll Synod's endeavours were extended to the whole of Scotland. More than £15,000 was quickly raised, (142) and the Free Church schooner 'Breadalbane' — built to carry ministers around the Hebrides — was used to ship provisions to the more destitute islands. (143) Although many of these were Free Church strongholds, the Church's response to the famine was notably and laudably free of sectarianism — no-one speaking more highly of its efforts than the Roman Catholic crofters of Moidart and Arisaig. (144) But charitable feeling was not a Free Church prerogative, and at public meetings in Edinburgh and Glasgow on 18th December and 6th January influential and undenominational committees were formed to raise funds for Highland famine relief. (145)

To the government's harassed officials these developments were a godsend. Coffin believed that the various relief organisations represented the Highlands' only chance of averting a catastrophe similar to that occurring in Ireland; (146) while Trevelyan — who was of the opinion that the Irish crisis had 'proved to demonstration that local distress cannot be relieved out of national funds without great abuses and evils, tending, by a direct and rapid process, to an entire disorganisation of society' (147) — treated their emergence as a glorious opportunity for the government to extricate itself from the Highland morass. Declaring it to be obvious that 'the temporary evil ought to be met by the temporary expedient of private charity', he instructed Coffin to furnish the various committees 'with all the information ... calculated to direct their exertions into useful channels'. (148) Under government pressure, therefore, the relief organisations were quickly unified as the clumsily entitled Central Board of Management of the Fund for the Relief of the Destitute Inhabitants of the Highlands, a body which held its first meeting in February 1847 and which was speedily assured by the Treasury that it could 'depend upon receiving all the countenance and assistance which it is in our power to give'. (149)

Although the Central Board of Management took overall responsibility for fund raising and food distribution, its component parts retained a considerable degree of independence, the Glasgow committee — or 'Section' as it was now called — taking

charge of the Board's operations in Argyll, western Inverness-shire and the Outer
Isles while the Edinburgh Section was entrusted with Wester Ross, Skye, the eastern
part of the mainland and the Northern Isles. (150) Under the Sections were Local
Committees which were appointed for each parish or district from lists of names
supplied by local clergymen and which were entrusted with the actual distribution
of meal to the hungry — the stipulated allowance being 1½ lb. of meal per adult
male per day, with women receiving ¾lb. and children under twelve ½ lb. each. (151)
Although this ration was calculated to do no more than prevent starvation it was, by
contemporary standards, not ungenerous. When the potatoes failed in Lewis in the
spring of 1837 the estate authorities' allowance to crofters had been only ½ lb. per
adult male per day — even 1 lb. being considered 'far too high' by Seaforth's factor. (15
And in Ireland, as Trevelyan informed the Board, 'one pound of good meal, properly
cooked' was thought 'amply sufficient for an able bodied person'. (153) For crofters
and their slowly starving families there was understandably little comfort in such
comparisons, however. And the weekly or fortnightly distributions of 'destitution
meal' were accordingly cheerless affairs:

> At the appointed time and place the poor creatures troop down in hundreds,
> wretched and thin, starved and wan. Some have clothing, some almost none, and
> some are a mass of rags. Old and young, feeble and infirm, they take their stations
> and await their turn. Not a murmur, not a clamour, not a word — but they wept
> aloud as they told of their miseries. (154)

The Board did not, therefore, end the crofting population's sufferings. On its own,
the government's — and indeed any — criteria, however, its immediate achievement
was remarkable. In the spring and early summer of 1847 — the dangerous period
before the new harvest — the Board supplied the greater part of the Highlands'
emergency provisions, the Glasgow Section alone despatching 7047 bolls of wheat-
meal, 5696 bolls of oatmeal, 1980 bolls of peasemeal and 690 bolls of Indian Corn
meal in the first three months of its existence. (155) All this was made possible by
a veritable flood of contributions. By 10th April 1847 the Board's resources amounted
to £138,175 and they eventually totalled more than £250,000. (156) Most of these
funds were raised in Scotland. But large donations were also received from England
and from Scottish emigrants in Canada and the U.S.A., the latter sending several
thousand barrels of meal, flour and even beef as well as cash. (157) And although
the strange new cereals, especially Indian Corn meal, were initially suspected, even
by people who had nothing else to eat, crofters and their families soon adapted to
life without potatoes and made good use of the seeds sent them by the Board as
partial substitutes for their former staple crop. By the summer of 1847, 'flourishing
crops of the most useful roots and other vegetables ... some of them previously unknown in the country', were to be seen all over the Highlands. (158) And the government — not alone in crediting the Board with the prevention of many thousands of
deaths from starvation — had decided that it could safely end its 'unnatural' intervention in Highland affairs. Its meal depots were accordingly closed and their remaining stocks sold to the Board which thus inherited the task of warding off renewed
famine. (159)

The Board's original intention had been that its operations should last for only
one season — and cease 'as soon as the harvest will enable the people to have their

wants supplied by the new crop'. (160) As the summer advanced, these optimistic expectations were encouraged by the prospect of an unusually good harvest – in Mull, for example, 'There never was ... in the memory of the present generation, so luxuriant and promising a crop.' (161) The Board's calculations, however, turned out to be based on a false premise – for even if the harvest had come up to expectation insufficient food would have been provided. Only about a sixth of the usual quantity of potatoes had been planted and the replacement crops of oats and barley could not possibly make good the deficiency since, on a conservative estimate, it took at least three acres of grain to equal the food value of one acre of potatoes. (162) Although those crofters who occupied larger than average holdings were therefore at an advantage, almost all crofters were bound to run short, and as Coffin remarked before leaving the Highlands in September, 'the only point undetermined was the probable extent of the deficiency'. The nutritional value of the forthcoming harvest, he believed, would be between 50 and 75 per cent of normal. (163) And even that estimate proved unduly optimistic. In the early autumn the weather broke and for several weeks the whole of the north-west Highlands and islands were swept by almost incessant rain and gales. Crofters' corn was flattened and practically destroyed, while a new outbreak of blight devasted the already scanty crop·of potatoes. (164)

Having suspended its food distributions as planned, the Board soon found itself pressed to resume them. Thus Norman MacLeod who visited the Outer Isles in August was in no doubt about the people's need for renewed assistance:

> The scene of wretchedness which we witnessed as we entered on the estate of Col. Gordon was deplorable, nay heart-rending. On the beach the whole population of the country seemed to be met, gathering the precious cockles ... I never witnessed such countenances – starvation on many faces – the children with their melancholy looks, big looking knees, shrivelled legs, hollow eyes, swollen like bellies – God help them, I never did witness such wretchedness! (165)

As the summer of 1847 gave way to a wet and stormy autumn it became clear that hunger and malnutrition were not confined to a few unfortunate localities. In Skye the potatoes had 'absolutely gone' by November. Destitution was reported to be 'fast increasing'. The entire population of Wester Ross was in serious difficulty by December and not a few families were 'on the verge of starvation'. In these areas, as in Arisaig, Tiree, Barra, the Uists and Harris where the position was 'so deplorable as to cause serious apprehension', the situation was, if anything, worse than it had been a year before. And the Board's resumption of its duties in December was therefore something of a foregone conclusion. (166)

The Board's assumption of a role that was considerably more permanent than that originally envisaged for it by its members and supporters was accompanied by its adoption of a mode of management which, if more efficient than that which it replaced, was also more autocratic and therefore less in touch with the needs of the people for whose benefit the Board's funds had been provided. The Local Committees, declared the Board, had been unhealthily democratic. Some had included crofters who were themselves in receipt of relief. And all had shown a lamentable tendency to act as 'the representatives and advocates of those seeking relief ... rather than of the relieving party'. (167) That crofters should have even this meagre influence over their own fate was something that the Highlands' ruling class was not prepared to concede. And it is no coincidence, therefore, that from landlords, factors, sheep farmers and other 'respectable people' the Board's representatives heard 'the same tale about the indolence and worthlessness of the people, and how poor ignorant lotters were sitting in committee distributing meal to themselves'. (168) Which side in the north-west Highlands' rapidly developing social conflict had most influence over the Board was made clear by its instructions concerning the appointment of the paid staff of Inspectors, Sub-Inspectors, Relief Officers and Overseers who, it was decided, would replace the Local Committees: 'They must be men of intelligence and firmness, who will do their duty as representing the Board, and not by sympathising with the people.' (169)

Within a few weeks of its formation, Sir Charles Trevelyan had informed the Board that

> Next to allowing the people to die of hunger, the greatest evil that could happen would be their being habituated to depend upon public charity. The object to be arrived at, therefore, is to prevent the assistance given from being productive of idleness and if possible, to make it conducive to increased exertion. (170)

In accordance with these instructions and prevailing concepts of the purpose of poor relief, the Board had initially tried to ensure 'that money or labour shall be extracted from those supplied with food' by ordering the Local Committees to provide employment on road construction works and similar projects. (171) This the Committees had signally failed to do, their general attitude being summed up in the reply received by a poor law official who 'expressed surprise that relief was ever given without requiring labour'. 'There is no work to give them,' he was told, 'and they cannot starve.' (172)

In order to ensure that such old-fashioned humanitarianism should not continue to triumph over the economic and moral assumptions of the Victorian middle class, the Board began its new season by introducing what it liked to refer to as its 'labour test'. The meal ration remained the same as before — although the adult male's 1½ lbs. could now be reduced to 1 lb. 'as a penalty upon idleness' — but meal was only to be distributed in return for eight hours' work a day, six days a week. The recipient of such relief received an automatic allowance for each child under twelve years of age. But older children got their meal only 'in return for such work as they can give', while wives and mothers were required to take up knitting and spinning in order to qualify for assistance. (173) Trevelyan of course approved. Others were less appreciative, the editor of the *Inverness Advertiser* arguing, for example, that 'The cruel and demoralising principle has been to exact a maximum of labour for a minimum of wages.' (174) That wages — which were paid in meal or in tokens which could be exchanged only for meal — were very low was unchallengeable. For three of the four years during which the Board's 'test' was in operation in the Highlands the price of meal was 1d. a pound. A married man with six children (for large families were the rule) therefore received for his day's work the equivalent of 1½d. for himself, 1d. for his wife and ½d. for each of his children, making altogether 5½d. The lowest wages paid on the open market at this time were about 6s. a week and even the crofters labouring on the Duke of Sutherland's privately organised famine relief projects were paid about 1s. a day. And if the married crofter's plight was bad, that of the single man was much worse. For his six days of often back-breaking work he received exactly 9d. worth of meal. (175) That this was a pittance, even the Board admitted. But their object, they added, was to make relief 'necessarily unpalatable', 'a test of destitution', a last resort. (176)

This at least they achieved, the much vaunted 'test' arousing widespread discontent and bitterness, emotions which were intensified by the fact that it was administered by a well-paid staff. Crofters, wrote the laird of Dunvegan's sister, Emily MacLeod,

feel the injustice of being paid at a very low rate out of what they not unnaturally consider their own money and are exasperated at seeing gentlemen living in comfort on what they know was subscribed for them, while they have to walk, often without shoes and always in insufficient clothing ... to the source of labour where, after working for eight hours, they receive the value of 1½d. (177)

That many crofters preferred to endure their 'many privations' rather than submit to the 'test's' degrading indignities is not really surprising (178) — still less the fact that the Free Synod of Argyll, which had taken the initiative in raising the relief fund, should feel moved to comment on

the inadequacy for the comfortable support of human life of the allowance ... given to families and individuals, in many cases who have no other means of subsistence [; and] to memorialise the Central Relief Board to represent to them the necessity of distributing with a more liberal hand the funds placed at their disposal by a generous public. (179)

To such appeals, as to more immoderately worded allegations that the half-starved recipients of relief were collapsing on the roads they were constructing, the Board paid little heed — even when they received corroboration of the validity of their critics' accusations from their own staff. 'The people are very willing to work,' wrote the Board's Lochalsh inspector in a report that was in essence a criticism of the rules he was paid to enforce, 'but so much are they weakened by insufficient food that much work cannot be got out of them.' (180)

The Board's new system of management, according to its most outspoken denigrator, consisted of 'a huge staff of stipendiaries on liberal pay, and multitudes of starving supplicants receiving a modicum of meal'. (181) It was, wrote a Skye minister, 'nothing more' than a means of 'spending the fund of the charitable and starving those for whom it was intended'. (182) The Board's members, however, were well satisfied. Expenses admittedly were higher. In 1847, for example, relief operations in Skye had been administered by eight committees, each one consisting of a number of unpaid volunteers. In 1848, an inspector, thirteen relief officers and a dozen overseers were required to do the same job, and their wage bill alone amounted to about £100 a month. (183) In a comparison of the amounts of meal distributed in the two years, however, is to be seen the effect of the 'test' and the cause of the Board's gratification. Despite 'an equal amount of destitution', the average fortnightly allowance of meal to Skye crofters fell from 1,280 bolls in 1847 to 330 bolls in 1848. In Wester Ross the figures were 938 and 254 bolls respectively. And in Tiree, although there was 'much more destitution' and a consequent increase in the number of recipients, a similar reduction was achieved. (184)

As in the previous year, the Board's operations were temporarily suspended in September. But prospects for the winter of 1848-49 were even more dismal than those of twelve months before. The potatoes failed more or less completely and the grain crop was so late that in many areas it remained unharvested. In Wester Ross, for example, crofters' corn was still green when the first snow fell in October. (1 Matters were made worse by an 'unusually unproductive' herring fishing and a falling away in the demand for labour in the south — a development which meant that temporary migration to the lowlands no longer provided crofters with a way out of their troubles. (186) While not unwilling to recommence its activities in the autumn of 1848, the Board was uncomfortably aware that its resources, though still con-siderable, were not unlimited — especially since it was now called upon to extend its operations into areas such as Lewis and Sutherland whose proprietors, tempted by the prospect of getting something for nothing, had overcome original scruples about the damage that might be done to their carefully cultivated 'improving' images by a tacit admission that charitable aid was needed to bail their tenantries out of their difficulties. (187) In 1849, therefore, the Board changed direction yet again, the aim on this occasion being to make the West Highlands more self-sufficient and thus prepare crofters for the eventually inevitable cessation of external assistance.

The Board's new policy depended on the development of the Highlands and islands' economic infrastructure and on getting the region's landowners to take an active interest in that development. And it had its origins in the Board's decision — of February 1848 — to provide the Gairloch estate with half the £2,500 required for the construction of a road along the southern shore of Loch Maree, the money being made available on condition that the estate management assumed responsibility for the welfare of the property's population by providing crofters with work on the building of the road. (188) This 'system of co-operation', as it was called, was ideally suited to the Board's new requirements: it involved proprietors in famine relief pro-jects, allowed the Board to reduce its staff and, theoretically at least, helped to develop the Highlands' natural resources. On a less favourable view it was 'a monstrous malversation of a charitable fund ... giving largesse to noblemen and gentlemen who ... have improved their estates by means of public subscription'. (189) But either way, the new mode of management was as popular with Highland landlords as it was with the Board and in 1849, when every proprietor in Gairloch and Lochbroom received funds for road construction and when the Board agreed to meet half the cost of a thirty-four mile road from Lairg to Loch Laxford on the Sutherland estate, it was extended to most parts of the north-west mainland. (190) About a thousand people were employed on Wester Ross road works during 1849 and by 1850 the area's landlords were in possession of a ninety mile network of new roads, linking Ullapool, Poolewe and Gairloch to Dingwall. (191)

These 'destitution roads' were the Board's great practical accomplishment, its other development efforts making little tangible impact on the Highland scene. Between 1848 and 1850, for example, the Board made a strenuous attempt to modernise the region's fishing industry by building a considerable number of piers and jetties and by supplying local fishermen and crofters with boats, gear and free instruction in deep sea fishing techniques. But despite these fairly massive invest-ments no general increase in efficiency and productivity was reported. (192) The

Board's piers, according to the fishery authorities, were 'spoken of alightingly' —
which was hardly surprising if the jetties built in Loch Torridon and Loch Kishorn
were at all typical: 'Both of them were small and insubstantial erections. The first,
it was said by the fishermen, had been erected too far up the loch to be of service
to them. The second had been left unfinished.' (193)

Attempts to establish a hosiery industry in Skye were, in productivity terms at
least, more encouraging. Having originated as a suitable female employment under
the infamous 'test', the industry got off the ground in 1848 when the Board entered
into a marketing contract with an Aberdeenshire businessman. At a cost of over
£1,500 the latter gentleman was provided with a spinning and carding mill at
Portree. And by 1850 ten women were employed in the mill itself, while about
1,050 outworkers were given the task of producing more than 1,600 pairs of stockings a month. (194) To fulfil their production quotas the crofters' wives and
daughters who were thus employed had to 'knit along the road, oftentimes with
their creels full of peats on their backs... Thus a good knitter may earn with diligence
and industry something less than one penny a day'. (195) And the immense profits
that resulted from such gross exploitation went into the pockets of a man who —
thanks to the Board — had not even had to capitalise his venture.

The Board's policies thus made little impression on the overall Highland situation
which, instead of improving, showed every sign of deteriorating still further. 1849
brought even more poverty and hunger than 1848 had done, the position in Skye
where 'notwithstanding a management even more strict ... than that of last year'
the maximum number of people receiving relief rose from 5,559 to 8,162 being
not untypical. (196) That summer a deputation from the Board's Glasgow Section
visited the Outer Isles to see the effects of famine for themselves. They found the
islands' people 'living in miserable hovels — not a few miserably clad — children
looking half starved and prematurely old — in short, misery, wretchedness and
destitution in many a form'. (197) A better harvest and a more successful herring
fishing meant that the winter of 1849-50 was a little less bleak for crofters. But
the crisis was by no means over when in September 1850, its funds exhausted, the
Board suspended its operations for the last time.

At the beginning of the Highland famine Sir George Grey, who was then in charge
of the Home Office, had expressed a hope that 'permanent benefit may ultimately
be derived from the calamity by the introduction of a better system of agricultural
management and by a consequent improvement in the social condition of the
people'. (198) And the hope of effecting such a transformation clearly underlay
the Board's original statement of its objectives:

> to improve the condition of the people and to develop the resources of the
> country ... to prevent the recurrence of so great a calamity and convert the suffer-
> ings of the people into the germ of their future amelioration. (199)

These goals the Board had manifestly failed to achieve. An official enquiry into the
Highland situation in the spring of 1851 concluded that 'no sensible progress has been
made, and the state of the population continues to decline'. (200) And the prevalent
feeling of disillusionment was adequately summed up by the editor of the *Inverness*

Courier. The result of this splendid fund has altogether been so unpopular and so unproductive generally... that we are convinced no such subscription will ever again be raised for the Highlands.' (201) As events of the 1880s and 1920s were to show, that last prognostication proved unduly pessimistic. (202) But that it could be made at all is a measure of the Board's inability to measure up to its own aspirations.

One reason for the Board's lack of success was that its programme was simply too ambitious. Such an organisation, no matter how enthusiastically conceived and managed, could not bring about the social and economic revolution which it envisaged. (203) But even within the limits of the possible the wrong objectives were often pursued – road construction on which so much money was spent being a case in point, not least because the Board's roads were usually undertaken with landlords' rather than crofters' needs in view. Thus the principal function of the road from Lairg to Loch Laxford was to open up the remote southern and western portions of the Duke of Sutherland's Reay deer forest, its completion being quickly followed by the erection of shooting lodges at Stack and Lochinver. (204) And in an underdeveloped economy, as was pointed out by a critic of Sir James Matheson's roads in Lewis, the last people to benefit from such developments were crofters: 'The tangible benefits in the shape of improved communications do not come home to those who ... wish nothing to be brought to them, and have nothing to send away.' (205) As the *Inverness Advertiser*'s editor remarked at the time, more permanent good would have been done by injecting much needed capital into crofting townships through a concerted effort to improve access roads, provide agricultural instruction, and encourage draining, fencing and other improvements. (206) But far from changing crofting agriculture for the better, the Board's activities often served merely to aggravate the damage already done to it by famine and by negligent land management.

In charge of the Board's policies were a small group of Edinburgh and Glasgow lawyers and businessmen 'with an admixture of small Lowland proprietors'. (207) These men knew very little about the Highlands and still less about crofting. But on the subjects of poverty and poor relief they possessed all the prejudices of the classes to which they belonged – prejudices which were all the more unyielding as a result of the current debate on the new Scots poor law. The inevitable outcome was that, instead of taking a wide and sympathetic view of the situation, the Board – encouraged and supported by Treasury officials like Sir Charles Trevelyan whose views were equally circumscribed – subjected crofters to a regime based on what one irate Skyeman referred to as 'petty workhouse rules'. (208) A classic example of the sort of idiocy that resulted is provided by one of the Board's 1848 directives:

Parties who possess means of their own, or who have not consumed the produce of their ground or stock, or whose property is sufficient to enable them to render their credit available, are not Destitute until their means are exhausted. (209)

Crofters' attempts to conserve seeds and stock were thus nullified. They were compelled to eat the former and sell the latter before being granted relief. And although this particular rule was eventually rescinded, (210) most of the Board's regulations – often enforced by utterly unimaginative officials, and consequently as 'unalterable as the laws of the Medes and the Persians' (211) – proved quite immutable. Crofters who worked their own holdings instead of labouring on the Board's projects were refused meal and in many instances, therefore, starving tenants had to virtually abandon their crofts in order to obtain food for themselves and their families. (212) The hostility originally engendered by the 'test' was thus increased and their consequent bitterness made crofters unwilling to co-operate with the Board's officials on the more sensible aspects of its policy, notably fishery development. (213) And the fact that many crofters' cattle had to be sold and savings not already spent on government meal had to be converted into food meant that the work which had been well begun by three decades of steadily growing poverty was completed: the crofting population was bereft of almost all its capital resources. One consequence was that many of the marginally more affluent crofters who could once have raised the funds needed to emigrate were no longer able to afford even this way out of their difficulties. (214)

The Board's members, to be fair, were not entirely unaware of the importance of the Highland economy's agrarian base. But they could do very little to promote the better utilisation of the land without the wholehearted co-operation of the men who owned it — a fact recognised by no less a personage than Sir Robert Peel, who expressed the hope that Highland landlords would show sufficient 'public spirit ... and enough of sympathy with the position of their crofting tenants' to take the lead in a programme of agricultural inprovement. (215) Peel, however, did not know his Highland landowners. The proprietors, declared the Board in one of its more exasperated moments, showed 'an entire want of faith in the possibility of improving the position of the people, or any desire to aid in the attempt'. (216) Supported by sheep farmers who, as Sir Edward Coffin discovered, were only too eager to oppose any scheme 'which promises to have the effect of confirming the people in the tenure of land which they would prefer to see in their own occupation', Highland landlords consistently refused the Board's pleas to grant leases to crofters — not least because of the fact that most of them were engaged in the wholesale eviction of their crofting tenants. (217) And because they had no leases the Board felt unable to encourage crofters to carry out improvements which might well be followed by the improver's ejection from his holding. Some sort of security of tenure, declared one of the Board's more intelligent inspectors, was 'the keystone to every exertion on the part of the crofter' — an opinion which was shared by the economist G.P. Scrope who visited the Highlands in 1849, (218) and one that received striking confirmation in the spring of that year when a reluctant Lord MacDonald promised one of the Board's representatives that he would grant eight-year leases to crofters who improved their holdings by draining and enclosing them in return for the regulation allowances of meal. As the Board's Edinburgh Section was informed by its delighted inspector in Skye:

The immediate effect of this new annunciation was the betrayal of an enthusiasm so long and unexceptionably dormant that there was a general doubt of its existence, but which took the true and practical direction of a general change, from vegetative apathy and stagnant indifference, to the bustle and industrious business which new hopes, opening prospects, confidence, and self interest engendered. I myself, in the course of an 8 mile drive... found that the people were at work, without superintendence, from before six in the morning, until the shades of evening fell, and I counted something more than 100 new drains opened on the second day of the new system in the same district. (219)

But while most other Skye proprietors entered into similar contracts in 1850, (220) these arrangements were never extended to other districts; and even in Skye the landlords' agreements were so hedged about with unnecessarily complicated conditions that they were easily broken when the Board's inspectors had departed for the last time. Lord MacDonald's own estate was to be the scene of some of the most extensive clearances of the 1850s. And the enthusiastic activity of the spring of 1849 thus remained only a momentary glimpse of what might have been, a forgotten precedent for the widespread improvements which followed the passing of the Crofters Act in 1886.

5. Fewer People, Less Land, 1850-1857

FAR from leading to a regeneration of the crofting economy — as the Relief Board and some politicians had hoped in their more sanguine moments — the famine of the 1840s served only to intensify Highland proprietors' hostility to the crofting system and to make 'redundancy of population' an even more 'prominent topic of lamentation' in landowning circles. (1) A tenantry that could scarcely prevent its own starvation was unlikely to produce a worthwhile rental, (2) and it therefore seemed to landlords that the famine had conclusively demonstrated the complete bankruptcy of crofting as a way of profitably organising their estates. If a very large number of people were not at once removed from the Highlands, warned MacLeod of Dunvegan's factor in 1850, several great and famous landlords would 'very soon bid adieu to their properties' and join the growing list of historic families who had already sunk in a sea of debts. (3) Of the imminence of such a fate the region's landowners were only too well aware, and the immediate effect of the famine on land management policies was thus to accelerate and intensify the already existing tendency to make sheep farming the main prop of estate economies in districts where kelping, and therefore crofting, had once been predominant — a development that was necessarily accompanied by the clearance of many of the areas still occupied by crofters. In a consequent reversal of long established demographic patterns, the Highlands' population, which had been growing for at least a hundred years, began to fall — the immediate cause of the decline being a new wave of emigration. (4)

The proprietors' evident conviction that emigration was the answer to their problems stemmed from the belief that it would free them 'at once and for ever from the care of their burthensome dependents'. And the cost, it was hoped by the more optimistic spirits among them, would be minimal because 'any large plan of emigration must become a national undertaking, and therefore be conducted at the public expense'. (5) To interest the government in such a scheme it was necessary to argue that it would benefit the colonies and the crofting population alike — by adding to the talents at the disposal of the former and by removing the latter from a life that had little to offer but poverty, hunger and distress. The Highland proprietors' undoubted propaganda skills were accordingly deployed to this end almost from the moment that the famine began. But for men whose professedly sole concern was their tenants' welfare they showed a rather suspicious tendency to maintain 'against all assurances and evidences to the contrary' that the colonies 'afforded an unlimited field for the reception of an emigrant population without discrimination of age, sex, or capacity', while simultaneously denying that the industrial areas of southern Scotland offered more than the most transient and unattractive prospects. Sir Edward Coffin, who noted this phenomenon with wry amusement, drew the appropriate conclusion:

As it is plainly the desire of those who press for a reduction of numbers that the emigrant ... should not have the *power* of returning, their indisposition to promote that form of removal which gives him the option leaves room to doubt the entire disinterestedness of the motive. (6)

And that Coffin's assessment of landlords' intentions was broadly accurate is borne out by subsequent events.

By the end of the 1840s – to give one example of the type of calculation involved in the promotion of emigration – Lord MacDonald's debts amounted to no less than £218,000 and his creditors were becoming increasingly impatient. (7) The family fortunes, it was clear, could be saved only by fairly massive borrowing. But the necessary loans proved difficult to raise – not least on account of Lord MacDonald's bankers' objections to his rental being 'spread over such a number of small tenantry'. (8 And it was left to Lord MacDonald's factor to draw the obvious conclusion. During the preceding forty years, he pointed out, the value of those sheep farms which had been extended by the simple expedient of evicting the crofters who happened to live beside them had been greatly enhanced, thus demonstrating 'the immense advantage to the proprietor of encouraging the system of clearing croft farms adjoining the larger possessions'. Lord MacDonald's chaotic finances, he believed, could best be repaired by a more widespread and thorough application of the same principle. And since the same could be said of every estate in the north-west Highlands and islands, mass emigration, which as one observer accurately remarked, 'they never regarded as beneficial to their tenants until it began to appear advantageous to themselves', came to be more and more assiduously canvassed by landlords as the only possible solution to the problems of the region. (10)

Highland sheep farmers, well aware that their industry was entering a period of unprecedented profitability, (11) adopted a similar stance, thus ensuring a further diminution of their standing among the crofting population. Of one Lochcarron sheep farmer 'it was commonly reported among the people that he never saw a green spot of earth but he coveted it as his own'. (12) And that characterisation, if unduly unkind, was by no means unfounded – the rather immoderate contemporary view that 'the larger farmers of the Highlands ... [were] the scourges of the people' (13) being supported by a considerable weight of more sober testimony to the same effect. Thus Sir Edward Coffin 'constantly' heard from sheep farmers that emigration was 'the sole remedy for the distress of the country'. Their 'evident aim', he reported, was 'to depopulate the districts which they occupy'. And because their rents constituted the largest and most dependable part of their landlords' income, sheep farmers could exercise an influence that was out of all proportion to their numbers – an influence that was considerably increased by the fact that they, unlike crofters, had the ear of estate managements. The typical factor was invariably of the same social standing as the sheep farmers on the estate he administered, had many friends among them and was always willing to listen to their opinions – in many instances, indeed, he farmed sheep on his own account, his greatest source of income often consisting of the very favourable lease granted to him by the proprietor in return for his services. (14) Since crofters' feelings counted for next to nothing, all those who mattered on Highland estates were therefore in favour of clearance and emigration.

But while there is thus no reason to doubt the judgement of the Skye factor who subsequently declared that 'the great rise in the value of sheep' was 'the real cause' of the widespread evictions of the mid-nineteenth century, (15) there was another important reason for landlords' and farmers' all too evident desire to be rid of the crofting population: the working of the new Scots poor law.

Throughout the northern and western Highlands and islands the aid available to paupers from official funds was — before the passing of the new poor law in 1846 — so small as to be almost negligible. Poor rates being unknown, annual allowances to the poor were sometimes as low as 2s. and seldom exceeded 10s. even in cases of special necessity. Persons classified as paupers thus depended on the charity of friends and relatives who — though by no means affluent themselves — maintained the traditional view that the destitute had a natural right to food and clothing and spoke of a person in need not as a beggar but as someone *ag iarraidh a' chodach,* seeking or asking his portion. (16) Such communality held little attraction for Victorian poor law reformers who were generally steeped in the principles of self-help and of Benthamite philosophy. And it was in any case outmoded — its main effect in the circumstances of the 1830s and 1840s being to drag everyone down to the same level of hopeless and helpless poverty. In 1846, therefore, the Highlands were treated in exactly the same way as the rest of Scotland, a legally enforced poor rate becoming the rule rather than the exception. And by 1850 only the parishes of Ardnamurchan and Bracadale — the one on the mainland of Argyll and the other in Skye — retained the old system of voluntary contributions. (17) Crofters derived considerable benefits from the change. But proprietors and sheep farmers — who had been united in opposing it — were forced, as the major ratepayers, to shoulder a new and unwelcome burden which was made all the heavier by the impact of the famine. (18) By the beginning of the 1850s the poor rate in three of the parishes on the MacDonald estate in Skye amounted to 15 per cent of the gross rental and the local rate had become one of the subjects meticulously enquired into by prospective buyers of the many Highland properties that were then appearing on the market. (19) In Skye and the Outer Hebrides as a whole, it was calculated in 1852, the poor rate stood at around 2s. 8d. in the pound as compared to the Scottish average of 1s. 1¼d. (20) And, it was feared, much worse was to come.

On the Relief Board's final withdrawal from the Highland scene in the autumn of 1850, the government had received numerous and not infrequently frantic appeals for renewed assistance. These however were rejected on the grounds that the aid made available in the 1840s had not produced 'any permanent improvement in the condition of the people' and that the time had come for Highland expenditure to be met from Highland resources. (21) In the implementation of such a policy the poor law seemed at first destined to play little part, for the simple reason that under its provisions the victims of famine and destitution counted as 'able-bodied' and 'occasional' poor who were not entitled to assistance. No doubt prompted by the government the Scottish poor law authorities had determined by 1851, however, to take advantage of the provisions made by the 1846 Act for the 'temporary relief' of such persons. Under these provisions, the Highland poor law boards were informed, they had clearly to accept responsibility for famine relief and they were accordingly instructed to extract from landlords, farmers and other ratepayers 'the largest amount

of assessment' which the latter were 'able to pay'. (22) This highly dubious interpretation of the 1846 Act was eventually and successfully challenged in the courts.
But by that time the damage had been done. The decision that Irish landlords should
help to meet the cost of famine relief was a major stimulus to clearances and evictions
in Ireland. (23) And the imposition of a heavy Highland poor rate, combined with
the threat of still heavier rates in the future, undoubtedly contributed to the same
result in north-west Scotland. (24)

As had been the case since the Highland clearances began some fifty years earlier,
evictions and removals had their apologists and rationalisers among some of the most
influential sections of southern public opinion. In the Highlands as in Ireland, declared *The Economist,* the famine had shown that: 'The departure of the redundant
part of the population is an indispensable preliminary to every kind of improvement.' (2
And though the small but growing band of pro-crofter pamphleteers (26) could take
some comfort from the writings of the one or two economists – notably G. Poulett
Scrope and W.P. Alison – who were prepared to argue that the Highlands' economic
salvation lay not so much in the deportation of small tenants as in the development of
a reformed crofting system which would incorporate greater security of tenure and
other incentives to agricultural betterment, it was the *Economist* viewpoint that
found most favour at an official level where a rapid reduction in the region's population was coming to be seen as the only way of permanently improving the Highland
situation. (27)

This attitude – in marked contrast to that prevailing in 1846 and 1847 when,
despite the pleas of MacLeod of Dunvegan and other proprietors, there had been no
question of paying for emigration out of public funds (28) – is partly attributable to
the disillusionment caused by the Relief Board's obvious failure to do more than
prevent the actual starvation of the crofting population, a disillusionment which, by
1849, had led to some of the Board's own members advocating the deployment of
a part of the famine relief fund in the emigration sphere. Although the Board had
subsequently assisted no fewer than 1,155 people to make their way to Canada, they
had done so only on condition that crofts vacated by emigrants were used to enlarge
neighbouring holdings, aid being refused, for example, to Gordon of Cluny on the
grounds that lands relinquished by Uist and Barra emigrants were being added to
sheep farms. (29) To its own satisfaction at any rate, the Board thus succeeded in
squaring its advocacy of emigration with its obligations to the crofters for whose
benefit its funds had been collected. But the Board of Supervision, the body charged
with the task of administering the Scottish poor law, had to contend with no such
scruples. Impressed by the Relief Board's lack of success and convinced – with a zeal
that would have done justice to characters in a Dickensian satire – that generous
assistance to the poor was more debilitating than poverty itself, the poor law authorities had, by the early 1850s, become firmly attached to the idea of emigration. They
decided, to put the matter bluntly, to starve crofters into emigrating. And their
determination to make the Highland poor law boards responsible for the relief of
destitution in their own areas was in part designed to bring this about. (30)

That the government shared the poor law administrators' views was borne out in
January 1851 by the appointment of Sir John MacNeill, chairman of the Board of
Supervision, to conduct an enquiry into the state of the Highlands. MacNeill's

prejudices were well known and Highland landlordism's few public critics immediately forecast that the result of his investigations would be more emigration, paid for perhaps by the taxpayer. (31) The same critics considered MacNeill, who was the third son of the then laird of Colonsay, to be little more than a landlords' spokesman (32) — an opinion that was scarcely modified by his conduct of the enquiry. The bulk of the evidence taken into account was provided by proprietors and their representatives, and to the openly expressed disquiet of, among others, the Free Church Destitution Committee, and the Edinburgh economist, W.P. Alison, emigration in fact turned out to be the only remedy for Highland distress which Sir John felt able to propose. (33)

The legislative consequence of his recommendations was the Emigration Advances Act. Introduced into the Commons on 22 July 1851, the Act had an unopposed and unusually rapid passage through both Houses of Parliament, receiving the royal assent on 7th August. (34) The Highland problem, according to its preamble, was most likely to be 'officially relieved by affording Facilities for the voluntary Emigration of a Portion of the Population of these Districts'; and the sums to be provided for this purpose could be conveniently and appropriately deducted from funds originally voted under the Drainage Act. (35) Emigration, in short, was deemed to improve an estate in much the same way as draining and ditching. And though the Act came too late to affect some of the major emigrations from Highland properties, it set the seal of official approval on landlords' policies and no doubt helped to quieten any remaining qualms of conscience about what was being done to the crofting population. (36)

In the summer of 1847, the year after the beginning of the famine, the Duke of Sutherland helped 380 of his tenants to emigrate to America. (37) And during the next ten years at least 16,000 people emigrated from the north-west Highlands and islands to Canada, Australia and the U.S.A. Most were assisted by their landlords, by the government, or by public subscriptions raised for the purpose. Some emigrated at their own expense. And many thousands more made their own way to the lowlands. (38) Now many of these people were forced to remove themselves; how many went voluntarily? These are moot points, not least because the distinction is in some respects unreal. Starvation and poverty, no less than eviction, imply some degree of compulsion, and the issue is further confused by the fact that it was in the interest of those who favoured emigration, whether landlords or the officials of central government, to represent the people affected by it as being in favour of it also. There is, however, no reason to suppose that crofters as a class were completely opposed to emigration. America was their traditional refuge from poverty and oppression, (39) and the traumatic experience of the famine not unnaturally awakened a new interest in escaping to the other side of the Atlantic. As early as October 1846 one of Sir Edward Coffin's subordinates reported that 'the lower orders' were 'turning their hopes to emigration', (40) and the subsequent deterioration in their circumstances made many crofters and their families only too eager to get away. In 1848, for example, several families left the MacLeod estate for the United States; and a great many more, it was said, were prevented from accompanying them only by their inability to raise the necessary funds. (41) The one obstacle to mass emigration, apart from crofters' poverty, was their belief that something would be done to improve their position at home. That hope, however, was finally dashed by the winding up of the Relief Board in 1850 and by the government's refusal to resume its own relief operations. And as the Board of Supervision's secretary remarked with obvious satisfaction, there was 'reason to believe' that as a result of the latter decision 'the reluctance of the people to emigrate has greatly diminished, and will probably be altogether overcome by a just appreciation of the hopelessness of their prospects'. (42) Thus a crofter from Creich in Mull told Sir John MacNeill in 1851 that 'not one in three would remain if they could find the means of emigrating', (43) and Sir John himself calculated that more than half the population of some crofting parishes would emigrate 'if they could find the means'. (44)

Finding the means was no easy task, however, Assisted passages, it is true, did exist; for as a consequence of an acute labour scarcity in the Australian colonies, colonial funds had been set aside to help pay the fares of certain classes of emigrants. Administered by a body known as the Colonial Land and Emigration Commission, (45) these funds were doled out only sparingly, prospective emigrants having to pay a deposit whose size was determined by the extent to which they met the colonies' requirements. Thus a single man paid £2 and a single woman £1 — wives being in short supply; while a married couple under forty-five years of age, paid £2 with 10s. being added for each of their children. People who were over forty-five paid between £5 and £11. And all emigrants, irrespective of age or status, were required to provide a suitable outfit for the voyage and to make their own way to the nearest port of embarkation. Intending emigrants thus needed a considerable capital sum and in the 1840s and 1850s most crofters were prevented from taking advantage of the Emigration Commission's terms by the virtually absolute poverty to which the famine had reduced them. In 1849, for example, many of the people who were willing to emigrate from Skye could not afford to make their way to Greenock — the nearest port from which the Commission's transports sailed — far less pay the deposits demanded of them. (46) And quite apart from financial considerations, Highlanders were generally less than enthusiastic about going to Australia. Earlier emigrants to New South Wales had sent back letters which 'did not at all give a favourable account of the place'. And since information from such sources received more credence 'than anything written in newspapers or sent from England', the widespread preference for Canada, the traditional destination of Highland emigrants, was never completely overcome — despite the dissemination of semi-official propaganda of a decidedly pro-Australian nature. (47)

So acute were their sufferings by the early 1850s, however, that many crofters wanted only to shake the Highland dust from their feet — their ultimate destination being relatively immaterial. The potatoes continued to be regularly blighted. And conditions along the north-west coast and in the islands continued to be deplorable — a not untypical plight being that of the evicted family who lived, or at least existed, at that time in a makeshift lean-to of boards and sailcloth on the outskirts of Portree and depended for survival on 'a few half-pence from the steamer'. (48) In the winter of 1850-51 the now commonplace hunger and distress were aggravated by the absence of any relief measures; while the following winter brought conditions that were, if anything, even worse. (49) By 1852 it was possible to observe of the north-west Highlands that 'the great bulk of the population in those parts of our land are ... on the verge of pauperism, with no immediate visible prospect of their distresses being alleviated'. (50) And in Skye that summer there was said to be 'more squalid misery and positive starvation' than at any time since 1846, (51) an Emigration Commission agent who visited the island in June reporting that 'Any description that can be given must fall short of the sad reality. It is not too much to say that many of the swine in England are better fed and better housed than are the poor of this island.' (52) Conditions on Lord MacDonald's estate he found particularly appalling. He was, he wrote, forced to turn down appeals for assisted passages from several MacDonald tenants because they had 'suffered so much from starvation'. (53) And from Sir Edward Coffin, who in the summer of 1852 revisited the scene of his endeavours of five years before, there came further confirmation of the seriousness of the crofting population's predicament:

> Nothing convinces me so much of the present poverty of the people as the general falling off in the state of their clothing. In 1846 and 1847 I scarcely saw any, however ill off for food, who were not on the whole better dressed than our peasantry in the West of England: while now ... rags are no longer uncommon, and many declare that they have only the covering in which they stand. (54)

Despite the overwhelming and inescapable misery of their lives, wrote the Sheriff of Portree, crofters were still convinced that their prospects could be dramatically brightened 'by properly devised remedial measures'. But by 1852, he added, they had come to 'despair of such measures being adopted'. Their savings and other resources having long since been converted into food, they had come to look on emigration as affording 'the only sure means of escape' from an otherwise hopeless situation and had even ceased to care whether or not they were being removed to make way for sheep. (55) But while many crofters were therefore willing to accept ✔ emigration as a preferable alternative to starvation, it was clear — as was remarked by several contemporary observers — that if their departure was to help solve the Highlands' problems it would have to be accompanied by the enlargement of the holdings occupied by the crofting tenants who chose to remain. (56) That vacated land be utilised for such a purpose had been a condition of the Relief Board's sponsoring of emigration. (57) And because the arguments in favour of such a procedure were quite overwhelming it was one to which landlords felt obliged to pay lip service. Implicit or explicit in all the pro-emigration propaganda which emanated from Highland proprietors and from official and semi-official sources, therefore, was the contention that emigration would benefit crofters by relieving congestion and by making possible the provision of larger, and consequently more viable, holdings.

The more outspoken critics of Highland landlordism — such as Donald Ross the Glasgow advocate and pamphleteer, and Hugh Miller the editor of *The Witness* newspaper — were quite unconvinced of the genuineness of such pronouncements and openly declared that the proprietors' advocacy of mass emigration betokened nothing more than a desire to extend and consolidate the sheep farming system. By 1849, a year which, according to Hugh Miller, 'added its long list to the roll of Highland ejections', (58) these men were convinced that an all out assault on crofting was under way — and their views were substantiated by G. Poulett Scrope, an M.P. and economist who toured the Highlands that summer. As something of an authority on Ireland's agrarian problem, Scrope was not given to idly involving Irish parallels. But in many parts of north-west Scotland, he reported, 'ejectments and house levellings' were 'almost as frequent as in Clare or Galway'. (59)

Clearances on such a scale implied that little, if any, more land was being made available to crofters, an inference borne out in the 1860s by the results of an unofficial but fairly painstaking enquiry into the effects of emigration on the Highlands' agricultural system. In most instances, it was concluded, 'the lands of emigrating tenants are added to some existing sheep farm and the small tenants, whose holdings are altogether inadequate for their support, are left just as they were'. (60) Subsequent and much more detailed analyses of the crofting system were to confirm the validity of that verdict (61) – and it was one from which crofters themselves never dissented: 'I have never seen that emigration gave more room to people, though it did to sheep. The tendency has been to add more families to places already overcrowded.' (62) Thus the Free Church minister of Kilmuir in 1883 and thus a crofter from Lochalsh: 'Emigration has not, in any case we know, improved the condition of ... those who remained in the country. The reverse was the result ... they were reduced to poverty, their lands being added to sheep farms.' (63) And a Skye crofter's conviction that tenants were never 'removed from townships for the purpose of bettering the condition of those who [were] left behind', was echoed by the son of a crofter from Sutherland: 'Those emigrations were not carried out in order to effect an improvement in the condition of the crofters. They were carried out in order to convert the land into sheep farms.' (64) With these contentions the first royal commission of enquiry into crofting affairs saw little reason to disagree. 'The residuary population,' it concluded, 'received little benefit from the emigrations' because most emigrants' holdings were given to sheep farmers rather than to crofters. (65) And that such was indeed the case is evident from even the most cursory examination of the events of the 1840s and 1850s.

Sir James Matheson, tea magnate and owner of Lewis, helped 1,771 people to emigrate from his island estate between 1851 and 1855. (66) His treatment of these emigrants was, by the standards of the time, decidedly generous – a model to other proprietors according to immigration officials in Quebec. (67) But his attitude to those of his tenants who were unwilling to exchange their crofts for an uncertain future in Canada was notably less benevolent. In the spring of 1851, for example, it was announced that any crofter who owed more than two years' rent to the estate and who rejected Matheson's offer of a free passage to Canada would be 'served with a summons of removal at Whitsunday and deprived of his lands'. (68) The subsequent evictions were accompanied by the wholesale clearance of several townships. At least forty-eight crofters were removed from Reef and Carnish in 1851 alone; and in the next few months there were fairly extensive evictions from the island of Bernera, on Lewis' west coast, and from the township of North Tolsta, a settlement established in the wake of Seaforth's clearances in the 1820s. Evicted tenants were moved into other uncleared townships, thus adding to the already serious problem of congestion and overcrowding. And as had been the case in Seaforth's time, the parish of Uig was particularly badly affected. Its population had more than doubled since the mid-eighteenth century but its crofters had, by the 1850s, been deprived of almost half the land that their fathers and grandfathers had occupied. (69)

A Lewis crofter once remarked with a bitterness that was not unjustifiable that out of Matheson's enormous expenditure on his estate not 'one single shilling was spent in improving our crofts and houses'. (70) But because he had equipped his emigrating tenants with the funds they needed to establish themselves in Canada, Matheson — in the 1850s at least — enjoyed an excellent reputation in all but the most anti-landlord circles. The same cannot be said of his fellow purchaser of Hebridean islands, Gordon of Cluny. The latter, wrote Sir Charles Trevelyan — by no means an intemperate critic of Highland proprietors — was 'notorious ... for his indifference to the feelings and interests of those connected with him'. And his notoriety, it was generally acknowledged, stemmed from the circumstances surrounding the transportation of no fewer than 2,715 of his tenantry to Canada in the years between 1848 and 1851. (71)

Of all the many thousands of people who left the north-west Highlands and Hebrides during the famine none were more brutally driven out than the people of Barra, South Uist and Benbecula. Prospective emigrants who refused to board the transports which Gordon had chartered for the occasion were hunted down with the aid of dogs, bound and despatched willy-nilly. (72) The sufferings of the men, women and children who were the victims of these proceedings can now only be guessed at; but something of them is preserved in the recollections of Catherine MacPhee of Iochdar, South Uist, who as a girl had witnessed the events which she so graphically described:

> Many a thing have I seen in my own day and generation. Many a thing, O Mary Mother of the black sorrow! I have seen the townships swept, and the big holdings being made of them, the people being driven out of the countryside to the streets of Glasgow and to the wilds of Canada, such of them as did not die of hunger and plague and smallpox while going across the ocean. I have seen the women putting the children in the carts which were being sent from Benbecula and the Iochdar to Loch Boisdale, while their husbands lay bound in the pen and were weeping beside them, without power to give them a helping hand, though the women themselves were crying aloud and their little children wailing like to break their hearts. I have seen the big strong men, the champions of the countryside, the stalwarts of the world, being bound on Loch Boisdale quay and cast into the ship as would be done to a batch of horses or cattle in the boat, the bailiffs and the ground-officers and the constables and the policemen gathered behind them in pursuit of them. The God of life and He only knows all the loathsome work of men on that day. (73)

As Catherine MacPhee indicated, the emigrants' troubles did not end with their eviction. When the first batch of South Uist emigrants were landed at Glasgow en route for Quebec in the summer of 1848, for example, they were so destitute that they had to bivouac in the open air for several nights. (74) And subsequent groups fared no better. The medical officer in charge of the Grosse Isle quarantine station in the St. Lawrence river — a man who had coped with the massive influx of refugees from the Irish famine — wrote of one contingent from Gordon's estate that he had never seen 'a body of emigrants so destitute of clothing and bedding; many children of nine and ten years old had not a rag to cover them'. And because they were almost all 'without the means of leaving the ship, or of procuring a day's subsistence for their helpless families', Canada offered them little prospect of immediate betterment. (75)

To landlords and to the British government's officials in London and Edinburgh, the emigration of the Highlands' 'surplus population' was a self-evidently beneficial measure. The Canadians who were in daily contact with crowds of ragged, starving Highlanders, able to speak only enough English to beg for bread, found it considerably easier to question the rightness of the policy which had brought them there:

> We have been pained beyond measure for some time past, to witness in our streets so many unfortunate Highland emigrants, apparently destitute of any means of subsistence, and many of them sick from want ... There will be many to sound the fulsome noise of flattery in the ear of the generous landlord who has spent so much to assist the emigration of his poor tenants. They will give him the misnomer of *benefactor,* and for what? Because he has rid his estates of the encumbrances of a pauper population. (76)

The *Dundas Warden,* the newspaper which contained that passage, was most unlikely to have come to the attention of Gordon of Cluny. But the main burden of its editor's complaint — that Highland emigrants were 'often so situated' as to make their emigration 'more cruel than banishment' — was taken up by A.C. Buchanan, a Quebec immigration official, in a letter to Gordon's factor. 'The mere transfer to this port of an indigent tenantry,' he pointed out, 'gives no reasonable grounds for expecting their subsequent successful progress.' Besides, he added, those who had already arrived in Canada would naturally make 'unfavourable representations' to their friends and relatives at home and the result would be a general 'disinclination to follow'. (77) That letter was not received in the Uists until the controversial emigrations were over; and it is, to say the least, doubtful if Gordon's estate management would have taken any heed of its contents even if it had arrived some months before it did — Gordon having already declared that he considered himself 'neither legally or morally bound to support a population reduced to poverty by the will of Providence'. (78) In the long run, however, at least one of Buchanan's prognostications proved correct. When, in the 1880s, emigration was again canvassed as a solution to the crofting problem, the suggestion was greeted with particular hostility in Benbecula, South Uist and Barra. (79)

Had the miseries endured by these emigrants or by the parties of people, 'lately expelled from the island of Barra', who arrived — 'in a starving state' — in Edinburgh and Inverness in the winter of 1850-51, (80) been compensated for by a generous redistribution of the land they relinquished, the events of these years might have been remembered with less resentment in the islands where they took place. In practically every case, however, the emigrations from Gordon's Hebridean properties were accompanied by renewed clearances. The Benbecula townships of Balivanich, Aird, Uachdar, Griminish and Torlum lost arable and pasture lands to Nunton farm. (81) The South Uist sheep farms established by Clanranald in the 1820s and 1830s were further enlarged and consolidated, Askernish and Milton being the principal beneficiaries. (82) And in Barra, where there had been relatively few clearances hitherto, at least ten townships were obliterated and a third of the island put under sheep. (83)

Although Gordon's clearances were unrivalled in brutality, they were not unparalleled in scope. Lord MacDonald's estate management's commitment to the clearance ideal has already been noted; (84) and the strength of their attachment to it is testified to by the fact that the shipping of over 2,500 of Lord MacDonald's tenants to Canada and Australia between 1849 and 1856 was accompanied by extensive removals and evictions. On the MacDonald estate in North Uist there were in 1830 well over 350 small tenants. By 1854 there were only 243 and the thirty-six crofting townships of 1830 had been reduced to twenty, the greater part of the island — including most of the best land — having been converted into sheep farms in the process. (85) On Lord MacDonald's Skye possessions sheep farming was of much larger standing. (86) But in Skye as elsewhere, the lesson of the famine seemed to be that the time was ripe for its extension. In the parish of Sleat, wrote Lord MacDonald's factor in 1851, 'many of the croft farms by the removal of the people might with great propriety be added to the tacksmen's possessions'. (87) And there followed a series of evictions which, in the words of the then minister of Sleat, were 'attended with circumstances of heartless cruelty'. (88) Not the least notorious of these clearances was the removal of the tenants of Boreraig and Suishnish in the autumn of 1853. Witnessed by the geologist Sir Archibald Geikie, it was described by him as follows:

> I had heard some rumours of these intentions but did not realise that they were in process of being carried into effect, until one afternoon, as I was returning from my ramble, a strange wailing sound reached my ears at intervals on the breeze from the west. On gaining the top of one of the hills on the south side of the valley, I could see a long and motley procession winding along the road that led north from Suishnish. It halted at the point of the road opposite Kilbride, and there the lamentation became loud and long. As I drew nearer I could see that the minister with his wife and daughters had come out to meet the people and bid them all farewell. It was a miscellaneous gathering of at least three generations of crofters. There were old men and women, too feeble to walk, who were placed in carts; the younger members of the community on foot were carrying their bundles of clothes and household effects, while the children, with looks of alarm, walked alongside ... Everyone was in tears ... When they set forth once more, a cry of grief went up to heaven, the long plaintive wail, like a funeral coronach, was resumed, and ... the sound seemed to re-echo through the whole wide valley of Strath in one prolonged note of desolation. (89)

Boreraig and Suishnish were converted into a sheep farm consisting of 2,761 acres of hill grazings and 183 acres of formerly arable land. The latter, it was subsequently noted, was 'of fair quality' while the hill pasture was 'of good quality and some of it may be described as superior'. (90) Several of the families evicted in order to establish this altogether desirable holding emigrated to Australia. The remainder — about 120 people in all — were moved to other townships, principally Isleornsay, Drumfearn, Tarskavaig and Breakish, where existing crofts were subdivided to make room for them. (91)

Developments at Boreraig and Suishnish were accompanied by the clearance of several townships which had the misfortune to march with Lord MacDonald's deer forest — the bulk of their tenants being moved into the already overcrowded settlement of Sconser, destined to become one of the most congested and unhealthy crofting townships in Skye. (92) The parish of Kilmuir — the northernmost part of the MacDonald estate — whose 'numerous small tenantry' Lord MacDonald's factor considered a 'scourge', was similarly affected, several of its sheep farms being extended at crofters' expense. (93) But despite one of MacLeod's principal tenants' belief that what he called 'the Emigration mania' would lead to the clearance of a large part of Glendale, (94) there were few further evictions on the MacLeod estate —

the main reason being that most of the land which was suited to sheep farming had already been adapted for such a purpose. (95) On the smaller Skye properties, however, Lord MacDonald's activities were assiduously emulated. Extensive evictions on the Strathaird, Greshornish and Lynedale estates (96) were accompanied by the clearance of a number of settlements on Raasay. Several townships in the southern part of that island were converted into a sheep farm and the sixty-three crofters who had formerly occupied them were forced to emigrate to Australia or to remove themselves to other parts of the estate. (97) The emigrants, one eyewitness recalled, departed 'like lambs separated from their mothers'; and with them they took handfuls of the soil which covered their people's graves in the island's churchyard. (98) Those who stayed behind fared little better. Several families were settled on subdivisions of already meagre holdings. (99) Others were moved to the neighbouring island of Rona, a place that was subsequently described by the Scottish Land Court as 'suitable for nothing else than a grazing for a very limited number of sheep'. (100)

To the people affected by them, clearances were utterly overwhelming catastrophes whose effects — psychological as well as physical — were profound and long-lasting. But while these effects are susceptible to analysis and discussion, (101) it is impossible to convey — in retrospect and in cold prose at any rate — the nature of the evictions' immediate impact on the crofting population. To give details of all the removals of the 1840s and 1850s would consequently be to reduce many thousands of intensely personal tragedies to a catalogue of superficially similar events. And the following paragraphs are therefore intended to do no more than make the point that almost no part of north-west Scotland escaped experiences of the type already described. The emigration of over 400 people from Harris in the early 1850s was accompanied by renewed clearances. (102) Most of Coll was cleared at about the same time. (103) And from Tiree in 1849 the Duke of Argyll shipped almost 600 people to Canada. Cholera broke out on the transports that carried them across the Atlantic and on their arrival in Quebec they could not afford to move on into the interior to look for work or land. With the emigrant sheds already crammed with the human debris of the Irish famine, they could obtain no shelter from the weather and, huddled together on the wharfs, many of them died of exposure and disease. (104) These and subsequent emigrations from the island were accompanied by scores of evictions, the Duke himself admitting to forty. (105) Half of Tiree was taken out of crofters' hands, a development paralleled on the Duke's property in the Ross of Mull and, indeed, on practically every other estate in the latter island. (106) In Mull, it was reported in 1849, the 'poverty and misery' caused by the famine were 'being daily added to by the evictions taking place'. (107) Dozens of ejected families settled in the 'wretched hovels' which sprang up in the neighbourhood of Tobermory; and there they supported themselves on the shellfish they scavenged from the beaches. (108) Other families emigrated or moved to the lowlands, not the least sweeping of the clearances which precipitated them into such courses of action occurring on the small island of Ulva, off Mull's west coast. A premier kelping property, (109) it was, in the 1830s, occupied by eighty-eight crofters settled in sixteen townships. (110) The kelp industry's decline was inevitably accompanied by a drastic fall in the island's rental. (111) And in the 1840s — spurred on no doubt by the famine — Ulva's owner, in the words of one of his admirers, made 'a decided stand against crofting', (112) proceeding, as Sir John MacNeill discovered in 1851, 'to warn off a certain number yearly and to convert the vacated lands into grazings, until in four or five years the population was reduced from 500 to 150'. (113) Within a few years even that small population had been removed and Ulva was left in the occupation of its landlord, his shepherds and two or three labourers. (114)

The proprietor of Ulva's conviction that 'the crofting system cannot be made an advantageous mode of occupying property in this part of the country' (115) was shared by landlords whose estates were situated on the north-west coast of the mainland. From north-west Sutherland — where considerable tracts of crofting land were added to sheep farms in the 1840s and 1850s (116) — to the parish of Ardnamurchan in Argyll — a district where, it was concluded in 1852, 'great advantages as regards returns would accrue by small possessions being thrown into Sheep Walks' (117) — emigrations and clearances went hand in hand. In Kintail, Lochalsh, Arisaig and Moidart there were numerous evictions, the expropriated tenants' lands being added to sheep farms in almost every case. (118) In Glenelg, a parish particularly badly affected by the famine, (119) the proprietor's motives in providing his crofters with free passages to the colonies are revealed by the fact that they were only made available to people who agreed to pull down their houses before leaving the district. (120) And in Knoydart, where its owner's death when his son was still a minor led to MacDonnell of Glengarry's estate being placed under the management of a group of trustees, there were very similar occurrences. On discovering that a part of the property was occupied by a number of crofters who had paid scarcely any rent since the onset of the famine, the trustees decided to eject them and let their lands to a sheep farmer. Over 300 people accepted the offer of a free passage to Canada. And in order to ensure that their holdings remained vacant their houses were demolished. In August 1853, a few weeks after the emigrants had sailed, those crofters who had refused to go to Canada were evicted, and their houses too were destroyed. Some were taken in by friends and relatives. But about thirty people who had nowhere else to go had the temerity to erect makeshift huts and tents among the ruins of their homes. 'With a view to compel them to remove,' as Sir John MacNeill found in 1854, 'their temporary shelters were pulled down, in some instances more than once.' (121) And although some of the refugees were still squatting on the estate in the summer of 1855, (122) their unequal struggle with the elements and with the estate authorities had eventually to be given up. When the Knoydart estate was sold in 1857 it was almost all under sheep. There remained only one small congested township of about a dozen crofters whose holdings consisted of a few acres of shallow, rocky soil on the shore of the Sound of Sleat. (123)

In 1852, as if Highland landlords and the British government between them were not doing enough to facilitate emigration, charitable endeavour, in the shape of the Highlands and Islands Emigration Society, stepped into the fray. (124) The Society — which was responsible for the greater part of Highland emigration after 1852 — had its beginnings in Skye in the previous autumn when, on the initiative of Sheriff Fraser of Portree, a committee of all Skye's resident proprietors and farmers had been set up to disseminate information about emigration and to help finance those crofters who were desirous of leaving the island. (125) When fund raising committees were established in Edinburgh and London in the spring of 1852, however, it became clear that control of the Society was not destined to remain for long with its originators, the committees being presided over by Sir John MacNeill and Sir Charles Trevelyan respectively. The latter, within a very few weeks, assumed overall command of the organisation thus provided for him. MacNeill became his willing lieutenant. And Fraser and his colleagues were quickly relegated to a distinctly subordinate position. (126)

No single event better illustrates the trend of official thinking on the crofting problem in the years that followed the famine than this take over of an emigration association by the two civil servants who had, since 1846, been most closely connected with Highland affairs. They hoped, in Trevelyan's words, to bring about an outflow of people that would match the 'wonderful exodus' from Ireland and effect 'a final measure of relief for the Western Highlands and Islands by transferring the surplus of the population to Australia'. (127) The number of people 'whom it would be necessary to remove from the islands and the west coast' was variously estimated to lie between 30,000 and 40,000 souls, (128) the Society meeting two-thirds of the cost (which was to be repaid by the emigrants after they had been settled in Australia), and the emigrants' landlords paying the remainder. (129) While thus re-cognising that emigration was to Highland proprietors' advantage, the Society, in its public pronouncements at least, made a great deal of the well-worn argument that the 'emigration of a part' was 'necessary for the welfare of the whole', Trevelyan going to considerable lengths to deny that his organisation had been founded to 'facilitate landlords' clearances'. (130) When proprietors or their agents were being confidentially addressed, however, rather different arguments were adopted. The Society's activities, it was pointed out, were less likely than those of individual land-owners to give rise to the 'clamours and complaints of evictions that tend very materially to render Highland property unpopular as an investment'. But with its assistance 'the superabundant population' of Highland estates could 'be transferred to Australia at a cost to the proprietors calculated not to exceed £1 per head'. (131) It was an attractive prospect and it is not at all surprising therefore that all the crofting landlords in the north-west — with the exception of Gordon of Cluny, on whose estate emigration had already been pushed to its limits — gave financial support to the Society. (132) That the body he had founded should have become entangled with evicting landlords was not, to Sheriff Fraser of Portree, a pleasing development; and he accordingly suggested that it should dissociate itself from them at least to the extent of ceasing to employ their factors as its agents. This idea Trevelyan treated with undisguised contempt. 'Fraser aimed only at administering a small charitable fund,' he wrote to MacNeill, 'but the matter has now assumed the character of an extensive social operation.' (133) Besides the end of depopulation, he believed, justified the means: 'Considerable estates belonging to the MacLeod and MacDonald families are in the market, but nobody will buy them while they are occupied by swarms of miserable tenants who can neither pay rent nor support themselves.' (134)

But while the Society succeeded in sending nearly 5,000 Highlanders to Australia in the five years of its existence, (135) Trevelyan's more grandiose ambitions remained unfulfilled, principally because 1852, the year of the Emigration Society's foundation, brought a harvest more productive than any since 1845. Blight was practically absent. Cattle prices began to rise. And renewed economic expansion in the south meant that migrant labourers were once more in demand. By the standards of immediately preceding years, therefore, 1853 was 'a season of universal prosperity' in the crofting areas. And although 2,605 people had sailed for Australia before the excellence of the crop became apparent, its ingathering was followed by an immediate and dramatic decline in the number of crofters willing to join them. (136) A bad harvest in 1854 brought a temporary recession into near famine conditions. (137) But subsequent years produced better crops and better fishings as well as the Crimean War, which imposed something of a check on every type of emigration from the British Isles. (138) Trevelyan having consequently concluded that crofters were now 'able to live comfortably at home', and his Society having in any case run short of funds, emigration from the Highlands to Australia was suspended in 1857. (139) And because the depression which began in the United States and Canada in the same year made transatlantic destinations less attractive also, emigration from the Highlands to the North American colonies petered out at about the same time. (140)

The crofters of the later 1850s were not living so comfortably as Sir Charles Trevelyan suggested — in 1857, for example, an official enquiry concluded that 'on the whole, the Highland population must be considered as poorly fed'. (141) But the worst, it is true, was over. In the ten years after 1846 the crofting population had plumbed the depths of hunger and deprivation. Driven from their homes by their own poverty and by their landlords' determination to extract profits from the land, many thousands of small tenants had left the north-west Highlands for the colonies and the lowlands. And the position of those who remained had not in consequence been improved. On every side, crofters' lands had been taken away from them. Whole townships had been obliterated. The common grazings of others had been drastically curtailed. Throughout the Highlands and Hebrides crofting had become an activity of only marginal agricultural and economic importance; and by the region's landlords its remaining practitioners were openly regarded as little more than a nuisance. In spite of everything, however, the crofting population had retained a hold — no matter how precarious — on the land. And for the first time in more than forty years crofters' prospects were improving. The fury of the blight was spent. The prices of produce, especially cattle, were rising. And prospects of remunerative employment were better than at any time since the failure of the kelp industry in the 1820s. But even more important than the ensuing improvement in the economic conditions of crofting life were the already discernible indications that crofters were becoming aware of common interests and objectives; and that they were becoming capable of uniting in pursuit of them. The latter development makes it possible to write, from this point forward, of a 'crofting community', a phrase that implies the existence of the sort of social cohesion that had hitherto been lacking among crofters. And its crucial significance in the history of crofting society is testified to by the way in which the historical initiative now shifts away from landlords — whose decisions dominated the early years of crofting – and moves towards crofters themselves. That such a decisive transformation was occurring was not at all apparent in the 1850s – and it did not, in fact, become so until the 1880s. Its origins are nevertheless to be found in the early nineteenth century. And it is with these origins that the following chapter is primarily concerned.

6. The Emergence of the Crofting Community

IN all the extensive literature about the Highland clearances no feature of them is more frequently commented upon than crofters' lack of resistance to evictions – the absence of violence, terrorism and intimidation being in quite striking contrast to their prevalence among the Irish peasantry whose situation was not dissimilar to that of their Highland counterparts. (1) That the existence of this relatively peaceful state of affairs in the Highlands was an important reason for official neglect of the region's problems is undoubted. It was, as is remarked in a recent study of rural disorder in Ireland, the endemic violence of the Irish countryside 'that made it difficult for the governing classes to ignore the poverty of the majority of the Irish people'. (2) But in the Highlands, as the normally pacific Hugh Miller remarked in the famine year of 1846, there was no such stimulus to concern:

> They [the Irish] are buying guns, and will be by-and-bye shooting magistrates and clergymen by the score; and Parliament will in consequence do a great deal for them. But the poor Highlanders will shoot no-one ... and so they will be left to perish unregarded in their hovels. (3)

This passiveness must not, of course, be exaggerated. As has recently been demonstrated, (4) it was often more apparent than real, many of the clearances mentioned in preceding chapters having been violently resisted by the crofters who were affected by them. Attempts to evict some six hundred people from the townships of Dunskellor, Mallaclete, Middlequarter and Sollas on Lord MacDonald's North Uist estate in the summer of 1849, for example, were vigorously opposed by the crofters concerned. Evicting parties of sheriff-officers and estate officials were, on three separate occasions, driven away by crowds of people who pelted them with stones and other missiles. And in order to successfully serve the summonses of eviction a force of about thirty policemen had eventually to be deployed. (5) Earlier and later clearances produced numerous examples of the same sort of response and in some cases – as at Borve in Harris in 1839 – crofters so successfully 'defied and severely maltreated' the officers sent to evict them that troops had to be called in to restore order. (6)

These and many other instances of a similar kind have been copiously described elsewhere; (7) and it is not proposed to re-examine them here. In form and intent they conform to the normal pattern of rebellion in pre-industrial societies. (8) And the recurrence of many of their common characteristics in the course of the much more highly organised uprising of the 1880s should not in itself be taken as an indication that these early protests marked the beginnings of a full scale crofters' revolt. All of them, in fact, were spontaneous and isolated acts of defiance, born out of utter desperation, and condemned to failure before they began. In every case the boundaries of township and locality represented the outer limits of the political universe and there was consequently almost no attempt to raise the standard of revolt among the crofting population at large. All this was in marked contrast to the situation prevailing in the 1880s, as was the virtual absence of links with the outside world. (9)

Contacts between crofters and southern radicals were not unknown in the early nine-teenth century. (10) But where they did exist they were extremely tenuous; and even in the 1840s and 1850s none of the radically inclined and vociferously anti-landlord propagandists who wrote so pungently and effectively about the clearances made any attempt to organise a protest movement among crofters themselves.

That such a movement did not appear was not due to the absence of causes for a crofters' revolt. The causes — as previous chapters have demonstrated — were so numerous, and the misery and degradation of crofting life so overwhelming, that it is difficult at first sight to see why no revolt occurred. As has been well said, however,

Human beings do not react to the goad of hunger and oppression by some standard and automatic response of revolt. What they do, or fail to do, depends on their situation ... on their environment, culture, tradition and experience. (11)

And in order to understand why there was no social and political uprising in the Highlands until the clearances were only a memory, it is to crofters' 'culture, tradition and experience' that reference must be made.

Until the eighteenth century a man born in the north-west Highlands or islands lived his life in much the same way as his father and grandfather, the essential continuity of past and present symbolised in genealogies and traditions which spanned several centuries. Then within the space of a lifetime all was changed. The crofter, working his single holding and labouring for a wage as a kelper, was in the Highland context a pioneer, and like his landlord had little use for much of what had gone before. He had not been born into a culture familiar with the capitalist order in which he found himself, for that order had come from outside — insidiously, through the operation of economic forces of which the crofter had no comprehension and over which he could exercise no control; violently, through military conquest and the deliberate and systematic destruction of his traditional way of life. (12) In attempting to cope with the situation created by commercial landlordism crofters were therefore at an acute disadvantage, not least because they were complete strangers to the social antagonisms which are an integral part of capitalism.

The traditional society of the Highlands, like all societies based on kinship, was by no means an undifferentiated or homogeneous mass. It was, on the contrary, highly stratified and contained several distinct layers of rank and position. (13) It was nevertheless a highly unified society, for although a great gulf was fixed, and was known to be fixed, between the chief and his tacksmen on the one hand and the lowly commons of the clan on the other, both sides — for reasons of military security if for no other — had an interest in maintaining all sorts of bridges across the chasm. Economic inequalities were consequently transcended by an egalitarianism expressed in terms of blood relationship, however remote, and encapsulated in the right of every clansman to shake the hand of his chief. (14) Class conflict between feudal lords and peasant masses, an important feature of the history of pre-capitalist Europe, was therefore unknown in the Highlands where it was only under the impact of capitalism and the associated imposition of a commercialised agricultural structure that a peasantry in the usual sense of the word was created from the lower strata of the traditional society. (15)

The crofter therefore inherited no popular tradition of resistance to feudal oppression and exploitation. Instead he inherited a folklore concerned with conflict between clan and clan, locality and locality — traditions which hindered rather than helped the creation of a sense of unity among crofters as a whole. And to the stultifying influence of such a folklore was added the confusing fact that, initially at least, most Highland landlords were the descendants of the traditional chiefs. That a nineteenth century Clanranald, Seaforth or MacLeod of Dunvegan was a landowning aristocrat rather than a tribal patriarch is obvious to the historian. For an unsophisticated people, however, the weight of traditional loyalty to the chief rendered more difficult the appreciation of the social and economic transformation than would have been the case if the landlord had been expropriated and swept into oblivion as happened in Ireland. Even in the 1880s, when a radical critique of Highland landlordism had been fully developed, there was still 'on the side of the poor much reverence for the owner of the soil', (16) an attitude enshrined in the Gaelic proverb,

> Ge dona an t-uachdaran
> 'S e tha truagh am bàillidh, (17)

as well as in the work of Mary MacPherson whose poetry was the most forceful to emerge from the land agitation of the later nineteenth century but who was unwilling or unable to criticise the traditional landowning families of her native island of Skye. (18)

The undermining of this belief that 'if our landlord knew our circumstances well he would give us justice' (19) was an immensely slow process which had its origins in the eighteenth century and is by no means complete even today. (20) Hastening it on in the early nineteenth century, however, were the clearances — which in their stark inhumanity and their terrible disregard for the traditions of clanship embodied all that Highlanders found alien and wrong in landlordism:

> Mo mhullachd air a' chaora mhór
> Càit bheil clann nan daoine còir
> Dhealaich sinn nuair bha sinn òg
> 'S mas robh Dùthaich 'c Aoidh 'na fàsach. (21)

In that and many other poems is to be found the awful anger that marked the beginnings of an effective anti-landlordism among crofters. Here, for example, is part of Derick Thomson's translation of one of the most penetrating of all the poetic condemnations of what was done to Highlanders by their former chiefs — Iain Mac a' Ghobhainn's *Spiorad a' Charthannais,* the Spirit of Kindness:

> They handed over to the snipe
> the land of happy folk,
> they dealt without humanity
> with people who were kind.
> Because they might not drown them
> they dispersed them overseas;
> a thralldom worse than Babylon's
> was the plight they were in.
>
> They reckoned as but brittle threads
> the tight and loving cords
> that bound these freemen's noble hearts
> to the high land of the hills.
> The grief they suffered brought them death
> although they suffered long,
> tormented by the cold world
> which had no warmth for them.

> Does anyone remember
> in this age the bitter day
> of that horrific battle,
> Waterloo with its red plains?
> The Gaels won doughty victory
> when they marshalled under arms;
> when faced with strong men's ardour
> our fierce foes had to yield.
>
> What solace had the fathers
> of the heroes who won fame?
> Their houses, warm with kindliness,
> were in ruins round their ears;
> their sons were on the battlefield
> saving a rueless land,
> their mothers' state was piteous
> with their houses burnt like coal.
>
> While Britain was rejoicing
> they spent their time in grief.
> In the country that had reared them,
> no shelter from the wind;
> the grey strands of their hair were tossed
> by the cold breeze of the glen,
> there were tears upon their cheeks
> and cold dew on their heads. (22)

And although poems have best survived the test of time they were, throughout the nineteenth century, supplemented by the personal recollections of those who had seen, or been involved in, evictions. (23) 'I think I hear the cry of the children till this day,' said a Lewis crofter of the clearances in Uig in the 1850s, his remark, like this comment about the Sutherland clearances of the early nineteenth century, being made to a royal commission in the 1880s: 'The accounts of old men living in Aird, and in the different townships about, are more graphic and vivid and harrowing than anything that has ever been written on the subject.' (24) And implicit or explicit in all such accounts was the contrast between what the Earl of Selkirk called 'the frequent removal of the antient possessors of the land' and the 'very opposite behaviour of their former chiefs'. (25)

Theories of lost rights, of a past and happy state, are common to the history of many communities and societies. The Fall of Man, the Golden Age, Arcadia, the myth of the Norman Yoke — so influential in the radical politics of seventeenth and eighteenth century England: all in their different ways express a belief that inequality, injustice and the exploitation of man by man have a historical origin and a hope that the better and fairer society preserved in the popular imagination will one day be restored. (26) The myth of the clan past — the notion that 'the old population of the country lived in some condition of Arcadian bliss, founded on the relation between Celtic clansmen and their chiefs' — was of this type. And in the nineteenth century it became 'very prevalent' in the Highlands. (27) Apparent even in the 1820s, (28) it tended — in the later years of the century at least — to take the form given to it by Peggy MacCormack of Lochboisdale, South Uist:

How we enjoyed ourselves in those far-away days — the old as much as the young.

I often saw three and sometimes four generations dancing together on the green grass in the golden summer sunset. Men and women of fourscore or more – for they lived long in those days – dancing with boys and girls of five on the green grass. Those were the happy days and the happy nights, and there was neither sin nor sorrow in the world for us. The thought of those young days makes my old heart both glad and sad even at this distance of time. But the clearances came upon us, destroying all, turning our small crofts into big farms for the stranger, and turning our joy into misery, our gladness into bitterness, our blessing into blasphemy, and our Christianity into mockery – O a dhuine ghaolaich, thig na deoir air mo shuilean le linn smaoininn air na dh'fhuilig sinn agus na duirb thainig sinn 'roimhe – O dear man, the tears come on my eyes when I think of all we suffered and of the sorrows, hardships, oppressions we came through. (29)

Embodied in such visions of the past (which are, incidentally, strikingly similar to those once held by Irish peasants), (30) and especially in claims that in the old Highlands 'the cattle were fat and plentiful and the land produced abundance for man and beast', (31) was a great deal that is obviously unhistorical. 'When enquiry is made as to when these happy times were,' declared *The Scotsman* in one of the editorials which made it the most widely hated newspaper in the Highlands of the 1880s, 'they are found to recede further and further back ... The truth is, of course, that the land never did flow with milk and honey.' (32) Highland landlords, not unnaturally, were of the same opinion. (33) And most historians would, on the whole, agree with them. It should be noted, however, that the uniformly crushing poverty of the early nineteenth century – a poverty epitomised in the famine of the 1840s – was worse, and potentially much worse, than anything that had gone before; and that it was accompanied by the virtual collapse of the old Highlands' social and cultural unity, qualities which had to some extent compensated for the economically harsh conditions of the past and thus gave to it a retrospectively attractive aura. When crofters spoke of the 'old people' as 'men of a very independent noble spirit, who were on the most cordial and friendly terms with their chiefs' and who 'looked upon their chief as their father and had no feeling of awe such as they have of proprietors nowadays', (34) they did no more than speak the truth. And what *The Scotsman* and most landlords failed to realise, moreover, was that the enduring significance of crofters' view of the past is not to be found in its historical accuracy or lack of it, but in the fact that it enabled crofters to set the grim realities of the nineteenth-century present against a vision of an older order in which material plenty was combined with security and social justice. Crofters were thus provided with an effective if unsophisticated critique of the social and economic system which was necessarily associated with commercial landlordism. And like their traditional beliefs about the nature of their rights to the land – beliefs which are examined in a subsequent chapter (35) – the myth of the clan past, though ostensibly backward-looking, therefore enabled crofters to define and articulate their by no means conservative demands in a language that all of them could understand. Among contemporary observers of the Highland scene, only the Napier commissioners seem to have grasped the importance of that fact:

The tendency to paint the past in attractive colours will not easily be abandoned, nor is it likely to be obliterated by contemporary education or political training. A comparison of the present with the past is a favourite and effective instrument for stirring popular aspirations for enlarged rights ... The delegates have accordingly not failed to bring all the features of distress and dependency in their actual existence into marked contrast with the happier conditions and higher privileges they believe to have prevailed in a preceding age. (36)

But while such beliefs helped crofters adapt to, and seek to change, the situation created by commercial landlordism, their existence does not in itself explain how the crofting community, considered as a social and cultural entity, was created from the commons of the clans; or how it was that crofters eventually gained the control over their own destinies which they so conspicuously lacked in the era of the clearances. In this process, it is clear, a large part was played by evangelical presbyterianism — still an important element in crofting life and in the past one of its vital components. For although the crofting community's decisive victories were won in the 1880s by means of political action and well organised social protest, (37) crofters — like many other people whose traditional way of life has been destroyed by capitalist civilisation (38) — initially sought relief from the frustrations and sufferings of their new existence in the sphere of religious experience.

Until the eighteenth century most Highlanders had little interest in protestantism of the presbyterian variety. Its individualist ethic was not calculated to appeal to a people for whom work and war were necessarily communal activities. And only in the heartland of Clan Campbell, already aligned with the Whig and Hanoverian ascendancies and consequently with the Established Church, was there a properly inducted and popularly accepted presbyterian clergy in the years immediately after 1700. Outside the Campbell pale and outside the belt of Catholic predominance which traversed the region from the southern part of the Long Island to Arisaig, Morar and Lochaber, Episcopalianism, like the Jacobitism with which it was usually associated, had survived the revolution of 1688 and its associated re-establishment of presbyterianism. (39) To put down episcopacy was the eighteenth century Kirk's main mission in the Highlands; and in the Highland context, therefore, the Established Church, like the Whig state whose support it enjoyed, was uncompromisingly modernist, committed not only to rooting out religious and political dissent but to destroying the society which underpinned that dissent. (40) Opening with the foundation of the SSPCK in the century's first decade and intensified after each of the Jacobite risings, the presbyterian offensive reached its climax in 1746 when many Episcopal chapels and meeting houses were destroyed by Cumberland's troops and the episcopalian creed officially proscribed. (41) Thereafter episcopacy ceased to be an effective force in the north-west and by the 1790s the Episcopal Church retained significant numbers of Gaelic-speaking adherents only in a narrow belt of territory stretching along the eastern shore of Loch Linnhe from Appin to Ballachulish. (42)

Although presbyterians were in undisputed control of Highland pulpits by the eighteenth century's end there was little sign of popular enthusiasm for, or attachment to, the Establishment. The latter, admittedly, laboured under immense difficulties. As the General Assembly was informed in 1760, many parishes in the north-west were 'so Extensive as to render the charge of them resemble a Province, requiring the Labour of a Body of Clergy'. (43) And everywhere there was a chronic shortage of churches — many congregations whose domiciles were remote from their parish church or whose parish church was in ruins being forced to worship 'in the open fields'. (44) Not until the 1820s, when government funds were made available for the construction of a number of 'parliamentary churches', was a serious attempt made to come to grips with this problem; and even in the 1830s it had by no means been resolved. (45)

But while it would be uncharitable to discount these and other problems, notably of finance, it must be said that many Highland ministers regarded the difficulties of their situation not as spurs to action but as convenient excuses for doing nothing. Whatever its performance elsewhere in Scotland, the record of the Kirk in the Highlands during the period of Moderate ascendancy was not a proud one. John Buchanan, whose accounts of his travels in the north-west in the 1780s contain a number of passages on the region's ecclesiastical affairs, drew a picture of a neglectful and apathetic clergy, out of touch and usually out of sympathy with ordinary people. (46) Not a few Hebridean incumbents held large tacks, and , 'like some other tacksmen', were 'too prone to treat their subtenants with great severity'. (47) And in this respect at least the nineteenth century brought no improvement. In the 1820s and 1830s several Skye ministers were also sheep farmers and some of them acted as factors on the larger estates (48) — pursuits scarcely calculated to enhance their popular appeal. Although the more extreme allegations made against such ministers must be treated with caution (49) there seems no reason, therefore, to doubt the general accuracy of the contemporary opinion — as stated to the General Assembly in 1824 — that the clergy of the north-west were for the most part 'inattentive to the interests of religion' — at least insofar as 'religion' was understood to incorporate a sense of evangelising mission. (50) Several of them did not even possess a working knowledge of Gaelic, (51) a state of affairs which in itself placed an insurmountable barrier between them and their congregations.

The irritating effects of such abuses were aggravated by the tendency for the Established Church to become identified in the popular mind with the interests of the landlords. In the old Highlands ministers had been drawn from among the tacksmen and like them had occupied something of an intermediate position in the social hierarchy. In the Highlands of the early nineteenth century, however, the clergy were inevitably drawn into the society of farmers, factors and proprietors and away from the small tenantry who constituted the bulk of the population. One vital consequence of this development was that ministers who objected to evictions were few and far between. One or two, notably Lachlan MacKenzie who was minister of Lochcarron from 1782 to 1819, earned a lasting popularity among the crofting population by denouncing removals. (52) But ministers who adopted such a stance were invariably Evangelicals who felt landlords' control of church patronage to be a threat to their own position, and their views were not shared by the Moderates who occupied most Highland pulpits. Donald MacLeod's claim that the ministers of Sutherland threatened 'the vengeance of heaven and eternal damnation on those who should presume to make the least resistance' to the evictors (53) might have been exaggerated; but there can be no doubt that most of the Established clergy gave at least tacit consent to landlords' policies and that their role during the clearances has ever since haunted the reputation of the Church of Scotland in the Highlands.

Disorientated and demoralised by social and economic change and bereft of their traditional leadership, the small tenantry could not, therefore, look to the Established Church for guidance and assistance. And in fact the religion to which they adhered was not the religion of the Establishment; certainly not the religion of the Kirk's

Moderate ascendancy. It was a popularly orientated and fervent evangelism which, in a series of dramatic 'revivals', swept through the north-west Highlands and Hebrides in the opening decades of the nineteenth century and eventually carried the greater part of the people of the region into the Free Church. As already suggested, the origins of this 'deep and stirring religious awakening' (54) are to be found in the social and psychological consequences of the collapse of the old order. The 'spiritual destitution' which nineteenth-century Evangelicals discerned in the Highlands was very real. It was the inevitable outcome of the absence — since the mid-eighteenth century — of any real sense of social cohesion or framework of moral reference. The evangelical faith helped make good this deficiency. It provided new beliefs and new standards. It created a new purpose in life and in an insecure world it gave some sense of security. A people, whose former way of life had been destroyed, found in a particularly fervent brand of Christianity 'a place to feel at home' (55) and a way of coping with the problems inherent in the commercial world into which they had been propelled.

In parts of the eastern Highlands, especially Easter Ross, the evangelical faith had gained a foothold in the seventeenth century. (56) In the north-west, however, the spark had to come from outside, its main bearer in the first instance being the Society for Propagating the Gospel at Home, founded in Edinburgh in 1798 and dominated by Robert and James Haldane and their particular brand of congregationalism. The Society's object was 'to supply the means of grace wherever we perceive a deficiency'. And since the Highlands seemed particularly lacking in grace as in much else, its missionaries at once turned their attention northwards, their efforts being quickly rewarded by a religious revival in southern Perthshire, the first of a northwards and westwards spreading series. (57)

The Establishment's reaction, however, was decidedly hostile. In 1799 the General Assembly adopted a resolution prohibiting 'all persons from preaching in any place within their jurisdiction who are not licensed' and in a Pastoral Admonition condemned the doctrines of 'false teachers' who assumed 'the name of missionaries'. (58) Apart from resentment about the latters' attacks on what they called 'the false doctrines of unfaithful ministers', there were fears that the revivalist movement might be socially subversive; (59) for while the Haldanes were no Jacobins, their congregationalism did have a mildly democratic aura, (60) and there hung about the popular nature of the movement they initiated enough of a revolutionary taint to make it suspect — especially in the neurotically repressive political atmosphere of the late 1790s. Thus the Society's missionaries included numbers of 'mechanics' and 'artisans' and in 1797 Neil Douglas, a former member of the Friends of the People acting independently of the Haldanes, preached in Argyll. (61) It is hardly surprising, therefore, that it should be remarked that

Some of these reformers of religion, as they wish to be considered, intermix their spiritual instructions with reflections on the incapacity and negligence of the clergymen of the Established Church and on the conduct of the landlords whom they compare to the taskmasters of Egypt. (62)

Stewart of Garth, the author of that comment, deplored the spread of new-fangled democratic ideas among his beloved Highlanders with all the considerable ire of which his romantic Toryism was capable. And the blame for this development he laid squarely on the shoulders of the itinerant preachers — those 'ignorant and fanatical

spiritual guides', he called them (63) — to whom Highlanders were increasingly turning. Even more significantly, there seemed to him to be an obvious connection
between the itinerants' degree of success and the discontent engendered by economic
change: 'Wherever the people are rendered contented and happy in their external
circumstances by the judicious and humane treatment of their landlords ... no itinerant
preacher has ever been able to obtain a footing.' (64) Much the same point was made
by James MacDonald in the perceptive account of Hebridean agriculture which he
published in 1811. This is what he had to say of the Western Isles' crofting population:

> The bond of connection and the ties of clanship which lately subsisted between
> these tenants and their landlords ... are dissolved. In many cases, indeed, they are
> replaced by a spirit of jealousy and hatred. Discontent and a desire for change are
> almost universal. The ancient attachment to church and state is grown very feeble ...
> Without fixed or definite ideas concerning any failure in duty of their clergy, they
> gradually relax in their respect for them, and have no small hankering after the
> pestilent fellows who under the name of different sectaries ... swarm over these
> neglected regions. Without any original tendency to bigotry or indeed any serious
> attachment to or predilection for any specific articles of faith, they frequently indulge
> in a disputatious vein of religious controversy. This, with political speculations, some
> of which would astonish a man not accustomed to the amazing powers of the common
> Hebridean in conversation, interlarded with reflections upon the character and con-
> duct of their superiors, and upon the hardships of their own condition, fills up their
> leisure hours. They have an idea that they deserve a better fate than that which has
> fallen to their lot ... They always suspect that they are peculiarly ill-treated, and
> live under an ungrateful government and oppressive landlords. In support of these
> charges they mention ... above all ... the dearness of land, and the shortness or
> absolute want of leases. (65)

On occasion, therefore, the apparent connection between religious revivalism and
social dislocation was manifested not only in the fact that small tenants — many of
whom were being subjected to removal and innovation of one kind or another (66) —
were particularly susceptible to the new religion, but also in the fact that the doctrinal
proclamations of the revivals' originators and adherents embodied some part of the
social aspirations just beginning to be formed by crofters. Thus in one early revival:

> Many of the converts became emaciated and unsociable. The duties of life were
> abandoned. Sullen, morose, and discontented, some of them began to talk of their
> high privileges and of their right, as the elect few, to possess the earth... The landlord
> was pronounced unchristian because he insisted on his dues. (67)

Such millennial visions of social justice were bound to appeal to the dispossessed and
demoralised lower strata of Highland society. (68) And though the number of small
tenants attracted by such notions is impossible to estimate, millential movements
could clearly be significant locally. Around 1800, for example, such a movement
was initiated in the Great Glen

> by certain religious itinerants who addressed the people by interpreters and
> distributed numerous pamphlets calculated, as they said, to excite a serious soul
> concern. The consequence was that men who could not read began to preach, and
> to influence the people against their lawful pastors... They next adopted a notion
> that all who were superior to them in wealth or rank were oppressors whom they
> would enjoy the consolation of seeing damned. (69)

Haldanite influence extended into north-west Sutherland, (70) and in 1805 John
Farquharson, an itinerant associated with the Haldanes, preached for some months
in Skye. (71) But for the most part the north-west was still outside the Haldanite

sphere of influence when, towards the end of the nineteenth century's first decade, the Society for the Propagation of the Gospel fell victim to its own doctrinal dissensions. (72) Almost at once, however, its evangelical mission was taken up by another body, the Gaelic School Society founded in Edinburgh in 1811. Although that society — as its name suggests — was primarily concerned with helping Highlanders become literate in their own language, it was also interested in the propagation of the gospel and seemed to attract men imbued with evangelising fervour. (73) Gaelic school teachers consequently played a prominent part in the religious life of the communities in which they were stationed, not the least of their contributions to it being the use they made of the Gaelic Bible, the only book used in the society's schools. (74)

The task of translating the scriptures into Scottish Gaelic was completed in 1801 and in the next twenty-five years 60,000 Gaelic Bibles and 80,000 New Testaments were distributed in the Highlands by the SSPCK and the British and Foreign Bible Society. (75) The Bible was thus the first and for long the only book to be widely available in Gaelic. Its appearance coincided with the highly successful literacy campaign launched by the Gaelic school movement. (76) And its importance to the nineteenth century crofting population can hardly be overestimated.

Until about 1800 the vast majority of the people of the north-west were dependent for their knowledge of the Bible on the clergy of the Established Church. They alone had access to the sources and their interpretation was, in consequence, almost impossible to dispute. After 1800 that situation changed. More and more crofters were able to read the Bible for themselves in their own language. In itself this development was bound to enhance the self-confidence of the small tenantry. More important, however, was their discovery that the Established clergy were not necessarily infallible; that the Bible appeared to have much to say that was relevant to their own predicament — not least to the land question; (77) and that, in short, the fundamental principles of Christianity could be applied to their own lives in a way that was very different from that usually suggested to them by their Moderate ministers. It is no accident, therefore, that religious revivalism in the north-west coincided with the spread of the Gaelic Bible and the growth of Gaelic literacy. (78)

Being well aware of this connection, Moderate ministers looked on the Gaelic schools with some disfavour; and many of the Society's teachers consequently found themselves hauled up in front of church courts on charges of irregular conduct of one kind or another. In 1829, for example, the Presbytery of Mull recorded its

regret... that two teachers of the Gaelic School Society of Edinburgh stationed in the parish of Ardnamurchan have assumed to themselves the office of public exhorters and are in the stated practice of abstaining from public worship... The presbytery find themselves called upon to put an effective stop to such practices — practices subversive of all established order and so calculated to produce the most pernicious consequences. (79)

A year later, however, several of the Society's teachers in the area under the presbytery's jurisdiction were persisting in 'schismatic and irregular practices'. They refused to attend worship in the Established churches 'on the ground that the Gospel is not preached' and were 'in the regular habit of publicly exhorting and expounding. Thus... exhibiting an example in all respects pernicious and engendering dissension among the people... and a spirit of disaffection towards all those in authority over them'. (80)

Elsewhere there were similar developments. In Lewis the establishment of Gaelic schools was quickly followed by a revival. (81) In Back, for example, the Society's teacher preached every Sunday to the people of the township. His activities, the minister of Stornoway reported, 'alienated the people from me in a great measure, so that on the Sundays I preached at Back they would in droves that day pass me on the road'. (82) The same result was produced by the Society's endeavours in Wester Ross and in this area a few of the local men employed as catechists by the SSPCK joined the more evangelically minded newcomers. Thus John Davidson, an SSPCK catechist in Lochcarron, set himself up as a 'public expounder of Scripture', attracted a mass following and, one Sunday in March 1820,

assembled the greater part of the population of Lochcarron to a place within sight of the Parish church, and there, while public worship was conducting regularly by the Parish Minister and such of the Parishioners as were with him... [he] employed himself in reading, lecturing, and praying with his congregation. (83)

The latter development indicates that while the revivalist faith came initially from outside the Highlands, the revivals very soon developed an impetus and produced a leadership of their own. Thus one result of John Farquharson's 1805 visit to Skye was the conversion to the evangelical faith of Donald Munro, a local man who was a catechist in the pay of the Establishment but who was more renowned for his ability as a fiddler than for his devotion to religion. After Farquharson's departure Munro put away his fiddle and began to conduct prayer meetings at various places in the northern part of Skye, (84) the eventual outcome of his activities being best described in a more or less contemporary account of it:

In the year 1812, by means of these meetings, an uncommon awakening took place among the people, which was attended with distress and trembling of the body... Some persons came under convictions when attending these meetings; others when they came in contact with awakened persons who attended them... These were days of power and of sweetness to as many as had spiritual taste and discernment; so that frequently when they met they were reluctant to part. (85)

At least one of the initiators of the Lewis revival of the 1820s — John MacLeod, the Gaelic schoolmaster at Uig — had been involved in the events of 1812 in Skye. (86) But in Lewis too local preachers quickly appeared and during 1823 the Established clergy began to complain of the 'religious frenzy which... has become so prevalent of late' and of the activities of 'the blind, daring fanatics who now infest this Island... disseminating wild unscriptural doctrines'. (87) The extent of the divergence between the popular religion and the Establishment was demonstrated at a communion service in the parish church at Lochs in the south-eastern corner of Lewis in August 1823. When the parish minister, Alexander Simpson — who, according to Evangelical tradition, was a drunkard as well as a Moderate (88) — began his sermon he was interrupted by several 'fanatics' who challenged the validity of the doctrines being propounded from the pulpit. On being asked to leave, Simpson's critics refused to budge and had to be 'dragged off'. Not a whit intimidated they then began to 'sing and expound Scripture and read it among themselves in the neighbourhood so near that their singing seemed meant to disturb the service'. Angered by this calculated defiance of his authority Simpson, with the support of the presbytery of Lewis, lodged a formal complaint with the civil authorities. Five men who had played a prominent part in the disturbances were promptly arrested and shipped to Dingwall where they were jailed for a month (89) — a proceeding which did nothing to quell the revival but which had the effect, as one of MacKenzie of Seaforth's Lewis correspondents remarked at the time, of setting the Established clergy firmly 'on the fair road to damn their popularity in the Lews'. (90)

Such events were not confined to Skye and Lewis. In Harris a revival began in the early 1820s under the leadership of John Morrison, a Rodel blacksmith — better known for that reason as Iain Gobha. (91) And by 1829 'Fanaticism and Sectarian-ism' were reported to be 'making rapid progress' on the island where Murdoch MacLeod, another '... lay-preacher or exhorter... had exerted all his influence to prevent the Parishioners from attending Divine Worship in the Established Churches'.(9 Throughout the north-west there were identical occurrences. In North Uist in the 1830s and early 1840s many people were following 'divisive courses' and organising their own Sunday services. (93) In parts of Mull dissent had 'proceeded to an alarm-ing extent'. (94) In Lochcarron by 1825 the leadership of the popular movement had devolved upon John Finlayson, another blacksmith, who was accused by the presbytery of 'following divisive and schismatic courses in absenting himself from attendance on the public ordinances of religion... and in collecting crowds at his house during divine service upon the Lord's day and in reading and expounding Scriptures to them'. (95) And there were stirrings of dissent in north-west Sutherland at about the same time. (96)

The emergence of the class of lay-preachers made up of John Finlayson, Donald Munro, John Morrison and their fellows was one of the revivalist movement's most important features, not least because these preachers — known as *na daoine,* the men, in order to distinguish them from the ordained clergy — constituted the first leadership of any sort to emerge from the crofting population's own ranks. Although they had a long history in those parts of the eastern Highlands where evangelical Christianity had been implanted in Covenanting times, (97) it was only in the early nineteenth century that *na daoine,* defined as a 'definitely recognised but ecclesias-tically unofficial order of evangelical laymen who won public veneration by their eminence in godliness', (98) made their appearance on the north-west coast and in the islands. In some cases, as in that of Donald Munro in Skye or John Davidson in Lochcarron, 'the men' had some previous connection with the Established Church or with the SSPCK — organisations which had long maintained a staff of lay catech-ists whose duty it was to assist the ministers of sprawling Highland parishes. For the most part, however, the lay-preachers seem to have been ordinary men drawn from the lower strata of Highland society. (99) Usually they were crofters. Occas-ionally they were craftsmen — blacksmiths seem to have been especially prominent. But their distinguishing features generally consisted solely of their own strength of character and the profound conviction of their religious beliefs, qualities which enabled them to preside over the popular religious movement from the start, con-ducting prayer-meetings, services, and above all the huge open air 'fellowship meet-ings' which became a feature of the Friday before communion throughout the evangelical Highlands. (100)

Well aware of their status in the community 'the men' cultivated a distinctive

appearance, wearing their hair long and in some areas adopting a recognised 'uniform'
− on the northern mainland this consisted of 'a camlet coat and a spotted handker-
chief tied over the head', while in Skye multi-coloured nightcaps were favoured. (101)
And their fervour had its counterpart in the emotional, often hysterical nature of
the movement which they led − a movement in which can be discerned at least a
shade of these vast and mysterious upsurges of chiliastic and millennial fervour which
occasionally gripped the imagination of the masses of medieval Europe and have
more recently erupted in widely separated parts of the Third World. (102) Thus one
contemporary observer, noting that it was 'known to every one conversant with
the Highlands that the recent degradation and misery of the people have predisposed
their minds to imbibe these pestiferous delusions to which they fly for consolation
under their sufferings', went on to describe how those affected by the revivals 'see
visions, dream dreams, revel in the wildest hallucinations'. (103) In Skye, for example,
many people − especially women − were said by contemporaries to have become
'fanatical' and fallen prey to fits or religious ecstasy. (104) In Lewis too many
people were 'seized with spasms, convulsions, fits, and screaming aloud'; (105) and
bliadhna 'n aomaidh, the year of the swooning, was long remembered in the island. (106)

The millennial character of the revivals had its counterpart in 'the men's' religious
teaching. Their theology was of the most elemental type, combining a harsh and
pristine puritanism with a transcendental mysticism that had less to do with nineteenth-century protestantism than with an older faith. Visions of heaven and hell,
prophetic utterances, intensely personal conflicts with the devil and his angels:
these were integral to their creed and a common pact of their experience; while
in their preaching homely illustration was combined with mysticism and allegory. (107)
And while 'the men' were often fully literate, knowing their Bibles 'as few besides
have known them', (108) they did not hesitate to introduce into their Christianity
concepts which were clearly derived from the neo-pagan cultural heritage of the
Highlands. Many 'men', for example, believed themselves to have the power of
second sight, (109) and even Lachlan MacKenzie of Lochcarron, one of the earliest
of the north-west Highlands' Evangelical ministers, was considered a prophet by his
congregation. (110)

'The men' were no primitivists, however. They had, on the contrary, a very low
opinion of much of the traditional culture of the Highlands; and indeed their
onslaughts upon that culture undoubtedly destroyed much that was valuable in it. (111)
What is not generally recognised in all that has subsequently been written about the
devastating effect of Highland puritanism on Gaelic culture, however, is that the
society which supported that culture was destroyed in the eighteenth century and
that 'the men's' attack upon the Highlands' cultural heritage can consequently be
interpreted as a more or less conscious attempt to come to terms with the realities
of a social and economic system dominated by landlordism rather than by clanship.
Thus the revivalists' social teachings were considerably more relevant to the actual
situation of the early nineteenth century crofting population than were those
which are embodied in the secular poetry of the period − much of which, in the
opinion of at least one authority, is dominated by a weak, romantic nostalgia for
the old order. (112) As early as the 1760s, for example, Dugald Buchanan of
Rannoch − perhaps the greatest evangelical poet to write in Gaelic -- included in

An Claigeann, The Skull, a telling indictment of the commercial landlordism which
was just beginning to make its mark on the Highlands. Several bitter verses are
devoted to the rackrenting laird who flays his people and thins the cheek of his
tenants by his excessive exactions. If the rent is delayed the cattle are seized, no
heed being paid to the cries of the poor. Before the landlord stands an old man,
his head uncovered in the bitter wind. His petition is ignored. For striking down
such a tyrant, Buchanan concludes, death is to be praised. (113)

Here is no anachronistic reluctance to admit the exploitative role of the former
chief. And indeed Buchanan's tirade marked the beginning of a long association
between Highland evangelicalism and anti-landlordism. Alexander Campbell, the
leader of an early secessionist movement in Argyll, thought it worthwhile to
record his 'testimony against covetous heritors that oppress the poor'; (114) and
not least among the faults of the Moderate clergy, according to *na daoine,* was that
they 'dined with the laird' and generally associated with the upper strata of Highland
society. (115) And at another level, the social protest implicit in the vision of hell
accorded to David Ross of Ferintosh, Ross-shire, requires no elucidation:

> In one spot David saw a poor soul surrounded by busy devils. 'There is a rich
> miser for you,' said the angel. 'They are pouring buckets of molten gold down his
> throat. There again,' said he, pointing to another, 'There is a laird who has been
> driving out tenants from their farms, squandering his means after strange women,
> rendering poor people miserable and himself so miserable that at last he had to
> take away his own life. He is now for ever doomed to be alternatively bitten by
> serpents and have his wounds licked over by hell hounds. Poor fellow! Little did
> he think during his moments of heartless pleasure and dissipation that he was sowing
> for himself the seeds of such an eternity of woe.' (116)

'The men' and their movement thus posed a threat to all those whose interests lay
in maintaining the social and economic status quo in the Highlands, whether
Moderate ministers, landed proprietors or sheep farmers. As far as the Church of
Scotland was concerned, only the comparatively small number of Evangelical
ministers — whose own beliefs at least approximated to the tenets of the popular
religion — had anything approaching a cordial relationship with 'the men'. Of the
Evangelicals the most popular were probably *Maighstir Ruairidh* — as Roderick
MacLeod of Bracadale was popularly known — and Alexander MacLeod who
became minister of Uig in Lewis shortly after the commencement of the revival in
that island. These men's churches were regularly filled to capacity with the evangelically minded people in their own congregations and in the congregations of neighbouring parishes. (117) But elsewhere, as already mentioned, 'the men' and their
adherents simply abandoned the parish churches. In Skye in the 1820s, for example,
there were only two parishes — one of which was Roderick MacLeod's Bracadale
and the other the neighbouring parish of Duirinish — in which there was no 'meeting
held for social worship on the Sabbath distinct from that carried on in the parish
church'. (118)

In view of 'the men's' obvious leanings towards anti-landlordism it was inevitable
that the Established clergy's concern about these developments should be shared
by landowners and their associates. Not only did 'the men' articulate crofters'
growing dislike of landlords, the very existence of a profoundly popular movement
equipped with its own leaders clearly constituted a threat to the latter's hitherto

undisputed dominance in the Highlands. The opinion of the minister of Barvas in Lewis, a man who thought it 'easy to see that no good can come to society from the raving effusions of... ignorant men who, with consummate effrontery, assume the character and office of public instructors', (119) was accordingly echoed by many proprietors. 'No gentleman,' it is recorded, 'associated with Donald Munro;' (120) while at his meetings and those of his fellows there might be seen, among the hundreds of crofters and their families, 'an occasional sheep farmer, if a native of the district, but never a factor'. (121) Lord MacDonald's estate manager, in fact considered 'the men' to be 'an evil influence', an opinion shared by MacLeod of Dunvegan who thought that 'the influence of lay preachers... was injurious to the people'. (122) And a group of Skye sheep farmers reacted to the 1812 revival in the island by making representations to Lord MacDonald, 'soliciting his Lordship's power and authority to suppress these meetings and to proceed against those who held them'. (123) Though somewhat premature, the apprehensions underlying such requests were not without foundation. (124)

In the context of the history of the popular religious movement in the Highlands the Disruption of the Church of Scotland in 1843 was a largely fortuitous event. The internecine conflict between Evangelicals and Moderates which led eventually to the former's secession and to the formation of the Free Church had nothing to   · do with Highland affairs and was, on the face of it, of little interest to the mass of the crofting population. As the ecclesiastical crisis approached, however, the Evangelical leadership made a determined effort to win popular support in the Highlands. Gaelic pamphlets were circulated. Evangelical deputations toured the region. And most important of all, the local Evangelical ministers strenuously endeavoured to win to their side the adherents of the indigenous evangelical movement. (125)

On their side the Evangelicals had many advantages. They were the only ministers for whom crofters felt any respect or affection and they were consequently able to draw on a fund of popularity built up over many years — *Maighstir Ruairidh,* for example, was able to draw large and enthusiastic crowds to his pro-Evangelical meetings in the winter of 1842-43. (126) The Moderates had no such advantage. For them there was only a deeply felt animosity. It is not really surprising, therefore, that 'the men' adhered unanimously to the Free Church (127) and that throughout the north-west Highlands the secession amounted to 'a tidal wave which... carried the population en masse'. (128) The situation in Lewis where fewer than 500 people out of a population of some 20,000 remained in the Established Church was not untypical. (129) There as elsewhere the parish churches were 'swept bare of worshippers', their congregations being reduced to a handful of sheep farmers and their shepherds. (130) When on the first Sunday after the Disruption the Durness church bell was muffled with an old sock and a dead dog hung over the pulpit in Farr (131) the symbolism was therefore very apt. The Established Church had ceased to have any claim to authority over the crofting population.

The immediate cause of the Evangelicals' withdrawal from the Establishment having been their opposition to landlords' control of church patronage, the Free Church held decidedly anti-landlord views. Landlords, in their turn, were intensely suspicious of the new denomination, their antipathy towards it manifesting itself in a campaign of obstruction and harassment which usually took the form of a refusal to sell sites for Free churches. Although not confined to the Highlands, the latter practice was more widespread and effective there than anywhere else simply because the sheer size of Highland estates enabled their owners to deny the Free Church access to whole parishes and in some cases to entire islands or even counties. (132) In one famous episode caused by Sir James Riddell's persistent refusal to provide a site for a Free church at Strontian, the problem was overcome by the provision of a floating church which was moored in Loch Sunart. (133) Elsewhere persecution was more difficult to counter. In Mull a Free Church congregation was obliged to worship in a gravel pit below the high water-mark; (134) while Lord MacDonald, the owner of the largest estate in the Hebrides, refused sites to no fewer than seven congregations. (135) When in the winter of 1845 the people of Paible on the MacDonald estate in North Uist attempted to build a Free Church meeting house on the township's common pasture, the building was promptly pulled down by the estate management and nine of the crofters involved in its construction evicted. A subsequent attempt to hold services in the lee of a large rock on the common grazing was countered by the simple expedient of ploughing and sowing the ground around it. (136))

Visiting the north-west Highlands five years after the Disruption, Robert Somers made the following comments about it. In the Highlands, he wrote,

There are only two ranks of people – a higher rank and a lower rank – the former consisting of a few large tenants... and the latter consisting of a dense body of small lotters and fishermen... The proverbial enmity of rich and poor in all societies has received peculiar development in this simple social structure of the Highlands. The clearances laid the foundation of a bitter animosity between the sheep farmers and the lotters; and as these violent changes were executed by the authority of the lairds, they also snapped the tie which had previously, amid all reverses, united the people and their chiefs. One link still bound the extremities of society in formal, if not in spiritual union. The parish church was a common centre where all classes met... But even religion... was converted at the Disruption into a new fountain of bitterness... There is thus a double point of collision between the two ranks – an ecclesiastical as well as an agrarian enmity... It is consequently almost impossible to find an individual in the upper rank who has not a grudge against the people, either on the score of their Free Churchism, or on the score of their hostility to the sheep walk system. (137)

Although the link between social conflict and religious dissent went back farther than Somers realised, his remarks contain an essential truth. In the Highlands the Disruption was not just an ecclesiastical dispute. It was a class conflict. Its battle line was the line of class demarcation, the line between the small tenantry on the one hand and sheep farmers, factors and proprietors on the other. In that fact is to be found the explanation of what is otherwise inexplicable: the intensity of proprietorial opposition to the Free Church.

Highland landlords' experience of the popular religious movement had done little to convince them that its institutionalisation in a Church founded on an essentially anti-landlord principle would be to their advantage. The Free Church, declared Sir James Riddell, proprietor of Ardnamurchan, would lead the people 'astray from the ministrations of the regularly ordained clergy who were placed over them for their spiritual good and edification' and make them more than ever dependent upon 'the teaching of illiterate laymen'. Besides, he added — and the argument must have seemed a powerful one in the politically troubled world of the 1840s — once one part of the established order had been successfully challenged, there was no knowing where the process might end. Already, he thought, the Free Church had 'bid defiance to the powers that be' and 'broken up society from its very foundations'. (138)

Such expectations were exaggerated. Ultimately dependent on the urban middle class of lowland Scotland rather than on the small tenantry of the Highlands, the Free Church was inherently unlikely to sanction a serious challenge to private property in land or in anything else. The real threat posed to landlords' interests by the Free Church was therefore more subtle — though nonetheless serious in the long term — than the red revolution suspected by Sir James Riddell in his more fevered moments. It was, as was pointed out by Hugh Miller — editor of the Evangelical newspaper *The Witness* and one of the most effective and influential of Highland landlordism's early critics — that the Free Church threatened to end crofters' political isolation: 'to translate their wrongs into English and to give them currency in the general mart of opinion'. (139) Broadly speaking, this was in fact what occurred. Among the Free Church's southern membership there immediately appeared a feeling that 'the enthusiastic adhesion' of the crofting population to their cause imposed upon them a special charge and responsibility, (140) a feeling that made possible the financing of the Free Church in the Highlands and greatly contributed to the success of charitable relief efforts during the famine. (141) At the same time and through the medium of the Free Church — which a recent historian has described as 'the bulwark of the Scottish Liberal Party' (142) — the first concrete links were established between the incipient agrarian radicalism of the crofting population and the mainstream of Scottish Liberal and radical politics. It is not without significance, therefore, that the crofting population, acting in concert with an important and vociferous section of southern public opinion and the Liberal and Evangelical press, was able, through the medium of a parliamentary enquiry which unreservedly condemned the landlords' conduct, (143) to force the site-refusing proprietors to give way. The passing in 1886 of the first Crofters Act was the outcome of a very similar sequence of events. (144)

Of more immediate importance, however, was the fact that in the north-west Highlands and islands the Free Church came into existence as a profoundly popular institution, the heir to a long tradition of religious dissent. It was, and still is, the church of the mass of crofting tenants and in a very real sense it was their creation, a victory for their interests over those of their landlords. It was in this way above all that the achievement of 1843 contributed to the more important victory of 1886, for the Disruption and the revivals which preceded it were largely instrumental in welding a disparate collection of small tenants into a community capable of acting collectively and possessing a distinctive character and outlook. That the future of the Gaelic language is still bound up with the fate of the Free Church is not accidental; (145) nor is the fact that even the socialism and anticlericalism of a modern Gaelic poet like Sorley MacLean is expressed in a language reminisecnt of that of the evangelical revivals. (146) Evangelicalism and the emergence of the modern crofting community are inseparable phenomena, if only for the reason that it was through the medium of a profoundly evangelical faith that crofters first developed a forward-looking critique of the situation created in the Highlands by the actions of the region's landowning and therefore ruling class. And although the principles at stake in 1843 were ostensibly religious, they reflected the deep-seated social antagonisms which eventually erupted in the more explicitly political conflict of the 1880s. In 1843 a majority of the crofting population stood up to their land-lords for the first time. And they won. Not even the famine and the clearances which followed it could obliterate the significance of that victory.

7. The Years of Recovery: Crofting Society, 1858-1880

DURING the famine Highland proprietors and central government were convinced that the solution to the problems of Scotland's north-western fringe lay in a drastic reduction of the region's smallholding population. The ostensible aim was to ease congestion and enlarge crofters' holdings. The real objective — as far as landlords at least were concerned — was to consolidate and extend the sheep farming system: hence the clearances and forced emigrations of the late 1840s and early 1850s. The inevitable outcome, as a royal commission discovered some thirty years later, was that crofters were everywhere 'confined within narrow limits' and that congestion was consequently as bad, if not worse, than it had ever been. (1) That confinement was the logical outcome of the developments outlined in the first part of this book. And the crofting community's long struggle to break free of it constitutes the theme of the remainder. Before that theme is taken up, however, it is necessary to give some account of crofting society as it emerged from the terrible years of the mid-century.

By the mid-1850s on the north-west coast and in the Hebrides sheep farmers occupied most of the best hill grazings as well as a good deal of the land formerly cultivated by small tenants. Although most of the consequences of this state of affairs were decidedly detrimental to crofters, one of its more paradoxical and quite unforeseen effects was that the position of the crofting tenants who had escaped eviction in the famine's aftermath was rendered more secure than hitherto. Once the latter ceased to require assistance to keep them alive, their removal from the 'inferior and exhausted soil' which they almost invariably occupied (2) would have caused their landlords more trouble and expense than could have been outweighed by the profits to be made from putting still more land under sheep. And the consequent tendency to leave crofters in undisputed occupation of their meagre plots and scanty grazings was enforced towards the end of the 1860s by a falling away in sheep farmers' profits. (3) Thus while there were in that decade a few more instances of the once prevalent practice of adding crofters' common grazings to sheep farms these were exceptional and when, in the 1870s, Highland sheep farming entered a period of severe depression, they ceased completely. (4)

In the 1850s, therefore, an era of crofting history came to an end. Since its beginnings crofting had existed in a state of flux: whole populations had been uprooted and removed while evictions, clearances and expropriations of every kind had gone on more or less continuously against a background of growing poverty and misery. The 1860s and 1870s were, in contrast, a period of unprecedented stability. The clearances were over and crofters' incomes were rising for the first time since 1815. The British economy was once more expanding. Agriculture was booming. And though crofters did not do as well as their sheep farming neighbours — many of whom amassed considerable fortunes in the early 1860s as the price of wool soared to record heights (5) — they did experience a fairly rapid expansion of their agricultural returns. Above all they benefited from the rise in cattle prices, for though crofters had been deprived of most of the pastures on which the eighteenth century's huge herds of black cattle had been reared, the proceeds from the sale of their cattle still made up the greater part of the revenue derived from the typical croft.

By the early 1880s, for example, crofters' stirks — worth less than £1 a head in the 1840s — were being sold for between £6 and £9, while prices for two and three year olds ranged up to £10 and £14 respectively. (6) Few crofts were large enough to grow the winter fodder needed in order to take advantage of the higher prices fetched by more mature animals. (7) But most holdings were capable of raising one or two stirks a year — the importance of the latter to the crofting economy of the time being attested to by the common contemporary saying: 'the stirk pays the rent'. (8) And as already indicated the rise in cattle prices was paralleled by a steep increase in the prices to be obtained for sheep. The flocks which crofters pastured on their common grazings were of course miniscule — especially when compared to those maintained by sheep farmers with several thousand acres at their disposal. But even in Lewis, where the smallholding population was most congested, the average crofter owned about eight sheep, one or two of which were sold each year. (9) And though worth less than those reared by sheep farmers, the three year old wedders which were most commonly marketed by crofters were, by the early 1880s, capable of fetching around 35s. apiece. (10)

Despite steadily rising stock prices, however, crofters — apart from the fortunate occupants of the unusually large crofts that were to be found here and there on the mainland (11) — remained part time agriculturalists, as dependant as their fathers and grandfathers on earnings obtained away from their holdings. Kelping, the industry originally responsible for this state of affairs, was little more than a memory by the 1860s. (12) And apart from the few remaining kelpers and those tenants who combined the management of their crofts with a trade of one kind or another — of the latter there were a fair number, for every district had its smiths, joiners, masons, shoemakers and so on (13) — crofters had to leave home to find work. Some crofters — and more sons and daughters of crofters — still went south each summer to look for casual employment as harvesters on lowland farms. And their success is testified to by the remark made about certain crofters in Skye in the 1880s: 'It is by their work in the south country that they are making a living.' (14) A more permanent stake in the southern economy was represented by the growing number of crofters' daughters who left home to enter domestic service of one kind or another. The Skye crofter who remarked that he had 'three daughters at service and they always assist me at the term' was by no means unique: many rents were paid and many bills met with money earned in the prosperous middle class households of Glasgow and other southern cities. (15)

The sporting estates that began to proliferate in the Highlands in the 1870s provided similar, if more temporary, opportunities; as well as creating jobs for large numbers of stalkers and ghillies, jobs that were often filled by crofters or by crofters' sons. (16) And on the sheep farms too there was seasonal work to be had, especially in the autumn when the sheep were 'smeared'. Smearing, the precursor of the modern practice of 'dipping' sheep in pesticides, involved working a mixture of butter, tar and grease into the fleece, in an attempt to give protection against vermin. Since one man could smear only about twenty sheep a day and since a quarter of a million were annually smeared in Inverness-shire alone, labour was obviously much in demand — and much of it was supplied by crofters. (17) During the 1860s and 1870s, moreover, the wages paid for casual labour of this type rose steadily, and more or less doubled between 1850 and 1880. (18)

But important as these sources of income were, they were completely dwarfed in size and significance by the fishing industry. The Napier Commissioners, whose 1883 enquiry into crofting conditions is the single most important source of information about the social and economic situation in the Highlands in the later nineteenth century, were of the opinion that crofters derived a larger annual income from the sea than they did from the land — a state of affairs which, in view of what was said about the Highland fishing industry in earlier chapters, seems little less than astounding. (19) The money that made it possible did not, however, come from crofters. The latter, though better off than their predecessors, still possessed no more than a fraction of the capital needed to develop the west coast fisheries. That capital came from outside the crofting community and crofters shared only indirectly in the industry's profits. Although they received greater rewards for their labour, their position was not in fact dissimilar to that of their kelping forebears and, like them, crofter fishermen were disastrously vulnerable to market fluctuations. (20) But in the 1860s and 1870s, as the typical crofter's returns from his maritime activities expanded even more markedly than those from his work on the land, that fact was by no means readily apparent.

As far as crofters were concerned, the fishing industry was divided into two quite separate branches: the white fishing and the herring fishing. The first of these, the coastal fishing for cod and ling which went on during the winter months, was given a new lease of life after the mid-century by improved marketing facilities resulting from the provision of steamer services to the Clyde and by the capital injected into it by the curers who established themselves at its main centres, Castlebay and Stornoway. In Stornoway, for example, there were in 1853 only some half dozen persons engaged in the curing business. By the 1880s there were around fifty. And as well as purchasing the catch these men provided the capital needed to buy boats and gear. The result was that by the 1880s there were between 500 and 600 Lewis boats engaged in the winter fishings off the island — a figure that was twice that of the 1850s and was made up of boats which were two or three times larger than those of the earlier period. (21) Returns to crofters were limited by the impossibility, in the absence of adequate rail links, (22) of transporting fresh fish to southern markets and by the control exercised over the industry by the curers. The latter operated a truck and credit system of payment which ensured that fishermen were almost perpetually in debt to them and which made it easy for curers to fix low prices and otherwise manipulate the market to their own advantage. (23) Despite the disadvantages under which they laboured, however, it was possible for crofters to derive a considerable income from the cod and ling fishings. In Lewis in the 1870s, for example, the six or eight men who made up a boat's crew could clear £15 to £20 apiece in a good winter besides providing themselves and their families with fish for consumption. (24) Such returns were unlikely to be equalled outside the Outer

Isles, the industry's main centre, but in most of the north-west, especially in Tiree, Skye, Wester Ross and Sutherland, crofters were assured of at least some income from the winter fishings. (25) But it was to the summer herring fishings that they looked for real financial rewards.

Between 1850 and the early 1880s the west coast herring industry experienced a spectacular expansion, the average annual total of barrels cured at west coast ports rising from under 80,000 in the period 1844 – 1853 to over 180,000 in the ten years after 1874 – by which time herring landings at Stornoway were exceeded only by those at Wick, Fraserburgh and Peterhead, the main east coast ports. (26) Crofters, it is true, were even less directly involved in the organisation of the herring fishery than in that for cod and ling, the former being the preserve of east coast fishermen who alone possessed the technical sophistication and the capital equipment – in the shape of boats and nets – needed to make a financial success of deep water herring fishing. When the east coast drifters arrived in the Minch in May, however, they almost all took on one or two local men as extra crew members; (27) and though crofters from the Outer Isles got the lion's share of these jobs, it was not uncommon for crofters to travel to Castlebay and Stornoway from Skye or even from the mainland in order to obtain employment. (28)

The west coast herring season lasted for six to eight weeks, the crofters hired for its duration earning from £7 to £10 on average. (29) But this was only a beginning. When the drifters followed the herring to the North Sea in July thousands of West Highlanders went with them to provide the temporary labour force that was required to man the huge fleet engaged in the much more extensive herring fisheries around the northern isles and in east coast waters. Originating in the early nineteenth century, when a few crofters from Sutherland, Wester Ross, Skye and Lewis began to spend a few weeks of each summer in Wick, (30) this seasonal migration grew rapidly in size after 1850. And by the 1870s practically the whole adult male population of some districts participated in the summer exodus – in Lewis, for example, 'only a few old men and boys' were left behind. (31) The crofters of the Outer Isles, and of Lewis in particular, had a greater stake in the east coast fishings than tenants elsewhere. But though some Skye crofters favoured the summer fishings off the Irish coast, (32) others went east in 'hundreds' each July and it is altogether probable that the annual influx of Gaelic speaking Highlanders experienced by fishing ports from Fife to Caithness included crofters from almost every township in north-west Scotland. (33) And as the herring industry boomed throughout the 1860s and 1870s so the demand for labour increased; wages rising by leaps and bounds. In the 1850s average earnings at the east coast fishings were in the region of £3 to £3.10s. By the 1880s the average wage was at least £12, and it was not uncommon for a Lewis crofter to come home in September with £20 or £30 in his pocket. (34) In the 1870s and 1880s, too, a growing number of women and girls – most of whom obtained their initial training in Castlebay and Stornoway curing stations – began to travel to the east coast with their menfolk in order to get work as herring gutters, their gross earnings contributing about £4.10s to the family budget. (35) The steady rise in income from such sources, coupled with the fact that outside a few rack-rented properties – of which the Kilmuir estate in Skye was the most glaring example (36) – rents remained at their old levels, (37) meant that the typical crofter of the 1870s was much better off than his father had been. Once blight died down in the 1850s potatoes again became the most important foodstuff. (38) But dependence upon them was everywhere less complete than before the famine, the staple diet of boiled potatoes being supplemented by fairly large quantities of fresh and salted fish. And though meat was still a rarity — sheep and cattle being too valuable to be slaughtered for food — a chicken or two might be put on the table on a special occasion, while milk and eggs were usually quite plentiful. (39) Grain crops were generally used as winter fodder for cattle. (40) But when crofters' potatoes ran out in spring and early summer there was usually enough money available to buy meal — imports of which rose steadily between the 1850s and 1880s (41) — a situation in marked contrast to that prevailing in the early nineteenth century when nothing but their potatoes stood between the crofting population and starvation. (42)

Expanding cash incomes meant that more money could be spent not only on necessities like meal but also on all kinds of 'shop produce', crofters' name for manufactured goods. (43) In the thirty years after 1850, therefore, manufactured clothes and shoes steadily replaced the home made varieties, while tea, sugar, jam and tobacco ceased to be thought of as almost unobtainable luxuries. (44) Until the mid-nineteenth century, for example, tea had been an infinitely rare and expensive beverage in the north-west Highlands; and a crofter's family would have counted themselves lucky to have one cup a week. But by the 1880s, when 'the poorest houses' in districts where tea had been virtually unknown before the famine brewed a pot of it 'twice a day at any rate', the *strupag* was already institutionalised as a vital component of crofting life. (45) And the dramatic rise in tea consumption is but one obvious example of a much wider change in the crofting way of life, a change reflected in Lewis crofters' habit of spending up to £30 a year on imported goods. (46) Their predecessors of thirty years before could not have found a sixth of that amount. (47)

Facts such as these, as the minister of South Uist remarked in 1883, show that after the famine the crofting community shared 'in the general progress of the country'. (48) It should not be forgotten, however, that crofters seemed prosperous only because they had recently lived in penury and that, although crofting conditions were very much better in the 1860s and 1870s than they had been in the first half of the nineteenth century, crofters' living standards did not compare at all favourably with those prevailing elsewhere in Britain. That this was the case is most apparent from Highland housing conditions, which were as bad, if not worse, than those to be found in all but the most wretched urban slums. To a stranger in fact — as the following passages from the autobiography of a South Uist schoolmaster make clear — crofters' houses could be almost unrecognisable for what they were:

> I shall not forget the shock I had, after a mile or so searching the road right and left for dwelling houses, and only seeing in the fast failing light what I took to be large isolated heaps of stones or earth, lying well back some hundreds of yards or so from the road we were travelling. I burst out: 'But where are the houses?' Pointing to one of the black-looking heaps I had noticed, my companion replied, 'These are the houses!' (49)

Such were one man's first impressions of the black houses in which, in the 1870s, the bulk of the crofting population still lived.

Varying somewhat in design from one locality to another, the black house's

principal architectural feature was an enormously thick outer wall made by building
two dry stone dykes, the one inside the other, and filling the space between them with
earth and rubble, Seldom more than six or seven feet high, the walls were as many
feet in breadth at the base but tapered slightly towards the top. On them was raised
a framework of rafters, often consisting – especially in the Outer Isles where timber
was almost unobtainable – of a nondescript collection of old oars, masts and pieces
of driftwood. The rafters were covered with 'divots' or large turfs – the cutting of
the turfs considerably damaged the land, but estate regulations designed to prevent
the practice were resented and usually flouted (50) – and these were thatched with
straw from the householder's corn. The thatch was secured by heather ropes weighted
with large stones, and the roof as a whole rested on the inner edge of the outer wall,
the absence of eaves ensuring that it would not be blown off by the frequent Atlantic
gales.

Long and low with a rounded roof, the crofter's house, according to one observer,
resembled nothing so much as a potato pit – a resemblance most striking in the case
of the more lowly hovels which were constructed of turf rather than stone and which
were propped up by the simple expedient of piling earth against their walls. Nor was
the unprepossessing outward appearance of the black house compensated for by in-
ward comfort. The floor was of earth and because there were no eaves the walls were
perpetually damp. In the 1870s, admittedly, the availability of a little more money
led to the appearance – on Skye and the mainland at least – of black houses equipped
with windows, floorboards, more than one door, a modicum of decent furniture and
perhaps two apartments. (51) The older type of dwelling, which was still much as it
had been in the 1830s or, for that matter, in the 1770s, (52) had none of these re-
finements, however; and in the 1870s and 1880s it was still to be found all over north-
west Scotland, especially in the Outer Isles where its predominance was almost completely unchallenged.

The traditional Highland habitation had no windows and no chimney, the smoke
from the peat fire which burned day and night, winter and summer alike being left to
find its way out through the thatch. Furnished with some planks and barrels, a few
three legged stools, and a box bed which was often roofed over to shelter its occupants
from the sooty rainwater which dripped from the thatch, the archetypal black house
consisted of a single apartment. The crofter and his family lived at one end; their cattle
inhabited the other; and, as if that were not diversity enough, the crofter's hens
roosted in the rafters above the fire. Animals and humans entered by the same door an
only rarely was any attempt made to erect an internal partition between their respectiv
halves of the dwelling – the only general concession to sanitation consisting of an
effort to incline the earthen floor towards the 'byre' in the hope that dung and urine,
if not the stench they emitted, could be confined to that end of the house. Dung was
seldom so confined, partly because of droppings from the hens in the rafters, partly
because the interior midden was removed only once a year – when it was spread on
the fields in spring. (53) In winter, when the weather was wettest and when the cattle
were confined for long periods, conditions were particularly appalling. A newspaper
correspondent who visited Lewis in January 1878 reported that in the crofters' houses
'Cows stand... knee deep in a dung heap'. (54) And five years later a Free Church
minister in the same island told the Napier Commission that when visiting his congrega

he frequently knelt in mud while praying with them. (55) Damp, dark, and dirty inside, crofters' dwellings were usually surrounded by domestic refuse of all kinds, the general squalor and discomfort being added to by the frequent non-existence of paths and approach roads and by crofters' enforced habit of building their homes in the least attractive and often wettest part of their holdings in order to conserve their all too precious arable land. (56)

The unhealthy effects of dampness and insanitation were aggravated by the tendency — especially prevalent in the more congested townships — for one croft's midden to foul the well of the holding beside it. (57) And in such conditions, as a poor law official remarked in 1885, 'It is not surprising that... typhus and typhoid fevers and other forms of disease... should be of frequent occurrence; it is more surprising that any person should escape.' (58) Typhoid and tuberculosis were, in fact, fairly common among the crofting population, the former being fairly prevalent in the Western Isles even at the end of the nineteenth century — by which time it had more or less been eliminated from the rest of Scotland. (59) And even in the 1920s the tuberculosis mortality rate in Lewis, where the black house lingered longest, was two and a half times greater than the Scottish average. (60) In the 1860s and 1870s, therefore, contagious disease was kept in check only by the relative isolation of many communities and the traditional practice of shunning its victims. (61) But even when it was absent, conditions were far from ideal; and the health of children in particular suffered badly from the conditions in which they were brought up. The logbooks of the schools established in the Hebrides after the Education Act of 1872 record a great deal of sickness and ill-health among their pupils (62) — the report of a *Scotsman* correspondent who visited Skye in December 1877 making the point more adequately than any statistics:

At the top of the village [of Torren], gathered in a listless way on a bit of moss land before an almost ruinous cottage were a dozen children — as squalid and as miserable as any that could be produced from the innermost dens of the Cowgate... What I saw at Torren I have seen at many places since. Children — not the bronzed, healthy urchins such as one meets in Lowland country districts — but puny, uncombed, blear-eyed, shivering little objects... This sorrowful index to the condition of the crofter forces itself very strongly on a stranger's notice as he passes through this island. (63)

Although its standard of living was rising, the crofting community was not, therefore, in a position that could be described as satisfactory. And even the economic situation was not one of unimpeded progress, higher stock prices and bigger incomes being at least partly offset by the deteriorating capacity of crofters' arable land. 'For the last fifty-four years I have been continuously cropping the same ground,' a North Uist crofter told the Napier Commission in 1883. 'And how,' he asked, 'can you expect good crops out of that?' (64) The answer, as crofters were only too well aware, was that you could not. Yet in many townships the same tiny plots had been incessantly cultivated since the abolition of the runrig system in the early years of the nineteenth century — a measure which, because it eliminated the inbuilt redistributive arrangements of traditional Highland husbandry was not so self-evident an 'improvement' as its proponents believed. (65) It was not, it must be said, that crofters were unaware of the benefits of allowing land to lie fallow. In one township in North Uist, for example, crofters made strenuous efforts to practice some sort of rotation. But so small were their holdings that if they left more than about a tenth of their arable land out of cultivation they could not produce the fodder needed for their cattle. (66) Their complaint was that of crofters everywhere, a complaint made thus by the tenants of Connista in the Trotternish district of Skye: 'The smallness of the crofts renders it imperative on us to till the whole of our ground from year to year, and by so doing the land is growing inferior and less productive.' (67) A steady decline in arable capacity was therefore inevitable. (68) And while it remained possible, with the aid of lavish applications of seaweed and manure, to obtain as many as seven or eight returns of potatoes in a good year, (69) cereal crops fell to almost ludicrously low levels.

In the parish of Kilmuir, a district containing some of the most fertile land in Skye, crofters' fields were reckoned in the 1880s to yield only two or three returns of oats. (70) In one more than usually prosperous township near Portree ten or eleven bolls of oats harvested for every five bolls sown was considered a fair return, and was achieved only by changing the seed every two years — more often than most crofters thought necessary. (71) In areas where the land had deteriorated even more markedly or where it had not been so good to begin with, yields were even more pitiful; with the result that in the 1870s and 1880s many crofters expected little more than a single return of corn from their impoverished holdings. (72) And since poor harvests were the rule even in good years, a wet summer meant no harvest at all. In the spring of 1877, for example, the twenty crofters in the township of Earlish, about a mile south of Uig in Skye, sowed seventy-seven bolls of oats. That autumn they harvested only twenty bolls. (73)

Few crofts had ever been large enough to produce all the food needed by their tenants and their families. (74) But the marked decline that occurred in their productive capacity in the nineteenth century's third quarter meant that crofters had to spend a steadily growing proportion of their incomes on meal and other provisions. In the early 1880s, for example, many Skye crofters had to buy from £8 to £12 worth of meal every year. (75) And throughout the north-west there were individual crofters who had to set aside £20 or more annually in order to purchase the food their impoverished holdings could not provide. (76) The experience of one Barra crofter was typical. In thirty-five years he brought home more than £500 from the east coast fishings; but, as he told the Napier Commission, he 'spent the whole of that in meal and in other things to support the family, all for want of land'. (77)

Despite their increased incomes, therefore, crofters remained unable to accumulate any capital. They were, on the contrary, in debt to meal dealers and to merchants and travelling salesmen of every kind. 'Our liabilities are so great that supposing we sold all our cattle we would still be left in debt,' declared the crofters of Carinish, North Uist, in 1883. 'The property that we have does not belong to ourselves,' a South Uist crofter similarly remarked. 'It belongs to the men who supply us with food and clothing.' (78) In the parish of Snizort in Skye by the early 1880s one township of seven tenants owed £54 to their meal suppliers, while larger townships of around thirty tenants owed between £150 and £300 to the same men. Elsewhere in the Highlands and islands the picture was the same: (79) the crofting community's new found prosperity rested on very insecure foundations. Much of it depended on credit. And crofters' credit was good only for as long as wages and stock prices continued high. As a Skye crofter pointed out in 1883: 'want of success at the fishing, or other work we go to, for even one year, means either ruin or starvation.' (80)

Although the clearances were over, therefore, his own insecurity was still the dominant fact of the crofter's life. In part that insecurity was financial; in part it derived, as it has always done, (81) from the natural difficulties of his situation – the Highland tenant, as the Napier Commission pointed out, being

exposed to unusual risks and vicissitudes. A good harvest or a good haul may make him comfortable for a season. A blight, an early frost, a wet autumn, a long winter, a gale of wind, a wayward movement of the herring, may deprive him of food for his family, funds for his rent, and seed for his ground. (82)

Of equal significance, however, was the fact that the crofter's tenurial position gave him no encouragement to try to overcome the natural obstacles in his way, but acted, on the contrary, as a strong disincentive to improvements of any kind. Not for nothing did at least one early nineteenth century traveller remark on the difference between crofters and their Norwegian counterparts. The latter laboured under geographic and climatic conditions that were even worse than those confronting tenants in the north-west of Scotland. But their ownership of the land and the fact that they received 'the advantage of their own exertions', gave them an interest in making all sorts of ambitious improvements. Not only were their small farms better cared for, their houses – in contrast to the 'dark one-room hovels' of the Highlands – were commodious residences with several apartments, wooden floors and glass windows. In Norway, in short, were to be found 'the Highland glens without the Highland lairds'. (83)

The obvious deficiencies in the crofter's condition his landlord and many writers – even in modern times (84) – blamed solely on his innate idleness and conservatism. The first was, and is, a slur. That the latter existed, and still exists, is obvious:

It does not matter to the Gael that a changed practice will reap him a bigger material reward. That is not recompense for having to that extent placed himself outside his group. If the material reward is real, he will be envied by his fellows and that is not a good state to be in, even for one growing season. If the reward is illusory, he will be ridiculed, and that is not good either in a society where there is no privacy. (85)

Such feelings are discernible, however, in practically every rural society on earth, and though they produce a situation in which 'progress' is less of a self-evident good than in urban societies, they do not make it impossible. Their existence in the Highlands, therefore, does not in itself explain why, for example, crofters lagged so far behind their peers in Norway. The real explanation of that state of affairs – as many nineteenth century writers and many more crofters suggested, and as is indicated by the subsequent history of crofting society (86) – is to be found, in fact, in the tenurial arrangements with which these paragraphs began: arrangements that were as agriculturally bad as they were socially unjust.

'If you give a tenant a rock in perpetuity he will make it a garden before long,' Arthur Young, eighteenth century English traveller and agriculturalist, once remarked. 'If you give him a garden for a limited time it will become a wilderness.' (87) And the relevance of that diagnosis to the nineteenth century crofting problem would have been very obvious to the author of the following comments about it, the parish minister of Glenshiel in Wester Ross:

The lotters holding their lands only from year to year, having no meliorations allowed them, and having learnt from experience that to improve their houses or lots, instead of producing any permanent advantage to themselves is only holding out an inducement to others to offer a few shillings of additional rent, and to deprive them of the fruit of their labour, are discouraged from attempting improvements. (88) Made in 1836 and preceded by proverbs such as, 'Mur b'e eagal an da' mhail, bheiread Tiridhe an da bharr', (89) the burden of that complaint echoes down the years to 188 'If we had the assurance that our rents would not be raised, or ourselves removed,' a Skye crofter told the Napier Commission, 'we would have encouragement to improve our holdings better than we do.' But as things stood, he went on, '... if I should improve my holding the landlord can have my improvements valued to increase the rant, and if I don't pay such a rent I will be warned and sent off at the May term.' (90 That man spoke from personal experience. (91) And as was borne out by Sheriff David Brand — who in his role as chairman of the first Crofters Commission knew as much as anyone about late nineteenth century crofting conditions — his experience was by no means unique:

A gain and again I have had cases brought under my own observation where old men were able to give the history of successive holdings occupied and improved by them, but taken away after a certain term of years and the benefit of the improvements passed on to someone else or to the landlord. (92)

Equally debilitating was the constant serving of eviction summonses on small tenants. These, as a Lewis crofter remarked, awaited anyone who dared to 'transgress the laws of the chamberlain'; (93) for they were — to quote Sheriff Brand again — 'the ordinary and normal mode of bringing a crofter to book for some real or supposed shortcoming on his part'. (94) Between 1840 and 1883, for example, 1,740 notices of eviction — affecting some 7,000 families — were issued in Skye alone. Most were intended to enforce the payment of rent arrears and the majority were not acted upon (95) — if they had been there would have been no crofters left on the island. But their effect can well be imagined in a society where attachment to and dependence on the land was such as to make eviction — to borrow Gladstone's famous utterar on the Irish land question — 'equivalent to a sentence of death'. (96) Estate manageme however, seldom took their tenants' susceptibilities into account. Thus in 1874, when the factor on Sir James Matheson's Lewis estate served eviction notices on no fewer than fifty-six Bernera crofters, he considered his action to be 'a little detail... too small a matter to bother Sir James about'. (97)

Occasional voices were raised in criticism of such policies. Thus the author of a treatise on Highland estate management which was published in 1858 noted that he had 'met with hundreds of instances of the earnest desire crofters have to improve if they have fair opportunity'. Urging landlords to interest themselves in their small tenants' welfare by granting leases, modernising houses, and giving instruction in scientific agricultural techniques, he continued:

We have a peasantry in the Highlands whom we lodge in hovels of mud — whom we drive out of their native glens and straths... and crowd into these parts that are not so capable of supporting sheep; we extort rents for the miserable plots allotted to them — give them no stated employment — leave them as ignorant as cattle — and then abuse them because they are not all that we wish them to be. (98)

Other writers made similar points. (99) But their recommendations, like those made by the Relief Board during the famine, (100) were generally ignored. Assured of massive incomes from the currently booming sheep farming industry, (101) most landlords wished only to forget about the crofters whose expropriation had made these incomes possible. And in the few cases where leases were offered to small tenants they seemed designed to weaken rather than enhance the latter's position. Thus the leases proffered to some Lewis crofters in the 1870s contained no less than fifty-four separate regulations, the infringement of any one of them immediately cancelling the rights of the lessee. An old man from Ness summed up the general feeling. He could not, he said, keep ten commandments for a mansion in the heavens, far less fifty-four for a black house in the Lews. The leases were accordingly turned down. (102)

Because they had no security, crofters made few improvements to their homes and holdings; while their landlords — from lack of interest, avarice, or both — made none either. Here and there, admittedly, crofters were helped and encouraged to build better houses. (103) But such enlightened actions were exceptional; and the few crofters who dared to commence improvements on their own account ran the risk of losing not only the benefit of them, if removed, but also the capital invested in them — for the landlord was not legally obliged to compensate the evicted tenant. Some land-lords paid a little compensation — but never enough. Others paid nothing at all — the history of John Gillies, a crofter on the Kilmuir estate in Skye being, in this respect, quite typical. On being ejected from one holding he 'got £7 as the value of the house I left. The wall of that house cost me £15 to build... At the next place from which I was removed I quarried all the stones for the house which I built and I got no com-pensation for it'. (104) And even more serious, in the long term, was landlords' neglect of crofting agriculture.

For the whole of the nineteenth century crofting agriculture was notoriously back-ward and inefficient; and it was clear that radical improvement could come only from above or outside the crofting community. Crofters could not, as one commentator put it, 'drink in agricultural theories from the clouds'. And if their landlords gave them no instruction, no one else was likely to make good the deficiency. (105) 'To carry on the business of improvements in this island to advantage,' it was observed of North Uist in 1799,

> it will be necessary to set a proper example. The greatest part of the people have never been out of the island and are altogether unacquainted with agriculture or improvement of any kind whatever, and without some instruction it cannot be supposed that they will do anything out of the common road. (106)

That advice was never taken, however — estate authorities making no effort to pro-mote a more scientific utilisation of crofting land. Seeds were seldom changed more than once in a dozen years; and what crofters knew of crop rotation they had picked up for themselves. (107) Drains were seldom dug; fences seldom built. To have done such things would have been to risk a rise in rent, or perhaps eviction if the additional rent could not be found or if the factor was looking for a good croft for a favourite. Thus, though the arable land had long since ceased to be held in common, there was little to differentiate each skimpy plot from its neighbour. In Lewis, for example,

> A few small stones erected at intervals form the only divisions, so that in autumn when the crop is housed and the potatoes pitted, one common stretch of barren looking land, over which the cattle and sheep roam at will, surrounds the various cottages. (108)

Such a system, of course, favoured the most traditionalist and least progressive crofters, for if a man did improve his holding by a judicious application of seed or fertiliser, he was quite unable to protect his improvements from the ravages of his lazier neighbours' stock. (109)

The autumnal dreariness of the typical township was added to — in the opinion of outside observers at least — by the ubiquitous lazybeds, those ineptly named and laboriously constructed mounds and ridges of earth which were thrown up in rocky and marshy land in order to supplement the produce of the tiny fields. 'Of every shape and size,' a journalist wrote of lazybeds at Keose in the Lochs district of Lewis,

> these grave like patches give the place on a dull day an almost sepulchral appearance Some of them, two or three yards in breadth, run in straight lines from the road away up the hillside, divided from one another by trenches more than a foot deep and several yards in width; others curve round corners in crescent form; a fourth kind straggle about in serpentine fashion; yet another variety have an irregularity worthy of the most neglected country churchyard — all speak to not a little labour on the part of the occupants. (110)

In essence a response to an environment that was frequently uncongenial to normal modes of cultivation, lazybeds or *feannagan,* as the above description suggests, varied in design according to the terrain; while their numbers varied in inverse proportion to the amount of naturally fertile arable land. In townships situated on the machair land of the Outer Isles' Atlantic seaboard, therefore, they were few and far between. In districts such as the south-eastern corner of Lewis and eastern Harris, on the other hand, they constituted almost all the arable land available to crofters. (111)

On lazybeds and in fields alike, the main crops were oats and potatoes — the latter giving way gradually to the former as more money made it possible to buy alternative foodstuffs and as higher stock prices made cattle rearing, and therefore fodder growing, an increasingly attractive proposition. (112) And throughout the crofting area at this time the land was still cultivated by spade or *cas chrom,* the traditional agricultural implement of the Gael. Although frequently despised by 'knowledgeable' observers, the *cas chrom,* or foot plough, produced better crops than the mechanical plough of more modern times by making possible the intensive cultivation of marginally arable land. (113) Turning over the land by hand was nevertheless a laborious task, and one that was made all the more unpleasant by the speed with which it had to be performed. So weak and shallow was the soil, so heavy and persistent the winter rains, that crofters could not cultivate their holdings in winter — as was the custom further south — without causing serious erosion. All the work on the land had consequently to be done in the few brief weeks between the winter's end and the crofter's departure for the herring fishings. For the crofting tenant, therefore, the spring was an acutely difficult time. If he planted his crops too early he chanced losing them in a cold, wet April and May; while if he delayed too long they might not ripen at all. Once made, however, his decision ushered in a busy and not uncheerful time for himself and his family. With the help of his wife and children he carted the winter's accumulation of dung from the 'byre' to the field, added to it the soot impregnated thatch and turf from the roof of his house — which had then to be rethatched — and his share of the tangle thrown up on the beach by the winter's gales or cut by the people of the township. And then with spade and *cas chrom* he worked the accumulated fertilisers into the famished land. (114)

The relatively unsophisticated nature of the crofter's system of cultivation was paralleled in his stock rearing activities. In most crofting districts the quantity of stock owned by a tenant was determined by fixing a 'souming' for every holding, the complex and unstandardised process involved being roughly as follows. The 'carry' of a township's common grazing — that is, the numbers of cattle, sheep, etc. which it could pasture — was initially established by the factor or by a land surveyor. And from the total township stock which was thus arrived at, a fixed proportion was allocated to each tenant, individual soumings being determined with reference to the wintering capacity of a croft's arable land or to the rent paid for it — the two, in theory at least, being closely related. (115) Since they involved a whole series of equations in which, for example, one horse equalled eight foals or two cows, while one cow equalled eight calves or four stirks or eight sheep or twelve hoggs or sixteen lambs, (116) souming regulations were inherently difficult to enforce; and the Crofters Commission was not exaggerating when it concluded in 1912 that 'The greatest source of trouble in the crofting area has been, and is, the management, or rather mismanagement, of common grazings'. (117) Even today, despite the existence of a veritable host of Acts and Orders on the subject, souming regulations are frequently ignored and abused. (118) And in the nineteenth century, needless to say, the abuses were greater and more numerous. Over-stocking was rampant and, combined with the effects of declining soil fertility, produced a situation in which there was seldom enough winter fodder to go round. The outcome — except in unusually open winters — was that the springs found crofters' cattle in very poor condition. (119)

The principal cause of over-stocking and kindred sins was ignorance rather than cupidity. In the 1860s and 1870s, nevertheless, there were indications of some sort of agricultural enlightenment among crofters. By the 1880s, for example, crofters' cattle and sheep were generally better cared for than they had been some twenty or thirty years before — a fact which accounted for a considerable part of the higher prices obtained for them. (120) Most crofters, however, still knew very little of the principles of stock management or of modern breeding techniques, and few landlords or factors attempted to make good the deficiency. (121) And even when the necessary knowledge was available it was seldom applied, for crofters, being far from wealthy, were invariably confronted with an 'almost irresistible' temptation to sell their best and most valuable animals rather than retain them for breeding purposes. (122) Little attention was thus paid to the quality of bulls and still less to the quality of tups, for if crofters were not greatly concerned about the pedigrees of their cattle they were, as a contemporary observer remarked, 'still less careful in the management of their sheep' — usually 'a nondescript class of blackface'. (123) The not unsurprising result was that common grazings, which if pastured by the proper number of correctly bred stock would have been capable of yielding fine animals, were generally grazed by sheep and cattle of obviously indifferent quality and value — a fact that was all too apparent in the difference between the market price for crofters' stock and that fetched by animals reared by sheep farmers. (124)

In comparison with what had gone before and with what was to follow, the 1860s and 1870s were an indeniably prosperous period for the crofting community. From the foregoing account of their circumstances, however, it is clear that crofters had little cause to be satisfied with the conditions in which they lived. Their houses were little more than hovels. They had no security of tenure. On being deprived of their holdings they received no compensation. They depended for their livelihood on wages earned far from home. Above all, they did not have enough land. In the 1880s, when crofters at last launched a concerted attack on Highland landlordism, all these grievances came very strongly to the fore. And all of them, especially the lack of land, stemmed ultimately from the agrarian system which commercial landlordism had itself created.

In the decade before the outbreak of the land agitation in the north-west Highlands the region's agrarian structure was dominated, as it had been since the eighteenth century, by great estates. Some of these were quite literally gigantic. Many sizeable islands were entirely owned by one man; while one mainland property, that of the Duke of Sutherland, occupied the greater part of a county. The proprietor of Lewis, Sir James Matheson, owned 424,560 acres, valued in 1872 at £19,488 a year. (125) Lord MacDonald and MacLeod of Dunvegan, owners of the two largest estates on Skye, had been forced — by their reduced financial circumstances — to sell off large tracts of their ancestral possessions in the years around 1850. Twenty years later, however, the former still owned 129,919 acres worth £11,614 a year, while the latter had at his disposal a grand total of 141,679 acres, thought capable of bringing in an annual income of £8,464. Properties of comparable size were to be found on the north-west coast of the mainland — Alexander Matheson's estates in Kintail and Lochalsh extending to 220,433 acres, and those of Cameron of Locheil in north Argyll and western Inverness-shire amounting in all to 125,754 acres. And large though these possessions were they were completely dwarfed by the colossus of the Sutherland estate which, in the early 1870s, extended to 1,362,343 acres worth £68,398 a year.

Although fairly small estates — small in this context meaning from five to twenty thousand acres — were to be found here and there, especially in Mull, Morvern and parts of Skye, the general pattern was, therefore, one of a few wealthy landlords controlling vast expanses of territory. The whole of the Outer Isles from the Butt of Lewis to Barra Head, for example, was divided into only five estates; (126) while the islands of Tiree and Iona together with the large peninsula known as the Ross of Mull constituted an important part of the Duke of Argyll's 168,315 acre domain. And though Skye in the 1880s was shared out between ten landlords, four of these — Lord MacDonald, MacLeod of Dunvegan and the proprietors of the Glendale and Kilmuir estates — owned about 90 per cent of the island's land surface, leaving only 10 per cent, or 38,000 acres, to be distributed among the remaining half dozen. (127)

The rate of absenteeism was high throughout the region. And it was invariably highest on the large estates. In Skye in 1882, for example, the five resident proprietors owned 24,045 acres between them. The rest of the island, 365,762 acres in all, was owned by absentees, (128) Absentee landlordism was, and still is, a highly emotive issue. But economically and socially at least it was of no great matter to crofters. Small tenants had little contact with their landlords, whether resident or absentee; and though the former probably re-invested a greater proportion of their rentals in their properties, it was sheep farmers — from whom Highland proprietors derived the bulk of their revenues — rather than crofters who were most likely to be the beneficiaries. As a gross violation of the typically Victorian notion that property had duties as well as rights, absenteeism attracted a great deal of adverse comment from nineteenth century radicals of every hue. And by highlighting the immensity of the gulf between their own lives in the squalid, restricted townships of the north-west Highlands and Hebrides and those enjoyed by their landlords in the high society of London and the south of France it may have done something to foster discontent among crofters themselves. But on the whole it seems to have made little direct contribution to fuelling the fires of rebellion.

Since landlords could not effectively manage their properties from a distance — ᴘ and since few of them, in any case, had any real interest in the day to day running of their lands — absenteeism was, however, responsible for the important role on Highland estates of the proprietor's factor and his assistants who, as a Tiree crofter bitterly remarked, 'had all the power in their own hands'. (129) 'There can be no doubt,' George MacKenzie of Coull had declared in the *View of the Agriculture of Ross and Cromarty* which he published in 1813,

> that the less a factor has to do with the management of an estate the better. The temptations to which he is constantly exposed when full powers are given are some- times greater than a man of ordinary virtue and fortitude can resist. (130)

But such strictures went unheeded and factorial abuses multiplied accordingly — the process being hastened by the fact that in a society composed of a handful of resident proprietors, a few sheep farmers and a multitude of crofting tenants, who were consid- ered beyond the pale of social respectability, factors easily — indeed inevitably — accumulated into their own hands practically every one of the public offices in the districts they administered. (131) In his estate management capacity, for example, Donald Munro, who was factor on the Lewis estate from 1853 until 1875, brought complaints against crofters to the attention of the legal authorities. And then, as Stornoway's procurator fiscal, he conducted prosecutions against the crofters whose alleged misconduct he had reported to himself. (132) Another Hebridean factor, Alexander MacDonald — who was known to crofters as the 'uncrowned King of Skye' and to civil servants at the Scottish Office by the less flattering soubriquet of 'Pooh-Bah' (133) — simultaneously managed no less than five of Skye's estates, thereby holding sway over 85 per cent of the island's population. MacDonald's factorial functions were combined with his professional activities as a bank agent and as Skye's only lawyer; and with his official duties as principal collector of rates and taxes in Skye, member and clerk of the school boards in six parishes, and captain of the Portree volunteers. (134)

The power and influence wielded by such men was immense and, as far as crofters were concerned, quite unchallengeable: 'He who is factor, banker, farmer, J.P., and so forth, has very little sympathy to spare for those whom he considers in his way'. (135) And rank injustices could thus be perpetuated with impunity. Donald Munro, 'a name still spoken of with loathing in Lewis', (136) distinguished himself by annually appropriating a specified nunber of hens from each household — hence his nickname *Domhall Ruadh nan Cearc,* Red Donald of the Hens. (137) Other estate managers were more tyrannical. There are, for example, authenticated cases of factors whose policy it was to increase a crofter's rent by 6d. on every occasion that he omitted to touch his cap or otherwise show his respect for them. (138) Corrupt, inefficient, riddled with favouritism and nepotism, dependent at a local level on 'ground-officers' drawn from among the crofter class and consequently more despised than the factor himself, (139) Highland estate managements were both hated and feared by the crofting community. 'Na'm bu tig a' la dh'eireas tu-sa as a sin,' a Hebridean crofter is said to have remarked at a factor's graveside. (140) And a verse composed at another factor's funeral reflects the same very general sentiments:

> Cuiribh air! Cuiribh air!
> 'S e chuireadh òirnne;
> 'S ma dh'éireas e rihist,
> Cuiribh e 'n còrr oirnn! (141)

It was thus no coincidence that during the troubles of the 1880s these proprietors who managed their own estates experienced considerably less 'inconvenience' than landlords whose properties were looked after by virtually unsupervised estate administrations. (142)

Most of the estates presided over by Donald Munro, Alexander MacDonald and their fellows shared the same broad characteristics. On the mainland, it is true, there were one or two properties such as the Knoydart estate in western Inverness-shire where the clearances had been pushed to their logical conclusion and almost all the available land put under sheep. (143) And there were other areas — Morvern, Glenelg, and parts of Mull and Skye, for instance — where crofters' share of the land was so minute as to be almost negligible. The parish of Bracadale on the MacLeod estate in Skye was one of these. Described by a Skye crofter as 'practically a desert', (144) it consisted almost entirely of six sheep farms, three of which, Glenbrittle, Talisker and Drynoch were enormous holdings whose tenants in 1883 paid annual rents of £1,800, £1,575 and £1,260 respectively. (145) More typical of the north-west coast and the Hebrides, however, (146) were these districts where the effects of clearing extensive tracts of land and cramming the evicted tenants into the less desirable corners could be observed side by side. Four such localities were the widely separated, but by no means untypical, parishes of Farr in Sutherland, Uig in Lewis, Duirinish and Waternish in Skye, and the islands of South Uist and Benbecula. (147)

The aggregate land rental of the parish of Farr was £6,492; and in Farr as elsewhere the proportions paid by the various classes of agricultural tenants provide a fairly accurate guide not only to the value of the lands occupied by them but also to the nature of the social and economic system which the land supported. Of the total of £6,492, then, seven farmers paid £5,810 and 293 small tenants £682. Of the latter group none paid more than £10 a year in rent, five paid between £6 and £10, 160 paid between £2 and £6, and the remainder paid under £2. The smallest farm was valued at £290 a year, the largest croft at £7.16s. And while almost three hundred crofters occupied holdings whose aggregate value was only £682 a year, a single sheep farmer — who was not even resident in the district — held lands for which he paid an annual rent of £1,688. Such was the end result of the much vaunted 'improvements' on the Sutherland estate. The parish which had witnessed the clearance of Strathnaver now contained, as the Napier Commissioners observed, 'the extremes of subdivision and consolidation; there is a striking absence of intermediate positions; the small farmer and the substantial crofter disappear entirely'. (148)

The total land rental of the parish of Uig in the south-western corner of Lewis was £3,698. Although less extensive than those in Sutherland, the clearances in Uig

had not been inconsiderable. (149) And as a result, the tenants of two deer forests —
which, by the 1880s, were replacing sheep farms all over the Highlands (150) — held
lands valued at £1,120 annually. Four sheep farmers whose annual rents were over
£100 apiece paid £887 a year to the estate. And two farmers whose rents were below
the £100 mark paid £170. The total annual rent of the 420 crofts in the parish was
£1,521. Five crofters occupied fairly substantial holdings worth between £10 and
£30 a year. A further 22 held crofts valued at between £6 and £10. But the vast
majority, 393 in all, had to be content with holdings worth less than £6 a year. Because clearance had been less complete, the social and agricultural extremities were
not, therefore, so far apart as they were in Farr. As the Napier Commissioners pointed
out, however,

2 small farms below £100 in annual rent and 5 crofters' holdings between £10
and £30, out of an aggregate number of 426 agricultural tenancies, is a miserable
representation of that system of substantial and graduated tenancy so desirable in
a community of which the vast numerical majority are associated with the cultivation
of the land. (151)

In Duirinish and Waternish and in Benbecula and South Uist the situation, though
different in detail, was similar in kind, and particulars of it need not be provided
here. (152) What is really important is the picture of north-west Scotland's agrarian
system that can be derived from a study of all four areas.

The gross land rental of the four districts was £22,180. And of this amount 28
sheep farmers and two tenants of deer forests paid £13,982. Half a dozen tenants
whose holdings were classified as small farms — that is, they were worth between
£30 and £100 a year — paid £345. The 2,090 small tenants whose holdings were
worth less than £30 a year paid a grand total of £7,853, which represented an average
rent of £3 15s. 1d. per head as compared with the sheep farmers' average of £488.
Of the more than two thousand small tenants only 56 whose holdings were worth
more than £10 a year could be considered substantial crofters. A further 256 occupied
moderately sized holdings for which they paid between £6 and £10 a year. But the
overwhelming majority, 1,778 in all, paid annual rents of under £6 for what were at
best insufficient holdings and at worst mere scraps of sterile land. The population
of the area in question was 15,816, and was made up of 3,226 families of whom
3,091 were the families of small agricultural tenants. Of the latter, as already mentioned, six held small farms; 56 or 1.7 per cent of the total population held substantial crofts; 256 or eight per cent of the total occupied moderate crofts; 1,778,
55 per cent of the total, were the tenants of small crofts; and the remaining 825
families, who paid no rent at all, must be considered as landless cottars and squatters.
Taken together, these figures show that the sheep farmers and deer forest tenants,
who numbered only 30 in all and constituted less than one per cent of the population,
paid 63 per cent of the aggregate rental, while the small tenants, who made up almost
90 per cent of the total population, paid only 35 per cent of the rent. At the same
time, and even more significantly, *the 30 tenants in the first category occupied
nearly two thirds of the available land leaving little more than one third for the
other 3,061.*

These figures are stressed because they encapsulate the consequence of the
clearances, a consequence which underlay the discontent which erupted into violence
in the 1880s. On one side a large population lived on tiny holdings in conditions of

acute congestion and squalor. On the other, a few wealthy men occupied vast emptinesses on which they grazed sheep or stalked deer. Nor could it be argued that crofters, being cultivators of land, were not so badly affected by this situation as might at first appear. The amount of pasture available to a crofting township was and is of crucial significance to its occupants, for crofters — considered as agriculturalists — were and are pastoralists first and foremost. (153) And not only had they lost the bulk of their homeland's hill pastures to sheep farmers, they had lost the best and most valuable portions of them. In Uig, for example, the cleared areas incorporated some of the best wintering ground, including all the machairs except those of Valtos and Kneep; while the East Loch Roag and Carloway districts — less attractive to sheep farmers because their grazings are of a poor, boggy type — were left in the occupation of crofting tenants. (154) All in all, as *The Times* remarked on the day following the publication of the Napier Commission's report, it was 'an economical condition scarcely consistent with agrarian content and social stability'. (15
And it was one whose ill effects were seriously aggravated by the high proportion of absolutely landless families.

In the four parishes referred to in preceding paragraphs, about a quarter of all resident families were classified as landless and subsumed under the generic titles of cottars and squatters. The former, in technical terms, were the inhabitants of dwellings built on holdings whose officially recognised occupants were usually close relatives of the cottars concerned; while the latter usually lived in houses built on the edge of a township's common grazings. Cottars generally cultivated a part of the croft on which they resided and occasionally paid a share of the rent. Squatters, however, paid no rent, despite the fact that they had frequently brought a part of common pasture into cultivation. Because their position was utterly insecure and their very existence a violation of estate regulations, precise numbers of cottars and squatters are difficult to determine, as is the point at which the lowlier crofters became cottars — a fact which led the Napier Commissioners to observe with considerable accuracy that the distinction between the various groups was 'more easily felt than delineated'. (156) About the origins of landlessness, however, there was no debate. It was the consequence of congestion and subdivision pushed to their ultimate conclusion: when holdings became too small to be further divided, and when there was no land on which new holdings could be created, some unfortunates were necessarily left without any land at all. The dictates of the kelp and fishing industries, combined with the effects of clearances and population pressure had begun the process. (157) And though these had ceased to be operative by the 1860s and 1870s — except in Lewis where the latter still existed — the landlessness created before the mid-1850s remained, as did a tendency for the number of cottars to go on increasing if only for the reason, to quote an Arisaig crofter, that it was 'a hard thing for any man to rear a family and expel them... It is the young people who support the old.' (158)

As was to be expected, the problem of landlessness was most acute in the areas where the crofting population was most dense. On the mainland and in Mull, therefore, cottars and squatters were fairly few and far between. On Skye, where the MacDonald estate alone contained 122 cottars in 1883, they were more numerous. (159
And in Tiree and the Outer Isles it was not uncommon to find 'crowds of squatters who construct hovels, appropriate land, and possess and pasture stock, but pay no

rent, obey no control, and scarcely recognise any allegiance or authority'. (160) In Tiree, for instance, the Duke of Argyll's policy of consolidating crofts at every opportunity — while benefiting those lucky enough to become the tenants of the enlarged holdings — led to the frequent dispossession of the families of deceased crofters. Having nowhere else to go, they joined the landless population originally created by the Duke's clearances in the 1850s. And by 1904 there were over 200 cottars and squatters in the island. (161) In Barra, South Uist and Benbecula where, in 1883, there were at least 400 landless families, the situation was equally bleak. But while the ratio of cottars to crofters was also high in North Uist and Harris it was in Lewis, the only part of the Highlands in which population expansion was maintained after 1850, that landlessness took on the dimensions of a virtually insoluble social and agricultural crisis. (162)

Supported less by the land than by money earned at the various fishings, the population of Lewis rose from 19,684 in 1851 to 29,352 in 1911. (163) In 1883 there were over 800 cottar families on the island and so rampant was the consequent subdivision that in the fifty years after 1844 the Matheson estate management was forced to recognise that, without any resettlement, the number of holdings had increased from 2,110 to 3,105 — 483 of the latter being little more than allotments worth under £1 a year. (164) Many crofts were divided between two, three or even more occupants (165) in the manner outlined in the following description of a not untypical holding in the township of Keose:

On an uneasy, undulating site there was apparently erected by the original holder a primitive hut with windowless walls... Alongside the father's hump-backed hut there had been run up by the elder son a second dwelling in all respects identical with the old family nest to which it joined so as to do away with the need for one of the side walls. Then, again, there has been swung out behind this pair of cottages a third low-walled house which grows in a crooked way out of the stonework of its neighbours and there another member of the family has taken up residence. (166)

The occupants of these dwellings, like cottars and squatters everywhere, were economically dependant on the fishing industry and on casual labour of every kind. And having little or no land on which to fall back in times of crisis, they were particularly vulnerable to downward fluctuations in money incomes from such sources. When during the famine, for instance, many of the crofters from whom the landless families obtained their potato patches had put the whole of their crofts under corn, cottars had suffered more than usually severely; and they were to do so again in the 1880s. (167) The obvious way out of their predicament, as cottars and squatters saw it, was for them to be given crofts of their own. (168) They could then raise their own crops and regularise the position by which — in defiance of souming regulations — they pastured considerable numbers of cows, stirks and sheep on township common grazings. (169) In a society in which the occupation of land was the be all and end all of everything it was an inevitable aspiration and one that was particularly strong amongst cottars and squatters whose forebears had occupied a relatively lofty social position.

There were innumerable cottars whose families, like that of Ronald MacDonald, a cottar at Hynish, Tiree, had occupied a recognised holding 'from time immemorial and paid the rent' only to be 'evicted to make room for sheep.' (170) And there were not a few who, like John Matheson, a cottar at Achnahannait on the MacDonald estate near Portree, could look back to a time when their people had been the comparatively prosperous joint tenants of a traditional farm. 'My own great-grandfather was a tenant in Achnahannait,' John Matheson told Lord Napier and his colleagues in 1883,

and had a fifth part of it... My grandfather succeeded him and had a fifth part... My father succeeded my grandfather and had an eighth part of the land and in his lifetime he came to be reduced to a sixteenth of the land. My father had six sons of whom I am the eldest, and not one of them would get a sod from Lord MacDonald. (17

In the 1880s and in subsequent decades men like Ronald MacDonald and John Matheson were — not unsurprisingly — prominent in raids on land from which their fathers and grandfathers had been cleared. (172) But while land hunger was most acute amongst cottars and squatters it was not confined to them. Among crofters themselves, as the Napier Commissioners discovered, 'the principal matter of dissatisfaction' was 'the restriction in the area of holdings'. (173)

Crofters possessed no statistical analyses of their position. Their grievances were entirely subjective, derived from their own experience of their own particular situations. But as is illustrated by the statement made to the Napier Commission by the crofters of Tarskavaig, a township in the parish of Sleat in Skye, they were none the less real for that:

A good number of years ago but within the memory of some of the oldest inhabitants Tarskaveg was inhabited by only four tenants... They were in a pretty comfortable condition... Subsequently, as evictions and clearances became prevalent throughout the parish, sheep farming got the preference, people evicted from other townships began gradually to crowd in upon us till, at the present day, our township is inhabited by forty tenants, occupying patches of ground varying from 1½ acres to 3½ acres. It therefore stands to reason that, out of such a small portion of land, it is an utter impossibility to make a livelihood... What we desire... is a reasonable share of the land, whereof we can make a livelihood, without being obliged to go to distant parts of the country to earn a living... There is sufficient land to distribute, and land formerly cultivated by tenantry, but of late converted into sheep farms. (174)

What was true of Tarskavaig was true of practically every township in north-west Scotland; and the 'question of the restriction of crofts' was consequently the 'capital grievance' of crofters everywhere. (175) 'The place in which we are is so straightened,' complained the tenants of Glashvin on the Kilmuir estate in Skye:

We are crowded into a space of one mile between two tacks on which there are twenty-three families of us without land... There are thirty-six crofters besides on that strip of a mile and the place must needs be poor. (176)

The township of Husabost on the western shore of Loch Dunvegan, declared its tenants, had until 1838 been 'held in common by eight tenants, paying a yearly rental of £8 each'. By the 1880s, however, 'the third and least profitable part' of it was 'overcrowded by twenty-six crofters paying yearly rents varying from £1 to £6'. (177) And Castlebay in Barra, said a sixty year old cottar in 1883, was in his 'first recollection' tenanted by ten families:

They kept a stock of from two to seven cows each family... Now they have only about the fourth part of that place, and there are twenty-two families paying rent in it. There are thirty families in addition to these without land at all located among them. (178)

In these circumstances, to obtain more land, to reverse the clearances — 'to return to the land which my father tenanted', as one South Uist crofter put it (179) — was for crofters an ambition so natural as to be almost instinctive. 'The peasant,' it has recently been written of nineteenth and early twentieth century Russia, 'naturally saw the root of all his difficulties in the shortage of land, his only salvation in an increase of land.' (180) Exactly the same could be said of the Highland and Hebridean crofting population of the same period:

> This is the cause of it all – that we see the land which our fathers had brought under cultivation by the sweat of their brows put under tacksmen, or, as they should more properly be called, desolators of the land, and ourselves heaped upon one another upon small patches of the very worst portions of the land, and many without any land at all, while upon the land which they possess as grass from one year's end to the other my father saw fourteen oat crops raised in succession... Now, in so far as I can understand the mind of the people, and especially of the younger portion of them, I fear that there is a danger that they may rise as the clans of old rose, if they don't get a hold over the land of which they are deprived... If some will say it is not right that we should be seeking these things, I shall not regard these as the poor man's friend; for if it is unlawful for us to ask it now, it was quite as unlawful for them to deprive us of it formerly. (181)

The sentiments contained in that statement by Donald Martin, a crofter at Back in Lewis, were universally held. 'The only thing that would remedy our ills,' remarked a Skye crofter, 'is that we should get more land.' (182) 'If we had plenty of land,' declared another, 'there would be no poverty in our country' – an opinion echoed by the North Uist crofters who believed that if more land was made available to them 'there would be peace and plenty instead of living from hand to mouth and contracting debts'. (183) All that a Harris crofter wanted, he told the Napier Commission, was 'More of the land which God created for man to take his living out of'; while the crofters of Uig in Lewis made their position clear by declaring that they had 'no hope' of their condition being improved 'except by getting enlarged holdings'. (184) And as was indicated by Donald Martin, the universal craving for more land was given force and direction by the fact that the overcrowded crofting townships were invariably hemmed in by huge and practically uninhabited sheep farms, all of which, as a landless Skyeman observed, contained 'green places on which crofters lived before'. (185)

Throughout the north-west Highlands and islands, wrote Lord Napier in 1885, 'the vacant land' and 'the starving multitude' were to be found side by side. (186) A currently common Gaelic saying put the matter more succinctly:

> Na biasta mor ag itheadh nam biasta beag,
> Na biasta beag a deanamh mar dh'fhaodas iad. (187)

And a particular example of the general situation is provided by conditions in the township of Solitote on the Kilmuir estate in Skye. A visitor to that 'miserable place' in the 1880s discovered that

> the patches of ground which the tenants cultivate vary in size from three roods to two acres. The township has no right of grazing. There are 17 families in the township and only three cows, and two of these are fed with grass purchased from the tenants of Conista while the third picks up its living at the roadside.

Given these circumstances, it was not unnatural that the tenants of Solitote 'pointed to the green fields of the sheep farms lying around, and asked why they should be huddled together while so much of the best land in Skye was under sheep'. (188) Not every township was so constricted and so depressed as Solitote. But there were few localities which knew nothing of the problems and frustrations of its tenants.

'When I open my door,' declared a Lewis crofter, 'there is no place within the range of my sight except where there are big sheep.' And these sheep, as one of his neighbours pointed out, grazed on 'land which our fathers had'. (189)

Like Lord Napier, these crofters had grasped the essential contradiction of the situation created in the north-west Highlands and islands by the clearances: the enclosure of constricted, congested, deprived and squalid townships by vast tracts of empty, uncultivated and not infrequently fertile land. So profound were the social tensions created by such a pattern of land use that, even if it had existed quite unaltered for a hundred years or more, some sort of uprising would not have been improbable. And because it had not so existed, rebellion was practically inevitable. The sheep farms laid out in Park and Uig in Lewis in the thirty-five years after 1820; the farms created on South Uist in the aftermath of the kelp industry's collapse; the farms established on Tiree in the 1840s and 1850s; those set up or enlarged on Lord MacDonald's estates in Skye and North Uist at the same time: these are but a few of the areas designated by crofters as suitable for settlement. (190) And all of them – as can be seen by reference to earlier chapters – had been brutally and forcibly cleared of their original occupants. Of that fact and its significance, the crofters who – in the 1880s and in the first quarter of the twentieth century – laid claim to the lands in question by illegally reoccupying them, (191) were very well aware. In the 1880s, after all, many witnesses and many victims of the clearances of the famine period were still alive. And where living memory failed there were the carefully preserved traditions of earlier expropriations. In north-west Sutherland in the 1890s, for example, 'the names of the townships... from which the people were driven' in the nineteenth century's opening decades were widely remembered – as were clearance songs and stories in South Uist in the 1930s. (192) In the folk memory, therefore, the sense of expropriation was undoubtedly vivid and strong, thus adding greatly to the consciousness of injustice and wrong that the agrarian system could not, by its very nature, have failed to produce. And even if that memory lapsed – which it seldom did – the tangible evidence of removals and evictions, was, and still is, there for all to see. 'Standing on any one of the great heights,' wrote a traveller in the Highlands in the 1870s, 'you see on every side of you the green slopes marked with the old ridges.' (193) These, together with ruined houses and the other signs of relatively recent cultivation and habitation which were discernable on practically every sheep farm in the Highlands, constituted – as the Napier Commissioners observed – a record of the clearances which was 'written in indelible characters on the surface of the soil'. (194) And where there had been small tenants before, it was not unreasonable to suppose, there could be small tenants again.

In the 1860s and 1870s the relatively high degree of security that resulted from the cessation of the clearances and the steady rise in crofters' incomes ensured that the discontent engendered by the Highlands' agrarian order remained below the surface. But while actually broken on only c ʼe occasion – by the disturbances that followed an attempt to evict a number of Lewis crofters in the spring of 1874 (195) – the social peace of these decades was an essentially fragile and precarious creation. Even a modest deterioration in crofters' financial circumstances was bound, for reasons examined in this chapter, to precipitate a new crisis in crofting society – a crisis

whose effects would be all the more unsettling because of its following a period of
rising living standards and of correspondingly increased expectations of life. Most
affected by such a crisis would be the generation which had grown up since the
famine. Used not to the absolute poverty of the past but to a situation in which
each year was usually a little easier, a little more prosperous than its predecessor,
that generation would not take kindly to any threat of a return to the conditions
that had prevailed in the first half of the nineteenth century. And younger crofters,
moreover, were undoubtedly better equipped to defend their interests than their
fathers and grandfathers had been. Not only had they inherited that growing feeling
of community whose emergence has already been discussed, (196) they were slowly
but surely developing a political consciousness of a type never before seen in the
Highlands. Better educated and more aware of the outside world than their predecessors (197) and possessing a hitherto unparalleled confidence in themselves and
their own abilities, they had taken, for example, to reading newspapers — newspapers,
it was noted, of a radical and antilandlord kind. (198) Most prominent of these was
The Highlander, founded in Inverness in 1873 by John Murdoch who, more than
anyone else, must be given the credit for arousing the crofting community to a
sense of its own potential power.

Born in Nairnshire in 1818, Murdoch was brought up in Islay where he acquired
a deep and enduring interest in Gaelic culture and an equally enduring hatred of
Highland landlordism. (199) In the course of a long and varied career in the revenue
service, Murdoch observed and was influenced by a number of radical political movements, not the least important of his experiences being his involvement — during
several years spent in Dublin in the 1850s and 1860s — in the politics of Irish nationalism. In Ireland he discovered Fintan Lalor's analysis of that country's land question
— an analysis which gave pride of place to the peasantry as the main agent of agrarian
change and one which Murdoch himself elaborated in a series of articles in *The
Nation,* the principal vehicle of Ireland's national aspirations. (200) When he retired
to Inverness to found *The Highlander,* therefore, it was the concept of creating a
Highland land reform movement rooted securely in the crofting community that was
uppermost in Murdoch's mind. The task was a formidable one. But Murdoch's contribution to its successful accomplishment was decisive and twofold: he forced
southern Gaelic societies and kindred bodies — usually composed of middle class
Gaelic revivalists who, though often the sons or grandsons of crofters, had little real
knowledge of crofting affairs — to align themselves behind the crofting population
in its struggle for a more equitable agrarian order in the Highlands; (201) and he
unceasingly encouraged, exhorted and cajoled crofters themselves into taking the
initiative in that struggle — with the ultimate aim of destroying the 'vicious land system'
which he believed to be the cause of all the Highlands' ills. (202)

Murdoch's objective, then, was to 'awaken' among crofters 'an intelligent and
vigorous public spirit and afford opportunity and encouragement to the inhabitants
of the Highlands to be heard on their own behalf'. (203) This he achieved, not only
through the columns of his newspaper, but also by tireless campaigning in the crofting townships themselves where, in the 1870s, the kilted figure of *Murchadh na
Feilidh* became increasingly familiar and influential. (204) The kilt — which then as
now was more identified with the synthetic Celticism of Highland lairds than with

the genuine Gaelic culture of the crofting community — was a part of Murdoch's endeavour to 'encourage the people to set a higher value on things pertaining to their country and particularly to their race, lore and language'. (205) And that, in turn, was but one of the ways in which he attempted to increase crofters' self-confidence and to inspire them to action on their own behalf. Such action, his Highland expeditions showed him, was much needed:

> As I went along I saw something of the poverty of the people: the poor land they held and in such small quantities, while there were so many large and good farms... and the poor congested just to make room for these. Then their husbandry was slovenly, their houses uncomfortable, and their crops, they could be nothing but poor on such land. (206)

To get crofters to protest about their conditions was far from easy, however. Thus in South Uist, Murdoch noted, 'the poor people were in such a state of slavish fear' of the estate management that they dared not attend his meetings, let alone act on his advice. But on finally obtaining a captive audience at a 'clipping' at Iochdar (since they could not leave their sheep they were obliged to listen to what he had to say), he succeeded in persuading the tenants of several townships to embody their more important grievances in a petition to the proprietor:

> I took care in the course of it that I was not teaching them; not telling them what to do, not putting grievances into their heads, not exciting their discontents... Small though these proceedings were they were the breaking of the first links in their chains. (207)

From such an occurrence to the effective challenging of the entire basis of Highland landlordism was a long and fateful step. But by 1881, the year in which *The Highlander* succumbed to the last of a long series of financial crises, that step was about to be taken.

8. The Highland Land War 1: Beginnings, 1881-1883

THE 1880s in the Highlands were a decade of severe, occasionally chronic, agricul- ʘ
tural depression. (1) As wool prices collapsed, sheep farmers' profits and landlords'
rentals fell back sharply from the heights they had reached in the balmy years of
the 1860s and early 1870s. Confronted by diminishing revenues and by a growing
number of sheep farmers who refused to renew their leases, landowners sought
financial salvation in a massive shift in land utilisation patterns which — because it
turned upon the wholesale transformation of sheep farms into deer forests — involved
a radical reshaping of the agrarian structure established in the early nineteenth century. But while sheep farmers could pull out of the Highlands and while the region's
landlords could look for new and equally profitable uses for the grazings thus vacated,
the crofting community — more prone to the effects of a recession than were either
of these classes — could do little to protect its own position; little, that is, that was
within the generally accepted norms of economic and political behaviour.

As far as crofters were concerned, the 1880s began with a sharp reminder that the
recent improvement in their living standards rested on essentially insecure foundations.
The Highland harvest of 1881 was uniformly poor; (2) and though the following
summer began with the promise of an unusually abundant crop it ended with
crofters' potatoes being more completely destroyed by blight than at any time since
the 1850s. (3) To the loss of the potato crop were added the consequences of an
unremunerative east coast herring fishing — the 4,290 Lewismen who spent the
summer on the drifters came home in September with only about £3 apiece, while
some Skyemen thought themselves lucky to return with £1 in their pockets. (4) And
on 1st October matters took yet another turn for the worse. Crofters' corn, most
of which had remained unharvested because of prolonged rain in August and September, was largely flattened and destroyed by an exceptionally severe southerly
gale. All the islands and the entire north-west coast of the mainland were affected
by the storm which, as well as adding to the agricultural havoc already wrought by
the blight, caused no less than 1,200 boats to be damaged or destroyed and brought
about the loss of an immense quantity of nets and other fishing gear. (5)
    The inevitable outcome of this series of catastrophes was that in the winter of
1882-83 the crofting population was plunged into conditions reminiscent of those
that had prevailed during the famine of the 1840s. By the New Year, therefore, the
effects of scarcity were everywhere apparent, especially in Lewis where 'numerous
families in every district of the island' were reported to be 'in absolute want'. (6)
And though mainland areas suffered a little less severely than the Hebrides no
crofting district escaped unscathed, (7) the general misery being added to by economic
developments similar to those which had occurred in 1846 and subsequent years. (8)
The potatoes having failed, the price of meal soared upwards as demand for it reached

unusually high levels. To obtain the funds needed to purchase it many crofters had
to sell their cattle — for which there was, in any case, a shortage of fodder; while
others were forced to add to debts which were already dangerously large. (9)

As the seriousness of the situation became apparent, appeals for aid were launched
in Glasgow and London; and in the early months of 1883 over £10,000 was collected
and distributed to crofters and their families. (10) From central government, however,
no assistance was forthcoming. The Scottish poor law authorities admitted the existence of unusual distress amongst the crofting population but did nothing to alleviate
it; (11) while Gladstone's Liberal administration refused to countenance parliamentary
proposals that crofters be supplied with badly needed seed oats and seed potatoes at
the taxpayers' expense — a private member's Bill incorporating these provisions
accordingly failing to be passed into law. (12) Those sections of the press which
reflected the opinions of the political establishment were equally unsympathetic. The
Liberal *Scotsman* believed that crofters should at once be 'disabused' of any notion
that they were 'entitled to government aid' and joined with the Tory *Times* in recommending officialdom's fifty year old answer to the Highland problem: emigration. (13) In the centres of political power and and influence, it thus appeared, there
was little interest in, and less knowledge of, the crofting community's problems and
aspirations. But at the very moment when their prospects seemed bleaker than for
many years crofters, by their own initiative, at last forced their grievances on the
attention of the British parliament and people.

In the 1880s, as had been the case for most of the nineteenth century, crofters'
economic troubles were closely paralleled by those confronting small tenants in
Ireland, where the agrarian structure at least approximated to that of north-west
Scotland. The winter of 1879-80 had brought near-famine conditions to a large part
of the Irish countryside. And the ensuing distress had greatly facilitated the remarkable rise of the Irish Land League, an agricultural tenants' movement founded in
1879 by Michael Davitt, Irish nationalist, ex-Fenian and, not insignificantly, the son
of a smallholder evicted from an estate in County Mayo in 1852. The League had as
its president and principal parliamentary spokesman, Charles Stewart Parnell, then
at the start of his meteoric career as leader of the Irish party in the House of
Commons. Its strength, however, lay not so much in its considerable parliamentary
representation as in its mass following in rural Ireland where rent strikes and other
forms of direct action organised by the League quickly threatened to undermine,
and even destroy, the enormous power of the Irish landlord class. Having failed to
crush the League by the deployment of all the coercive apparatus at its disposal,
Gladstone's administration, on the prime minister's initiative, responded to its
challenge by resolving to reform the Irish agrarian system — the outcome being the
Irish Land Act of 1881. Although not the final solution to the Irish land question,
the Act was a landmark in agrarian legislation. In conceded several of the League's
demands, notably those for security of tenure and judicially determined rents, and
was, in sum, a scarcely less than revolutionary attempt to remedy small tenants'
grievances at their landlords' expense. (14)

Irish unrest and its legislative consequences did not go unnoticed in the Highlands.
The government's publishers received an order for a copy of the Irish Land Act from

a remote part of Lewis; (15) and at least one group of Skye crofters, on 'hearing of good news from Ireland', expressed an inclination 'to turn rebels outselves in order to obtain the same benefits'. (16) Their reaction can scarcely have been unique. For after 1881, as one of their spokesmen subsequently observed:

> It was impossible that the intelligent crofter should not contrast his condition with that of the Irish tenant and ask to what the difference was due — whether it was due to violent agitation in the one case, and to peaceful, quiet, law-abiding habits in the other. (17)

And it was no coincidence, therefore, that in the winter of 1880-81, when the no-rent tactics of the Irish Land League were receiving wide publicity in the press, the crofters of Valtos and Elishader on the Kilmuir estate in Skye intimated their intention to cease paying rent to their landlord. (18)

The 46,142 acre Kilmuir estate, bought from Lord MacDonald in 1855 by a Nairnshire gentleman, Captain William Fraser, (19) was one of the few places where crofters could claim to suffer, like their Irish counterparts, from rack-renting. Under Fraser's ownership, the crofting rental of the property had almost doubled — despite a substantial reduction in the amount of land available to crofters — and the rents of some crofts had risen from around £5 to over £13. (20) As early as 1877 a visitor to Skye had observed that the repeated increases in their rents had led to widespread murmurings of discontent among Fraser's tenantry, (21) and it is not at all surprising, therefore, that the crofters of Kilmuir proved particularly receptive to the lesson implicit in events in Ireland. Their new departure was not matched by any sudden change in estate policy, however — the initial response of Fraser and his factor to the rent strike being that traditionally associated with Highland landlordism when it was confronted with the slightest hint of crofting insubordination: a petition calling for a rent reduction was rejected and summonses of removal taken out against the crofters who had dared to put their names to it. (22) But then, in the spring of 1881 — and for reasons that remain obscure — the Kilmuir estate authorities switched from a coercive to a conciliatory policy. Rents in Valtos and Elishader were reduced by 25 per cent, on the ostensible grounds that Fraser had discovered a small error in their soumings. (23)

In the wider world, these small beginnings of effective direct action by crofters passed practically unobserved. Before twelve months had elapsed, however, the crofting problem had become a matter of national concern.

The crofting townships of Gedintailor, Balmeanach and Peinchorran which constitute the district known as Braes or the Braes are situated on the east coast of Skye about eight miles south of Portree. Braes — of whose setting a *Scotsman* correspondent wrote in 1882 that it 'would be difficult to imagine anything more romantic' (24) — is a fairly typical, if somewhat isolated, crofting community delineated on the south by Loch Sligachan, on the east by the Sound of Raasay and on the west by a ridge of hills of which the highest is Ben Lee. Though unspectacular by the standards of the island containing the Cuillins, Ben Lee effectively separates Braes from Glen Varragil which carries the main, and nowadays very busy, road from Kyleakin to Portree — thereby ensuring that Braes can be easily approached only by a narrow, winding road that runs southwards from Portree. In 1882, as will become apparent, that fact was of some importance. But of still more importance was the status of

Ben Lee itself.

Like most other hills in the Highlands Ben Lee, which was capable of carrying between 1,200 and 1,400 sheep, (25) had once been part of the common pastures of the townships at its foot. That much was generally agreed. All else, however, was in dispute. The representatives of Lord MacDonald, whose estate included Braes and Ben Lee, admitted that until 1865, when the hill was leased to a sheep farmer for an annual rent of £128, the Braes crofters had been allowed to graze their stock upon it. But since the reorganisation of the MacDonald estate in the early nineteenth century, (26) they added, Ben Lee had been outside the officially recognised marches of the Braes townships whose tenants, therefore, had had the use of the hill 'merely ... on sufferance', had 'no right or claim to it', and were not entitled to any abatement of rent because of its loss. (27) The crofters' view of the situation was much simpler, one of them summing it up thus:

I and my father before me, and my grandfather, great-grandfather, and great-great grandfather have been living in the township of Balmeanach, and the hill of Benlee was all that time connected with our township. (28)

In 1865 the Braes crofters — whose account of events was eventually recognised as the correct one (29) — had submitted, as had many thousands of crofting tenants before them, to the loss of their grazings. (30) That they raised the issue again in the autumn of 1881 owed something to the fact that the current lease of the hill was about to expire, (31) and a good deal more to the passing of the Irish Land Act — Lord MacDonald's factor's contention that 'There was no combination till after the Irish affair', (32) being borne out by the comments of the crofters themselves. 'What made us raise the question just now,' one of them remarked, 'is that we were hearing that there were new laws passing about lands.' (33) Nor was their considerable knowledge of Irish events derived exclusively from newspapers — several Braes crofters having been employed, in the summer of 1881, on fishing boats working out of ports in south-west Ireland. (34) The extent of their contacts with their Irish counterparts is impossible to estimate, but they almost certinly saw something of the conflict raging in the Irish countryside and from it drew their own conclusions. On their return to Braes, at all events, they were instrumental in drawing up a petition which demanded that Ben Lee be restored to them as of right. Signed by almost all the tenants of Gedintailor, Balmeanach and Peinchorran, the petition was presented to Alexander MacDonald, Lord MacDonald's factor, (35) in November — only to be at once rejected. It was at this point — only a few weeks after Parnell had issued his famous no-rent manifesto from Kilmainham Jail in Dublin, a manifesto which called on Irish tenants to 'choose... between the Land for the Landlords and the Land for the People' (36) — that the Braes crofters took a crucial decision. They announced that they would immediately cease paying rent to Lord MacDonald. And a few days later, on the Martinmas termday of 1881, the tenants of Braes marched into Portree, halted outside Alexander MacDonald's office and informed him 'that their rents would not be paid that day, or any other day, until Ben Lee was returned to them'. (37)

Crofters at Valtos and Elishader had already made effective use of the rent strike, a fact of which the Braes men could not have been unaware. On the Kilmuir estate as in Ireland, however, a refusal to *pay* rents had been used to force a landlord to *reduce* rents. And that, in the Highland context, was a tactic of limited value, if only for the reason that relatively few crofters suffered from grossly extortionate rents. Almost all crofters, however, suffered from a scarcity of land. (38) And by recognising that a rent strike could be used not merely to enforce a rent reduction but to coerce a proprietor into giving more land to small tenants, the Braes crofters had adapted the principal weapon of the Irish Land League to Highland circumstances. They therefore began a movement which, if at all successful, was bound to appeal to crofters everywhere.

The significance of events at Braes was not lost on the landlords of Skye. Obsessed by the Irish precedent, they feared at best some sort of legislative intervention on the crofters' side and at worst agrarian revolution. (39) Strenuous attempts were accordingly made to have a number of Braes crofters arrested on charges of intimida- tion. And when these failed from lack of evidence — the bulk of the collected testi- mony having served merely to demonstrate the tenants' unanimous and almost entirely voluntary adherence to their cause — it was decided to evict a number of them on the grounds that, as a result of their rent strike, they had fallen into arrears. (40) Summonses of removal were consequently taken out against a dozen of Lord MacDonald's tenants at Braes. And on 7th April 1882 a sheriff-officer left Portree to serve the eviction orders which, though entirely legal, were clearly designed to intimidate their recipients. This they equally clearly failed to do. At Braes the luckless sheriff-officer was accosted by a crowd of about 150 people and assaulted. And although he was not seriously injured, the summonses were taken from him and burned on the spot. (41) The crime of deforcement — the name given in law to an attack made upon a sheriff-officer or any other legal official in the course of his duties — had clearly been committed. And since the names of five of the crofters who had taken a prominent part in the proceedings were known to the authorities, warrants were immediately issued for their arrest.

The forcible destruction of the hated eviction notices was a traditional response of Highland tenants to their landlords' attempts to remove them from their holdings. But in the past, as noted in a previous chapter, (42) such actions had been little more than desperate gestures of defiance in the face of virtually irresistible force. At Braes in the spring of 1882, however, the crofters' campaign was well organised and was, moreover, offensive rather than defensive. Its circumstances being thus entirely novel, the Braes' crofters' resistance to their landlord and to the law did not at once collapse as had that of their predecessors at Kildonan, Borve, Sollas and a dozen other places between the 1790s and 1850s. Their morale, on the contrary, remained high. They posted sentries on the hills overlooking the road from Portree and sat back to await developments. (43)

Until April, the tenants of Braes had conducted their campaign in an entirely peaceable manner. (44) Their deforcement of the unfortunate sheriff-officer, how- ever, made it possible for the authorities to move against them, the opportunity thus provided being especially welcomed by William Ivory, Sheriff of Inverness-shire, whose instinct it was to crush the crofters' movement — an objective which was to preoccupy him for the next six years. Because Inverness-shire did not possess a police force large enough for the type of action he thought necessary in Skye, Ivory appealed for assistance to the local authorities in Glasgow, home of Scotland's largest and most efficient constabulary. With surprisingly little fuss, his request was granted. And before dawn on 19th April, a day of cold, incessant rain, a detachment of over fifty policemen, most of whom would have been more at home in the streets of the empire's second city, marched from Portree with Ivory at their head or — to sacrifice drama to truth — at their rear; for he was always one to exercise discretion in such matters.

The expedition, whose task it was to apprehend the men wanted in connection with the deforcement of 7th April, passed through Gedintailor without encountering any resistance; and though the police were met outside Balmeanach by a crowd of about a hundred men, women and children, the Braes crofters, who had not expected to be raided at such an hour and on such a day, were not so well prepared as they might have been. Guided by the local ground officer, a police contingent was consequently able to arrest the wanted men without undue exertion. While the arrests were being made, however, the local tenantry had gathered in some strength and as the police attempted to withdraw with their captives they were surrounded, stoned and otherwise assaulted. About a dozen constables were more or less seriously injured and, on the police drawing their batons and repeatedly charging the crowd in an attempt to regain control of the road to Portree, one or two crofters and their wives were severely cut about the head. For a few minutes it seemed as if the captured crofters might be rescued by a detachment of their comrades who had occupied the Portree road at a point where it traverses a hillside which rises almost sheer from the sea — the place is known locally as An Cumhang. But in the end the police were victorious. A final desperate charge took them through the encircling mass of crofters and, at a run, they escaped towards Portree through a last barrage of mud and stones. (

Such, in outline, were the events which passed into legend as 'The Battle of the Braes'; events whose immediate effect was to give unprecedented publicity to crofters' grievances. Within a few days of the 'battle' having occurred there were in Skye no fewer than eleven journalists, representing newspapers as far apart geographically and politically as the *Inverness Courier, The Scotsman,* the *London Standard* and the *Freeman's Journal* of Dublin. (46) Their reports, not least their descriptions of the conditions in which Hebridean tenants lived, undoubtedly helped to swing public — and especially radical — opinion in the crofting community's favour. (47) But public opinion would not of itself have moved the government to make concessions to crofters. That was achieved only by further agitation and above all by the development of a crofters' political movement.

In April 1882 that movement had not been founded. But in the aftermath of the Braes affair John Murdoch's long campaign for a political union between crofters and the adherents of the Gaelic revivalist movement then flourishing in the south at last began to bear fruit in the emergence of a pro-crofter coalition headed by men like John Stuart Blackie, professor of Greek and passionate Celticist; Dr. Roderick MacDonald, president of the Gaelic Society of London; John MacKay, a member of that society and a prominent Gael; Angus Sutherland, pesident of the Glasgow Sutherland Association; Alexander MacKenzie, a founder member of the Inverness Gaelic Society and editor of the influential *Celtic Magazine;* and G.B. Clark, a Scottish doctor residing in London where he had had a long career in radical and socialist politics. This increasingly effective pressure group had as its parliamentary spokesmen, Dr. Charles Cameron, a Glasgow Liberal M.P. and the chairman of the

Federation of Celtic Societies; Charles Fraser-MacIntosh, Liberal M.P. for Inverness and a leading Gaelic scholar and antiquarian; and Donald H. MacFarlane, Irish nationalist member for County Carlow but a Highlander by birth. Here then, was the nucleus of a potentially powerful political alliance. (48) But though Cameron, Fraser-MacIntosh and MacFarlane at once set about the task of bringing the Highland land question to the attention of the House of Commons, (49) they still laboured under the difficulty of having no organisational links with crofters themselves. That particular problem was soon to be overcome. Until it was, however, developments on the wider political stage and those occurring in the Highlands proceeded in virtual independence of each other; a state of affairs which did not, admittedly, prevent Highland landlords and other upholders of north-west Scotland's agrarian status quo from attributing the unrest in the region to a Dublin based conspiracy whose principal agents were held to be the Glasgow branches of the Irish Land League. That the latter took an active interest in Highland discontent is undoubted. But the cool reception accorded to their emissary to Skye indicates that while crofters were willing to draw on the Irish example they were not, at this stage at least, prepared to encourage direct Irish involvement in their affairs. (50) And the subversive 'agitators' — Irish or otherwise — who, it was widely suggested at the time, (51) were responsible for disturbances in crofting areas, prove, on closer inspection, to have been no more and no less than the mythical creations of understandably frightened members of the possessing classes.

In Skye itself, meanwhile, the movement initiated at Braes was — without any assistance from Ireland or anywhere else — attracting growing support among the island's crofting population. Some months before the dramatic happenings of 19th April 1882 had drawn the attention of the outside world to events in Skye, crofters in the north-west corner of the island had commenced their own campaign of protest. The districts affected by it were the Husabost and Glendale estates: the former a small property on the western shore of Loch Dunvegan; the latter a 35,022 acre estate centred on the fertile strath of Glendale which runs southwards into the hills of Duirinish from the head of Loch Pooltiel, a small inlet on Skye's west coast about five miles south of Dunvegan Head. Glendale was owned by the trustees of Sir John MacPherson MacLeod who — some thirty years before his death in 1881 — had bought the property from a financially stricken MacLeod of Dunvegan. Husabost, an estate of some 5,000 acres which had passed out of MacLeod's hands at about the same time, was owned by a Dr. Nicol Martin who, though a resident landlord and a native of Skye, (52) was held in very little esteem by his tenants — largely because his management of his estate was principally distinguished by his maintenance of quasi-feudal services of a type long obsolete elsewhere in Britain. Ten days' unpaid labour was required each year from crofting tenants on Martin's estate, and failure to answer the landlord's summons — which usually came at seed-time or harvest when crofters were busiest on their own holdings — was punished by a fine of 2s. 6d. a day. (53)

But while the situation on Martin's property was clearly such as to heighten the discontent produced by crofters' universal grievance, lack of land, it fell to the Glendale estate management to arouse the district's crofters to action. In January

1882 the factor on the Glendale estate, himself a sheep farmer, issued a series of edicts designed to promote local sheep farmers' interests at the expense of those of the crofting population. Crofters were forbidden, for example, to keep dogs and ordered to cease collecting driftwood on the seashore, a practice which, it was alleged, involved them in trespassing on sheep farmers' lands. (54) Announced at a time when news of the rent strike at Braes was no doubt sweeping across Skye, these impositions had the effect of inducing a group of Glendale crofters to call a public meeting at which their grievances, new and old, were to be discussed. Attended by crofters living on Martin's estate as well as by most of the Glendale tenantry, the ensuing assembly was a resounding success. Pledging themselves to present a united front to their landlords, those present resolved that the tenants of the various townships on the two estates should at once draw up petitions embodying their respective complaints and send them to Martin and to the Glendale trustees. (55)

Martin's tenants not unnaturally requested the abolition of 'the slavery called day's work' as well as asking 'that the hill ground which was taken from us be now duly restored to us'. (56) But the demand for more land was common to all the petitions, the crofters of Skinidin, for example, asking for the restoration to them of two islands in Loch Dunvegan — islands which had been added to a sheep farm in the 1840s but which, as an eighty year old crofter remarked, were 'ever since my recollection... looked upon as part of the grazing belonging to the township'. (57) Like those made by the tenants of Braes a few months before, these requests were rejected by the estate authorities to whom they were addressed. A letter to Donald MacDonald, the Glendale factor, encapsulated the crofters' reaction:

Sir,... We received a letter from the trustees from whom we were expecting to obtain pleasure for our petitions, but misfortunately we were disappointed... We conclude that you shall be without the rents until we receive what we are wanting, and that shows you that we are all the same as one man. Certainly you need not put any to the trouble of going out with summonses. None shall quit the estate until all demands are arranged.

We are, yours respectfully,
The Tenants of Milovaig and Borrodale,
including all the Glendale Tenants. (58)

Although the rent strike thus announced affected the entire area encompassed by the Glendale and Husabost estates, tension was highest in the townships named in the crofters' letter, Upper and Lower Milovaig and Borodal. The tenants of these townships had petitioned the Glendale trustees to let to them the nearby sheep farm of Waterstein, the current lease of which was due to expire at Whitsun 1882. (59) But their request had been refused and the farm handed over to the factor, Donald MacDonald. (60) The latter, while not refusing this excellent opportunity to add to the extensive lands he already occupied, felt his position to be so dangerous that he armed himself with a revolver; while the crofters, for their part, declared that at the Whitsun term they would occupy Waterstein with or without permission. (61) Convinced that their threat was a serious one, the late proprietor's trustees visited Glendale at the beginning of May and urged their tenants to give them a little more time to enquire into the situation on the estate. The reply they received summed up the spirit and significance of the entire revolt in Skye in 1882:

We told them that our forefathers had died in good patience, and that we our-

selves had been waiting in patience till now, and that we could not wait any longer —
that they never got anything by their patience, but constantly getting worse. (62)
By the end of May the Milovaig and Borodal crofters' sheep were being pastured on
Waterstein. (63)

From the Court of Session the trustees obtained an order instructing the offending tenants to remove their stock from the disputed grazings. But the order was
ignored and the factor's shepherds threatened with violence should they make any
attempt to clear the farm. On such an attempt being made in November a shepherd
was in fact severely mauled by crofters. (64) And although warrants for the arrest
of twenty-five of his assailants were subsequently issued by the authorities, the
wanted men remained at large for the simple reason that in the sort of pitched battle
likely to be produced by an attempt to apprehend them the small force of police
then stationed in Skye would be no match for the crofters. (65) Less dramatic, but
equally indicative of the strength of feeling among the Glendale and Husabost tenantries, was the outcome of the Martinmas rent collection on the two properties. No
rents at all were paid at Husabost. And at Glendale only five of the estate's five
hundred crofting tenants came forward to settle their accounts — the feeling of the
overwhelming majority being demonstrated in December by the burning of a corn
stack belonging to one of the crofters who had broken faith. (66)

While these developments were occurring in Glendale, the crofters who had borne
the brunt of the authorities' first clumsy attempt to quell the growing unrest in
Skye remained quite uncowed. Of the five Braes crofters arrested in April, two were
fined 50s. and three 20s. by an obviously sympathetic court in Inverness. (67) They
came home to a heroes' welcome and, thereafter, events at Braes closely paralleled
those in Glendale — the Braes crofters driving their cattle on to Ben Lee in the
month that Waterstein was similarly invaded, and Lord MacDonald's estate managers,
like their counterparts at Glendale, obtaining a Court of Session order which instructed the rebellious crofters to desist from actions which, in the Court's judgement, were
quite illegal. (68) Copies of the order, which was to be served on no fewer than fifty-
three of Lord MacDonald's tenants, were entrusted to a messenger-at-arms who
arrived at Braes on 2nd September. And since most of the menfolk were away at
the east coast herring fishings, the defence of the townships devolved upon their
wives and daughters. They rose manfully to the occasion. 'Howling in a frightful
manner', and with their shawls pulled over their faces to prevent their identification,
they pelted the messenger and his party with stones and other missiles and forced
them to retreat to Portree. (69)

Graham Spiers, sheriff-substitute at Portree, had, since the first hint of violence
at Braes in the spring, been of the opinion that Skye could be satisfactorily pacified
only if the police received military assistance. (70) Subsequent developments, he
thought, had served only to confirm the accuracy of his original prognosis and by
September he was accordingly convinced that unless troops were at once deployed
on the island law and order would not be restored and there would, consequently,
be nothing to prevent 'feeling in Skye... coming to the climax which Ireland has got
to'. (71) With this view Spiers' superior, Sheriff Ivory, was in full agreement, and on
21st September he asked the government for a hundred troops 'to act as a protection
and aid to the civil authorities in serving... the interdicts and other orders of the
Court of Session'. (72) Although J.B. Balfour, who as lord advocate was the foremost
Scottish minister in the government, supported Ivory's request, the majority of
Gladstone's administration, with their Irish experience fresh in their minds, had no

desire to be embroiled in another agrarian uprising. Ivory's appeal for aid was accordingly turned down. Instead of applying for help from the army, it was suggested to him, the Inverness-shire authorities should immediately set about strengthening their own police force. (73) This they agreed to do. And in November fifty constables were added to the county constabulary — a step which brought its total strength up to ninety-four men. (74)

While showing that the crofters' movement was being taken more and more seriously, these developments did little to solve the problem confronting the authorities in Skye. Any police force, a Highland sheriff was to observe on a future occasion — and revolutionary tacticians of modern times would no doubt agree with him — was likely to prove 'quite insufficient to prevent resistance to the law... where the sympathy of the people is against the enforcement of the law'. (75) And in Skye in the autumn of 1882 the truth embodied in that remark was becoming rapidly apparent. On 24th October, for example, the forces of law and order in the shape of a messenger-at-arms, a police inspector, a superintendent and nine constables were prevented from entering Braes by a large and 'determined' crowd. (76) For Lord MacDonald's agents, who had hitherto demanded that 'prompt steps' be taken to put down what they referred to as the 'illegal combination' at Braes, (77) that particular incident was the last straw. Concluding that 'the law is no longer respected in Skye', they decided that the advantages of an immediate settlement at Braes outweighed the risk of a continuing conflict. And in December they accordingly agreed to lease Ben Lee to the tenants of Braes in return for an annual rent of £74.15s. (78) The Braes crofters were soon to conclude that they had been more or less duped into paying a not inconsiderable rent for 'the hill which was part of their holdings in time past', and the December agreement consequently proved to be no more than a temporary truce. (79) But in forcing Lord MacDonald to come to terms with them the crofters seemed, at the time, to have won something of a victory — as indeed they had done. They accordingly called off their rent strike and brought Braes' year of troubles to an end. (80)

As tranquillity returned to Braes the authorities turned their attention to Glendale where, behind a cordon of sentries posted on the narrow and winding hill road which crosses into the glen from Dunvegan, the district's crofters were reported to be preparing to defend themselves against an expected police incursion with crude but effective pikes consisting of scythe blades lashed to poles. (81) The reports of these weapons' existence may or may not have been mere rumours. But it was all too manifestly obvious that Glendale had effectively passed out of civil and criminal jurisdiction — in January, after all, the crofters who had assaulted the Waterstein shepherd in November were still at large. (82) For Ivory and his subordinates to have indefinitely countenanced such an admission of their own helplessness would have been unthinkable. And on 16th January an attempt was accordingly made to station a police sergeant and three constables at Hamara Lodge in the centre of the Glendale estate. The property's crofting population, however, were quite determined to prevent any arrests and, if possible, to preserve the virtual autonomy which they had recently won for themselves. Alerted to the approach of the police detachment by the sound of horns blown by their sentries on the hills to the east of the glen, they therefore gathered in strength; and about a quarter of a mile short of their destination the four policemen were set upon by a crowd of about five hundred men, many of them armed with stout sticks. Knocked down, kicked and beaten, the sergeant, his constables and the inspector who was accompanying them were driven like cattle to the estate boundary and left to make their own way back to Dunvegan. (83) On the following day, by way of consolidating their command of the situation, the Glendale crofters deforced a messenger-at-arms and drove him off the estate. (84) And on 20th January several hundred men armed with sticks, scythes, graips and other weapons marched from the glen to Dunvegan — with the aim of forcing the police to completely evacuate the district. This they achieved with spectacular ease. Some hours before their well drilled column arrived in Dunvegan the police abandoned the village and fled across the hills to Edinbane. (85)

Initially limited to a refusal to pay rents, the crofters' movement — as these events made clear — had grown spectacularly in scope in the nine months which followed the first clash between crofters and police at Braes in April 1882. Lands had been seized, the courts defied, officials manhandled and substantial areas closed to the police. The agitation, in short, had assumed something of the status of a revolutionary challenge to the existing social and agrarian order in those parts of Skye where it had begun. But even more worrying, from landlords' point of view at least, were the signs that the unrest was unlikely to remain for long confined to one or two localities. In the closing months of 1882, for instance, crofters on the Kilmuir estate began a new rent strike, and the tenants of several townships on Lord MacDonald's property threatened to withhold their rents until hill pastures which had long since been added to sheep farms were restored to them. (86) Still more significant were the increasingly numerous manifestations of discontent in districts outside Skye.

In 1880 John Murdoch, Angus Sutherland and several kindred spirits had hailed as a glorious opportunity to launch a Highland land reform movement an attempt to evict a number of crofters from Leckmelm — a township situated on the northern shore of Loch Broom about three miles from Ullapool. (87) On that particular occasion, however, little had come of their endeavours. But as the autumn of 1882 gave way to by far the worst and most difficult winter experienced by the crofting population for many years, (88) there were a number of indications that such a movement — sparked off by events in Skye rather than by paragraphs in the radical press — might at last be about to appear. Thus an attempt to evict a crofter at Rogart on the Sutherland estate was resisted by a crowd armed with sticks; while at Lochcarron a sheriff-officer was deforced while trying to serve summonses of removal on two crofting tenants. (89) And in the islands there were still further reaching developments. Tiree crofters, for example, petitioned the Duke of Argyll for a reduction in their rents; and the tenants of one of the island's townships, Balephuil, demanded the restoration of pastures on Ben Hynish which had long since been incorporated into a neighbouring farm. Crofters on Barra — in January 1883 — made a similar request for grazings on sheep farms once enlarged at small tenants' expense. (90) And the tenants of several townships in Uig, Lewis, began to hold public meetings at about the same time. The hardships suffered by them that winter, they declared in a letter to Lady Matheson, widow of Sir James Matheson and owner of the island, stemmed ultimately from the existence of 'huge possessions in the hands of sportsmen and tacksmen'. They had, they added, 'no desire at present to follow the example of the Skye crofters'. But they could not 'vouch for the course the crofters of Lewis may pursue, judging from the views expressed at their recent meetings'. (91)

The proliferation of events such as these, the Home Office concluded in February 1883, showed that there was 'much discontent and excitement' among north-west Highland and Hebridean crofters — a contention for which there was indeed abundant evidence, not least in the existence of the 'intimations... made to various proprietors that, if demands put forward by crofters for additional lands are not voluntarily conceded, forcible possession of the lands will be taken'. (92) And in view of these occurrences it is not really surprising that in the opening months of 1883 the British government decided to actively intervene in crofting affairs for the first time since the famine of the 1840s.

The expulsion of the police from Glendale had, as the lord advocate remarked with evident satisfaction, 'brought matters to a crisis'. And by the end of January he had at last persuaded the cabinet to accede to Ivory's requests for troops. (93) The military's immediate objective was to be the apprehension of five Glendale crofters — all of whom were to be charged with offences arising out of the recent affrays in the glen. As a conciliatory gesture, however, it was decided that a final attempt should be made to persuade the wanted men to surrender themselves voluntarily — the man charged with this delicate task being Malcolm MacNeill, the official in charge of administering the poor law in north-west Scotland. (94) MacNeill was conveyed to Loch Pooltiel in a gunboat, and on 9th February he met about five hundred crofters in the Glendale Free Church. A prolonged debate ensued; and though MacNeill's participation in it was greatly facilitated by the fact that he was fluent in Gaelic, his mission at first seemed likely to end in failure. All the crofters in Glendale, he was informed, had participated equally in the events of the previous few months and while they were ready 'to go in a body' to jail they were not prepared to give up five men of whom the authorities clearly desired to make a salutary example. In order to avoid a potentially bloody and obviously unwinnable confrontation with the army, however, they eventually agreed to adopt the course advocated by MacNeill. The five wanted crofters consented to stand trial in Edinburgh where, on 15th March 1883, they were sentenced to two months' imprisonment. (95)

For the moment, therefore, military intervention was avoided — something for which the government at least were duly grateful. But as a means of putting an end to the protest movement in Skye the sentences imposed on 'the Glendale martyrs', as the five imprisoned crofters were soon dubbed, were an undoubted failure. In Glendale itself, for instance, the crofters' rent strike remained solid — an attempt to break it by evicting forty-five crofters failing on 10th April when the sheriff-officer charged with delivering the summonses of removal was deforced and driven off the estate by a large crowd. Neither he nor any other officer could be induced to make a second attempt. And since, in order to take effect at the Whitsun term-day, the summonses had to be served before 15th April, the Glendale crofters had clearly won another victory. (96)

As this type of skirmishing between landlord and tenant continued in Glendale, the political campaign launched by the crofting community's parliamentary allies began to gain in momentum and effect — assisted, no doubt, by the fact that the unprecedented publicity given to crofting affairs had resulted in the emergence of what J.B. Balfour subsequently called 'a considerable body of vague and floating sentiment in favour of ameliorating the crofters' condition'. (97) The pro-crofter feeling thus delineated by the Liberal lord advocate was strongest amongst the more radically inclined members of his own party. (98) And in January 1883 twenty of the latter — none of whom sat for a crofting constituency — joined Fraser-MacIntosh in putting their names to a Commons motion which called for a royal commission of enquiry into crofters' grievances. (99) Earlier moves in this direction had been frustrated by the government's determination to avoid its own entanglement in Highland affairs — as recently as the previous November, for instance, Gladstone had informed D.H. MacFarlane that 'no such question' was 'under the consideration of Her Majesty's Government'. (100) In the opening weeks of 1883, however, events in Glendale, coupled with political pressures, of which Fraser-MacIntosh's resolution was the most notable example, forced a change of policy. On the 26th of February the government announced that it would, after all, set up a royal commission ' to inquire into the condition of the Crofters and Cottars in the Highlands and Islands of Scotland'. And on the 8th May that commission, under the chairmanship of Lord Napier, began taking evidence from crofters at Braes. (101)

The setting up of the Napier Commission, though clearly a considerable victory for the crofters' cause, did not at the time seem quite as momentous an event as it does in retrospect. Suspecting that the Commission was merely a delaying tactic and that its activities would be confined to the few areas where violent outbreaks had already occurred, many of the crofting community's southern sympathisers regarded its appointment as a reason for more rather than less agitation. And it was with this object in view that they founded in London in February 1883 the unwieldily named but politically portentous Highland Land Law Reform Association. (102) The Association's programme was loosely modelled on that of the Irish Land League. But to the League's demands for 'fair rents, durability of tenure and compensation for improvements' the HLLRA added a call for 'such an apportionment of the land as will promote the welfare of the people throughout the Highlands and Islands' — the latter being explicitly designed to remedy crofters' most pressing grievance, lack of land. And the fact that the Association was largely an institutionalised version of the already existing crofting lobby was reflected in its choice of office bearers: D.H. MacFarlane was elected president, and among his numerous vice-presidents were prominent Gaelic revivalists such as John Stuart Blackie, Fraser-MacIntosh and Dr. Roderick MacDonald, as well as radical land reformers like G.B. Clark. (103)

Although the HLLRA at once declared its membership 'open to all who approve of its objects and subscribe to its funds' and proclaimed its intention to become the political voice of the crofters' movement, it could not, in the nature of things, immediately rally the crofting community around its banner. (104) But while MacFarlane and his colleagues were organising themselves in London, the Napier Commission — at first thought by the HLLRA leadership to be grossly biased in favour of the landlords (105) — was having the quite unexpected and unintended effect of galvanising crofters into action on their own account. (106) Until the Commission's appearance, a crofter remarked, 'We were afraid we would be persecuted if we should speak out'. (107) As was demonstrated by a statement made by the Commission's first witness, and still more strongly by attempts that were subsequently made to evict crofters who had given evidence to Lord Napier and his colleagues, (108) that fear was very real:

Q. ... you will have the goodness to state what are the hardships and grievances, if any, of which the people whom you represent at this place complain.
A. I would wish that I should have an opportunity of saying a few words before I tell that, and that is that I should have the assurance that I will not be evicted from my holding by the landlord or factor, as I have seen done already ... I want the assurance that I will not be evicted, for I cannot bear evidence to the distress of my people without bearing evidence to the oppression and high-handedness of the landlord and his factor. (109)

With very conspicuous reluctance Lord MacDonald's factor and most of his fellows agreed to provide the required assurances. (110) And crofters were thus enabled, and even exhorted, to publicly state their grievances for the first time – not merely by land reformers like John Murdoch and Alexander MacKenzie who visited township after township urging crofters 'to give expression to their own opinions', (111) but by the commissioners themselves. In every crofting district, for instance, there were posted up impressively official notices which instructed tenants to meet and elect delegates to the Commission. (112) And at the mass meetings held for that purpose, as well as at the Commission's own sessions in the crofting townships, discontents were discussed and aspirations articulated in a way that was quite new. Crofters who had been hitherto uninvolved in the movement initiated in Skye thus gained their first – and undoubtedly intoxicating – experience of organising themselves in an attempt to better their own conditions. And alongside their consequent increase in self-confidence there developed a growing awareness of the latent power of the crofting community – for was not the Napier Commission itself the outcome of the agitation in Skye? Gradually, therefore, the crofting population became attuned to the idea of marshalling itself for a wider and more far-reaching struggle than that originally envisaged by tenants at Braes and Glendale – a crucial stage in that process being reached in August 1883 when some two thousand crofters, who were gathered at Fraserburgh for the summer herring fishing in the North Sea, met to discuss the land question. On their return home, they resolved, they would set up 'Land Law Reform Associations ... in their various parishes'. (113)

The effect of the Fraserburgh resolution, news of which was contained in crofters' letters home to their wives, (114) was reinforced in the autumn by support from the editorial columns of the *Oban Times* – which had recently acquired in Duncan Cameron a young and intensely radical editor who was passionately devoted to the crofters' cause (115) – and by the HLLRA's decision to begin issuing Gaelic and English circulars which urged crofters to organise themselves within its constitutional framework. (116) 'The object of the HLLRA,' a typical circular declared,

is to effect by unity of purpose and action such changes in the land laws as will promote the welfare of the people... The cause has many friends... but the success of the movement must necessarily depend upon the unity and determination of the Highland people... Unity is might, and with might on their side the people will soon succeed in obtaining their rights. (117)

In order to be affiliated to the Association in London, a local branch of the HLLRA
had to have a membership of at least twenty, each member paying an annual subscription of one shilling to central funds and also helping to meet any expenses incurred by his own branch. Control of the branch was vested in an eight man committee
which included a chairman, secretary and treasurer, all of whom, like the rest of the
committee, were elected by the branch members. (118) To establish an HLLRA
branch was, therefore, a fairly simple process, requiring no more effort than had
been needed to elect delegates to, and prepare evidence for, the Napier Commission.
And in those areas where crofters were already engaged in active confrontation with
their landlords the procedure was even more straightforward: all that was needed
was the adoption of the title HLLRA by one of the regular mass meetings which
crofters had themselves evolved in order to direct and control their agitation.

The ground having been well prepared for it, the success of the HLLRA's initiative
was more or less assured. Its first Highland branch was constituted at Glendale on
5th December, and although landlords, factors and several clergymen joined in denouncing the Association as a 'fenian fraternity', other crofting districts quickly
followed suit. (119) By the end of 1883, in other words, the nascent crofters'
movement had been given a political dimension and an organisational framework —
attributes which were to enable it to transcend the limitations initially imposed on
it by geographical circumstance. In 1884, therefore, the Highland land war entered
a new and more decisive phase.

9. The Highland Land War 2:
Is Treasa Tuath na Tighearna, (1),1884-1886

THE Napier Commission, by arousing expectations of immediate legislation on the crofting question, (2) had the effect of temporarily stilling the violence which had preceded its appointment – a development reinforced in Glendale, the principal centre of that violence, by the estate management's decision to let one third of Waterstein farm to the crofters of Milovaig and Borodal (3) and, more generally, by the departure of crofting tenants to their summer jobs in the Lowlands or on the herring drifters. The onset of the winter of 1883-84, however, was accompanied by a growing realisation that an officially imposed solution to crofters' problems was far from imminent; and unrest accordingly manifested itself once more. On the Glendale and Kilmuir estates rent strikes were consolidated and intensified. The part of Waterstein still held as a sheep farm was reoccupied by crofters. Other lands were seized near Hamara, Glendale, and in the neighbourhood of Garrafad on the Kilmuir estate. (4) And attempts to remove tenants who took a leading part in these proceedings failed when the sheriff-officers charged with the task of delivering their eviction orders were assaulted and deforced in what was rapidly becoming the standard manner. (5) Elsewhere in the Hebrides there were similar developments. The tenants of several Tiree townships began a rent strike and threatened to occupy grazings on Ben Hynish and Ben Hough. (6) In South Uist lands were seized in the neighbourhood of Stoneybridge. (7) North Uist crofters petitioned the island's proprietor for more land, (8) and grazings at Melbost in Lewis were occupied by crofting tenants. (9)

On the political front, meanwhile, the Napier Commission's report – published in April 1884 – proved, as G.B. Clark admitted, 'more sympathetic... and more advanced in its recommendations than was generally expected'. (10) And by lucidly exposing the more glaring inequities of the Highland agrarian system – as well as by recommending a fairly sweeping reform of it – it gave the crofting community's cause a considerable boost. The Commission's attempt to devise a unique and specifically Highland solution to the crofting problem – an attempt which turned on proposals to give legal status to the traditional institutions of the crofting township and a planned phasing out of all holdings of under six acres(11) – was not, however, to the liking of crofters themselves. Most of the latter had set their hearts on legislation on the lines of the Irish Land Act of 1881; and at mass meetings throughout the crofting area the Commission's recommendations were consequently condemned as complicated, impractical and, above all, inadequate. (12)

By the spring of 1884, therefore, the optimism engendered by the setting up of the Napier Commission had largely faded away – a development hastened by the Liberal government's evident lack of anxiety to pass, or even bring forward, crofting legislation of any kind. (13) Some understandably exasperated crofters in Glendale were heard to remark that the only way to obtain a land act was to follow the Irish example and shoot a few landlords. (14) And if that suggestion was not meant to be taken very seriously, the same was not true of the underlying intention to step up direct action. At a mass meeting held before their departure to the summer herring fishings the Glendale men resolved that if no governmental gesture was forthcoming by the autumn, more sheep farms would be forcibly appropriated. (15)

As discontent increased, so did the prestige and influence of the HLLRA. By June 1884 the Association's membership included some five thousand crofters, and a vigorous recruiting drive organised by the HLLRA's recently appointed 'lecturer', John MacPherson — acknowledged leader of the Glendale crofters and one of the 'martyrs' of 1883 — was bringing in more members almost daily. (16) Declaring that 'the time had now arrived that crofters should unite together and agitate their cause for freedom and more land', MacPherson spent the summer addressing meetings and helping to establish HLLRA branches in Skye, Mull, north Argyll and the Outer Hebrides. (17) His tour was everywhere successful — in Barra, for example, he was escorted from township to township by a procession of some six hundred crofters. (18) And those members of the HLLRA's executive who joined their representative in the islands in the early autumn were quickly swept up in the general enthusiasm. Thus D.H. MacFarlane, drawing on his experience of Ireland's land reform movement, thought that the Irish peasants'

feeling upon the subject was weak and vacillating in comparison with the deter- mined spirit of the people of the Highlands. The Highland eeople are convinced that their cause is just, that their demands are just, and they are determined to seek re- dress. (19)

The HLLRA's star being undeniably in the ascendant, MacFarlane's heady optimism was not unjustified by events. The Association's membership was soaring. Its conten- tion that the Highlands' agrarian order was archaic and unjust had been at least tacitly acknowledged by a royal commission. And speaking in Edinburgh in August Gladstone had publicly pledged his government to legislate on the crofting question. (20) It was therefore in an atmosphere of enthusiasm bordering upon euphoria that the HLLRA convened its first annual conference at Dingwall in September 1884. The conference was attended by crofters' delegates from all over the north-west Highlands and Hebrides and its principal outcome was the HLLRA's adoption of a manifesto soon to be known to the crofting community as 'the Dingwall Programme'. (21)

The Programme, while welcoming the Napier Report, largely rejected its proposed reforms in favour of a more radical approach involving not only the granting to crofters of security of tenure and compensation for improvements but also the estab- lishment of 'a Land Court with judicial and administrative functions' — a measure incorporated in the Irish Land Act of 1881 but specifically disapproved of by the Napier Commission. (22) Such a court, it was envisaged, would determine fair rents and be empowered to 'enlarge crofting townships and form new townships ... on any land which the court may consider suitable'. It would, in other words, redistribute the land in crofters' favour.

The Dingwall Programme, dismissed by *The Times* as 'a piece of pernicious non- sense', (23) was thus a very radical document which, not content with proposing a drastic modification of the landlord-tenant contract, went on to propound a scheme of compulsory land settlement — a concept which the lord advocate thought to be 'attended with far-reaching and... dangerous consequences'. (24) And in so doing the

Programme transcended even Gladstone's Irish Land Act of 1881, a measure which had itself been widely condemned as a revolutionary interference with the rights of landed property. (25) Finally, and still more significantly, the HLLRA appended to its manifesto an announcement that its members would, at the next general election, 'only support Parliamentary candidates for the northern constituencies who approve of this programme and promise to support a Bill to give it full legislative effect'. (26) In conjunction with the imminence of the Third Reform Act which gave crofting tenants the vote for the first time, this declaration amounted to a knell of doom for landlordism's long dominance of Highland politics.

Although the electoral effects of the challenge thus thrown down to the Tory and Liberal parties in the Highlands did not become apparent until the end of 1885, the months immediately following the Dingwall conference were marked by a rapid escalation of the conflict between the crofting community and its landlords. At HLLRA meetings in Tiree it was demanded that 'the land be justly divided' and in that island and in South Uist wire fences around sheep farms were clandestinely destroyed. (27) In November, moreover, 'the crofters and cottars' of South Uist resolved at a mass meeting to pay no rent to their proprietrix, Lady Gordon Cathcart, (28) until she instituted a general rent reduction and restored 'the arable and pasture land forcibly and unlawfully taken from them to enlarge big farms'. (29) Since no rent reductions or land redistributions were forthcoming, crofting tenants on South Uist and Benbecula paid almost none of the rents that were due at Martinmas. (30) And in accordance with another resolution adopted at their November meeting – namely, 'that unless the land be justfully divided at the New Year the nearest tacks will be taken possession of and appropriated' (31) – the crofters of the two islands marked the commencement of 1885 by occupying lands from which their forebears had been evicted between the 1820s and 1850s. (32) Typical of these occupations was that conducted by the crofters of Stoneybridge in South Uist. With a blissful disregard for the dire warnings emanating from the estate authorities, they took possession of lands on Ormaclett farm – a substantial holding from which some of them had once been evicted – allotted the illegally occupied fields amongst themselves, and began to prepare their new 'crofts' for cultivation by spreading seaweed on them. A subsequent attempt to serve forty-two of the offending tenants with court orders instructing them to withdraw from Ormaclett led only to the deforcement of the sheriff-officer concerned. (33)

Elsewhere in the Outer Isles there were virtually identical occurrences. Barra crofters met to demand more land. North Uist tenants pegged out new 'crofts' on Balelone and Balranald sheep farms. And in Lewis crofting rents were withheld, farm fences destroyed and lands seized. (34) The Shawbost branch of the HLLRA, for example, organised the occupation of part of Dalbeg farm, the branch secretary's announcement of their action summing up the general feeling of Hebridean crofters in that eventful winter:

We have put up with these grievances for a long time, but now we venture to lay hold of that piece of our old grazings with the strong hand of the people united for their rights... Now the fence is broken down in several places and our sheep and cattle are feeding on our old possessions. (35)

In Lewis, too, a sheriff-officer was deforced. (36) But here as elsewhere in the islands

the distinctive feature of the new wave of unrest was the increasing use by crofters
of terrorist tactics of one kind or another. The overnight destruction of fences and
dykes became commonplace. In South Uist telegraph wires were cut and a boat
belonging to a farm manager destroyed. In that island and in Lewis boulders were
placed on the roads in order to harass farmers, factors and landlords — the only people
who could afford to travel by carriage. (37) And at the same time, the boycott — the
social ostracisation which the Irish Land League had developed into a formidable
weapon of agrarian conflict (38) — made its appearance in the Highlands. Crofters
in Skye and South Uist were instructed by their HLLRA branches to do no work for
sheep farmers. And it was made abundantly clear that anyone who dared to occupy
the holding of an evicted tenant would be made to feel the displeasure of his fellow
crofters in no uncertain fashion. (39) The latter threat, as was demonstrated by
events, was not at all an idle one. In Kilmuir, Skye, for example, a boat belonging to
a crofter who refused to take part in the agitation was destroyed, his windows smashed
and his byre burned down. (40) The corn stacks belonging to two North Uist crofters
who refused to join the HLLRA were similarly sabotaged and their cattle mutilated. (41)

By the end of 1884, therefore, the crofting population of north-west Scotland, so •
long quiescent in the face of oppression and exploitation, were actively engaged in a
campaign of subversion, of which agrarian crimes of the type mentioned above were
merely a small if particularly striking part. To landlords and their allies the spectacle
was a decidedly alarming one. Throughout the Hebrides, *The Scotsman* declared in
October,

> men are taking what does not belong to them, are setting all law at defiance, and
> are instituting a terrorism which the poor people are unable to resist ... Rents are
> unpaid, not because the tenants cannot pay them, but because in some cases they
> will not, and in some cases they dare not.

If the law was not quickly and firmly enforced, the paper concluded, 'the condition
of the islands will soon be as bad as that of Ireland three years ago'. (42) The terrorism
and intimidation which were thus condemned by Scotland's leading Liberal newspaper
were genuinely deplored by the HLLRA's urban leaders. (43) But there was little they
could do to control their Highland and Hebridean branches whose members' struggle
with their landlords and the law had long since assumed a quite unstoppable momentum
of its own. Estate owners and local authorities — who did not need the clarion calls of
The Scotsman to arouse them to the seriousness of their predicament — were equally
helpless. The picture of a few evil and unscrupulous 'agitators' engaged in the terroris-
ing of a fundamentally law-abiding population whose fervent desire it was to be allowed
to pay rent to their landlords was one that had no reality outside the fertile imaginat-
ions of Whiggish leader writers in Edinburgh. The vast majority of the crofting community sympathised quite openly with the terrorists, fence breakers and land raiders. And
it was for that reason that the one or two crofters who were opposed to lawlessness
were afraid to give evidence against them. The result, as the proprietors of one Hebridean
estate complained, was that 'the perpetrators of these crimes could not be discovered'. (44)

As was always the case in the early years of the land war, unrest was most acute in
Skye where, in the autumn of 1884, crofters occupied several sheep farms on the
Glendale and Kilmuir estates. (45) Terrorism and intimidation were reported to be
particularly rampant on the latter property and towards the end of October an attempt
was consequently made to station a police superintendent and ten constables in the

Trotternish peninsula. All eleven men were driven off the estate by a large crowd. (46) At the beginning of November 1884, therefore, the Kilmuir tenantry were the un- challenged masters of their landlord's estate — a position which, it seemed, they were reluctant to give up. The Kilmuir crofters, the distraught chief constable of Inverness- shire reported to the home secretary on 9th November,

> have for the past week been assembled in hundreds, day and night, armed with sticks for the purpose of assaulting an expected body of police, and declare that they will attack any number of constables... At present a reign of terror exists in the district and nothing short of Government aid or protection for the Police in restoring order and maintaining the law will suffice. (47)

In September the Inverness-shire authorities had asked to be allowed to arm their police in Skye, and they had subsequently received fifty service revolvers and a thousand rounds of ammunition from the War Office. (48) Confronted with what was, from their point of view, an unsupportable situation in Kilmuir, they now decided to march a detachment of forty armed police on to the property. (49) Con- temporary press reports that some of the crofters guarding the approach roads to the Kilmuir estate were armed with rifles as well as cudgels may have been erroneous. (5 But there is, nevertheless, every reason to suspect that an incursion of newly armed and recently recruited police into a district where tension was high, tempers frayed and the police detested would have resulted in a bloody confrontation. And it was pro- bably as well, therefore, that the government at last agreed to make troops available for duties in Skye. (51)

The outcome of that decision was the arrival off Skye in mid-November of a small flotilla consisting of a gunboat, a troopship carrying three hundred marines, and the MacBrayne's steamer, *Locheil* — the latter chartered to serve as a mobile police barracks when it became apparent that none of the island's innkeepers were willing to identify themselves with the forces of law and order by providing accommod- ation for policemen. On being informed of the nature of their mission, the *Locheil's* captain and most of her crew resigned; while the Kilmuir crofters reacted to the government's display of superior force by announcing that they would not rest 'until they got justice done and until the iniquitous land laws [were] reformed'. (52) Having issued this defiant statement, however, they prudently resolved to refrain from con- fronting the marines — partly in order to avoid a battle which they knew they could not win and partly because their hatred of the police who, as the lord advocate observed, they 'regarded ... as the agents of the landlords rather than as part of the constituted authorities of the Country', (53) did not extend to the troops who were very cordially received. (54)

Crofters' professions of non-resistance notwithstanding, the redoubtable Sheriff Ivory was determined to make the fullest possible use of the troops who had at last been placed at his disposal. And he accordingly began the task of pacifying Skye by marching two hundred and fifty fully armed marines around the northern part of the Trotternish peninsula from Uig to Staffin — a route carefully chosen to take in some of the most disturbed parts of the Kilmuir estate. The outcome of these en- deavours was a propaganda triumph for the crofters. The marines' manoeuvres, *The Times'* correspondent reported,

> were intended as an imposing military spectacle to overawe the natives. Few of these, however, were stirring and those that were abroad seemed to be amazed rather

than intimidated by the display... Taken as a whole, today's proceedings can only be described as an extravagant display of force, the effect of which was to excite the astonishment, and mirth even, of the crofters but not to cow them. (55)

The government took a similar view, Ivory being curtly informed that the home secretary, Sir William Harcourt, was 'somewhat surprised' at the scale of his initial operation. (56) But though they made Inverness-shire's luckless sheriff their scape-goat, Ivory's difficulties were largely of government ministers' own making and they constitute an important testimony to the vacillating and indecisive nature of the Liberal administration's Highland policy.

Because Gladstone's cabinet could not, despite its distinctly Whiggish hue, afford to offend too severely the crofting community's sympathisers in the Liberal party's radical wing, the troops in Skye were not, on Harcourt's instructions, allowed to perform duties that were normally carried out by the police. They could not, for example, be used to escort sheriff-officers engaged in the serving of eviction orders; (57) and when such officers were deforced, as they almost invariably were, the military were consequently forbidden to intervene except as police escorts in any subsequent attempt to apprehend the deforcers. (58) Thus, while it undoubtedly convinced the crofting community and the political leadership of the HLLRA that the Liberal government was not to be trusted, the military presence in Skye did absolutely no-thing to help the island's landlords to enforce their will on their dissident tenantries. In the last week of December 1884 — to give only one example of an increasingly common pattern of events — sheriff-officers were deforced while attempting to serve summonses of eviction on crofters in Kilmuir and Glendale. (59) But a full month elapsed before any attempt was made to arrest the crofters concerned — the atmosphere in which the arrests were made being illustrated by the fact that the police involved had to be protected by marines who, at one stage, were ordered to fix bayonets in order to ward off an angry crowd. (60) The persistence of this sort of situation had a predictable outcome: an attempt to evict crofters who had occupied lands on Dr. Martin's Husabost estate failed in January, because a sheriff-officer, for whom no military escort could be provided, decided that he could not serve the summonses of removal 'without great risk of personal injury'. (61) Following further deforcements in the spring, (62) refusals by sheriff-officers to serve writs, court orders and eviction notices became commonplace. But despite renewed appeals to Harcourt — who, for all his desire to maintain law and order, strongly sympathised with crofters and had, for personal as well as political reasons, no wish to lay himself open to the charge of aiding and abetting Highland landlordism (63) — permission to provide the officers with military escorts was not forthcoming. The result, since police escorts were more likely to provoke than to prevent disturbances, was that legal notices remained unserved and legal proceedings against crofters became, for all practical purposes, valueless. (64)

With military protection the police were able to regain access to the areas from which they had recently been excluded. (65) But as a means of putting an end to rent strikes and other manifestations of crofting discontent, military intervention in Skye affairs was, for the reasons mentioned above, a costly failure. (66) At the Martinmas rent collection on the Kilmuir estate — the area where the marines were most active — almost no rents were paid by crofters. (67) And from Glendale and

Kilmuir the no-rent movement spread, in November and December 1884, to the rest of Skye. In township after township it was resolved that no rents would be paid until grievances were redressed. Thus crofters at Sconser demanded that lands which had been added to Lord MacDonald's deer forest during the clearances of the 1850s be restored to them. (68) At Braes, meanwhile, a new rent strike was instituted, the tenants of Balmeanach, Gedintailor and Peinchorran now claiming that the additional rent being paid by them for Ben Lee should be cancelled and the hill restored to them as of right. (69) In Sleat, a district previously unaffected by the agitation, crofters petitioned Lord MacDonald for more land; and at Elgol on the Strathaird estate, rents were withheld and fences around sheep farms were destroyed. (70) On the Dunvegan estate, too, the winter brought indications of unrest, with some of MacLeod's tenants initiating their own rent strike. (71)

That rents were withheld on such a scale was partly due to the damage done to crofters' domestic economies by the steep fall in cattle prices which began in 1884 and continued for several years. (72) By the late 1880s stirks which would have fetched £7 or £8 in 1883 were worth only about £1 10s; and many could not be sold at all. Prices for more mature cattle fell proportionately; while crofters' wedders declined in value by about 50 per cent. (73) After 1883, therefore, the happy state of affairs in which 'the stirk paid the rent' (74) came to an end. Within two or three years the returns on cattle sales had fallen so drastically that they did not even equal the cost of the winter fodder which many crofters bought to supplement the grain they produced on their usually inadequate holdings. (75) Debts increased and credit became more difficult to obtain. (76) But though one poor law administrator remarked that the solution to the crofting community's economic problems lay in Highland tenants learning to curb the 'extravagant habits' which they had contracted in the relatively prosperous 1870s, (77) the crofters of the mid-1880s, unlike those of half a century earlier, could not be cowed and intimidated into paying rent to a landlord while their own living standards were declining. A letter from the tenants of Fasach to the Glendale trustees encapsulated the new, defiant attitude:

> Our poverty is not our fault. We have worked... to pay you for what should be our houses. But we are now so poor that we must first obey the law of nature to feed and clothe ourselves, and we cannot therefore pay you the rent which you wish to exact from us. (78)

In the context of the crofting community's long history of non-resistance to a particularly exploitative landlordism, such proclamations, together with the rent strikes and land seizures they announced, smacked of little less than revolution. And though the north-west Highlands quietened down as usual in the summer when the menfolk left for the herring fishings — thus allowing the marines to be withdrawn from Skye in June 1885 (79) — the climate of crofting opinion was such as to make it obvious that the agitation was far from finished. The winter of 1885-86 brought renewed outbreaks of unrest. In districts as far apart as Ardnamurchan and Lewis, peatstacks and haystacks were burned and other acts of terrorism committed. (80) In Skye it was still 'impossible to get officers to serve writs', (81) with the result, as Lord Lovat informed the government in October 1885, that 'the Queen's writ ... does not now run in the island. The lands seized are still mostly in the hands of the law breakers, rents and taxes are unpaid, and many defaulters are still at large'. (82)

To landed proprietors the most worrying aspect of the general lawlessness among their tenantries was the rapid proliferation of rent strikes. In September 1885 Lord MacDonald's estate management appealed to crofters to pay such rents as they could afford — that such an appeal was made at all is an indication of growing desperation. But as Alexander MacDonald ruefully observed, 'not a single farthing was paid, and not a tenant appeared', a phenomenon repeated all over Skye at that year's Martinmas rent collection. (83) In 1880 the crofters of Kilmuir had owed their landlord only £63. In 1883, some three years after the first rent strike on the estate, they had owed him £990. By the end of 1885, however, their arrears totalled £5,718. (84) On the MacDonald estate the same pattern was repeated, crofters' arrears rising from £464 in 1883 to £4,816 in 1885. And in the Outer Isles the situation was, from landlords' viewpoint, no better. (85)

Applied locally, as in Braes and Glendale in 1882, rent strikes were mere irritants — significant in terms of the protest they registered but quite incapable of inflicting serious damage on landowners' finances. But applied on a massive scale, as it was in all of north-west Scotland in 1885-86, the rent strike was a potentially deadly weapon, especially in the context of the serious slump produced in estate revenues by the current collapse of wool prices. (86) When in September 1885 a Skye factor declared that 'unless the law is enforced a good many west coast proprietors must succumb', (87) his warning, though perhaps a little premature, was not without foundation in fact. As a result of the crofting community's rent strikes on the one hand and the effects of agricultural depression on the other, Highland and Hebridean landlords were undoubtedly facing the most serious economic crisis they had known since the early nineteenth century. (88)

It was, no doubt, their growing awareness of and concern about this crisis which induced in Highland landowners that 'general desire ... to come to terms with their crofting tenants' which was noted by Locheil in December 1884, (89) and which assumed a concrete shape in the following month when about fifty Highland proprietors or their representatives met at Inverness to discuss the crofting question. The outcome of their deliberations was an offer to provide crofters with leases, revise their rents and guarantee the payment of compensation for any improvements made by crofters to their houses or holdings. (90) Made two or three years earlier, these proposals would almost certainly have evoked a favourable response — for even in 1883, as the minister of Glenelg had remarked to the Napier Commission, many crofters would have been satisfied with 'some little concession' from their landlords. (91) By 1885, however, that time had passed. The proprietors' offer was universally — and correctly — interpreted as a sign of weakness rather than generosity, the *Oban Times'* pronouncement that 'The Highland lairds are on their knees' being echoes by crofters everywhere. (92) 'No concessions of the landlords can settle matters,' a Kilmuir crofter declared at an HLLRA meeting in January 1885. 'We want no concessions. We want our just rights.' (93) That such opinions were widely held and that they were capable of receiving political expression was convincingly demonstrated by the results of the general election held towards the end of 1885. With no fewer than four of the five crofting constituencies falling to its candidates rather than to the Liberal or Tory lairds who were their traditional incumbents, that election was an outstanding victory for and vindication of the HLLRA (94) — the crofting community celebrating the occasion by staging torchlit processions and lighting bonfires on the hilltops. (95) 'The enemy have left the spoils and fled before the conquering hosts of land law reform,' proclaimed the ecstatic editor of the *Oban Times*. 'From the Mull of Kintyre to the Butt of Lewis the land is before us.' (96)

What were the reasons for this remarkable success? The Liberal and Tory discomfiture in the Highlands, *The Scotsman* informed its readers whom it had previously assured of the certain defeat of HLLRA 'carpet-baggers', (97) was attributable to the fact that crofters, knowing 'nothing of politics', had been 'deluded with promises of nearly everything they desire'. (98) An alternative explanation – and one that is at once more convincing and less insulting to the collective intelligence of the crofting community – is to be found in the strength and effectiveness of the HLLRA's Highland organisation. As was shown by a confidential investigation carried out for the government in the summer of 1886, the majority of the mainland crofting population were members of the HLLRA. And in the islands the Association's strength was even more impressive. In Skye, for example, it was 'probable that every man of the crofter and cottar classes, with many merchants and artisans besides, [was] an enrolled member'. (99) It was this almost unanimous adherence of the crofting population to its aims and objectives which made possible the HLLRA's spectacular triumph at the polls.

As a political organisation – and it has some claim to the title of first mass political party in Britain (100) – the HLLRA was clearly organised from above and outwith the crofting community. But for its existence the crofters' movement would not have achieved such a wide unity, such a well developed sense of political purpose; while the fact that they possessed allies more able than they in the arts of politics and publicity greatly strengthened the crofting community's position vis-a-vis that of their landlords – something of which both sides in the conflict were well aware. In 1886 John MacPherson, Glendale crofters' leader, 'could say in all truth and sincerity that if it had not been for the ... H.L.L.R.A. he would have lost heart long ago'. (101) Two years previously one of the trustees of the Glendale estate had had made essentially the same point in a letter to Sheriff Ivory. 'The people could easily be dealt with,' he wrote. 'But the London agitators cannot.' (102)

The HLLRA, however, was more than a political party. It was a social movement; and as such its inspiration and organisation came from below, from the crofting community itself. Of the many thousands of people who took part in the Association's campaign of protest in the rural Highlands only a handful were not crofters or cottars. A few teachers – of whom the best known was Donald MacRae, an effective organiser of direct action in Lewis in the later 1880s (103) – played some part in the agitation. And in Catholic areas like Barra, South Uist and Arisaig the local priests gave occasionally outspoken support to the movement. (104) The vast majority of the protestant clergy were, however, opposed to it. An occasional Free Church minister, of whom the Rev. Finlay Graham of Sleat was the outstanding example, urged his congregation to join the HLLRA. (105) But most of his colleagues – while refraining from following the example of the Rev. Hector Cameron of Barvas, Lewis, a man who denounced rent strikes as sinful (106) – did not hesitate to join the Church of Scotland's parish ministers in what the *Oban Times* called an 'unholy alliance' against the Association. (107)

That the HLLRA was able to overcome the clerical opposition to its policies and programme is another tribute to its own strength — a truth grasped by D.H. MacFarlane when he remarked that he won the 1885 election in Argyll 'with the powers of heaven and earth against him. The landlords were the earth and the ministers were the heavens.' (108) In view of what was said in an earlier chapter about the Free Church's part in promoting a sense of community among crofters, its role in the land war might seem a strange one. By the 1880s, however, the Free Church had generally lost its initial identification with the forces of antilandlordism. Its ministers had no wish to change the social status quo. They felt themselves, on the contrary, indebted to landlords who had rendered them valuable services. Thus the Free Church minister of Kilmuir, in his evidence to the Napier Commission, went out of his way to express his gratitude to William Fraser, the parish's owner and arguably the worst landlord in the Highlands, for all that he had done for the Free Church. (109) The 1880s therefore witnessed a partial reversal in the earlier roles of the Free and Established Churches. It was the ministers of the latter body — many of whom had practically no congregation — who had least to lose by joining the HLLRA. And the clerics who took the most active part in its activities were, therefore, Church of Scotland ministers led by the young and fervently radical Donald MacCallum who was minister at Waternish at the height of the troubles in Skye. (110) But though the latter greatly distinguished themselves — Donald MacCallum enjoyed the double distinction of having been tried before the presbytery of Skye on a charge of having 'incited crofters to class hatred', (111) and of having been subsequently arrested during a round up of HLLRA 'agitators' in Skye in the autumn of 1886 (112) — their part in the land reform movement was quite minimal compared to that of crofters themselves.

Most committed to the HLLRA and to the cause it represented were those men who had grown up in the relatively prosperous and secure 1860s and 1870s and who were not prepared, as some older crofters undoubtedly were, to fatalistically accept a relapse into social and economic uncertainty. 'The old men had not had the same advantages of education that the young men had,' a Lochcarron crofter told an HLLRA conference in 1886:

They must put the fear of the landlord and his satellites, the factors ... out of the old men. They must try and make them realise that the powers that be are nothing to the powers that the generality of the people possess. (113)

The younger generation of crofters were thus more receptive than their elders to the politically radical notions transmitted into the Highlands by John Murdoch and his associates. (114) Their movement did not, however, represent a complete break with the past. Its local organisation, though standardised in accordance with HLLRA instructions, was broadly developed by crofters themselves in the early days of the agitation and in it the influences of the crofting community's earlier and formative experiences were clearly visible. HLLRA meetings, it was observed at the time, were 'always held in the open air in defiance of rain and tempest' and at them, 'the person selected to preside opens and closes the proceedings with prayer'. (115) The resemblance between these gatherings and the assemblages convened by 'the men' during the heyday of the religious revivals of the early nineteenth century was not coincidental; (116) nor was the fact that the local leaders of the Association — men cast in the mould of John MacPherson whose meetings were punctuated by passionately delivered Gaelic prayers and whose eloquence in his native tongue was said to be such as to move men to tears or to fury (117) — occupied positions in the townships that were in all respects analogous to those held by *na daoine* of a preceding generation. By the 1880s, when the Highland land war was at its height, 'the men' had largely faded from the scene and their populist religion had been institutionalised within the framework of the Free Church. But while the Free Church inherited Highland evangelicalism, it was John MacPherson and a host of other HLLRA activists who inherited 'the men's' leadership of and influence over the crofting community. And the contribution of the crofting population's historical heritage to the Highland land reform movement of the 1880s was as obvious in what its local leaders said as it was in the ways in which they said it.

That traditional beliefs and customs, notably those which enshrined the bond between chief and clan, could be, and undoubtedly were, a retarding influence on the development of a radical challenge to Highland landlordism constituted the theme of a previous chapter. (118) Not every aspect of the crofting community's traditional culture fell within this category, however; and there were in existence in the nineteenth-century Highlands a number of concepts — most of them derived from the more or less remote past of the Celtic peoples — that were quite capable of being transformed into important components of a distinctive critique of landlordism. Crofters, for example, never became reconciled to the right of private ownership of game, a fact which caused Highland landlords no little trouble — especially in the second half of the nineteenth century when sporting preserves came to occupy an important place in estate economies. (119) 'It is not easy to convince a Highlander that a landlord has a better right to a deer, a moor fowl, or a salmon than he has himself,' it had been despairingly noted in 1802, 'because he considers them the unconfined bounty of heaven.' (120) And in the face of all that landed proprietors could subsequently provide in the way of game laws and gamekeepers, those notions — enshrined in the Gaelic saying that all Highlanders have a right to a deer from the hill, a tree from the wood and a fish from the river (121) — exhibited a remarkable power of survival and were eventually incorporated into the corpus of myth, belief and opinion by which the crofters of the 1880s justified their onslaught on their landlords. 'The fish that was yesterday miles away from the land was claimed by the landlord the moment it reached the shore,' declared a crofter at an HLLRA meeting in Skye in 1884:

> And so also were the birds of the air as soon as they flew over his land. The law made it so, because landlords were themselves the lawmakers, and it was a wonder that the poor man was allowed to breathe the air of heaven and drink from the mountain stream without having the factors and the whole of the county police pursuing him as a thief. (122)

Of similar derivation, but of much greater importance, was the concept that the tribe, clan or community which lived and worked upon the land had a right to permanent occupation of it. (123)

The latter belief, as far as landlords were concerned, had no historical or legal validity. Throughout recorded history, they thought, their ancestors — as chiefs and feudatories — had been the outright and recognised possessors of the land. Thus the Duke of Argyll, writing at the height of the crofters' agitation, saw in the earliest feudal charters of the Highland nobility 'all the well known powers and obligations of ownership in land' (124) — a view shared by MacLeod of Dunvegan who could see no historical grounds for the 'extraordinary assumption' that the Highland people had ever had any recognised rights in the land. (125) Of the Duke's theories crofters held a very low opinion — a Lochaline crofter remarking to the Napier Commission that 'We are not to be bamboozled by his Grace's scientific conundrums.' (126) And with a complete disregard for the claims of their chiefs and landlords, the commons of the clans and their crofter descendants have, in fact, always clung steadfastly to the notion of the indissolubility of their ties with the land from which they have scraped their often precarious subsistence.

In the medieval and early modern Highlands this belief usually took the form of an idea that prolonged occupation of land gave a right to a 'kindness' or permanent tenancy of it. Referred to in Gaelic as *duthchas,* a 'kindness' was generally thought to have been established when a family had maintained the effective occupancy of a township or joint farm for three generations or more; and, being recognised by the whole community, it was supposed to be inviolable. Thus the tacksmen of such farms followed each other in patrilineal succession and any attempt by the feudal superior of the land in question to establish another family on the farm was apt to be resisted by the entire clan, even to the point of bloodshed. (127) Especially strongly expressed among clans like the MacGregors or MacDonalds of Islay and Keppoch whose feudal rights were inadequate or uncertain, (128) this ancient concept of the inalienability of the land of the kindred persisted into the eighteenth and nineteenth centuries. In 1750, for example, it was noted that

> throughout Lochaber, and the adjacent Wild Countries, the Farms have always been given to the Cadets of the Lesser Families that are the Heads of Tribes, which they possess for Ages without any Lease, and look upon them as their right of Inheritance; and when they are not able to pay their Rent and are turned out, they look upon the Person who takes these Farms after them, as usurping their right. These people have often Refused to take a written Lease, thinking that by so doing they give up their right of possession. (129)

The latter notion, that to accept a lease was to surrender a recognised right — here observed amongst the tacksmen of the 1750s — was resuscitated by the crofters of the 1880s, the Portree branch of the HLLRA declaring in March 1886, for example,

> that the land of the Highlands, belonging as it does to the people of the Highlands, the acceptance of leases by crofters is not necessary, and is besides a tacit admission of rights which they repudiate as inconsistent with the security of tenure to which they are entitled. (130)

This frequently observed belief that Highland tenants had 'a kind of hereditary right' to their holdings (131) survived the state-supported enforcement of private property in land for the simple reason that, as far as small tenants were concerned, legal rights to land ownership had no moral sanction whatsoever. Highland tenants, as the Earl of Selkirk observed in 1805,

> well know of how little avail was a piece of parchment and a lump of wax under the old system of the Highlands. They reproach their landlord with ingratitude and remind him that but for their fathers he would now have no estate. The permanent possession which they had always retained of their paternal farms they consider only as their just right from the share they had borne in the general defence, and can see no difference between the title of the chief and their own. (132)

Another early nineteenth century writer, John MacCulloch, went so far as to attribute all crofting discontents to this one — according to him outmoded — belief:

But all these complaints, against servitudes as against rent, are the remains of those ancient feelings, from which the Highland people were used to consider the lands as their own; a feeling which was in full force in many places not many years ago ... [when ... the people considered themselves the proprietors of their farms; as not liable to be ejected at the will of their Chief, and scarcely even to compulsory rent. (133) Transmuted from one generation of crofters to the next, these beliefs were as strongly held in the 1880s as they had been when the tenants of Kildonan told Patrick Sellar and his associates 'that they were entitled to keep *their* Grounds'. (134) Thus the delegates who came forward from the crofting townships to give evidence to the Napier Commission 'often expressed' the opinion 'that the small tenantry of the Highlands have an inalienable title to security of tenure in their possessions', an impression which, the Commissioners recorded, was 'indigenous to the country though it has never been sanctioned by legal recognition and has long been repudiated by the actions of the proprietors'. (135) And as was recognised by land reformers in the Highlands and in Ireland — where the peasantry had inherited the same Celtic traditions (136) — these sentiments were quite capable of being accommodated into the radical anti-landlordism of the later nineteenth century.

Thus the fact that the British parliament recognised the validity of the customary landholding system of Ulster — a region where tenants had long been held to have some sort of permanent stake in the land — and incorporated it in the Irish Land Act of 1870 seemed, to John Murdoch, 'to show very forcibly the importance of cherishing at least some of the traditions which have been handed down from father to son'. (137) 'It would never do,' he wrote in 1876, 'for Highlanders to lose sight of their ancient rights ... in the land.' (138) And nine years later, when the land war which Murdoch had done so much to precipitate was well under way, he was still hammering home the same message. 'Highlanders had never forgotten,' he declared in a speech at Portree in September 1885, 'that the land was theirs and that landlordism was a violent encroachment upon the divine rights of the people.' (139) It was a doctrine that integrated very neatly not only with the longstanding belief in a popular claim to the land but also with the commonly held view — examined at some length in a previous chapter (140) — that clan society had been distinguished by equity, harmony and plenty. Until 1745, according to Dr. Charles Cameron, the Liberal M.P. who was one of the crofting community's earliest parliamentary advocates, 'the cultivators of the soil had a proprietary right in it'. Like the other features of the Highlands' golden age, however, that right had been destroyed at Culloden: 'It was only after the Highland rising in 1745, when the tribal jurisdiction was swept away, that the Highland chief was transformed into a position analogous to that of the English landlord'. (141) To a clan historian like Alexander MacKenzie, such a sweeping claim appeared 'crude and inaccurate'; (142) and as a piece of historical analysis it did, indeed, leave a lot to be desired. (143) As its propagators were well aware, however, such an interpretation of the past corresponded very closely to the beliefs of crofters themselves — beliefs which, as Joseph Chamberlain discovered during his tour of the north-west Highlands in the spring of 1887, existed 'deep down in the minds of the people. You find it universal. They are all of the opinion that they have claims which no lapse of time can possibly extinguish'. (144)

To such notions statesmen like Gladstone and — much more surprisingly — Lord Salisbury paid lip service; (145) and if confirmation of their validity was needed it could be found in the writings of liberal economists like John Stuart Mill whose opinion that 'the land of every country belongs to the people of that country' was viewed very favourably by John Murdoch and other Highland land reformers. (146) These and similar precepts of nineteenth-century political economy the Irish Land League had attempted, with some success, to relate to the Celtic tradition — Parnell, for example, saying of the speech that launched the land war in Ireland that

> We went down to Mayo and we preached the eternal truth that the land of a country, the water of a country, the air of a country, belong to no man. They were not made by any man and they belong to all the human race. (147)

The leaders of the land agitation in the Highlands undertook a similar task, the Rev. Donald MacCallum proclaiming, for instance, that 'The land is our birthright, even as the air, the light of the sun, and the water belong to us as our birthright.' (148)

Such declarations could be substantiated by reference not only to the writings of Mill and other economists but also to the works of eighteenth-century philosophers like Rousseau. (149) As far as most crofters were concerned, however, the obvious source of confirmation of the rightness of their beliefs about the land was the Bible — whose important place in crofting life has already been mentioned. (150) In it, and especially in the Old Testament, they found apparently instructive parallels between their own plight and that of the Jews (151) — a point well made in an 1884 pamphlet about the Highland land question:

> By the Mosaic legislation the land was to be held under a tribal tenure, the soil being apportioned among the families by whom it was cultivated or used for pasturing their flocks and herds; and this also appears for ages to have been the custom among the Celtic population of the British Isles... These ancient Hebrew land laws ... were set aside by the greedy selfishness of nobles and princes... And if the land secured to the tribes of Israel could be filched from the people in such a manner, it is not to be wondered at that the Scottish Highlander, whose Bible is his *vade mecum* ... should come to view his present condition in respect to the land as somewhat analogous to that of the poorer Jews in the later days of the Jewish monarchy. (152)

The accuracy of that analogy may be subject to dispute. But about the sincerity of crofters' belief that the Bible both sanctioned the notion that landlords had usurped the land and confirmed the validity of their own claim to the land, there can be no question.

The declaration of a Tiree crofter who was imprisoned for his part in a land raid on the Duke of Argyll's Tiree estate in 1886 speaks for itself:

> He held that he was standing on the side of justice and he had the Bible as his authority. The earth belonged to the people and not to the Duke of Argyll or any landlord. (153)

The texts on which these views were based were the common currency of HLLRA politics and were to be seen at any one of scores of crofters' meetings:

> The earth is mine ... The earth is the Lord's and the fulness thereof ... Woe unto them that join house to house, that lay field to field ... The earth He hath given to the children of men. (154)

'Unless landlords can prove that we are not of Adam's race at all,' wrote John MacPherson to MacLeod of Dunvegan, there were to be found in the Bible 'letters of agreement from God pronouncing our claim and right in the land.' (155) And the same point was made by Norman Stewart, a crofter at Valtos on the Kilmuir estate in Skye, and a branch president of the HLLRA. 'If the landlords consulted Moses or Joshua,' he told a mass meeting at Valtos in 1885, 'they would find there substantial evidences as to who are the rightful owners of the soil. The Lord Advocate and

Sheriff Ivory can quote Acts Georges and John, but we can quote the Act of God –
the Bible.' (156)

The 1880s were a time of widespread agrarian unrest. Within the confines of the
British Isles alone, existing tenurial arrangements were being effectively challenged in
Ireland and Wales as well as in the Highlands. (157) Land reform and land reformers
were consequently much in vogue, the latter ranging from Joseph Chamberlain, the
radical politician who hoped to tie the rural vote to the Liberal party, (158) to Henry
George, the American propagandist to whom land nationalisation seemed the obvious
panacea for all social and economic ills. (159) Both Chamberlain and Henry George
took an active interest in crofting affairs. (160) But Georgite ideals made little impact
on the crofters' movement which, as preceding paragraphs make clear, was, in its
philosophy as well as in its organisation, a distinctively Highland creation. (161) And
while it would be unwise as well as unjust to minimise the contribution made to that
movement by men who were not crofters – John Murdoch, D.H. MacFarlane, G.B.
Clark and their colleagues to mention only a few – it evidently embodied aspirations
and reflected experiences that were uniquely those of the crofting community.

By the mid-1880s, in short, the crofting community had emerged as a coherent
political – as well as social – entity, and crofters had at last begun to take control of
their own destinies. It is that fact that made the 1880s – on the face of it, a period of
increasing poverty and misery – a time of hope for crofters. The commercial landlordism introduced into the Highlands in the eighteenth century was at last on the retreat.
Change was in the air. And for the first time in the nineteenth century Gaelic poetry
took on an optimistic tone – best exemplified in the work of *Mairi Mhor nan Oran,*
that committed and outspoken land reformer whose songs, it is said, contributed
significantly to the HLLRA's success. (162) Small tenants everywhere in the north-
west acquired a new and striking self-confidence. 'The crofters,' a *Scotsman* correspondent reported from Skye on polling day in the parliamentary elections of 1885,

> were most enthusiastic and each approached the polling station with an air of
> independence which would have seemed singularly strange to any visitor who had
> not seen a Skye crofter during the last five years. (163)

The political consequence of that 'air of independence' was the arrival of a 'Crofters'
Party' at Westminster in January 1886. (164) Too few to wield much parliamentary
power, the four members of that party represented a mass movement which had
thrown down the gauntlet to Highland landlordism and had plunged north-west
Scotland into its greatest political, administrative and social crisis since the demise of
Jacobitism. It was the extent of their support among crofters that gave D.H. MacFarlane
(Argyll), Charles Fraser-MacIntosh (Inverness-shire), Dr. Roderick MacDonald (Ross
and Cromarty), and G.B. Clark (Caithness) their political significance. (165) And it
is a measure of the success of the crofting community's campaign that they took
their seats in a parliament preparing to devote more time to Highland affairs than any
of its predecessors since the 1740s.

By 1885 it had become apparent to Gladstone's government and indeed to every
thinking observer – with the exception of Highland landlords (166) who should not,
perhaps, be included in the latter category – that the only possible solution to the

crofting question lay in a legislative reform of the Highland land system. (167) The requisite legislation should logically have been based on the recommendations contained in the Napier Commission's report. The problem, as the home secretary remarked on more than one occasion, was that these recommendations had not met with acceptance in any quarter. (168) One landlords' spokesman thought the report 'hardly worth discussing'. (169) Another dismissed it as 'full of inconsistencies and anomalies'. (170) And crofters, as already mentioned, had indicated a very strong preference for a measure more akin to the Irish Land Act of 1881 than to the proposals of Lord Napier and his colleagues. To this the cabinet were not averse. Gladstone, like Harcourt and Joseph Chamberlain, felt a great deal of sympathy for crofters and was anxious to do something for them. (171) Besides, the Act by which crofters set so much store was the prime minister's own creation and one of which he was inordinately proud. It was consequently resolved, in Gladstone's words, to endorse 'the substantial application of the Irish Land Act to the Highland parishes'; and a Bill to that effect was introduced in the Commons in May 1888. (172)

That particular Bill fell with the government in June. (173) By the New Year, however, a new Liberal administration was in power, there were four crofters' M.P.s in the Commons, and so effective had the agitation in the Highlands become that even *The Scotsman* — the paper most committed to the landlords' cause — felt obliged to admit that 'the condition of some parts of the Highlands has become so serious that the urgency of the crofter question can scarcely be exaggerated'. (174) Conservatives and Liberals alike having consequently concluded that some sort of remedial legislation was urgently required, (175) the refurbished version of the previous year's Bill which was hastily introduced by the government met with little opposition. Even the Duke of Argyll — who had resigned from Gladstone's cabinet in protest against its Irish land legislation and who had subsequently become the Highland landlords' principal parliamentary spokesman and an arch-opponent of all land law reform — agreed not to oppose the new measure, 'not because he thought it was a good Bill', but because 'he could not deny that they were in a position that compelled them to agree to something being done'. (176) Arthur Balfour, soon to be secretary of state for Scotland and already the Conservative party's principal spokesman on Highland affairs, took a similar line. (177) And on 25th June the Bill passed into law.

The Crofters Act of 1886 — the only major piece of legislation to be successfully enacted by Gladstone's short-lived third administration (178) — applied to parishes in Argyll, Inverness-shire, Ross and Cromarty, Sutherland, Caithness and the northern isles where there were in 1886, or had been in the preceding eighty years, holdings consisting of arable land held with rights of common pasture, and in which there were tenants paying annual money rents of under £30. The Act therefore affected almost every crofter in north-west Scotland — the exceptions consisting of the tiny minority who held leases; a state of affairs very different from that envisaged by the Napier Commission which, in an attempt to promote the enlargement of holdings, had recommended that legal protection should be bestowed only on the relatively small number of crofting tenants who paid annual rents of £6 or more. (179) Subject only to certain easily fulfilled conditions, the Act guaranteed security of tenure to crofters and gave them the right, on their relinquishing a holding, to claim compensation from the landlord for improvements made to it by themselves or by their family predecessors.

The Act also enabled a tenant to bequeath his croft to a member of his family and, in the most important of its provisions, set up a land court, the Crofters Commission, which was empowered to fix fair rents for crofters' holdings, subject these rents to a septennial revision, cancel all or part of any accumulated arrears, and generally administer the Act and any subsequent crofting legislation. (180)

By the standards of an age accustomed to regarding landed property and private contracts between landlords and tenants as inviolable, even sacrosanct, the Crofters Act was a measure so radical as to be little short of revolutionary. Thus *The Scotsman* condemned it as 'a great infringement of the rights of property'; while Fraser of Kilmuir owner of one of the most disturbed districts in the Highlands, discerned in it an indication of 'communism looming in the future'. (181) Such shrieks of alarm from the propertied classes were inevitable and not very important. Of more significance, however, was the reaction of the crofting community and its parliamentary representatives. Should the Act meet with their approval, peace would return to the Highlands. Should they reject it, unrest would inevitably continue. And from the first it was clear that crofters regarded the Act as far from satisfactory.

Because it was explicitly modelled on the Irish Land Act of 1881, the Crofters Act met many of the demands embodied in the HLLRA's Dingwall Programme for the simple reason that the Programme had been drawn up with Irish legislation very much in mind. (182) In one crucial respect, however, the 1886 Act fell seriously short of meeting crofters' wishes: it contained little provision for making more land available to them. In part, perhaps, this was the fault of the HLLRA leadership. By continually harping on the similarities between the Irish tenantry's case — a case whose justice had already been conceded — and that of the crofting community, they had obscured the vital difference between the Irish and Highland situations. Irish agriculture was essentially arable and the Irish smallholders' greatest need was for freedom from rack-renting and capricious eviction. These things, it is true, were not unknown in the Highlands. But Highland agriculture was essentially pastoral and crofters' greatest need was for more land (183) — something that was little appreciated by some of the HLLRA's urban adherents. (184)

The government, on the other hand, were not unaware of the peculiarities of the Highland situation. Both the lord advocate and the home secretary well understood the divergences between the agrarian systems of Ireland and north-west Scotland. The former, at least, thought that crofters' calls for land redistribution were 'by far the most important' of their demands, and was 'sensible that the expectations, or at all events the hopes, which the crofting class ... cherish, will not be satisfied unless legislative provision is made for giving them more land'. (185) The Liberal administration. however, felt unable to make any such provision. Crofters were too poor to buy land. The only conceivable alternative, therefore, was that the government should itself buy the necessary land and lease it to crofters. The latter procedure was, in fact, eventually and successfully adopted. (186) But to the Liberal party of the mid-1880s it seemed to involve too damaging a departure from the cherished principles of laissez-faire. That, at least, was the opinion of the lord advocate. He did 'not suppose', he informed the Commons, that such a proposal 'would be entertained'. (187)

The 1886 Act consequently made only one very minor concession to crofters' demands for more land. Where land was available for the enlargement of crofts and where its owner refused to let it to crofting tenants on reasonable terms, any five or more tenants whose holdings were near or adjacent to the land in question could apply to the Crofters Commission for the compulsory enlargement of their crofts. The amount of land that could be regarded as available for such a purpose was very restricted. Land subject to existing leases and certain types of farm land were, for example, excluded − provisions which had the effect of placing most sheep farms and deer forests outwith the measure's already limited scope. (188) Thus, although even this weak gesture in the direction of land settlement made the Crofters Act more daring than the Irish measure on which it was modelled, (189) the enlargement clause proved quite ineffective in practice (190) and, from the outset, did nothing to mollify the land-hungry crofters whom it was intended to appease.

In the Commons, therefore, the crofters' M.P.s declared that, as conceived by the government, the Crofters Bill of 1886 was 'of no advantage to the Highland people' and was likely to prove itself no more than 'a sham and a delusion'. (191) Supported by the Irish nationalists who recognised the crofting community's struggle against landlordism to be analogous to that in which their own rural constituents were engaged, (192) they opposed the Bill through all its parliamentary stages. But since both front benches were determined to accept no amendments to it, the Bill passed into law without the far-reaching land settlement clauses which the four HLLRA members attempted to attach to it. It did so, however, in the midst of an angry chorus of rejection from the crofting community. Thus Kilmuir crofters resolved to 'utterly condemn the so-called Crofters Bill ... and to continue the agitation till the full measure of their just rights to the soil of their ancestors [was] recognised and secured to them by the legislature'. (193) Glendale crofters similarly pledged themselves 'not to rest satisfied without getting all the land of the Highlands for the people of the Highlands'. (194) And though these declarations were made in districts of above average crofting militancy, virtually identical resolutions were carried unopposed at scores of HLLRA meetings from Mull to Cape Wrath, and from Helmsdale to the western seaboard of Lewis. (195)

Most bitter of the crofting community's members were the landless people, the cottars. At an HLLRA meeting in Skye in December 1884 one of them had forcefully observed that

there was considerable talk about the crofters; but there was another class more needful of relief, the cottars ... It would not benefit the cottars a bit though others got a reduction in rent and more land unless they got land for themselves ... and he strongly urged that in any ... settlement of the land question provision should be made for giving land to cottars. (196)

The 1886 Act made no such provision, cottars, in fact, falling almost completely outwith its scope. Their anger and frustration were consequently intense and soon manifested themselves in a new wave of land seizures. In the spring of 1886, while the Crofters Bill was passing through parliament, twenty cottars living at Morvich in Kintail met and declared that they were 'in such a low condition that we must take the land which is lying waste into our own hands to provide food for ourselves and our families'. And in April they began ploughing fields near their landlord's residence, Morvich House, at the head of Loch Duich. (197) There were similar developments in Benbecula. (198) And at an HLLRA meeting in the Tiree township of Baugh on 16th April it was resolved

That as the Government has rejected all or any amendments proposed on behalf of cottars, some of the lands unjustly taken from themselves and their fathers and now lying waste be taken possession of and planted with potatoes. (199)

The land raid thus decided upon followed within a matter of weeks. (200)

These events, together with the decision of the three hundred delegates who attended the HLLRA's annual conference at Bonar Bridge in September to reconstitute the Association as the Highland Land League – the League's principal task being 'to restore to the Highland people their inherent rights in their native soil' (201) – made it clear that crofters did not consider their agitation to be at an end. By the autumn of 1886, however, the political context of that agitation had altered radically. Gladstone government had fallen on the Irish home rule issue; the Liberal party had split on the same question; and a Conservative administration headed by Lord Salisbury had been returned to power. Arthur Balfour, Salisbury's nephew, had taken over the recently created Scottish Office; while the Highland Land League, itself in some disarray on the question of home rule for Ireland, was already showing signs of the dissensions that were, within a very few years, to bring about its fragmentation and collapse. (202) The political disagreements of their leaders did not, it is true, affect crofters' and cottars determination to regain the lands lost during the clearances. But the new government was equally determined to put down disorder and make no more concessions. The passing of the Crofters Act, Balfour believed, had simultaneously deprived Highland unrest of any justification it might once have possessed and given him the moral authority to suppress it. He was, he told the House of Commons in August 1886, 'no fanatical admirer' of the previous administration's crofting legislation:

But one advantage of that Bill I foresaw ... it makes it quite certain that we can exercise the forces of the law and yet be guilty of no hardship to the tenants of the Highlands and Islands. (203)

The 1886 Act was followed, therefore, not by a return to tranquility but by a series of encounters between the crofting community and the forces of law and order that were more bitter and more violent than any which had hitherto occurred.

10. The Highland Land War 3: Coercion and Conciliation, 1886-1896

FIRST to feel the effects of Conservative coercion were the crofters of Tiree who, as already mentioned, (1) had resolved in April 1886 to reoccupy some of the lands of which the island's tenantry had been deprived some thirty or forty years before. (2) Adopted with the then tenantless farm of Greenhill very much in its proposers' minds, the April resolution was soon nullified by an unexpected turn of events: in early May it became known that the island's proprietor, the Duke of Argyll, had let Greenhill to an unusually prosperous crofter. By taking over Greenhill in this fashion, the farm's new tenant was widely considered to have betrayed his fellow crofters. And the consequent bitterness — considerably aggravated by the fact that the offending crofter was an HLLRA member and brother of the president of the Association's Tiree branch — played no little part in precipitating the confrontation which followed. On 22nd May the brothers were expelled from the HLLRA and a few days later Greenhill was occupied by over three hundred men who at once proceeded to allot the farm among the crofters and cottars of nearby townships. (3)

Because Gladstone's government — which was still in power when these events occurred — refused to sanction renewed military intervention in the Hebrides, (4) the forty policemen who landed on the island on 21st July to serve the writs which the Duke of Argyll had taken out against Greenhill's illegal occupants were unescorted by troops. And as such they were no match for the island's crofters. Confronted at Greenhill by a force of men and youths armed with sticks and clubs and outnumbering them by about six to one, the police were obliged to withdraw to the relative security of the inn at Scarinish, their mission unaccomplished. (5) The problem of what they should do next was solved for them by Tiree's crofting population. On the morning of 22nd July the inn was surrounded by the men responsible for the seizure of Greenhill. The police contingent, it was demanded, should immediately withdraw from the island. They left that afternoon. (6)

With the police in full retreat and the government informed, via the Duke of Argyll, that Tiree had passed 'under the rule of savagery', (7) military involvement became inevitable. And on 31st July 1886 — the day after Balfour took over the Scottish Office — a detachment of fifty police escorted by five times that number of marines was landed on the island. (8) Eight crofters, including the new president of Tiree's HLLRA branch, were promptly arrested; and all were subsequently found guilty of mobbing and rioting and deforcement — five being sentenced to six months' imprisonment and the others to four months. (9) Since crofters found guilty of similar offences in the past had been fined a few shillings or jailed for two or three weeks, (10) Balfour not unsurprisingly received a veritable spate of protests and representations about the severity of the sentences imposed on the Tiree men. (11) He ignored them. It was a fitting beginning to his Highland policy.

The Tiree difficulty behind him, Balfour turned his attention to Skye where, in the summer of 1886, the crofters' rent strike was as solid as ever — the total of outstanding arrears having passed the £20,000 mark. (12) And because factors invariably doubled as rate collectors, receiving rents and taxes at the same place on the same day, the non-payment of rents entailed an effective embargo on rate payment also. The outcome — seriously aggravated by Skye landlords' refusal to pay *their* share of the rates until they had received their rents — was that, from 1884 onwards, massive arrears of rates quickly accumulated. Deprived of funds, poor law and school boards were forced to borrow heavily until, in the spring of 1886, their credit was exhausted and local government in Skye threatened with complete collapse. (13)

As the ensuing crisis developed, cries of woe went up on all sides. Reginald MacLeod son of MacLeod of Dunvegan, declared Skye to be 'in a state of anarchy'. (14) *The Scotsman* — inevitably — agreed; and added that the chaos was entirely the fault of the Liberal government which had, it was alleged, conspicuously failed to restore some degree of order to the island's affairs. (15) Gladstone's ministers, however, had had their fill of Skye and its seemingly endless troubles, and appeals to them to use troops to enforce the collection of rates elicited only an uncompromising refusal. (16) This policy Balfour at once cast aside. The law enforcement agencies in Skye, the new Scottish secretary noted in September 1886, had been 'demoralised by the ill-usage they have received from the population of the island; ill-usage usually altogether unpunished and never punished adequately'. (17) To restore respect for the law accordingly became Balfour's immediate priority, a delighted Sheriff Ivory being consequently informed that Her Majesty's government considered it 'imperatively necessary' to take 'exceptional measures ... to restore order' in Skye — measures which involved the despatch to the island of a force of marines whose task it would be to ensure that the outstanding rates were paid in full. (18)

On being informed of his intentions, proprietors and their agents not unsurprisingly saw in Balfour the saviour of Highland landlordism from the embattled position into which it had been thrust by the success of the crofters' movement — their new-found optimism being reflected in the reception accorded to the Scottish secretary's proposals by Alexander MacDonald, 'the uncrowned King of Skye', whose many roles included that of solicitor to the island's school and poor law boards. At his instigation, summonses for arrears of rates were quickly taken out against crofters. But proprietors, most of whom owed more money to the local authorities than all the crofters of Skye put together, MacDonald left severely alone. 'Defaulting landlords,' he thought, 'should be proceeded against, if proceeded against at all, by some different and less summary process.' (19) By the 1880s, however, the political influence of the landowning class was on the wane even in the Tory party. And to MacDonald's chagrin it soon became clear that Balfour, who was subsequently to describe Irish landlords in terms that were little short of contemptuous, (20) had an equally low opinion of the pretensions of their Highland counterparts. Unless landlords and tenants were 'placed on exactly the same footing', the Scottish secretary declared, he would forbid the deployment of troops in Skye and leave the island's owners to sort out their own problems. (21)

Even with a Conservative administration in power, then, there was evidently to be no return to the days when a Highland landlord was almost automatically assured of government support in dealing with an unruly tenantry. And to that extent the first Crofters Act — itself the product of political pressures generated by the crofting community — marked a decisive decline in Highland proprietors' power to influence Highland affairs. That power was by no means eliminated. But after 1886 the pattern of events in the Highlands was increasingly controlled — or at least dominated by — central government or by official agencies established by it. These agencies (the first of which was, of course, the Crofters Commission), though seldom subject to democratic control in any real sense of the term, (22) have always been to some extent responsive to crofters' demands — especially when these demands have been vociferously expressed. Thus while British governments, after 1886 as before, have had an interest in maintaining order in the Highlands their policies — despite the continuing political influence of landlordism — have not always been the ones that landowners would have chosen. The great achievement of the crofters of the 1880s, in other words, was that they made impossible a continuation of the situation in which north-west Scotland was ruled in flat defiance of the interests of the crofting community. And in the autumn of 1886, in tacit recognition of this novel state of affairs, Skye landlords were forced to give way and pay their outstanding rates. (23)

At once, however, a new difficulty arose — one that showed that although the balance of power had shifted against them, Highland landlords were still able to act vindictively against their tenants. The military, it had originally been agreed on all sides, were not to be used to collect rents, as opposed to rates, until the Crofters Commission had fixed fair rents for crofters — a task that would obviously take several years to complete. (24) As soon as Skye landowners' rates had been paid, however, Alexander MacDonald informed the authorities that it was the proprietors' opinion that the payment of rates 'on rents not recovered' entitled them to enforce the collection of overdue rents and to expect military support in so doing. (25) MacDonald, Balfour angrily concluded, 'thinks he can presume on our known desire to restore law and order, and that once having got the troops he can use them in his way and for his purposes'. (26) Equally suspicious of MacDonald's intentions were Skye's crofting tenants who saw in their landlords' manoeuvrings an attempt to circumvent the provisions of the 1886 Act by forcibly collecting arrears of rent before the Crofters Commission had had time to decide what proportion of these arrears should be paid. (27) Eventually checked by fresh legislation — introduced, in Balfour's words, to mitigate the 'considerable local disturbance and political difficulty' which they provoked (28) — these activities were, in the autumn of 1886, largely unaffected by official appeals to Skye landlords to desist from the collection of outstanding rents. (29) And although only fifty-eight of the island's crofters were in fact proceeded against for arrears of rent, the tenants singled out for attention were, as Sheriff Ivory put it, 'those who had taken a prominent part in refusing to pay any rent whatever for the last 3 or 4 years' — in other words, the local leaders of the Land League. (30) Harassment of this type, while not uncongenial to the sheriff, undoubtedly contributed to the troubles which followed the arrival of Balfour's expeditionary force on Skye.

Under Ivory's personal command and consisting of forty policemen and seventy-five marines, the expedition reached Skye at the beginning of October 1886, the redoubtable sheriff commencing operations at dawn on the 7th by landing a contingent of

police and marines at Loch Pooltiel — their objectives being the serving of summonses
for arrears of rates on the crofters of Glendale. (31) Although Ivory and his men were
the targets for volleys of 'coarse epithets in Gaelic', (32) their mission was accomplished
without violence on either side — as were similar forays to other parts of Skye, 358
summonses being served in two weeks that were remarkably free from clashes of any
kind. (33) There remained, however, the delicate — and to most people offensive —
task of poinding and selling in lieu of rates the effects of the 243 crofters who, despite
all Ivory's endeavours, refused to settle their tax accounts. And a week before the
process of confiscation was due to begin there emerged a hint of the sort of difficulties
likely to be experienced by the authorities: a number of crofters whose rates were still
outstanding drove their cattle into the hills in an attempt to prevent their confiscation.

The expedition's second phase, like the first, opened at Glendale. But on this
occasion peace did not prevail, verbal abuse being supplemented with a few clods
and stones. And on the Kilmuir estate a few days later the 'uncompromising attitude
of hostility' observed among the Glendale tenantry (35) erupted into violence. At
Bornaskitaig on 25th October sheriff-officers were prevented from entering crofters'
houses and they and their police escorts were pelted with stones, mud and 'handfuls
of filth from the manure heaps'. An accompanying detachment of marines were
ordered to intervene and, while they held back an angry crowd at bayonet point, six
crofters were arrested. (36) At the nearby township of Heribusta, meanwhile, a
sheriff-officer and two policemen — who did not have the benefit of military protection — were being similarly assaulted. (37) And on the following day a crowd of
about thirty men and women armed with sticks, graips and other weapons successfully prevented a sheriff-officer from serving writs for arrears of rent on some of
Lord MacDonald's tenants at Woodend — a township some six miles to the west of
Portree. (38)

To Ivory these events were a godsend. Suspending the poinding operations, he
launched a purge against the crofters responsible for them. During the next few days
Heribusta was repeatedly raided by troops and police — on one occasion every house
in the township was searched at one a.m; on another the local Free Church was
surrounded by marines while the Sunday service was in progress. At first these
endeavours proved vain. The wanted men had fled to the hills in a manner reminiscent
of the aftermath of Culloden, and only one woman was arrested. (39) The fugitives
no doubt hoped that on this, as on former occasions, the authorities would eventually
abandon their quest. But Ivory persisted. And in the end the November weather
forced his elusive quarries to surrender. (40) At Woodend, meanwhile, Ivory had better
luck. Before daybreak on 29th October a strong force of police took up positions on
the hills above the settlement while another police contingent, commanded by the
sheriff himself, approached it along the road from Portree. Ten men and a woman,
all of whom had participated in the events of three days before, were apprehended
while trying to escape to the relative security of the hills. (41)

These arrests were the first of a whole series. At the beginning of November a
youth and two boys were apprehended for placing boulders on the road to Elgol,
and when crofters at Broadford demonstrated against their arrest, two men found
themselves jailed on charges of mobbing and rioting. (42) On 9th November a
speaker at a Land League meeting at Portree referred to Ivory as a liar. He was

promptly imprisoned on a charge of slandering a judge and magistrate; and next day two more Land League members were arrested on similar charges. (43) On 13th November John MacPherson and the Rev. Donald MacCallum — undoubtedly the two most prominent Land Leaguers on the island — were arrested on charges of 'promoting an unlawful agitation'. (44) The next day was a Sunday. It found the incumbent of Waternish parish church languishing in a cell in Portree Jail. (45)

To these events the Land League leadership reacted with an understandable bitterness. Alexander MacKenzie declared Skye to be in the grip of a 'veritable reign of terror'; while G.B. Clark compared Ivory's 'high handed proceedings' to those of 'a Turkish Pasha in Macedonia'. (46) But to criticism from such sources Ivory was quite immune. His conduct of affairs in Skye had the backing of the island's landlords — MacLeod of Dunvegan, for example, thought that Ivory had shown the Skye crofting community that 'law and order were only slumbering' and were now to be 'restored to life and vigour'. (47) And even more important, the sheriff had the Scottish secretary's unquestioning public support. (48) The whole-hearted endorsement of the Royal Irish Constabulary's brutal suppression of unrest in the Irish countryside which distinguished Balfour's conduct of Ireland's affairs on his being moved to Dublin in 1887 had its origins in his suppression of the Skye crofters' movement in the autumn of 1886. (49) It is not surprising, therefore, that the man to whom John MacPherson referred as 'that most heartily hated member Mr. Balfour', (50) was in Ivory's opinion, a heroic figure: 'the first to show the true way of restoring law and order in a disaffected district'. (51)

That law and order had been restored to Skye was undoubted. In December, with most of his numerous prisoners being despatched to jail for periods of one, two or three months and with the greater part of the crofting population's rates arrears at last collected, Ivory was able to inform a suitably gratified Balfour that the island was 'in a much more tranquil and law respecting state than it has been since the land agitation first commenced' — a diagnosis confirmed by the regular police reports from the 'disturbed districts'. (52) The winter of 1886-87 was the most uneventful that Skye had experienced for several years, the tranquillising effect of Ivory's campaign of repression being supplemented by a marked change in crofters' attitudes to the 1886 Act — a change wrought in January 1887 by the Crofters Commission's announcement of its first adjudications on crofting rents.

The crofters affected were the tenants of a number of Sutherland proprietors and their rents were reduced on average by about a quarter, while no less than half their arrears were cancelled. (53) The reductions were no larger than those currently being put into effect on Highland sheep farms. (54) But crofters and their allies had expected little from the Commission and were pleasantly amazed. 'It must be admitted,' remarked the *Oban Times* on reappraising the Crofters Act in the light of these decisions, 'that it inaugurated a new era for Highlanders', (55) a judgement reinforced in May by the Commissioners' publication of the results of their initial investigations in Skye. 262 of Lord MacDonald's crofting tenants were awarded an average rent reduction of 22 per cent. Half their arrears were cancelled. The average reduction granted to the Kilmuir crofters whose cases were reviewed by the Commission was in the order of 40 per cent. And, in a tacit admission of the accuracy of the long-standing allegation that Kilmuir was a rack-rented property, no less than 65 per cent of its tenantry's arrears were written off. (56)

Rent reductions of this magnitude were enormously symbolic as well as financially important victories for crofters. But even more significant, given the fact that few of Skye's crofting tenants had paid any rent at all since 1883, was the extraordinarily high proportion of arrears cancelled by the Commission. In a typically aggressive editorial printed on 2nd January 1886 the *Oban Times* had asserted that 'The landlords' game all along was to starve the people, and now the people can starve the landlords by adhering in a body to the No Rent Policy'. (57) And though landowners were in no danger of dying of hunger it was certainly the case, by 1887, that they were, as one of their representatives put it, 'reduced to great straits for want of money'. (58) To Skye's proprietors, therefore, the prospect of losing the greater part of three or four years' crofting rental was far from welcome and they consequently responded to it by making a new attempt to 'insist upon the payment of their rents'. (59) The outcome was renewed violence, most marked at Elishader, the township on the Kilmuir estate where the first rent strike of the land war had occurred, (60) and where in January 1887 a sheriff-officer serving summonses for arrears of rent was assaulted by crofters. (61) The Scottish Office was not prepared, however, to jeopardise the recently established and still fragile peace in Skye for the sake of landlords who were clearly acting contrary to the spirit, if not the letter, of the 1886 Act. Thus no attempt was made to apprehend the offending crofters. (62) And in the spring, the government considering it 'desirable that some restraint should be placed upon action by landlords', (63) the original Act was amended in such a way as to give the Crofters Commission the power to halt all legal proceedings involving crofters' rents until the rents concerned had been reviewed by the Commission. (64)

While undoubtedly helping to placate crofters, the 1886 Act, however amended, did absolutely nothing — as the Land League had predicted (65) — to alleviate the predicament of the landless. In 1887, in fact, the latter's situation and prospects were rapidly deteriorating. In the Outer Isles, where landlessness was a far from uncommon condition, the spring of 1887 was an exceptionally bleak and cheerless one. Stock prices were low. Supplies of food and seed were scanty. (66) 'There can be no doubt,' the sheriff-substitute at Lochmaddy observed in one of his regular reports to his superiors in Inverness, 'that the mass of the people are very poor, and I am unable to understand how a large portion of the cottar class manage.to keep life and soul together'. (67) One cause of hardship was the steep fall in cattle prices mentioned in a previous chapter. (68) But much more serious, as far as cottars at least were concerned, was the current depression in the herring fishing industry.

Between 1884 and 1886, as a result of record catches and the imposition of higher import duties in the industry's main European markets, herring prices fell catastrophically, boats were laid up and fewer additional hands hired for the summer fishings — a state of affairs which seriously affected the crofters and cottars who were accustomed to obtaining seasonal employment on the herring drifters. (69) At the same time and also because of the slump, herring curers abandoned the traditional practice of buying catches at prices fixed before the season opened — a practice which had involved them in heavy losses when prices collapsed — and insisted that the herring be sold at daily pierhead auctions. Losses were thus passed on to boatowners. And they, in their turn, ended the old system of fixed wages and adopted a method of payment which turned upon each hired hand receiving a small proportion of the proceeds resulting from the sale of his employer's catch. Designed to protect owners from the worst effects of the depression, the new wage structure took little account of the needs of fishermen-crofters who had long met the herring fleets' labour requirements. And with scarcely any warning, the migrant Highlander or Hebridean consequently found himself exposed to all the repercussions of a collapsing market — his earnings being 'at once reduced from an assured maintenance ... to a mere precarious subsistence if he were fortunate enough to obtain an engagement at all'. (70)

Although these developments affected almost all of north-west Scotland, the island of Lewis was undoubtedly hardest hit. Its crofts were smaller and its crofters consequently more dependent on the fishing industry than was the case elsewhere in the region. And, to make matters worse, the island's population contained a much higher than average proportion of landless families — families whose incomes consisted almost entirely of wages earned on the herring drifters. (71) In 1887, it was officially estimated, about £40,000 was lost to the crofting population of Lewis because of the slump in the herring industry, the average wage brought back from the east coast fishings falling from the £20 or £30 of the early 1880s to a mere £1 or £2. (72) The unavoidable social consequences of that catastrophe are illustrated by the predicament of Mary MacLeod, a widow and cottar who lived at Crossbost in the south-eastern corner of the island. Until 1884 her two sons had earned good wages on the herring fleets and the family had, by the standards of their time and place, lived fairly well. By 1887 they were reduced to poverty. (73) And what was true of Mary MacLeod's family was true of cottar families everywhere in Lewis. As the winter of 1887-88 set in, it became apparent that there was, as one official put it, 'a most lamentable state of destitution' among the island's landless population. (74)

One important consequence of the loss of the greater part of their non-agricultural income was to give a new edge to the perennial land hunger of cottars generally and of Lewis cottars in particular. 'Such are the straits of the people of this island owing to the want of land,' it was resolved at a Land League meeting at Garrabost in April 1887,

that the time has come for decisive action; and if relief is not obtained during the current year, it will be necessary to go at the large farms without waiting for the passing of a new law on the subject. (75)

Far from bringing relief, the ensuing months brought a further deterioration in cottars' already unenviable position. And with the onset of a winter of hunger and deprivation land raids became a virtual certainty.

The target in the first instance was Park, the hilly peninsula in the south-eastern part of Lewis which the Seaforth estate management had converted into a sheep farm by means of a series of particularly sweeping clearances — examined at some length in a previous chapter. (76) In 1882 the farm's current lease had expired and no new tenant could be found for it — a common experience at that time of steeply falling wool prices. Nearby crofters and cottars had asked Lady Matheson, owner of Lewis, to divide the farm among them. But their request was rejected and the

more remunerative expedient of transforming it into a deer forest adopted. (77)
The 80,000 acre forest thus established was let to an English industrialist by the
name of Platt; and nowhere, according to a contemporary sportsman's guide, was
there 'a more attractive sporting place'. (78)

Deer forests which, in the 1880s, were being set up or extended in almost every
part of the Highlands, were decidedly unpopular among the crofting community
and its political allies. They were, it was felt, swallowing up vacated sheep farms
which could and should have been made available for settlement by crofting tenants.
The proliferation of sporting preserves was consequently condemned by the Land
League; while crofters vented their feelings on the subject by destroying grouse
eggs and, at Sconser in Skye, slaughtering a number of Lord MacDonald's deer by
the simple expedient of driving them into the sea and drowning them. (79) The
envisaged action against Park was to be on a much grander scale, however. The
forest, it was resolved at a meeting convened at Balallan − one of the townships on
its fringe − on 12th November 1886, 'must be cleared and given to the people'. (80)

At further meetings during the next few days − most of them chaired by Donald
MacRae, schoolmaster at Balallan and an active Land Leaguer − plans were discussed,
duties assigned and firearms collected. (81) Rumours of these activities spread inexorably across the island. But it seems they were not believed by the authorities.
Nothing, at all events, was done to forestall the raid which began as intended on
the morning of 22nd November. (82) Fortunately for the raiders the day dawned
bright and clear, and before sunrise bands of young men, consisting for the most
part of the 'cottars and squatters' who had been 'represented in force' at the meetings at which the raid was planned, (83) set out from Balallan, Leurbost and other
townships within striking distance of the forest. Between them they carried about
fifty serviceable rifles, a number of red flags and a considerable quantity of
baggage − for they planned to camp out for more than one night. The old men,
women and children of the various townships they passed through turned out to
cheer the raiders on their way. And the only opposition they encountered came
from an understandably alarmed Mrs. Platt whose husband was in England on
business. Accosting several of the raiders on their way to the forest she pleaded
with them to turn back. Their reply was crushingly unanswerable. 'My lady,' said
one of them as he marched past her, 'we have no English.'

Having rendezvoused as arranged near the head of Loch Seaforth the raiders,
of whom there were about seven hundred in all, at once set about the task of killing
as many deer as possible. The riflemen were stationed on strategic ridges and passes
while their companions acted as beaters, driving the deer south-eastwards into the
forest, into the wind, and under the muzzles of the guns. All that day the slaughter
continued and as night fell the raiders made camp on the shores of Loch Seaforth.
Tents made from the sails of fishing boats were patched. Bonfires were lit and over
them were roasted haunches of venison − part of the day's kill. (84) The obtaining
of venison was in itself an important reason for participating in the raid − indeed
the sheriff of Ross-shire, who arrived in Lewis within twenty-four hours of the
raid's commencement and who personally interviewed a number of the raiders,
thought that 'many who took part in it did so mainly from a desire to get food for
their starving families'. (85) In that they certainly succeeded. At least a hundred

deer were killed, (86) and several boats laden with carcases destined for the townships from which the raiders had come were seen slipping away from Park. (87)

But more important than even hunger for food was hunger for land — a hunger
intensified by the fact that many raiders, although landless themselves, were the
sons or grandsons of men who had cultivated land in Park some forty or fifty years
before. Thus one of the raiders

stated that his father's family were among those evicted ... and it is impossible
to imagine with what intense bitterness he gave expression to the feelings with
which he said he gazed upon the ruins of his grandfather's cottage. (88)

That man and others like him hoped that as a result of the slaughter for which
they had been responsible, the sporting value of Park forest would be so drastically
reduced that its tenant would give it up, thus forcing Lady Matheson to reverse her
decision of 1882 and hand the forest over to the crofters and cottars of the parish
of Lochs. (89) And at worst, they believed, their craving for land, together with
the tragic state of affairs existing in Lewis that winter, would receive wide publicity
in the press. 'Their object,' a group of raiders told reporters, was 'to draw the
attention of the whole country to their case.' (90) More than thirty years were to
pass before any part of Park was resettled with official blessing, (91) and the
raiders' primary objective thus remained out of their reach. Publicity for their
grievances, however, they received at once and in full measure. And with this, they
decided to be content for the moment. On the raid's third day — and before any
of the police or troops who had been despatched to Lewis could be deployed against
them — the raiders withdrew from the forest, Donald MacRae and the thirteen
others for whose arrests warrants had been issued voluntarily surrendering themselves to the authorities in Stornoway. (92)

That their endeavours had not been in vain became clear in December when the
government agreed to enquire into the social and economic condition of Lewis. (93)
And that enquiry — as was noted by a newspaper correspondent who accompanied the
officials charged with the task of conducting it — at once laid bare the roots of discontent: 'In one township after another the same state of matters was met with —
half-clad and half-starved people living in squalor within wretched and overcrowded
houses.' (94) The landless population of Lewis, the report itself made clear, were
suffering acutely from the effects of the slump in the herring industry. (95) And
though some poor law administrators continued to believe that there was no more
to the crisis in Lewis than 'a spurious cry of destitution bolstered up ... by agitators', (96)
the report succeeded in convincing Lord Lothian, Balfour's successor at the Scottish
Office, that something positive would have to be done to tackle the economic basis
of the crofting problem. (97) The consequent shift in government policy did not,
however, materialise in time to prevent the months that followed the raid on Park
from developing into the most violent phase of the entire land war in the Highlands.

'The Crofters' agitation has come to an end,' wrote the *Oban Times'* Lewis correspondent in December 1887:

It is the cottars' turn now ... The cottars not only demand the restoration of
Park ... but all the other lands under sheep and deer, with compensation for the
loss suffered by themselves and their fathers through the conduct of the evictors
who ruined them and left them landless in pauperism. (98)

Because of the prevalence of such feelings, the withdrawal of the raiders from Park produced no diminution of tension in Lewis. A detachment of eighty Royal Scots, sent to the island while the deer raid was in progress, was retained at Stornoway, and was joined in December by a gunboat and a force of marines. (99) Goaded by hunger, poverty and official inaction, cottars throughout Lewis were meanwhile preparing to follow the example set at Park. A few days before Christmas about two hundred men from Shader, Borve and other townships on the island's north-west coast marched on the large sheep farm of Galson and informed its tenant that his lands would soon be taken from him. (100) Two or three days later another sheep farm — that of Aignish on the Eye peninsula near Stornoway — was visited by almost a thousand crofters and cottars who proceeded to inform its tenant 'that they required the farm ... to provide holdings for the starving landless cottars and their families in the district, whose ancestors had it under cultivation'. (101) And on 29th December at a mass meeting near Stornoway it was resolved that on 9th January Aignish, together with the neighbouring farm of Melbost, would be forcibly expropriated. The cattle and sheep on the farms, it was decided, would be driven to new pastures: the grounds of Stornoway Castle, residence of Lady Matheson. (102) That these were no idle threats was soon made clear. To make the raiders' task some-what easier, hundreds of yards of the Aignish boundary fence were torn down under cover of darkness. (103)

During the first week of January 1888 Stornoway's sheriff-substitute posted up Gaelic and English notices which warned that participants in the proposed occupation of the farms would be liable to heavy penalties. (104) His proclamations were without effect, however. On the appointed day a crowd of about a thousand people — 'a large, excited, and determined ... mob', the sheriff called them in a hastily despatched telegram to the Scottish Office (105) — marched on the disputed farms. There they were confronted by a strong force of police, Royal Scots and marines; and while the sheriff read the Riot Act in Gaelic and in English there began one of the bitterest and bloodiest of all the confrontations between the crofting community and the law. The strong military presence meant the abandonment of the original plan to drive the Aignish stock to Stornoway. Instead, a number of sheep were deliberately driven into the sea, while others had their backs and legs broken by the stout sticks and clubs wielded by the raiders. On the troops and police attempting to clear the farm they were pelted with stones and other missiles. Several policemen and the Royal Scots' commanding officer were more or less badly hurt while the local procurator-fiscal who, revolver in hand, was observing the scene from a nearby knoll found himself assaulted. In the midst of all the confusion thirteen men, picked at random from the crowd, were somehow or other arrested. A rescue attempt was quickly organised by their comrades but was eventually defeated by a group of marines who formed a cordon round the prisoners and — holding off an angry, yelling and jeering crowd at bayonet point — marched them off to jail in Stornoway while their colleagues gradually forced the main body of the raiders back across the farm's boundary. (106)

These arrests did absolutely nothing to restore tranquillity to the island. Four days after the Aignish fracas, cottars' delegates from every part of Lewis met in Stornoway and formally requested the government

to restore to the descendants of the clansmen ... the whole of the lands formerly

tilled by their ancestors for centuries, the restoration to the people of the said
lands being the only solution to the land question. (107)

The implementation of such a solution was still a long way off, however, and Lewis
cottars seemed decidedly unwilling to await it. In the face of threats to burn down
farmhouse and steading, Aignish was placed under permanent military protection. (108)
And elsewhere on the island direct action was increasingly being resorted to. On 5th
January some three hundred men from Barvas on Lewis' west coast made the long
journey to Stornoway in order to present Lady Matheson with a petition asking
that Galson farm be divided among them. 'These lands are mine,' Lady Matheson
told a wet and weary deputation, 'and you have nothing to do with them.' (109)
Events soon proved her wrong. By the middle of January the increasingly harassed
local authorities had found it necessary to station eight constables at Galson in an
attempt to prevent the nightly demolition of dykes and fences. (110) The men
responsible for the destruction were not so easily deterred, however; and while
patrolling the farm on the night of 16th January the unfortunate police detachment
encountered several of them busily engaged in tearing down a fence. A hand-to-hand
fight ensued. Several policemen were seriously cut about the face and the raiders
escaped. (111)

At about the same time as these events were occurring in the neighbourhood of
Galson, a part of the farm of Coll near Stornoway was occupied by cottars, while –
on the other side of the island – fences around Dalbeg and Linshader were destroyed. (112)
And when, on 18th January, an Edinburgh jury acquitted the fourteen Park raiders –
a development which the sheriff of Ross-shire found 'most disheartening', but which
was greeted with delight in Lewis (113) – a fresh impetus was given to the agitation.
'Lawlessness,' the Scottish Office was informed at the end of January, was 'prevalent
in almost every district in Lewis.' The overnight destruction of farm dykes and fences
had become so commonplace as to be hardly worthy of comment. Land League
meetings were being regularly held in almost every township on the island and at
them the 'wildest resolutions' were being freely adopted, 'the avowed object,' it was
noted, 'being to obtain possession, if necessary by violence, of land presently occupied
by sheep farms or deer forests'. (114)

Landlessness, it was all too clear, lay at the root of these and many other manifestations of unrest. 'A portion of the land which belonged to their forefathers,' a
Lewis cottars' spokesman had argued before the Napier Commission in 1883, 'should
be given to them.' (115) And in 1886 it had been noted that cottars provided the
backbone of the Land League organisation in the island. (116) In the winter of
1887-88, having gained nothing from the government and faced with a catastrophic
decline in their living standards, Lewis' cottar population made plain their need for
land in the only effective way that was open to them: they took it by force. And
since the younger men among them were almost invariably in the Naval Reserve,
which had a large membership on the island, (117) they were able to organise their
campaign on military lines. The thousand men who marched on Aignish did so in
line abreast with pipes playing and flags flying. At Galson, too, it was noted, the
raiders responded to military commands given by one of their leaders; (118) while,
by a blend of strict discipline and the fear engendered in every Land League member
by the knowledge 'that if he will offend against the rules of the League he'll pay for

it', the cottars managed to keep their movements and intentions quite secret from the police and the military. (119)

Developments in Lewis were mirrored by unrest among cottars in other parts of the Highlands and Hebrides. At Clashmore in the Assynt district of Sutherland, for instance, a farm of which crofters had been deprived as recently as the 1870s was raided by its former occupants. Dykes were demolished and the farm steading burned to the ground. Military intervention followed. (120) At Lochcarron and in Glenelg there was talk of seizing lands. (121) And in Skye — where the poverty caused by the fishing crisis and low cattle prices, though somewhat less acute than in Lewis, was nevertheless 'very widespread' (122) — there were indications that the year-old social peace was more precarious than had been thought. At the beginning of January 1888, for example, Glendale crofters resolved to take possess- ion of lands in Bracadale from which, as one speaker put it, their fathers and grand- fathers had been evicted 'in the days when sheep were more thought of than men'. (12 On the Kilmuir estate, too, there was renewed unrest. The crofters and cottars of Bornaskitaig, Hunglader and Kilvaxter petitioned their landlord for the restoration of their former grazings on Duntulm and Monkstadt farms which, it was pointed out, 'were in the hands of strangers while ... the rightful owners were huddled together on rocks and moss not fit for cultivation'. And on 17th January a party of about fifty men carried out a detailed survey of the disputed lands in order to allow old men to point out pre-clearance township boundaries to their sons and grandsons. (124)

Across the Minch in Harris, meanwhile, factors and landlords were presented with petitions requesting that more land be made available to small tenants — one particularly unpopular sheep farmer being informed by an anonymous letter that 'Some of the poor landless people ... are bent on making an example of you first'. (125 The letter's recipient escaped unscathed. But in Harris, as across the county boundary in Lewis, there was acute poverty and suffering among the landless population. And it is not really surprising, therefore, that the agitation in the island should be described as 'more of a cottar than a crofter one', or that representatives of the former group should openly threaten 'to imitate the Lewismen'. (126) In this, however, they were not alone. Throughout the Uists and Barra, according at least to the sheriff- substitute at Lochmaddy, 'the disturbances in the Lews have had a very serious effect; they are, of course, much talked of, and the conduct of the people applauded, and opinions held and expressed that it would be well to follow suit'. At meetings held in South Uist in the opening weeks of 1888, for example, the island's cottars resolved that they would not 'let ourselves or our families starve as long as there is cultivable land growing under sheep in Uist, or as long as there is anything in Uist that we can lay our hands upon to prevent such starvation'. They would, the cottars agreed, continue 'to agitate against policemen, and soldiers, and landlords, till big farms are demolished and granted to such crofters and cottars that are in need of them'. (127) And in Barra — and indeed at cottars' meetings throughout the Hebrides — similarly aggressive sentiments were very freely expressed. (128) But despite the existence of the very general unrest to which the making of so many violent statements testified, there were — outside Lewis and Clashmore — no actual seizures of land.

Partly, no doubt, this was due to what Alexander MacKenzie called the 'cruel sentences' imposed on the fourteen Lewismen who, at the High Court in Edinburgh on 30th January 1888, were found guilty of mobbing and rioting at Aignish farm three weeks earlier and were subsequently imprisoned for periods ranging from nine to fifteen months. (129) The pacifying effect of this unarguably repressive development — which, in the authorities' opinion, reversed the damage done by the Park raiders' acquittal (130) — was strongly enforced, however, by a quite unexpected upturn in the crofting community's economic prospects. The Hebridean white fishings having proved exceptionally good, the spring and early summer of 1888 brought crofter and cottar households more money than they had seen for several years. (131) And for the moment at least, the edge of the cottars' land hunger was decisively blunted. Only in Lewis — which had taken on Skye's earlier role of unchalleneged storm centre of crofting unrest — did trouble of any kind continue. In May, for instance, crofters and cottars from Balallan held a meeting inside the boundaries of Park forest, and some crofters' cattle were driven on to Aignish farm. (132) That month, too, the island's owner, Lady Matheson — under police protection since February when anonymous threats had been made on her life — left Stornoway to take up residence in the south of France. (133) But as the summer advanced and proved as prosperous as the spring, tranquillity returned even to Lewis. And in September the troops who had been stationed on the island since the celebrated raid on Park nine months before were finally withdrawn. (134)

The military withdrawal from Lewis in the early autumn of 1888 marked the end of the land war which had begun in Skye more than six years before. In comparison with the winters that had preceded it, that of 1888-89 was virtually uneventful. By the end of 1890 the Inverness-shire constabulary had been reduced to normal strength. And in that year, in the case of Skye, and in 1891, in the case of the Outer Isles, the police were instructed to cease submitting regular reports on crofters' activities. (135) The cessation of crofting violence was accompanied by a steep decline in the political activity which had commenced with the founding of the HLLRA in 1883. Some part of that decline can undoubtedly be attributed to the crofting community's disenchantment with the manoeuvrings of its erstwhile leaders — manoeuvrings which, in the expressive phrase of a Barra crofters' leader, had reduced the HLLRA's successor, the Highland Land League, to the status of 'a mere political Association'. (136) But of at least equal importance in explaining the Land League's demise, and of considerably more importance in accounting for the gradual disappearance of the agitation which had given rise to it, were the enhanced financial circumstances of the crofting population.

By the end of the 1880s, the worst of the crisis in the herring industry having been successfully surmounted, hired hands' wages were rising once again — as were the prices obtained by crofters for their cattle. (137) In the course of the subsequent twenty years, moreover, the crofting community's fishing earnings climbed to, and indeed above, the levels they had reached before 1884. And though cattle prices did not show the same improvement, the consequent loss of income was more than offset by the plummeting price of the meal which, as mentioned in a previous chapter, most crofters and all cottars had to buy to supplement the food they grew

themselves. (138) Caused by the massive expansion in grain imports from America
as well as by improved transport facilities in the Highlands themselves, the latter
development was of very great benefit to crofting tenants everywhere. In Scourie,
on Sutherland's west coast, to give a particular instance of a general process, the
price of a boll of imported meal fell from around 50s. in 1880 to 12s. 6d. in the
early years of the present century. (139)

Of even greater benefit, however, was the occurrence in the years around 1850
of a very significant shift in the government's Highland policy: away from the
virtually unrelieved repression of the years immediately following the Crofters Act
and towards the officially sponsored development of the Highland economy in
general and of its crofting sector in particular. From this development twentieth
century attitudes to the Highland problem largely stem. But given the magnitude
of the reappraisal involved, it was not something that could be accomplished overnight. And initially indeed it seemed that economic interventionism would be confined to the promotion of that age-old Highland nostrum, emigration — Lord Lothian,
for instance, declaring in May 1887 that 'the first step towards an immediate solution'
of the crofting problem lay in 'an attractive and well financed scheme of State-
aided emigration'. (140) Support for such a view could be found in the Napier
Commission's report and among north-west Scotland's landlords, to whom the
removal of the region's 'surplus population' seemed as needful and beneficial as it
had done to their predecessors in the 1840s. (141) To such a proceeding, however,
the crofting community was unalterably opposed. In 1883 a Lewis crofter had
remarked of his compatriots' feelings on the subject that

There is no doubt they are strongly against emigrating and is it not rather a
hard thing that they should be made to emigrate while sheep are being fed at
home? (142)

And five years later, when a government-sponsored emigration scheme was put into
operation, (143) such opinions were, if anything, more strongly held than ever —
crofters and cottars resolving at meetings held in all the crofting areas 'to oppose
with their might and main,.... any scheme of emigration ... until all the land available
for cultivation in the Highlands and Islands be used ... to form new crofts for the
landless'. (144) Emigration was not ruled out completely — Glendale crofters, for
example, announcing that they would not stand in the way of anyone proposing
to transport landlords and sheep farmers to Manitoba. (145) But a popularly supported
exodus, it was clear, would have to be preceded by a very complete redistribution of
the land.

Among the Conservative government's supporters there were, it is true, one or
two men — the most notable of whom was Joseph Chamberlain — who favoured the
granting of more land to crofters. (146) But as a Liberal Unionist and a radical of
a decidedly antilandlord turn of mind, Chamberlain's influence on Salisbury's
administration was not, in the 1880s at least, decisive. And for the moment, therefore, a Highland land settlement programme remained off the government's agenda.
The concept of massive emigration having been effectively abandoned, however,
there was an obvious need for an alternative and more constructive policy. And it
was his awareness of that need that induced the secretary of state for Scotland to
undertake, in the early summer of 1889, a personal tour of the north-west Highlands

and Hebrides — his objective, in his own words, being to discover what could be done 'to ameliorate the conditions of the inhabitants of these parts'. (147) The immediate outcome was Lothian's conversion to a programme of economic development in the Highlands. In August 1889 he recommended to the Treasury that no less than £150,000 should be spent on developing the fisheries and on the construction of roads, railways and piers. (148) A royal commission set up to conduct a more detailed enquiry made substantially similar recommendations. (149) By 1892, when the Conservatives fell from office, £237,291 had been assigned to development schemes in crofting areas. (150) The first of a continuing series of attempts to stimulate the Highland economy by means of judicious applications of financial assistance, that policy attracted considerable support in the Highlands and produced a lasting improvement in the region's communications system. (151) At the time, however, its undoubtedly beneficial effects on crofting life were completely eclipsed by the long-term consequences of the Crofters Act — consequences which did not become generally apparent until the 1890s.

Responsible for rent reductions of up to 50 per cent and the cancellation of the bulk of the arrears which had accumulated during the rent strikes and economic difficulties of the 1880s, the Crofters Commission was, by the mid-1890s, held almost in reverence — Donald MacRae, the man who had led the raid on Park in 1887, remarking of it, for example, that there was 'not an institution ..., except perhaps the Sabbath, that the Highland people cling to with more determination'. (152) And of even greater significance, it was generally agreed, (153) were the good effects produced by the decision to grant security of tenure to crofters. The enduring significance of that decision had been summed up thus by a Glendale crofter within a few months of the hotly disputed Crofters Bill of 1886 having passed into law:

> If a crofter formerly built a house it belonged to the laird; as well as other improvements affected by the crofter. Now the crofter could call the house and croft his own, along with any improvements which he made. Fifty years ago, could their fathers have believed that such a change could be effected? (154)

The great achievement of the Crofters Act, in other words, was to bring crofters' tenurial position into a close alignment with their traditional beliefs about the nature of their stake in the land — and it is for this reason that, even today, the surest way to arouse the crofting community to anger is to suggest an alteration in the 1886 Act's basic principles. Crofting tenants had always thought that they had a right to permanent occupancy of their holdings; and their landlords had no right to evict them at will. (155) To these notions the Crofters Act gave the force of statute law. And the consequences, as was pointed out by a royal commission in 1895, were both immediate and dramatic:

> Our opinion is that, speaking generally, the Act has had a beneficial effect, and particularly in the following directions. In the first place, the fixing of a Fair Rent has to a large extent removed from the minds of crofters the sense of hardship arising from the belief that they were made to pay rent on their own improvements, or otherwise made to pay at an excessive rate for soil of a poor quality. In the second place, the combination of a Fair Rent with Statutory Security of Tenure has not only taken away or allayed causes of discontent, but has imparted a new spirit to crofters and imbued them with fresh energy. The abiding sense produced that the permanent improvements which a crofter makes upon his holding will, if

he complies with certain reasonable statutory conditions, accrue either to himself
or to his family successor, will not be taxable by the landlord in the form of
increased rent, and moreover will have a money value under a claim for Compensation
on Renunciation of Tenancy or Removal from his holding, has led to vigorous efforts
towards improvement by crofters in many quarters. For instance, we found that more
attention is being paid to cultivation, to rotation of crops, to reclamation of outruns,
to fencing, and to the formation or repair of township roads; but most conspicuous
of all the effects perceptible, is that upon buildings, including both dwelling-houses
and steadings. In a considerable number of localities we found new and improved
houses and steadings erected by the crofters themselves since the passing of the
Act. (156)

In the twenty years after 1886, for example, nearly 1,600 of the 4,000 crofters in
the islands of Skye, Harris, the Uists and Barra built new homes on their holdings. (15
And in the report which it published on its being wound up in 1912, the Crofters
Commission itself recorded that 'the black hovels in which too many of the people
lived are now passing away, and have been largely replaced by smart, tidy cottages
that would do credit to any part of the country' – a state of affairs which in itself
justified the commissioners' conclusion that they left the Highland crofter in a better
position than they found him. (158)

Although a major pacifying force in the Highlands, and recognised by crofters as
the keystone of a new and more equitable social order in the region, the Crofters
Act was not the final solution to the Highland land problem. The crofting community'
original criticism of it – that it did nothing to restore cleared lands to the people –
remained as valid in the 1890s as it had been in the previous decade. Within the
confines of the very limited land settlement powers bestowed upon them by the
Act the Commission, admittedly, did their by no means negligible best, enlarging
2,051 holdings and making a grand total of 72,341 acres – most of it in the form
of hill grazings – available to crofters. (159) But in the context of the many millions
of acres then occupied as sheep farms and deer forests, the Commission's endeavours
were pitifully inadequate, the more so since, having no power to create new holdings,
the Commission could do nothing for the large landless population among whom the
universal craving for more land was naturally most intense. The Crofters Act, as they
themselves had bitterly remarked in 1886, (160) and as the *Oban Times* commented
in 1901, had 'left the cottars out in the cold'. The typical cottar, the paper continued,

lives in a circumscribed and discouraging sphere well calculated to create discontent and one that holds out no prospect of future betterment by the exercise
of self-exertion and enterprise. The claim of the crofter to an inherited title to the
soil has been recognised, but that of the cottar has never been acknowledged.

But despite, or perhaps because of, their privations, landless families continued to
hope that 'some day they [would] come into possession of holdings of their own', (16
a situation which – as had been obvious in the troubled winter of 1887-88 and was
to become so again in the opening years of the new century – was a perfect recipe for
renewed agrarian unrest. And if the discontent engendered by such a state of affairs
was relatively muted in the comparatively peaceful and prosperous 1890s it was not,
even then, entirely absent.

In Lewis, the undisputed stronghold of landlessness, for instance, the destruction
of sheep farm boundary fences became a perpetually recurring event; (162) while in

the spring of 1891 there took place a second, if less spectacular, raid on Park. The
raiders, about forty in all, settled for some weeks at Ornsay, one of the townships
cleared half a century before. Among them there was at least one man who had
witnessed his father's eviction from the place and it was with considerable justice,
therefore, that they claimed they had come 'to retake the homes of their ancestors'.
Reroofing one or two ruined houses, they set about planting potatoes on the long-
abandoned rigs and were eventually removed by the police – thirty-two of the
raiders being subsequently sentenced to one or two weeks' imprisonment on trespass
charges. (163) In the early 1890s, too, there were a number of raids by cottars on
the farm of Borve on the island of Berneray in the Sound of Harris where, in 1890,
a stable was demolished and a stackyard burned and where, some three years later,
the illegal occupation of a part of the disputed farm – from which small tenants had
once been cleared – led to four cottars being jailed for sixty days on charges of
mobbing and rioting. (164) Elsewhere in the region – in the Uists and in the neighbourhood of Clashmore (scene of a land raid in 1887), for example – fences and
dykes were destroyed. (165) And in Skye in 1893 a part of the Kilmuir farm of
Duntulm as well as a small island off Staffin were subjected to illegal incursions of
one kind or another. (166)

Such incidents, the sheriff of Ross-shire pointed out in 1891, were the inevitable
consequence of the existence in the Highlands, and especially in the Hebrides, of a
large and dissatisfied cottar population, and unless some provision was made to
give land to the landless he could discern 'little hope of entire immunity from disturbance ... for many years to come'. (167) The latter solution to the problem had,
of course, been determinedly convassed by crofters and their political representatives
throughout the 1880s. And it had then received no governmental encouragement
whatsoever. (168) By the 1890s, however, the concept of officially-sponsored land
settlement was gaining increasing support – some of it emanating from very surprising quarters. Like the preceding decade, the 1890s were a time of serious
difficulties for the Highlands' sheep farming economy. And as sheep farmers pulled
out and as estate rentals crumbled, the entire *raison d'etre* of the agrarian system
established during and in the wake of the clearances seemed on the point of vanishing. The moral was obvious. As the *Oban Times* remarked in 1889, there was no
longer 'keen competition on the part of capitalists for lands that may be claimed
by the people', and there seemed, therefore, to be no compelling reason for landlords to oppose the return of these lands to the crofting community. (169) In fact,
there was one such reason: the immense profits to be made from converting vacated
grazings into deer forests. These profits had led to the Park peninsula being denied
to its cottar claimants; and Park was but one instance of a very general phenomenon. (170)
Not every unprofitable sheep farm was a potential sporting paradise, however. And by
the later 1880s some landlords were consequently reaching the *Oban Times'* conclusion – though, of course, from a quite opposite direction. Thus in 1887, in a
petition which, as an astonished civil servant commented, 'practically asks for a
Land Purchase Bill for Skye', a number of that island's owners asked the government
to 'relieve them' of sheep farms that were of no further financial use to them and
hand them over to crofters for settlement purposes. (171)

The purchase of privately-owned lands by the government and their subsequent resale to their former tenants who were thus converted into owner-occupiers or — in the jargon of the time — peasant proprietors, was an important element in the Conservative administration's attempts to solve the Irish land question. On their being granted a permanent stake in the land, Irish peasants, it was hoped, would be rendered more prosperous, more contented and, therefore, less prone to involvement in political unrest and agitation. Irish landlords, for their part, were compensated with a generosity sufficient to ensure their general support for the scheme. (172) And it was, no doubt, the latter aspect of it which attracted the financially harassed proprietors of Skye to the concept of land purchase. They were, they told the government, quite willing to see the crofting system extended — as long as they received 'just and equitable' compensation for all or part of their possessions. (173)

The determination on Highland landlords' part to do very well financially out of any land settlement scheme — a determination evident even in 1887 when no such scheme was being seriously considered — was to prove the major obstacle in the way of achieving a quick and radical redistribution of north-west Scotland's agricultural land. (174) Thus the first and extremely tentative step taken in the direction of the creation of new holdings — the Conservative government's 1892 decision to bestow on the newly created Scottish county councils the power to provide allotments in areas where there was a serious demand for them — came to nothing in the Highlands, the principal reason for its failure being the strength of proprietorial opposition to it. (175) 1892, however, witnessed another and apparently more hopeful development: the setting up by the Liberal government which came to power that year — and did so in the Highlands with very strong crofting support (176 — of a royal commission whose task it was to report upon the amount of land in the crofting counties which, though then under sheep or deer, could be utilised for land settlement purposes. (177)

In its report, published in April 1895, the Commission not unsurprisingly concluded that there was, especially among the Highlands' landless population, a continuing and quite unabated demand for more land. 'Very many' cottars, the commissioners observed,

are deserving and intelligent, and owe their unfortunate position to adverse circumstances. Their ambition almost invariably was ... to get a croft such as their crofter neighbours possess. While the position of the crofter is one of difficulty ... the position of the cottar is still more difficult, and any scheme that would result in affording cottars the opportunity of obtaining crofts ... would operate a substantial relief both to the cottars themselves and to the neighbouring crofters. (178)

And the land needed for such a purpose, the Commission's painstaking enquiries had shown, was readily available. There were in the Highlands, it was concluded, no less than 439,188 acres that could be used to extend existing holdings; and a further 794,730 acres that were suitable for the creation of new crofts. (179)

By the spring of 1897, however, Lord Rosebery's Liberal government was tottering towards its imminent collapse, and instead of the sweeping land settlement measure expected by crofters, the Liberal administration reacted to their own Commission's report by introducing a lukewarm Bill which did not even mention the formation of new holdings. That measure, which fell with its promoters in the early summer, destroyed the credibility — in the Highlands at least — of both the Liberal party and the Land League which had nailed its colours firmly to the Liberal mast.

In the ensuing election, therefore, Liberal and Land League fortunes suffered a decisive reverse — the latter organisation now a tattered remnant of its former self, being finally and completely swept from the political scene. The field was thus left open to Conservative and Unionist candidates who based their campaign on their advocacy of land reforms similar to those carried out by the Conservatives in Ireland between 1886 and 1892. 'The real solution of the question,' declared one Tory manifesto,

lies in the intervention of the government with financial assistance on the principle of the Irish Land Purchase Acts — first, to take up suitable tracts of land and utilise them for crofters' holdings; and, secondly, to enable these crofters who are capable and desire to do so, to become owners of their land. (180)

Infinitely more imaginative than anything offered by the Liberal-Land League alliance, these proposals were welcomed as such by — among others — the crofters of Glendale, one of the places where the land war had begun some thirteen years before. (181) And in 1897 the Unionist government which came to power in the election in question did indeed implement the policy its Highland candidates had advocated by establishing the Highland Congested Districts Board. Its tasks included that of making more land available to the crofting community, and among its achievements was the conversion of Glendale's crofting tenants into the owners of their holdings. (182)

11. Land Raids and Land Settlement, 1897-1930

THE phrase 'congested districts' was originally and somewhat euphemistically coined to describe those parts of western Ireland where, as Lord Salisbury explained to Queen Victoria, 'a dense population of half starving multitudes' lived on frequently infertile and invariably constricted holdings and where hunger and even famine were consequently seldom absent for very long. (1) There, as in the western Highlands and Hebrides, the cheek by jowl existence of the peasants who clung determinedly to their miserable patches of unproductive soil and the well-to-do graziers who farmed a large proportion of the region's rolling grasslands produced a desperate land hunger which, it seemed, could be assuaged only by a far-reaching redistribution of the land. 'To look over the fence of the famine stricken village,' wrote one of Ireland's nationalist politicians in a passage that could have referred to any one of a hundred townships in north-west Scotland,

and see the rich, green solitudes which might yield full and plenty spread out at the very doorsteps of the ragged peasants was to fill a stranger with a sacred rage and make it an unshirkable duty to strive towards undoing the unnatural divorce between the people and the land. (2)

And it was in an attempt to eliminate or at least reduce the discontent thus engendered that the Conservative government included in its Irish Land Purchase Act of 1891 the clauses which set up the Congested Districts Board — the Board's function being to promote the economic development of the west of Ireland by financially assisting indigenous industries, by supplying instruction in farming techniques, and by providing new holdings on lands purchased for that purpose. (3) The Board, it was agreed by Irish nationalists as well as by its Unionist promoters, was a resounding success. (4) And it was not unnatural, therefore, that the latter should establish a virtually identical body to deal with the apparently similar problems posed by Scotland's 'congested districts' — an area defined in terms of its own under-development and reckoned to include parts of Mull, all other populated islands from Tiree and Barra northwards and the greater part of the mainland coastal periphery from Ardnamurchan to Caithness. (5)

Constituted in 1897, greeted by the HLLRA veteran G.B. Clark as 'a fair and honest attempt' to come to grips with the crofting problem, (6) and consisting of the secretary and under-secretary of state for Scotland, the chairmen of the Crofters Commission, Fishery and Local Government Boards, and two other persons nominated by the Scottish secretary, the Highland Congested Districts Board possessed powers and was assigned duties analogous to those of its Irish predecessor. (7) Under its auspices, roads, paths, bridges, piers and slipways were constructed; the inshore fisheries developed; and the Harris tweed industry aided by grants for looms and by the provision of technical instruction. Agricultural shows were sponsored, fencing and draining encouraged and financially assisted, improved varieties of seed provided, the spraying of crofters' potatoes to protect them from blight made possible, and the cultivation of turnips, kale and other crops promoted. And because the region was, as the Board noted, 'more suited to pastoral than to agricultural farming', its members and officials 'endeavoured throughout to encourage the improvement of stock by all means in their power' — attempting, with considerable success, to educate crofters as to the importance of keeping rather than selling good breeding animals and providing townships or groups of townships with bulls, tups and stallions for breeding purposes. (8) The fifteen years of the Board's existence thus constitute an undeservedly forgotten chapter in the history of Highland development. Its endeavours — continued by its successors — laid the basis of much of the comparative prosperity of modern crofting life and proved that, with appropriate assistance, the crofting community was quite capable of instituting improvements which Highland landlords had long believed — or at least said — to be beyond their tenantries' competence.

As its title indicates, however, the Board's principal function was to relieve congestion. And that could be done only by providing land for the landless — whose applications for holdings began to pour into the Board's offices within weeks of its being set up. (9) But unfortunately for the applicants and for the Board's eventual reputation, its efforts to provide the requisite crofts — either by buying land for resale as smallholdings or by financially assisting those proprietors who were willing to subdivide one or more of the farms on their estates (10) — were gravely handicapped from the outset: partly by financial restrictions imposed by the government; and partly by the fact that in its human aspect at least the Highlands' land problem was not, after all, the same as that of Ireland.

Able to help a settler to equip his new holding with buildings, fences and other permanent fixtures, the Board was not permitted to assist him to stock his land. And since few cottars could raise the funds needed to purchase the sheep they were expected to take over from the owner or tenant of the former sheep farm on which they were usually settled, this was a serious drawback — as was the Board's inability to buy more than a tiny proportion of the land required for settlement purposes. That the Board was not empowered to borrow money and had therefore to buy estates out of its very inadequate income of £35,000 a year was limiting enough. But equally restrictive was the Board's discovery that crofters had no strong desire to become the owners of their holdings, a state of affairs which rather paralysed the Board's activities because it could not — like its Irish counterpart — spend money on land purchase in the sure knowledge that it would eventually be repaid by the people who lived, or were settled on, the land in question. (11)

Unlike the Irish peasant, whose fervent desire it was to own his plot, the typical crofter was content with the recognition — enshrined in the Crofters Act — of his long-standing claim to a secure tenure of his holding. As early as 1887 — and in reply to Joseph Chamberlain's proposal that peasant ownership on the Irish model should be introduced into the crofting counties — the Lewis branches of the Land League had observed:

A fair rent is preferred to purchasing their holdings at 49 years purchase, when most of the existing tenants and claimants would be in their graves ... Moreover they consider themselves most solemnly now to be part owners, according to English [sic] law which granted them fixity of tenure. (12)

And to such considerations there had to be added the fact that ownership, in the Highland context, at least, was attended with marked financial disadvantages. The capital value of a croft rented at £5 a year — a by no means untypical holding — was considered, for purchase purposes, to be about £100. And the annuity by which this sum, principal and interest, was to be repaid to the Board over a fifty-year period was £3.14s. — an apparent saving of about 25 per cent. But the purchasing owner was held responsible for the payment of owner's as opposed to tenant's rates; and these, in almost every part of the north-west Highlands and islands, were so high as to practically extinguish the original saving. (13) As owners, moreover, crofters lost the protections and privileges of the 1886 Act — which applied to crofting tenants only — including the useful and highly esteemed right of appeal to the Crofters Commission for settlement of grazing and other disputes. And the not unsurprising upshot was that of all the crofting tenants on the estates bought by the Board — Syre in Strathnaver, Northbay in Barra, the island of Vatersay, and the large Skye properties of Glendale and Kilmuir — only those of Glendale, undisputed stronghold of antilandlordism, held to their original agreement to buy their holdings, the remainder opting for the status of tenants of the Board or its successor, the Board (subsequently the Department) of Agriculture for Scotland. (14)

These difficulties, coupled with the Board's lack of compulsory purchase powers — a lack much criticised by some Highland MPs in 1897, (15) made land settlement an unavoidably slow and expensive process. One effect of the consequent contrast between the few new holdings actually provided and what one Highland newspaper referred to as 'the glowing promises held out ... by the Tory party in the summer of 1895', (16) was a resurgence of crofting support for the Liberals whose 1906 election pledges included a promise of sweeping land reforms in the Highlands. (17) Another, produced by the Board's arousal of expectations which it was quite unable to fulfil, was the commencement in 1900 of another round of land seizures — destined to continue intermittently until the 1920s.

Like earlier and similar incursions, (18) these raids on north-west Scotland's sheep farms were a manifestation of the deep and enduring discontent produced by an agrarian system characterised by a gross imbalance between the amounts of land allotted to farmers on the one hand and to the crofting community on the other. But between the unrest of the present century's opening decades and that of the 1880s there was a vital difference. During the land war there had been — outside the ranks of the Highland Land League — little acceptance of the principle of land settlement. In the early twentieth century, however, the redistribution and resettlement of a good deal of the land that had been cleared a hundred years before was almost universally admitted to be the only real solution to the Highlands' agrarian problem. Since the 1890s, when the Liberals had set up a royal commission to investigate the region's land settlement potential and the Unionists had established the Congested Districts Board, the resettlement of landless families on lands purchased for that purpose had become an important component of the Highland policies propounded by both the major political parties. And the only — if occasionally profound — disagreement between them was about the methods by which resettlement was to be achieved: the Liberals being prepared to envisage a degree of compulsion that would have been anathema to their predecessors of the 1880s and was, until about 1917 at least, unacceptable to their Unionist opponents.

The political aspects of the cottars' fight for the land of which their ancestors had been deprived was thus generally conducted within the context of a Liberal-Tory confrontation. And though their southern supporters attempted on more than one occasion to revive the Highland Land League and to re-establish it as the accepted vehicle for the crofting community's political aspirations, they completely failed to gain a mass membership in the crofting counties — the new League being dominated by an exotic amalgam of socialists, Gaelic revivalists and Scottish nationalists whose careers, though not uninteresting in themselves, can safely be left out of a history of the crofting community. (19) All that is not, of course, to say that the struggle for more land had become altogether easier and more respectable than had been the case in the HLLRA's heyday. There was, admittedly, less violence than during the troubles of the 1880s — principally because the state's coercive apparatus was much less freely employed and because cottars and squatters, having no land in the first place, could not make use of landlord-provoking tactics like the rent strike. But land raids and the grievances which gave rise to them were quite capable of producing their own particular brand of bitterness.

As if to demonstrate that the nineteenth century's problems were still far from solved, the year 1900 was marked in Skye by the MacDonald estate management's decision to take legal proceedings against the crofters of Sconser whose sheep, it was alleged, were being deliberately pastured on Lord MacDonald's extensive — and by now very valuable — deer forest. Sconser's inhabitants claimed — accurately enough (20) — that the lands in question had belonged to the townships of Moll and Torramhichaig from which their forefathers had been evicted in the 1850s. And when a sheriff-officer arrived at Sconser to serve writs which instructed the offending tenants to remove their sheep from the forest, he was promptly surrounded by an angry crowd who pelted him with mud and stones before chasing him back the way that he had come. (21) The question at issue having thus achieved newsworthy status, the estate management then attempted to solve it by offering to remove Sconser's occupants to vacant lands in Sleat where, with the help of the Congested Districts Board, they were to be settled on holdings which, it was suggested, were in all respects superior to those they were being asked to abandon. This gesture the crofters interpreted as an attempt to further extend the forest at their expense. And they accordingly rejected it — making the telling point that the Board could as easily spend its money on a fence between their common grazings and their landlord's sporting preserves. (22) Sconser's tenants therefore remained where they were, the Board eventually acceding to their demands for a march fence. (23) And as a demonstration of the limits placed on Highland landlords' powers by the developments of the nineteenth century's last twenty years — limits that would have seemed inconceivable in the 1850s when townships could, quite literally, be cleared to order — their victory was not without significance. But more typical of the times, and certainly more indicative of the troubles to come, were occurrences in Barra in the same year.

The very small beginning of resettlement legislation represented by the Conservative government's Allotments (Scotland) Act of 1892 had been warmly welcomed in Barra where a very large landless population lived in appallingly overcrowded and squalid conditions. (24) And a considerable number of Barra's cottars — along with landless families in the Uists — at once put the measure to the test by applying to

Inverness-shire county council, the responsible authority in the matter, for the plots to which they now thought themselves legally entitled. There followed a protracted wrangle, distinguished by the council's allotments committee's conclusion that the cottars' claims should be met and by the council's landlord members' determination that no allotments should be conceded, and ending in 1899 when the question was finally shelved – an outcome which, as the *Oban Times* remarked, provoked 'a wide-spread feeling of disappointment and irritation'. (25) Their subsequent appeal to the Congested Districts Board having elicited no positive response, (26) Barra's cottars decided to take the law into their own hands. On 8th September 1900 the farm of Northbay – one of the largest on the island – was illegally occupied, the cottars responsible for its seizure 'holding that it is better to go to prison than suffer longer as they are doing', (27) and pointing out to Lady Gordon Cathcart, owner of Barra and South Uist,

> That all their efforts during the last five years to induce the County Council of Inverness-shire to help them to obtain some small portion of land ... have signally failed ... They feel that they are becoming an intolerable burden on their crofter friends upon whose lands, already much too small for their own needs, their cattle and horses drag out a half starving existence. (28)

One farm having been occupied, others quickly suffered the same fate, the most spectacular raid occurring on 26th September when a group of cottars from town-ships in the southern part of Barra landed on the adjacent island of Vatersay – then let as pasture to a sheep farmer – and on it proceeded to peg out a number of 'crofts' for themselves. (29) By the beginning of October the island was so unsettled that its owner's lawyers were demanding that some sort of action be taken to stop 'organised bands of cottars ... marching hither and thither marking out for their own occupation ground in the lawful occupation of other people'. (30) And though the crisis at Northbay was brought to an end in March 1901 when the Congested District Board bought the entire farm and a part of the neighbouring farm of Eoligarry and, on the land acquired, proceeded to provide almost sixty new crofts, (31) nothing was done to alleviate the plight of the many landless families living in and around Castlebay – some of whom again invaded Vatersay in the spring of 1901. (32)

The moral to be drawn from the decision to hand Northbay over to its illegal occupants was obvious, however, and its impact was not confined to Barra. Openly expressing their belief that 'they never had a better chance of having their congestion relieved seeing the Barra people got more land', more than a hundred cottars from the South Uist townships of Stoneybridge, Howbeg, Howmore and Snishival met in May 1901 and resolved to petition the Congested Districts Board for holdings on Ormaclett and Bornish farms. 'Why be cottars or landless squatters any longer,' asked a placard which was tied to a fence at the cottars' meeting place, 'while land in abundance is quite ready for instant habitation? ' (33) At that and similar gatherings in the next few months the restoration of the farms 'from which our forefathers were so illegally evicted' was repeatedly demanded; and the threat made that if the required land was not promptly made available, its cottar claimants would be 'reluctantly compelled' to take 'forcible possession' of it. (34)

The subsequent symbolic occupation of Bornish and Ormaclett (35) had its counter-part in events in North Uist where cottars had urged the Congested District Board to buy lands at Valley, Griminish and Scolpaig in the north-western corner of the island –

a district which North Uist's owner, Sir Arthur Orde, was then offering for sale. The Board having intimated that the area in question was quite unsuitable for settlement, the cottars concerned met at Bayhead, proclaimed that 'over half a century ago their forefathers were ruthlessly evicted from their homes at Griminish to make way for sheep' and — encouraged by an old man who had witnessed these and other clearances and who was of the opinion that 'it was all very good to talk of justice and agitating on constitutional lines, but he had seen nothing come of that for 65 years' — proceeded to occupy Griminish farm in order 'to show the Board' that it was 'well fitted' for crofts. (36)

While attempting to deal with these and other difficulties in the southern part of the Long Island, the Congested Districts Board's harassed officials received, from landless families living in the township of Tobson on the island of Bernera off Lewis' west coast, a request that the farm of Croir, adjacent to their township, be purchased and allotted among them:

It is ridiculous to have a farm on our small island when there are so many cottar fishermen on the land of others ... There are 43 souls of us and surely our lives are of more account than one man and his sheep. (37)

This appeal the Board and the proprietor of Lewis, Major Duncan Matheson, categorically refused to consider. (38) And in April 1901 the Board received the following letter from eight of Tobson's cottars:

Gentlemen, We have been seeking this farm from the factor and Landlord and Parliament for the last seven years and so far we have made no progress .... We are on the land of others and are not allowed to build a proper house and are in constant dread of eviction ... We now give you due notice that we shall take Croir Farm on the 17th April. If we break the law we are compelled to do so; so look out .... (39)

On the appointed day the eight petitioners appropriated a part of the farm and began to plant potatoes on it. (40) And having defied a court order to relinquish the land thus occupied, they were eventually removed by the police and bound over to keep the peace for six months. (41)

Elsewhere in the Hebrides there were similar manifestations of unrest. In Tiree, for instance, the large landless population's perennial aspiration for holdings of their own was intensified by events in Barra and the Uists. And an appeal to the island's proprietor, the Duke of Argyll, for a measure of land redistribution having elicited only an offer of assisted passages to the colonies — a traditional ducal response to difficulties in Tiree, but one that was hardly appropriate in twentieth-century conditions (42) — land raids were threatened in the early months of 1902 and again in the spring of 1903. (43) Among cottars on the island of Taransay — in West Loch Tarbert on the Atlantic coast of Harris — there was considerable talk of land raids at about the same time. (44) And in the spring of 1903 a number of South Uist's cottars translated identical mutterings into action by occupying Bornish and Milton sheep farms. (45)

Throughout this period, however, north-west Scotland's apparently endemic agrarian unrest remained centred on Barra where the Congested District Board's attempts to placate the island's landless population by buying and settling Vatersay came to nothing — the selling price being quite beyond the Board's resources. and where the consequent discontent was aggravated by a series of bad seasons for the island's numerous cottar-fishermen. (46) All they wanted, the latter declared, was 'a piece of land to plant a barrel or two of potatoes and grazing for a cow, to fall back upon when the fishing failed'. (47) In an attempt to obtain it Vatersay was again invaded in the spring of 1902. (48) In the following spring — in order to forestall renewed incursions of a similar nature — the Board bought about sixty acres of distinctly inferior land on Vatersay for the grossly inflated price of £600, divided it into some fifty potato plots, and let it to the landless families of Barra's more southerly and congested townships. (49) The peace thus achieved proved transient, however. In February 1906 about fifty cottars landed on the disputed island and declared themselves 'determined to get possession of the whole farm of Vatersay and to remove their dwelling houses to Vatersay as soon as possible' (50) — which intention they began to put into effect in June by ferrying their sheep and cattle across the Sound of Vatersay and by commencing to build houses on what they defiantly referred to as their crofts. (51)

As had happened in 1901, the Barra cottars' example proved contagious. Tiree's landless families renewed their appeals for holdings; (52) while the tenantry of the Kilmuir estate — bought by the Congested Districts Board in 1904 — met to demand the more rapid division of sheep farms and to threaten to 'take possession of the land'. (53) Demands for the resettlement of sheep farms were made at Glenshiel in Wester Ross. (54) And towards the end of February 1906 the cottars of the Stoney-bridge district of South Uist, with flags flying and with pipers at their head, marched in procession on to Ormaclett and Bornish sheep farms in order, as one of their spokesmen remarked, 'to let the authorities see that they were badly off and that more land was required'. (55) This at least they achieved. A sheep farm at Geirinish in the northern part of South Uist having been similarly invaded, (56) the sheriff of Inverness-shire — a man of a markedly more humane disposition than his predecessor, William Ivory — visited the island and had 'a friendly interview' with the raiders. He formed, he reported to the Scottish Office, 'a favourable impression of the people; but ... was struck by the indications of their poverty'. That their need for land was genuine and urgent he had no doubt whatsoever. The newly installed Liberal government, he accordingly believed, should honour its pre-election pledges on Highland land settlement and 'should introduce the [requisite] Bill ... as early as possible'. (57)

That the Liberal party had come to power committed to ambitious and radical land reforms was undoubted; as was the determination of the new administration's Scottish secretary, John Sinclair (later Lord Pentland), to transmute into effective legislation his party's good intentions towards the Highlands where it had secured a clean sweep of the crofting constituencies. Sinclair's proposals — which envisaged a wider and more sweeping land settlement programme presided over by a new body to be called the Board of Agriculture for Scotland — had the backing of the prime minister, Campbell-Bannerman, but were less welcome to the Liberal party's right wing (58) and utterly opposed by the Conservatives. (59) To the region's misfortune, Highland land reform thus became one of the victims of the rapidly developing conflict between the enormous Liberal majority in the Commons and the equally massive Tory majority in the House of Lords. And though the relevant legislation passed through the Commons in 1907 and again in 1908 it did so only to be destroyed by the recalcitrant peers in the Upper House. (60)

To the landless people of the Hebrides, whose hopes were thus shattered by men who knew little and cared less about their problems and predicament, the Lords became an object of the most bitter detestation and Sinclair something of a hero — Lewis cottars, for instance, thanking him 'for his faithful services' to their cause and declaring that the career of the 'selfish, cruel Lords ... should be ended' at the earliest opportunity. (61) Sinclair and his colleagues were eventually to come to the same conclusion. But until the constitutional crisis of 1910 and the subsequent abolition of the Lords' legislative veto, the Highlands' landless population, seeing little prospect of Sinclair's endeavours having a successful outcome, continued to assert their claims in the only way that seemed open to them — the prevalent attitude being reflected in resolutions adopted at a mass meeting in Skye in April 1908. Since the Lords were evidently determined to frustrate Highlanders' democratically expressed aspirations, it was concluded, 'the only weapon left for us is to take forcible possession of the land'. (62)

That was certainly the course adopted by Vatersay's illegal occupants. By the autumn of 1907 they had built more than twenty houses on the island where, it was clear, they were determined to remain. (63) 'Up to fifty years ago,' the secretary of state was informed,

> their grand-parents and remoter ancestors had crofts on Vatersay at the very place where the raiders' huts were now set up — and though their grand-parents had been evicted their descendants had never given up their claim. Throughout all the years their descendants down to this day have continued to bury their dead on Vatersay. (64)

Claims so securely rooted in history and tradition were not likely to be abandoned without a struggle — especially in view of the fact that the people making them had established a firm foothold on the land in question. And to Sinclair, whose sympathies lay with the cottars and who had absolutely no desire to provoke a confrontation with them, the obvious solution to the problem was to regularise the raiders' position by giving them legal as well as moral rights to Vatersay. Towards the end of 1907, therefore, he informed Lady Gordon Cathcart that if she agreed to set up a crofting township on Vatersay, the Congested Districts Board would be instructed to give her the financial and other assistance needed to make the project a success. This plan the island's proprietrix at once rejected; and offered instead to sell Vatersay to the Board — at a considerable profit to herself and at a price beyond the Board's resources. (65)

Their negotiations with the government having thus collapsed, the Barra estate management proceeded to take legal action against the raiders. And in June 1908 no fewer than ten of the latter found themselves imprisoned for two months. (66) A storm of protest followed. (67) The government was forced to reopen its talks with Vatersay's owner. And in October it was agreed that the Congested Districts Board should buy Vatersay for £6,250. (68) The raiders, all of whom were granted holdings on the island, thought the price extortionate — which it was. But they were, as they informed the Scottish secretary, 'genuinely grateful' to him for 'bringing about this settlement'. (69) Others were less delighted. Conservative spokesmen and newspapers alleged that in 'giving in' to the raiders the newly ennobled Lord Pentland was condoning and even encouraging lawlessness, (70) a contention which ignored their own party's decision to obstruct legislation designed to mitigate the Highland situation, but one which subsequent events did little to refute — the Vatersay settlement having the inevitable effect of precipitating a veritable spate of requests and demands for similar treatment. (71)

In Barra itself, for example, a number of landless families living in the undeniably congested east-coast townships of Bruernish, Balnabodach and Ersary pointed out that they were 'exactly in the same circumstances as the Vatersay people before they obtained the land'; announced that if their wants were not attended to they would 'by dire necessity ... be forced to take possession' of lands for themselves; and — despite Pentland's warning that illegal action would only 'prejudice their case' — proceeded, in March 1909, to occupy the part of Eoligarry farm unaffected by the Congested Districts Board's land purchases of eight years before. (72) In South Uist, where the farms of Milton and Glendale were raided, there were virtually identical occurrences. (73) And having previously declared that they would 'be compelled ... to take forcible possession of a farm as in the case of the Barra men', six cottars from the Lewis township of South Shawbost occupied a field on Dalbeg farm in order to provide themselves with land on which to grow potatoes. (74) On their defying a court order to quit Dalbeg, the raiders were jailed for a week. (75) When released, however, they returned to the farm because, as they said, they 'had nowhere else to go and could not live in the air or on the sea' — an attitude that led to their being imprisoned for another twenty-one days. (76)

Raids and threats of raids on Hebridean sheep farms having thus become a part of the accepted order of things, and the land settlement powers of the Congested Districts Board being demonstrably inadequate, there was by the end of the twentieth century's first decade an obvious need for new legislation on the Highland land question — legislation which at length materialised as the Small Landholders (Scotland) Act of 1911. Made possible by the curbing of the Lords' prerogatives, the Act — though a private member's measure — had the Liberal government's support and was in essence a refurbished, if somewhat watered down, version of Sinclair's ill-fated Bills of 1907 and 1908. (77) A new departure in agricultural policy, the 1911 Act extended many of the original Crofters Act's provisions to smallholders outside the crofting counties and abolished the Crofters Commission and the Congested Distrists Board — the functions of the former being taken over by the Scottish Land Court and those of the latter by the Board of Agriculture for Scotland, a body on which was bestowed a wide range of land settlement powers and an annual income of £200,000. The greater part of that income was to be expended on land settlement schemes in the north-west, and especially in the Hebrides. The owners and farming tenants of lands utilised for settlement purposes were, the Act laid down, entitled to sums of compensation which, failing agreement, were to be determined by the Land Court or — if the compensation claimed was in excess of £300 — by an arbitrator appointed by the Court of Session. Compulsory purchase of land by the state was still ruled out. But should a proprietor or tenant refuse to enlarge or to constitute smallholdings on his land, the Board was entitled to lay the case before the Land Court and, if the Court was satisfied that the Board's proposals were reasonable and designed to meet a genuine need, it was empowered to issue an order instructing the objectors to comply with the Board's wishes. (78)

At last, it seemed, the crofting community's demands for a redistribution of land in their favour — demands which had their origins in the clearances and which had been incessantly and vociferously expressed since the 1880s — were about to be met. The establishment of the Board of Agriculture in the spring of 1912 was accordingly welcomed at scores of meetings in the crofting areas. (79) And by the end of that year the Board had received 3,370 applications for holdings — almost half of them from cottars living in the Outer Isles. (80) Before the Board's first twelve months had elapsed, however, it was manifestly obvious that it was little better equipped than its predecessors to tackle the problem of transferring land from one class of occupant to another. Its funds were inadequate and — what was worse — its procedures, especially those regarding compensation claims, were woefully complex and slow as well as being notably generous to landowning and sheep farming objectors to its plans. (81) Without the willing co-operation of the latter, therefore, the Act was clearly liable to prove a dead letter. (82) And from the first it was clear that such co-operation was not to be forthcoming.

In part, Highland landlords' undoubted opposition to the 1911 Act derived from their Conservative politics. But political calculation was enforced, as is usually the case, by financial self-interest. Sheep farming, the traditional prop of Highland land-lordism, had, it was true, long ceased to be a profitable enterprise in many parts of northern Scotland. (83) But the region's landowners, while amenable to the idea of selling land to the state at prices that were — to put the matter mildly — conspicuously inflated, had no wish to see their properties settled by crofting tenants. The capital gains from such a development would, they feared, be small; and the possibility of cashing in on any subsequent improvement in the agricultural situation would be removed. Crofters, once established, enjoyed security of tenure and could not easily be shifted; while on a crofting estate, as was pointed out by a member of one distinguished Highland family, the landlord was

at the mercy of a commission whose sympathies are entirely with the tenants, and who, if they allow any increase of rent at all, will give the very smallest increase possible, while, if prices fall, they will give the most generous concessions in rent. (84)

Sheep farmers, though for different reasons, were as likely as the proprietors to obstruct settlement schemes. Writing from South Uist in 1909 one of the Congested Districts Board's agents had observed:

It seems to me that farmers in this district just now, even although they wish to leave, pretend they don't, in the expectation of the government asking for the farm for small holdings when compensation will be paid for break of lease. (85)

Like their landlords and like the latter's Edinburgh lawyers who, as a civil servant at the Board of Agriculture ruefully remarked, became 'very expert in the peparation of claims for every conceivable item connected with a farm', (86) sheep farmers tended, therefore, to react to the Board's land settlement proposals by initiating legal proceedings as to the amount of compensation to be paid to those adversely affected by the settlement scheme or shcemes in question. And the consequent thicket of writs, processes, claims and arbitrations in which the Board became entangled quickly nullified all optimistic expectations of a final and speedy solution to the agrarian problem in the Highlands — only 502 new holdings being created in the first seven years of the Board's existence. (87)

In the spring of 1914, to give an example of the difficulties that ensued, the Board requested the Land Court to authorise the establishment of 32 new crofts and

14 enlargements to existing crofts on the North Uist farm of Cheese Bay. Having inspected the farm and heard representations from the various parties involved, the Board issued the requisite orders in November 1915, at which point North Uist's owner, Sir Arthur Campbell Orde, intimating that his claim for compensation would exceed £300, asked the Court of Session to appoint the arbitrator to which the law entitled him. In April 1918, an arbitrator having at last been nominated, Sir Arthur lodged a claim for £16,852. And although he was eventually awarded only £4,770 the Board, as the 1911 Act had stipulated, was found liable for all the expenses of the case. (88) The inordinate amount of time taken to appoint an arbitrator was, in this particular instance, attributable to wartime circumstances. In other respects, however, the case was not untypical of those in which the Board was embroiled from its inception. And the ensuing and seemingly interminable delays — in the course of which neither the Board nor its prospective settlers knew whether or not the scheme in question would have to be abandoned — caused a great deal of bitterness and frustration among the many Hebridean cottars whose hopes of obtaining land had yet again been raised only to be eventually dashed. (89)

It was not altogether surprising, therefore, that by 1913 there was, as a Highland newspaper remarked, 'ample evidence of a coming revolt'. (90) In Lewis that year the island's proprietor, Major Duncan Matheson, opposed the Board's plans to create 131 new holdings on the farms of Galson, Gress, Carnish, Ardroil, Orinsay and Stimervay on the grounds that they were not suitable for crofts and that he would lose more by way of rent than he would gain by way of compensation. (91) Lady Gordon Cathcart adopted a similar stance with regard to the proposed subdivision of a number of farms in South Uist where, it was pointed out in the course of the summer, 'Some of the applicants in anticipation of getting land had kept stock for almost two years, and .... had to struggle hard to maintain that stock'. (92) Resolutions to the effect that 'if the Board of Agriculture would not hurry up there would be nothing for it but to seize the land' began to be passed at meetings in these and other areas. (93) And in December 1913 the Lewis farm of Reef was occupied by cottars from adjacent townships. (94)

A letter from the raiders to the Scottish Office made their position and predicament crystal clear:

We were applying for land since the year 1908. Applying to the proprietor at first and then to the C.D.B. and latterly to the Land Court .... We were getting replies giving neither encouragement nor discouragement, as if the whole proceedings were in mockery. The only reply we get now is 'that our applications are under consideration'. Anyhow we were believing we would get land and that caused us to remain at home in anticipation of getting to work on the land and that was not in our favour as we did not go elsewhere for work. If we won't have immediate possession we shall be compelled to dispose of our stock which we were diligently gathering and keeping together in order to have some for the new land ... As is well known an Act of Parliament was passed to give land to the landless and as is equally well known no land was received by anyone under the Act. Surely no one can blame us for the steps we have decided to take. But whether we get blamed or not is of no moment. We have suffered long enough as we are and though we were to suffer in another way we would hardly be worse off than we were. (95)

Reef, its occupants declared, 'was for ages cultivated by smallholders before the clearances'. (96) But whatever their moral and historical rights to it, their legal claims to the farm were non-existent and Matheson thus had no difficulty in obtaining court orders forbidding the offending cottars from trespassing on his property. The court's instructions, as was usual in such cases, were ignored and the raiders sentenced to six weeks' imprisonment. (97) But their actions, as the under-secretary of state for Scotland wrote at the time, were both 'a symptom and a warning' — a timely indication of the 'widespread dissatisfaction at the slow progress in acquiring holdings under the Act'. (98) And the troubles at Reef were not unsurprisingly accompanied by raids on farms in Barra and South Uist and followed, in the spring and early summer, by illegal occupations of lands elsewhere in the Hebrides. (99)

Like the Irish problem, the suffragette movement and the endemic labour unrest which belie Edwardian Britain's retrospective aura of prosperity and tranquillity, the growing discontent among the Highlands' landless population was submerged in the wider and more awful violence of the European war which broke out in August 1914. And when that war was finally over attitudes to Highland land, like attitudes to much else, were found to have undergone a number of not insignificant changes. The exigencies of the war itself, it was true, had caused land settlement to be practically suspended. (100) But its suspension had been accompanied by repeated assurances that once the war had been won 'the land question in the Highlands' would, as T.B. Morrison, lord advocate in Lloyd-George's coalition government declared at Inverness in 1917, 'be settled once and for all ... everyone is agreed that the people of the Highlands must be placed in possession of the soil'. (101) Such promises, like the rest of the 'homes fit for heroes' rhetoric of the time, were more freely made than kept. They did, however, represent a genuine realignment of opinion, typified by the new-found Liberal and Unionist unity on the need for a comprehensive land settlement policy in the Highlands and the waning of proprietorial opposition to such a policy; (102) and caused, in part at least, by a dawning realisation that land redistribution, though radical, even socialist, in origin and a vital component of the Bolsheviks' success in Russia, might help to preserve rather than destroy the existing social order which, in the years immediately following the war, more than once seemed in danger of imminent collapse. 'The dread of Marxism', as well as a sense of public gratitude to Highland servicemen, was — it was noted in a document drafted in the Scottish Office in the 1920s — responsible for the widespread advocacy of land settlement: 'a landholder had no time for revolution ... the holder feels he has a stake in his country and his face is turned towards stability and security'. (103)

Political commitment — even when inspired by fear of Bolshevism — was one thing; legislation another. The tentative additions made to the Board of Agriculture's land settlement powers in 1916 (104) did nothing to mollify irate feelings in the Highlands, where land raids, temporarily stilled by the war, showed every sign of commencing once again. In the spring of 1917, for example, lands were seized at Sconser in Skye and at Eoligarry in Barra. (105) And as was remarked in a police report on events at Eoligarry, the war had evidently done nothing to weaken the cottars' resolve to possess the land so long denied to them:

... there has grown up with the War a new feeling, a determination to cast aside legal methods and, by force of seizure, obtain what they deem their rights. They openly state their position thus. 'Why is it that our husbands and sons who are serving their country — some killed and some wounded — cannot obtain ... a place

to build a decent house upon? Why is it that the Government asks us to cultivate
the land, yet will not give us the land to cultivate? Why is it that two old bachelors
.... are allowed to have all Eoligarry lands for themselves, while we who are risking
our sons' lives to defend that land can by no means obtain an inch of it?' (106)
Asked by some of the women involved in the raid on Eoligarry, these questions were
soon to be repeated by people in Tiree and Sutherland.

In January 1918 a number of cottars from the Tiree township of Cornaigbeg
took possession of a thirteen-acre field on Belephetrish farm and at once proceeded
to prepare it for a spring planting of potatoes. Their actions, they said, were dictated
by their own poverty and by the government's injunctions to increase agricultural
production. The prime minister, they pointed out, 'had asked the people to get food
and that was what they were doing'. And they were doing it, moreover, on land which
would have been settled by the Board of Agriculture before the war, had not the
amount of compensation demanded by landlord and tenant been too high. The raiders
were all old men – two at least being in their seventies – and all had sons on active
service. But none of that prevented them from being sentenced to ten days' imprisonment as a result of legal proceedings initiated by the Duke of Argyll, the island's
owner. (107) Argyll's actions, however, were far from unique. That summer a group
of cottars from the Sutherland township of Portgower took over a small portion of
one of the very many sheep farms on the Duke of Sutherland's estate. One of the
raiders was a widow whose two sons were then at the front line in France. With her
companions she was jailed for ten days. (108) As far as the Highlands' nobility were
concerned, it appeared, not a great deal had changed since the clearances.

Between parliamentarians' pledges and the all too harsh realities of the cottar
population's existence there was thus a yawning gap of mutual mistrust. Events in
Tiree and Sutherland had their less dramatic counterparts in the Uists. And with
the demobilisation in 1919 of the very many young and landless Highlanders and
Hebrideans who had seen service in the war, the demand for holdings became, as
the Board of Agriculture reported, more insistent than ever. (109) 'When we were
in the trenches down to our knees in mud and blood,' remarked a Harris cottar, 'we
were promised all good things when we should return home victorious.' (110) 'We
returned home,' wrote another ex-serviceman, 'firmly believing that the promised
land would be given us.' (111) The reverse, however, proved to be the case. Excessive
costs, lack of powers, limited funds, unduly high expectations: these are the phrases
that characterised official thinking on Highland land settlement in the twelve months
following the armistice with Germany in November 1918. (112) And nowhere, during
this period, were the problems and frustrations of landlessness more acute than in
Lewis.

That there was not enough land in Lewis to provide holdings for all its people
was common knowledge – among the island's cottars as well as among the seemingly
endless procession of commissions of enquiry into Lewis' uniquely insoluble agrarian
problem. (113) But to the former, at least, that was a situation which made the
existence of the island's larger farms more, and not less, intolerable than it would
otherwise have been. And in 1917, when four Lewis seamen wrote to the editor
of the newly founded *Stornoway Gazette* to express the hope that his paper would
'help us to get the land of our forefathers, that they were deprived of cruelly to
make room for the sheep and grouse and the sporting Sasunnach', (114) the farms –

under pressure since the 1880s — were clearly due for division into crofts. That, at any rate, was the wartime government's opinion. In June 1917 the Board of Agriculture began preparing a Lewis land settlement scheme which was to be enacted at the end of the war and which was to involve practically every scrap of the island's potentially arable land. And the island then being up for sale, the government considered buying it in its entirety. (115) If Lewis had then passed into public ownership, its post-war history would undoubtedly have been more peaceful, if considerably less eventful, than proved to be the case. In the event, however, it was purchased for £143,000 by Lord Leverhulme, a man who had made a fortune from the manufacture and promotion of mass-produced soaps and who planned to spend a part of that fortune on the economic development of his large but by no means prosperous Hebridean estate — to the benefit, he hoped, of its inhabitants and to the eventual profit of himself. (116)

Unable to understand an attachment to the land that transcended the calculations of profit and loss which had ruled his own life, Leverhulme had little time for crofters and still less for crofting, which he thought of as a decidedly uncommercial mode of living. And that anyone should wish to *extend* such a system was, quite literally, outwith his comprehension. Land settlement, he informed the Board of Agriculture, was 'a gross waste of public money' and, in his opinion, 'the only solution of the land question in Lewis' was to be found in his own planned development of the island's fishing industry. (117) That Lewis was in need of economic aid of some description was certainly all too plain. Even before the war, Lewismen's by now traditional source of work and income, the herring industry, was beginning to fail them — largely because of the lower manpower needs of a fleet that was being remodelled around modern steam drifters. (118) And after the war, when the industry's long-established markets in central and eastern Europe were denied to it by revolutionary turmoil and politically motivated trade embargoes, there began a prolonged and disastrous slump officially summed up thus:

Formerly, Lewismen went in considerable numbers as hired men on the East coast fishing boats; but the general depression of the herring fishing industry now leaves fewer openings of this kind ... and taking ... the Summer and Autumn herring fishery as a whole it may be said that only a few hundred Lewismen now get employment in this fashion. (119)

So bleak were employment prospects on the east coast that, in the summer of 1920, not a few of the men who made their way there in search of work had to borrow the money they needed to get home again. (120) Emigration began to rise and the population of Lewis to fall for the first time in at least two hundred years. And with the island's inshore white fisheries also in trouble, (121) its crofters and cottars were consequently in no way opposed in principle to Leverhulme's employment-providing schemes.

They were, however, justifiably sceptical of their new landlord's claims that the development of Stornoway as a herring port equipped with canneries, processing factories and all the other paraphernalia of industrialised fishing, would bring economic salvation in its wake. Long used to the vagaries of the fisheries, and more aware than Leverhulme of the dimensions of the current crisis in the herring industry — a crisis which contributed more than his subsequent disputes with his island's population to Leverhulme's ultimate failure in the Hebrides — Lewis'cottars were not prepared to trust their island's owner to the extent of abandoning their claims to the land. (122)

And it was at this point that Leverhulme's ambitions and those of Lewis' large landless population came into — as it proved — irreconcilable conflict: a conflict beauti-
fully preserved in this account, by one of the Board of Agriculture's representatives,
of a meeting between Lord Leverhulme and a group of his dissident tenantry. Leverhulm
is addressing the crowd:

> And then there appeared in the next few minutes the most graphic word picture
> it is possible to imagine — a great fleet of fishing boats — a large fish-canning factory
> (already started) — railways — an electric power station; then one could see the
> garden city grow — steady work, steady pay, beautiful houses for all — every modern
> convenience and comfort. The insecurity of their present income was referred to; the
> squalor of their present houses deftly compared with the conditions in the new earthly
> paradise. Altogether it was a masterpiece; and it produced its effect; little cheers came
> involuntarily from a few here and there — more cheers! — general cheers!! ...
>
> And just then, while the artist was still adding skilful detail, there was a dramatic
> interruption.
>
> One of the ringleaders managed to rouse himself from the spell, and in an im-
> passioned voice addressed the crown in Gaelic, and this is what he said:
>
> *'So so, fhiribh! Cha dean so gnotach! Bheireadh am bodach mil-bheulach sin*
> *chreidsinn oirnn gu'm bheil dubh geal 's geal dubh! Ciod e dhuinn na bruadairean*
> *briagha aige, a thig no nach tig? 'Se am fearann tha sinn ag iarraidh. Agus 'se tha*
> *mise a faighneachd* (turning to face Lord Leverhulme and pointing dramatically
> towards him): *an toir thu dhuinn am fearann?'* The effect was electrical. The crowd
> roared their approbation.
>
> Lord Levershulme looked bewildered at this, to him, torrent of unintelligible
> sounds, but when the frenzied cheering with which it was greeted died down he
> spoke.
>
> 'I am sorry! It is my great misfortune that I do not understand the Gaelic language.
> But perhaps my interpreter will translate for me what has been said?'
>
> Said the interpreter: 'I am afraid, Lord Leverhulme, that it will be impossible for
> me to convey to you in English what has been so forcefully said in the older tongue;
> but I will do my best' — and his best was a masterpiece, not only in words but in
> tone and gesture and general effect:
>
> 'Come, come, men! This will not do! This honeymouthed man would have us
> believe that black is white and white is black. We are not concerned with his fancy
> dreams that may or may not come true! What we want is the *land* — and the question
> I put to him now is : *will you give us the land?'*
>
> The translation evoked a further round of cheering. A voice was heard to say:
> 'Not so bad for a poor language like the English!'
>
> Lord Leverhulme's picture, so skilfully painted was shattered in the artist's
> hand! (123)

In that confrontation are echoes of everything that this book is about — and many
of the reasons for the failure of Leverhulme, and of other planners before and since,
to develop the Highland economy while simultaneously winning the trust and respect
of the region's population.

Believing that 'the agitation for land was old fashioned and irrelevant', (124)
declaring that 'the retention of the whole of the existing farms in Lewis is an essential
foundation of the schemes I have for development', (125) and threatening that 'If the
farms are taken I shall be forced ... to stop the development work', (126) Leverhulme
was implacably opposed to land redistribution in general and to the subdivision of
the farms of Coll and Gress in particular. Situated within a few miles of Stornoway,
they were needed, he declared repeatedly, to supply the town with milk — an argument which, like his dislike of crofting agriculture *per se,* became something of an

obsession with him. (127) To Robert Munro, secretary of state for Scotland, to the Board of Agriculture and, above all, to Lewis' many hundreds of applicants for holdings, Leverhulme's anti-settlement stance was very far from being acceptable, however. (128) And it was perhaps unfortunate that the government, in the person of its Scottish secretary, allowed itself to be persuaded — in much the same way that the cottars' meeting described above was persuaded — that the Lewis land settlement programme should be suspended: 'until Lord Leverhulme should have an opportunity of showing whether by the development of his schemes he would convince the Lewismen that it was in their best interests to fall in with his proposals and cease their demands for smallholdings'. (129) From the first, however, Lord Leverhulme's chances of meeting these criteria seemed remote — not least because of the fact that in the spring of 1919 a number of cottars, most of them ex-servicemen, occupied Coll and Gress farms. (130)

The raiders' motives and justifications were simple: 'While we were engaged in our country's battles,' (131) said one man who had first applied for a holding in 1906,

promises without number were made that ... the land from which our forefathers were evicted would be placed in our possession ... While we were fighting nothing seemed too good for us, but now that the enemy has been overcome, through our help, these promises seem to take time in being fulfilled ... (132)

And the conditions in which they and their families lived, the raiders pointed out in a letter to Robert Munro, were no longer to be tolerated:

We were squatting under revolting conditions in hovels situated on other men's crofts. Into one of these hovels, containing two apartments, no fewer than 25 people were crowded. Our families were suffering unspeakably not only from insufficient accommodation but also from want of milk and other food while hundreds of acres of good land were lying untilled at our doors. (133)

The raiders thus considered that they had been 'reluctantly compelled to take matters into [their] own hands'; (134) and having once installed themselves they were not to be easily moved by all Leverhulme's appeals and blandishments. He was not at all opposed to the proprietor's plans, one raider remarked. But he 'wanted to have land whatever happened'. (135) 'We fought for this land in France,' declared another, 'and we're prepared to die for it in Lewis.' (136)

In April, therefore, the farm's occupants planted potatoes on their 'crofts' at Gress. And as if to show that Leverhulme's troubles were not to be confined to that particular locality, Galson — a farm on the other side of the island and the scene of considerable violence in the 1880s (137) — was again subjected to a number of illegal incursions. (138) Elsewhere in north-west Scotland, meanwhile, there were similar manifestations of steadily growing discontent. Before 1919 was over, lands had been seized in Harris and in North and South Uist (139) — developments that were accompanied by threats to occupy farms in areas as far apart as Tiree, Sutherland and Wester Ross. (140) And it was against this background of virtual guerilla warfare between the north-west Highlands' cottar population and the authorities that the coalition government's Land Settlement (Scotland) Bill finally passed into law on 23rd December 1919. (141)

The 1919 Act — which a Highland newspaper described as the first measure to have 'any real chance' of establishing 'a contented people on the soil of their native land', (142) and which the Duke of Sutherland hoped would finally lay 'that ghost of un-rest which has haunted the Highland glens for so long' (143) — greatly extended the powers and responsibilities of the Board of Agriculture to which it granted some £2,750,000 for settlement purposes. Enabled to advance substantial loans to holders in order to allow them to take over the stocks of newly settled sheep farms as well as to buy seeds, fertilisers and implements of every kind, the Board was also authorised to compulsorily purchase lands for settlement. And since purchase procedures, though by no means rapid, were much less complex than those involved in the Board's en-forcing — under the provisions of the 1911 Act — land settlement schemes on privately owned land, the majority of the crofts established after 1919 were constituted on lands bought for that purpose by the state, the settlers and any crofters already on the property becoming the crofting tenants of the Board of Agriculture. (144)

Despite the fact that 'instructions were given that land was to be secured as quickly as possible' and that the question of cost was 'to be a secondary consider-ation', (145) the 1919 Act provided no instant or automatic solution to the problem of landlessness in the Highlands and Hebrides. The complexities of the purchase negotiations in which the Board was then involved meant that in 1920 only 227 applicants were actually settled on new holdings; (146) while among the many land-less families whose ambitions seemed as far from realisation as they had ever been, 'suspicion and resentment' not unnaturally increased. (147) And from the time and money which the Board and its officials spent satisfying the claims of the landlords from whom it bought its growing number of estates, the crofting community drew an inevitable conclusion. 'From the conduct of the Board,' declared a group of Skye crofters, 'it can easily be seen that they are prejudiced against the landless people, doing their utmost to protect and please the landowners.' (148) It was an opinion that events in Lewis did little to refute.

In January 1920 the farms of Coll and Gress, from which the raiders had with-drawn the previous autumn, were reoccupied and, by way of confirming their intention of staying, their expropriators began to build houses upon them. (149) Leverhulme promptly retaliated by dismissing from his employment every man from the district of Back in which the disputed farms were situated — conduct that was as indiscriminate as it was dictatorial. (150) On this occasion, however, the raiding was 'on a larger scale and of a more determined nature' than at any time since the 1880s. (151) And far from intimidating the island's cottar population, Leverhulme's action merely generated more hostility — the happenings at Coll and Gress being quickly emulated on other farms in the south and west of Lewis. (152) Reverting to more conciliatory tactics, Leverhulme offered to provide the raiders with quarter-acre allotments of arable land or ten-acre crofts to be constituted on the common grazings of existing townships. But both plans were rejected. (153) Determined not to surrender, Leverhulme then attempted to split the Lewis crofting community and arouse public opinion against the raiders by halting all his building programmes — an action which meant the loss to Lewis of a weekly wage bill calculated to exceed £3,000, (154) but which had the good effect of causing the Scottish secretary to decide that something would have to be done to 'mitigate the situation' in the island. Since the passing of the Land Settlement Act, Munro pointed out in a letter to Leverhulme, settlement schemes had been initiated in a considerable, and steadily growing, number of places. Only in Lewis, where requests for holdings had been most strongly voiced 'and where expectations had been held out before the war of substantial concessions to the popular demand', had absolutely nothing been done. In such circumstances, the secretary of state concluded, 'the action of the raiders, while legally wrong and punishable, was at least intelligible'. (155)

That summer, however, Leverhulme won a series of notable victories in what he was increasingly prone to think of as his war with Munro, the Board of Agriculture and the occupants of Coll and Gress. Having conceded the need for land settlement schemes on the west coast of the island, he intimated his intention of keeping the east coast farms intact, announced that his development projects would not be resumed until Coll and Gress were vacated, and, on that basis, conducted a series of meetings in every part of Lewis at which he not unsurprisingly – considering the amount of employment at stake – succeeded in winning majority support for his stance. (156) The Board, however, remained unpersuaded:

> The situation appears to the Board to be that Lord Leverhulme is now endeavouring to prevent them from carrying out the duties of Land Settlement imposed upon them by Parliament by threatening to withdraw his schemes for developing the island unless the Board further suspend their operations in regard to Lewis. The Board feels that the time has now come when it is their clear duty to proceed with (at any rate) a partial scheme of land settlement in Lewis. (157)

With that view the illegal occupants of Coll and Gress would – had they been informed of it – have cordially concurred. Recalling how promptly the British government of 1887 had despatched its troops to put down unrest in Lewis, they contended, with understandable bitterness and cynicism, that 'the Government was always ready to enforce the law when unfavourable to the landless', and added that it had perhaps been too much to expect 'that when it is favourable to them it will be enforced without delay'. (158)

But in October 1920, aware of their growing isolation in Lewis, the raiders allowed the lord advocate – who visited the island for that purpose – to persuade them to withdraw from the disputed farms. (159) By leaving, they made clear, they were not abandoning their claims – merely giving the Board time to put a settlement scheme into operation and allowing Leverhulme to recommence his various activities on the island. Rightly or wrongly, they went with the belief that they had been given 'an undertaking that if we would withdraw ... the Board of Agriculture would deal with our demand for holdings'. The lord advocate was convinced he had given no such undertaking. (160) In such misunderstandings were the seeds of future troubles. But the truce thus achieved in Lewis did at least allow more attention to be paid to events elsewhere in north-west Scotland – events which showed that Lewis cottars' discontents were widely shared.

The spring of 1920 was marked by raids on lands in North Uist, on the MacLeod estate in Skye, and on a farm in Raasay. (161) And in the summer the focus of attention shifted to the north coast of Sutherland where cottars from the townships of Melvich and Portskerra took possession of a sheep farm promised them by the Duke of Sutherland in 1915 but sold by him four years later. (162) In conjunction with contemporary happenings in Lewis and the fact that almost fifty other farms were currently being threatened with illegal occupations or incursions of one kind or another, (163) these developments helped to justify the Duke of Sutherland's August declaration that there was a 'danger of the Highlands becoming something like Ireland' — then enmeshed in its people's violent struggle for independence — and certainly seemed to bear out his contention that the Board of Agriculture was 'displaying an attitude of helplessness in meeting the situation'. (164)

The winter of 1920-21, moreover, brought a rapid increase in tension and a more and more widespread tendency on the part of the Hebrides' landless population to resort to direct action against the farms which they had coveted for so long. In December, in what was said to be 'one of the largest raids that has taken place in the Western Isles', (165) several thousand acres of farmland in North Uist were occupied by a large number of cottars. (166) Hundreds of sheep and cattle having been driven off, an immediate start was made on building huts and houses and on preparing the land for cultivation. By March over 30 acres had been ploughed while an area twice that size had been thoroughly manured and otherwise made ready for turning over. Handed court orders which instructed them to quit the lands they had seized, the raiders refused to budge, one of them remarking with understandable asperity: 'We don't care a damn for the Sheriff. We are soldiers.' (167)

Having been eventually arrested, six of the more defiant of the farms' occupants were sentenced to two months' imprisonment. (168) But as a Skye cottar remarked in an exasperated letter to the Board of Agriculture — a letter which, like the statement of his North Uist compatriot, reflected his recent military experiences: 'It will not frighten us although people are imprisoned for land raiding — better that than four years under German fire.' (169) And in South Uist, where ex-servicemen were publicly declaring their intention to 'fight this time for ourselves and not for others' and where the sheep farms of Drimore and Dremisdale were occupied by cottars in the opening weeks of 1921, the same very general sentiments obviously prevailed. (170)

'From past experience,' the South Uist raiders announced, they were 'convinced that the only way to get the Board of Agriculture to move' was to 'take the law into their own hands' (171) — a view with which the Board naturally and vehemently disagreed, arguing, for example, that

Though the Board have in some cases promoted schemes on raided lands it is not the case that scheme has followed on raid as effect on cause, but rather that the raiders disturbed a situation which was tending towards solution. (172)

Such exercises in semantics, however, did little to shake the Board's many critics' conviction that its own dilatoriness was more than anything else responsible for the unrest in the Highlands, (173) and equally little to dispel the aura of mistrust and confusion surrounding its intentions in the Hebrides.

In 1921, admittedly, some progress was made in the Uists where settlement schemes were officially inaugurated on several of the recently raided farms. (174) In Harris, however, there were a number of raids on farmland in the vicinity of Rodel; (175) while in Raasay the ex-servicemen who had appropriated a field near Raasay House in March 1920 were joined, in the spring of 1921, by a party of raiders from the nearby island of Rona to which a number of families from the southern end of Raasay — the part of the island claimed by the raiders — had been removed during the clearances of the 1850s. (176) Conditions on Rona, the Scottish Land Court had reported in 1920, were 'miserable in the extreme', the land being of 'the poorest quality' and the houses of 'the most primitive description'. 'It is difficult to know,' the Court concluded, 'how anyone can carry on under such conditions, and still more so to understand how a living can be obtained.' (177) With that view, Rona's applicants for holdings in Raasay were in full agreement:

The circumstances under which we live here are most deplorable, the place being hardly fit for goats, far less human beings, while the good land on the south end of Raasay from which we could have a decent living and for which the best of our manhood has bled and died in Flanders and elsewhere is as a sporting ground for an independent English gentleman. (178)

The gentleman in question, acting in conjunction with Raasay's owners — the Glasgow firm of William Baird and Co. which had worked the island's ironstone deposits during the war (179) — at once initiated legal proceedings against the raiders who had begun to rebuild some of the ruined houses at Fearns (one of the townships cleared seventy years before) and to prepare their 'holdings' for immediate cultivation. (180) Instructed to relinquish the lands they had seized, the raiders refused to do so, whereupon five of them were sentenced to forty days' imprisonment (181) — an outcome which provoked an altogether understandable feeling of outrage on Raasay and Rona. A mass meeting was summoned. And to Lloyd-George and Robert Munro, to whom copies of the unanimously adopted resolutions were despatched, it was pointed out

that the offence of these men was that ... they reclaimed at their own expense for food production small patches of extensive arable land on the island of Raasay now devoted to the rearing of sheep and deer ... [and] that the sentences constitute an outrage upon and an insult to the memory of the gallant deeds performed by Western Islemen in this War and past wars. (182)

As far as the government were concerned, however, such sentiments counted for very little. And though Raasay was in fact purchased and its land redistributed by the Board of Agriculture in 1922, (183) the Scottish secretary reacted to the disquiet produced by the jailing of the raiders, not by issuing a conciliatory statement, but by proclaiming 'that in future land raiding is to operate as an absolute bar to land settlement, and that persons taking part in such raiding shall be removed from the Board's lists of approved applicants for small holdings'. (184) But despite such threats raiding continued, especially in Lewis where, in the course of 1921, the concordat established between Leverhulme, the government and the island's landless population broke down completely and irrevocably.

In December 1920 Lord Leverhulme had organised meetings in almost every township in Lewis in order to appeal to the island's crofting community to give him a guarantee that there would be no interference with his remaining farms for at least ten years — the time needed, he believed, to ensure the success of his plans. And except at Back — the district which contained the farms of Coll and Gress and where there were nine dissensions from the pro-Leverhulme resolution — he won unanimous approbation. (185) In response to the virtually irresistible pressure thus engendered, Munro had little option but to accede to Leverhulme's demands. And in January 1921 he assured Leverhulme that no part of his estate would be compulsorily acquired for settlement purposes until the stipulated ten years had elapsed. (186)

That agreement was of very dubious legality, however; and as far as the Highlands' cottar population was concerned served merely to confirm their growing belief that there was one law for the landlord and another for the landless. The 1919 Act had clearly stated that once the Board of Agriculture was 'satisfied' that there was, in a given area, a genuine 'demand for small holdings' and that 'suitable land' was available for their creation, it had a 'duty' to proceed with an appropriate settlement scheme. That the Back district of Lewis met all these requirements was impossible to deny. 'If one Act of Parliament can be overruled,' Munro was asked by an embittered applicant for a holding on Coll farm,

why not another? Why should some men be sent to prison for failing to comply with the law and others be paid huge salaries for the same thing? The Board cannot deny that we have satisfied them that there is a demand for small holdings and that there is suitable land available here to meet our demands. (187)

Convinced in the previous autumn that their claims to Coll and Gress were about to be sympathetically considered, (188) the cottars of Back felt betrayed. Nor were their feelings in any way mollified by Leverhulme's decision to make the farms of Reef, Carnish, Ardroil, Mealista, Timsgarry, Croir, Dalmore and Dalbeg available for settlement. All were situated in the south-western corner of Lewis, the nearest being thirty miles from Back and the most distant no less than sixty miles away. And though 67 new holdings and 166 enlargements to existing holdings were constituted on these farms at Whitsun 1921 they were awarded, naturally and fairly enough, to local applicants rather than to men from Back. (189)

That Gress and Coll were again raided in the spring of 1921 was not, therefore, very surprising. (190) More unexpected, however, was the slowing down and eventual suspension of work on Leverhulme's development projects on the island — ostensibly in response to events at Coll and Gress, but in fact because of the steadily increasing financial difficulties of Lewis' proprietor. (191) Matters came to a head at the end of August when Leverhulme announced his intention to leave Lewis to its own devices and to concentrate on Harris, which he had bought in 1919 and where he hoped to construct a large and profitable fishing port at Obbe, renamed Leverburgh in his honour. (192) Among Leverhulme's supporters in Lewis this announcement caused some consternation. (193) At Coll and Gress, however, the raiders were convinced that Leverhulme had abrogated his understanding with the government and with the people of Lewis and consequently believed themselves entitled to expect the Board of Agriculture to recommence its operations in the island. (194) With that view Munro could see no reason to disagree. 'In the circumstances as they now are,' he informed Leverhulme on 6th September 1921, 'I feel that I would not be justified in refraining any longer from putting into operation a generous measure of land settlement.' (195) And within the next few months land settlement schemes were drawn up for most of Lewis' remaining farms. (196)

By the end of 1921, therefore, the worst of the troubles in Lewis were at an end. And as the Board of Agriculture's settlement programme moved into high gear, it began to appear as if the process initiated by the establishment of the Congested Districts Board almost a quarter of a century earlier was at last approaching a satisfactory conclusion. Delays still occurred, however, and those affected by them not unnaturally felt that their claims were not receiving the attention they deserved. 'The Great European War was finished in about four years,' a group of Hebridean

cottars informed the Board in 1922,

> and the British Government through their Board of Agriculture has failed in about the same time to acquire small plots of land for those to whom they were promised ... We may be candid enough to tell you that our patience is now at breaking point, and that any untoward action on our part will be exonerated by every honest man in the kingdom, unless by your Board and its officials. (197)

The men who signed that letter occupied a farm in North Uist in the early part of 1923. (198) And their action was merely one of a long series of land raids which affected Sutherland, Lewis, Harris, Benbecula and Skye — where farms on the MacDonald and Strathaird estates were occupied by ex-servicemen objecting to the Board's tardiness in executing projected land settlement schemes in the area. (199)

By previous standards, however, these were mostly minor affairs and by 1924 the post-war crisis in the Hebrides was clearly over — if only for the reason that, as was pointed out in the Board of Agriculture's annual report for that year, practically all the potentially arable land in the areas where land hunger was, or had been, most acute had been resettled by crofting tenants. (200) In Skye, for instance, the Board had added 51,000 acres to the lands previously purchased by the Congested Districts Board and, by creating more than 200 new holdings, had practically eliminated landlessness on the island. (201) On the mainland, where cottars had always been fewer than in the islands, (202) the Board's activities had generally been confined to extending the pastures of coastal townships at the expense of neighbouring deer forests. In Sutherland, however, the congestion which had characterised the county's crofting townships since the clearances of a hundred years before was considerably eased by the breaking up of several sheep farms — a process carried to its ultimate conclusion in Tiree, Barra and South Uist where practically all the farms created between the 1820s and 1850s were restored to crofting tenants. More than a third of Tiree and Barra's populations gained holdings as a result; and though landlessness had been considerably more prevalent in these islands than in Skye, the problems caused by it were well on the way to being solved. (203) In North Uist and Harris, too, a considerable proportion of the long-deserted townships were repeopled; while in Lewis practically every one of the island's large farms was divided into crofts. In Lewis, of course, congestion and landlessness were so acute that resettlement failed 'to make such an appreciable difference to the welfare of the community ... as [was] noted in the case of some of the other islands'. But the awful and glaring injustices of the old agrarian order had at least been removed. (204)

Land settlement did not in itself provide an automatic answer to all the crofting community's problems. That more land had been placed under crofting tenure did nothing to mitigate the serious effects of the post-war collapse of stock prices and the continuing decline of the fishing industry — a decline that was not reversed until the 1960s. (205) The consequently precarious state of the crofting economy in general, and that of the island of Lewis in particular, was dramatically underlined by the crisis produced by the extraordinarily wet summer and autumn of 1923. The crops having failed, cattle prices being low and employment practically unobtainable, the following winter was distinguished in the Outer Isles by conditions which were more than faintly reminiscent of those that had prevailed in the region in the 1840s.

An emergency road construction programme was instituted to provide work and wages; while a government grant of £100,000, added to by various charitable contributions, was made available for the purchase of seed oats and seed potatoes. (206)

In one respect, however, the land settlement programme was an immediate and conspicuous success. Between 1886 and the early 1950s some 52,000 acres of arable land and 732,000 acres of pasture were added to the area occupied by crofters, a process which involved the creation of 2,742 new holdings and the enlargement of 5,160 previously existing crofts. (207) The Crofters Commission and the Congested Districts Board had contributed to this total. But the greater part of it must be attributed to the endeavours of the Board of Agriculture, in the years immediately following the First World War. And not only had more land been made available to crofters: sheep stocks had been taken over from outgoing farmers and managed with considerable success; financial and agricultural aid to crofters everywhere was increased; and the improvement in agricultural techniques and in housing conditions — first apparent in the immediate aftermath of the Crofters Act of 1886 — was maintained and indeed accelerated. (208) Although the effects of giving land to people who previously had none are psychological as well as economic, something of the benefits wrought by state intervention in crofting life can perhaps be deduced from some statistics concerning the Kilmuir estate in Skye, scene of some of the last clearances in the Highlands and of many of the violent events of the 1880s. The property was bought by the Congested Districts Board in 1904. After twenty-five years of public ownership the acreage under tillage had risen from 2,450 to 3,325, and the acreage occupied by crofters from 24,332 to 44,600 — ten large sheep farms being swept away, 85 new crofts created and 268 existing holdings enlarged in the process. Landlessness had been eliminated, and the number of thatched houses had fallen from 336 to 137, while the number of modern stone-built houses with slated roofs had increased from 20 to 304. (209)

By the end of the 1920s, therefore, the long struggle for the land, a struggle which constitutes the theme of the second part of this book, was virtually at an end. The agrarian and social injustices perpetrated by the creators of the land system that had taken shape during the clearances had been permanently removed — from the crofting community's Hebridean heartland at any rate. In the Outer Isles, in Tiree and in Skye, the majority of the farms so brutally established in the nineteenth century's first sixty years were occupied once more by crofting tenants — many of them former cottars whose ancestors had been evicted from the lands to which their descendants now returned. And if islands like Mull and the straths of Sutherland, Ross-shire and Inverness-shire are still deserted, that is not the crofting community's fault; rather it is an enduring testimonial to evictors more thorough, more ruthless and — by their own criteria — more successful than those that most of the Hebrides have known.

12. Postscript: The Crofting Community Today

TO end this history of the crofting community by reporting that all is well with contemporary crofting society would be pleasant. It would not, however, be true. Despite almost ninety years of officially inspired efforts to solve it, the crofting problem is with us still: changed in some respects, but all too recognisable in others. Thus, although the extreme poverty of the past has been eliminated, crofters' living standards are, in many respects, still below those prevailing elsewhere in Britain. In 1972, for instance, a survey of houses in North and South Uist and in Barra showed that 68, 58 and 74 per cent respectively were below the officially tolerable standard, many being quite unfit for habitation. (1) And in these depressing statistics is to be found one cause of the most alarming symptom of crofting decline: the departure of the young people, a development which, in the last forty or so years, has made depopulation rather than congestion and land hunger the universally acknowledged key to the crofting problem. (2) But the drift from the land is not solely the consequence of crofters' comparatively low standards of living. It is also the result of twentieth century circumstances – and especially of the changes which have occurred in the crofting community's relationships with the industrial and affluent society to the south of the Highlands. Immeasurably better educational facilities and increased communications with the south – in the social and intellectual as well as in the physical senses: all these have combined to bring the crofter more and more completely into the mainstream of British social and economic life. And in the process, his expectations and aspirations have changed fundamentally.

Throughout the nineteenth century crofters, as kelpers, migrant labourers and fishermen, continually participated in the capitalist economy. They did so, however, not in order to escape from their lives on the land but in order to obtain the funds needed to sustain that life. As long as he retained his hold on the land, in other words, the nineteenth-century crofter, in spite of his poverty, was fundamentally at east with himself. And until the 1920s the crofting community's efforts were accordingly directed not so much towards improving living standards as towards confirming and extending traditional rights in and claims to the land on which crofters lived or of which they had been deprived. This intense emotional attachment to the land – an attachment stemming ultimately from the place of the land in the kin-based society of the old Highlands and one that has often been commented on in this book – is still fairly prevalent among crofters. In the 1950s a royal commission described it thus:

Above all they have the feeling that the croft, its land its houses, are their own. They have gathered its stones and reared its buildings and occupied it as their own all their days. They have received it from their ancestors who won it from the wilderness and they cherish the hope that they will transmit it to the generations to come. Whatever be the legal theory they feel it to be their own – and in this respect the provisions of the Crofters Acts do no more than set the seal of Parliamentary approval on their own deepest convictions. (3)

Even today such feelings keep many crofters on their holdings in defiance of the dictates of financial self-interest — their attitude typified by the testimony of a crofting witness to the royal commission mentioned above. 'If I was not born there and the very dust of the place dear to me,' he concluded his account of the many disadvantages of his holding, 'I would quit tomorrow.' (4) But it is nevertheless the paradoxical crux of the contemporary crofting problem that, at the very time when the crofter's rights to his land were guaranteed, his increasing absorption into the wider society around him ensured that the land in itself could no longer be considered enough.

Unaccompanied by the living standards and amenities of the south, crofting life has, during the past thirty or forty years, become increasingly unattractive to a large proportion of the younger population of north-west Scotland. The steadily widening educational opportunities of the same period have provided these same young people with an alternative to crofting. And they have benefited immeasurably thereby. But because of the absence of local job opportunities, 'getting on' — whether in a profession or a skilled trade — has almost invariably meant 'getting out'. Individuals have benefited. But the crofting community as a whole has been impoverished as talent, enthusiasm, energy and leadership have been drained from it and into the urban and industrial centres of the south. (5) Throughout the crofting areas, for instance, the age structure of the remaining population has been grossly distorted. Thus in Scotland as a whole the proportion of people over the age of 65 to those under that age is 1:8. In parts of Lewis and Harris it is as high as 1:4 or even 1:2, and in some townships it is as high as 1:1. (6) The consequences of such a situation are as inevitable as they are disastrous. Enterprise and initiative are often lacking. The quality of social life has declined. And because of these developments still more people are tempted to give up the crofting life.

Given the social and economic difficulties currently confronting the crofting community — of which depopulation is easily the most serious — it is clear that the various measures which were taken between 1886 and the 1920s in order to give security of tenure and more land to crofters were not in themselves sufficient to ensure the survival of a healthy crofting society. And the contemporary crisis in crofting life has consequently led to a fairly widespread questioning of the validity of the crofting policy which has prevailed since the 1880s, and to attempts to evolve new and radically different solutions to crofters' problems. The essential weakness of the 1886 Crofters Act and of the land settlement programme of the early years of the present century, according to their recent critics, was that instead of reforming crofting agriculture they perpetuated and even extended the traditional crofting system. And being dependent on the fragmentation of arable land into a mass of tiny holdings that system, it is argued, is quite unsuited to modern conditions. Hence the conclusion of the last royal commission of enquiry into crofting affairs that crofting, 'as now organised, is fighting a losing battle against the social and economic forces of the day', and hence its members' decision to propose a series of explicitly 'modernising' measures — the most important of their recommendations being that everything possible should be done to amalgamate existing crofts into economically viable units. (7)

Expressing its regret that governments of the 1880s had not seen fit to implement the Napier Commission's virtually identical proposals, that commission – which
was chaired by Thomas M. Taylor, late principal of Aberdeen University, and which
reported in 1954 – proceeded to indict the 1886 Act as follows. In the 1880s, it was
ruefully observed,

> The legislature ... was concerned in the main with the individual crofter's position
> and the form which this protection took has in the long run created a rigidity in the
> crofting structure which is the cause of many of its difficulties today. (8)

Subsequent commentators have expressed the same verdict in even more forceful
language, declaring for example, that the first Crofters Act 'heralded the doom of
crofting life, insulating it from normal economic trends and *legally* ensuring that
crofting land could not now be developed into viable economic units'. (9) The
import of that contention is, to all intents and purposes, the same as that of the
Napier Commission's somewhat patronising recommendation that 'the most humble
and helpless class' of crofting tenants – i.e. the large majority who then paid annual
rents of £6 or under – should be denied immunity from eviction in order that they
might be 'resolutely though gently withdrawn' from the land and encouraged to
emigrate 'or take their position ... as labourers, mechanics, or fishermen'. (10) And
to the historian, in fact, the most striking feature of almost all the modern condemnations of the original Crofters Act is the resemblance they bear to the attacks made
upon it in the 1880s by the then Duke of Argyll and other opponents of the
crofters' movement. (11)

The principal weakness of the most popular critique of the 1886 Act – depending
as it does on the argument that the legislation in question tended to promote agricultural inefficiency and backwardness – is that while possibly sound *economically,* it
leaves social and political considerations out of account. The Act was Gladstone's
government's response to the very considerable political pressures generated by the
crofting community. And as such it laid aside the Napier Commission's economically
rational recommendations regarding the need for the consolidation of existing holdings and granted crofters' forcibly expressed wish that all tenants, no matter how
small their crofts, be granted security of tenure. The subsequent land settlement
programme was shaped by similar social and political forces. The sheep farms created
during the clearances were taken over and used not to provide a few large holdings
but to ensure – in response to the crofting community's demands – that as many
cottars and squatters as possible were provided with crofts. That *profits* might have
been higher if the land had been left in the occupation of farming, as opposed to
crofting, tenants was not denied:

> But the comparison is between two entirely different things. A sheep farm is a
> commercial undertaking and has to be judged as such; a crofting community is a
> way of living and cannot be judged in terms of a profit and loss account. The people
> were there and insisted upon staying there. Their conditions were a reproach to the
> nation of which they form part, and the only way to remove that reproach was to
> give them the available land. (12)

Nor was such a policy as divorced from economic realities as it may seem in
retrospect. The essential fallacy in the continuing quest for an economically and
agriculturally viable crofting system is that crofting, as was demonstrated in the
early chapters of this book, was created not as an agriculturally efficient method

of landholding but as a convenient means of disposing of a displaced population while simultaneously satisfying an urgent demand for labour. For better or worse, therefore, 'crofting has always meant the sum total of activities which yield the crofter some return — whether it is agriculture, fishing, public works, knitting, etc.' (13) The common factor has, of course, been agriculture. But in this century, as living standards have risen and the need to assiduously cultivate every scrap of potentially arable land has disappeared, its contribution to the crofting economy has declined rather than increased — a tendency that seems likely to continue. (14)

Unfortunately, however, the existing pattern of government aid to crofting, though praiseworthy and helpful in many respects, betrays a lack of sociological and historical insight into the realities of crofting life — the generous cropping and agricultural improvement grants for which provision was made in the Crofters Acts of 1955 and 1961 being unmatched by any like provision for crofters' non-agricultural activities. (15) The model croft, as far as recent legislators on the subject are concerned, is one which aspires to the status of a small farm. And the present grant structure consequently favours the crofters of areas like Caithness and Orkney where the land is more fertile and holdings larger than is the case in the north-west Highlands and Hebrides. In the early 1960s, for instance, the annual average payment of cropping grants to the 245 crofters of the Sutherland parish of Assynt was £146 as compared with an average payment of £12,585 to the 227 crofters of the Caithness parish of Watten and Wick. And the 535 crofters of Harris, to give another example, were then receiving an annual average of £3,772 from the same source — a sum which, when contrasted with the £29,848 being paid to the 532 crofters of Orkney, seems little better than derisory. (16)

At a superficial level these figures appear to add weight to the argument that crofting, in its present form on the north-western seaboard and in the Western Isles at any rate, is economically moribund and doomed to eventual disaster. What these and similar statistics really indicate, however, is that the crofting community of the region in question is still, as it has been since the heyday of the kelp industry, highly dependent for its livelihood on occupations that are essentially ancillary to the purely agricultural side of crofting. Indeed in a situation in which 85 per cent of existing holdings provide their occupants with less than the equivalent of two days' work a week (17) the crofter's non-agricultural employment — in fishing, weaving, tourism, forestry, construction, service industry, and so on — is usually of greater financial importance to him than his work on the land. A policy which involved the wholesale consolidation of smallholdings — apart from being of dubious commercial value insofar as the amalgamation of two, three or even more crofts would not necessarily produce financially viable farms in a part of the country where costs are high, markets distant and soil and climate unfavourable(18) — would, therefore, be socially disastrous in that its main effect would be to break the crofting community's historic ties with the land and thus accelerate the already alarming movement of people from the crofting areas to places where employment prospects are better and living standards higher. The probable outcome can be seen in Mull, an island where clearances were ruthlessly carried through to their logical conclusion, where large agricultural units consequently prevail and where depopulation has become critical — a state of affairs which may be contrasted with that prevailing in Lewis where a system of grossly undersized and uneconomic holdings maintains a relatively large and flourishing community. (19)

Had all previous attempts to 'modernise', 'rationalise' and 'improve' Highland agriculture been successful, in other words, the entire north of Scotland would have suffered the fate of the interior of Sutherland. And had not the crofting community successfully fought for its right to retain its hold upon the land Skye, Tiree and the Outer Isles would now be as empty as Mull. Nor is the retention of a large crofting population a romantic and unreal objective. As the decidedly unromantic Highlands and Islands Development Board (HIDB) has remarked of crofting, its vital contribution to the social and economic well-being of the region is that it

helps to maintain communities and their essential services in remote areas which might now otherwise be deserted. [And indeed] ... if one had to look ... for a way of life that would keep that number of people in such relatively untractable territory, it would be difficult to contrive a better system. (20)

To have a good chance of achieving economic success without at the same time causing social dislocation and cultural collapse, therefore, a development policy for the crofting areas ought ideally to be founded on maintaining the people on the land while simultaneously endeavouring to make every possible provision for the type of employment that can be combined with the management of a small croft.

It is consequently to the credit of the present Crofters Commission that, despite their having been constituted by an Act of Parliament which itself set great store by the need for an agriculturally viable crofting system, (21) they have pursued the objective of amalgamation and consolidation with considerable caution, attempting instead to promote and facilitate the crofting community's involvement in commercial and industrial enterprises of one kind or another and believing that the

willingness of crofters to work in industry combined with a desire to own their own homes and cultivate or stock a piece of land which they regard as their own, and which, for practical purposes is their own, gives us an opportunity in the Highlands of working towards a new form of industrial society which will be healthier and more stable than any community which is completely urbanised. This is the true value of the small croft, and as new opportunities for employment are provided it will increase rather than diminish. (22)

About such a vision of the Highland future there is nothing that is intrinsically utopian. It is merely an extension into present circumstances of the historic role of crofting as examined in this book. And when, on its being set up by the then Labour government in 1966, the HIDB adopted a similar policy with regard to crofting, long-standing hopes for the regeneration of the crofting community seemed on the point of realisation. But despite the explicit belief of its first chairman that 'No matter what success is achieved in the Eastern or Central Highlands ... the Board will be judged by its ability to hold population in the true crofting areas', (23) the HIDB has of late rather lost interest in crofting affairs. With the notable exception of its fishery development scheme, its attempts to provide crofters with non-agricultural employment opportunities have largely failed; while its endeavours in the tourist field have brought relatively few benefits to crofting tenants. (24)

Symptomatic of the Board's failure to make any real impression on the crofting problem has been its attitude to the land; for though the land cannot in itself provide crofters with more than a fraction of their economic requirements it is, to quote the Board's first annual report, the Highlands' 'basic natural resource'. (25) And it is by virtue of its unique relationship with, and claims to, the land that the crofting community exists. But in spite of its professed eagerness to learn from the experience of other countries and the fact that such experience has tended to show that the owning of an underdeveloped region's land by a few large landowners is inimic to its effective development, (26) the Board's policy on land reform has been practical non-existent and its policy on land use timorous and contradictory. In 1968, to give but one example of the latter characteristic, the Board proclaimed its intention to promote 'schemes for land reclamation and regeneration where the estimated return justifies the expense involved, or *where the social advantage in any comprehensive scheme is sufficiently strong to offset any doubt that the project is economically viable'*. (27) Two years later, when reporting on the development potential of the Strath of Kildonan, the Board observed that its planning was *'primarily economic rather than social in its orientation'* and concluded that land settlement in the strath could not be *economically* justified. (28)

That the HIDB can thus employ arguments which the Congested Districts Board of 1900 or the Board of Agriculture of 1920 would not have dared to use is indicative of the extent to which modern politicians – and those of the left in particular – have refused to grapple with the still contentious issue of landholding and land tenure in the Highlands. That Conservative administrations should have no desire to dismantle the apparatus of landlordism in the region is understandable. But that successive Labour governments have not advanced the good work begun by the Highland Land League and the Liberal party is considerably less comprehensible. And it is a failure which, in view of the recent enhancement of the Highlands' economic prospects as a result of the rapid expansion of tourism and, more important, oil-related industrial-isation, could prove disastrous for the crofting community. For the existing tennurial system gives crofters little opportunity to exercise control over, and reap benefits from, the changes which are undoubtedly imminent.

The crofting community's victories of the 1880s and subsequent decades – victor-ies enshrined in the 1886 Act and ensuing legislation – were won at a time of acute difficulty for Highland landlordism. Sheep farming was in decline. Farming tenants were difficult to find. It was easy and not altogether unprofitable to leave crofters in possession of the lands they already occupied and even to make more land available for settlement. Within the last few years, however, that situation has altered radically. Throughout the Highlands land values are soaring while changes in land use from agricultural to commercial and industrial purposes, once thought unlikely, are now inevitable and are, in fact, already occurring. And the crofter whose hard-won security of tenure applies only as long as his land is used for agricultural purposes can neither stop development nor benefit from it financially, since increased land values resulting from a change in land use accrue to landlord rather than tenant. Thus in a recent and notorious case in Skye a number of crofters were deprived of a part of their common grazings on which their landlord wished to build several houses. As in all such cases, compensation for the crofters was assessed by the Land Court with reference to the land's agricultural value only, and they received exactly £1.25 apiece. (29) The land-lord's profit was expected to amount to many thousands of pounds. It was in an attempt to enable crofters to cope with this sort of situation that the Crofters Commission proposed in October 1968 that crofters be given full rights of ownership to their crofts.

In essence, therefore, the revival of the concept of crofting owner occupation, or

peasant proprietorship as it used to be called, some sixty years after the Congested
Districts Board's failure to persuade significant numbers of crofters to buy their
holdings, (30) was the Commission's response to the changed economic circumstances
mentioned above. Their proposals, which they rightly claimed to constitute 'the most
important reform in crofting since the first Crofters Act of 1886', (31) and which
turned on the ownership issue, were designed to overhaul the entire crofting system
in order to make it more amenable to change and to give crofters a positive — and
hopefully profitable — role in developments which they could not, in any case, prevent.
Ownership, the Commission explained, would give crofters rights to the development
value of their holdings — rights which, if they had been incorporated in earlier legislation, would have multiplied the compensation awarded to the Skye crofters whose
case was outlined in the previous paragraph by a factor of several hundred. As owners
of their holdings, moreover, crofters would be better placed to participate in development on their own account. They could, for example, raise capital on the security of
their house and buildings — something they cannot do as crofting tenants.

The way in which the Commission intended their proposals to be implemented
was as simple as it was sweeping. On an appointed day all holdings held under crofting
tenure were to be compulsorily converted to owner occupation. Crofters' purchase
prices were to take the form of an annuity no greater than their current rents; and
landlords were to be compensated from public funds — the latter expenditure being
partially offset by the saving resulting from the abolition of the legal and administrative apparatus necessitated by crofters' unique tenurial status. The immediately
expressed fear that a free market in crofting land would lead to crofters selling out
to holiday home seekers and property developers the Commission partly dismissed
as misplaced paternalism and partly countered by proposing some degree of control
over the resale of croft land, such control to be accompanied by a 'Code of Land
Use' designed to ensure that no land lost its agricultural function without good
reason. And among crofters — from whose Federation of Crofters Unions the ownership proposals first emanated — there was a general, if understandably cautions,
welcome for the Commission's recommendations. (32)

Since 1968, however, the crofting community's enthusiasm for reform has noticeably diminished, a development due principally to the fact that the crofting reforms
contemplated by Mr. Edward Heath's Conservative government and by that government's Scottish secretary, Mr. Gordon Campbell — reforms which were embodied in a
Bill presented to parliament in 1973 (33) — bore little relation to the Commission's
original proposals and were, in fact, quite different from them in scope and intention.
The eventual rights and status of the crofter remained substantially as envisaged by
the Commission. But the means by which the change was to be effected had been
drastically revised. Along with several subsidiary reforms — of which land resale
controls and a land use code were two of the more important — the concept of compulsory conversion to ownership was abandoned. The crofter had now to elect to
buy his holding. And his purchase price, failing agreement with the landlord, was to
be determined by the Scottish Land Court in such a way as to include at least some
part of the holding's 'market' as opposed to 'crofting' value. Since purchase prices
thus calculated would include at least a proportion of a holding's development value
as well as a sum related to that likely to be realised by the sale of house and buildings —

assets which crofting tenants have always provided without assistance from their landlords — it seemed likely that crofters who opted for ownership would be asked to pay high, perhaps exorbitant, prices rather than the virtually nominal annuities originally proposed.

The Conservative Bill fell with Mr. Edward Heath's government in February 1974. Four months later Mr. William Ross, secretary of state for Scotland in the succeeding Labour administration, stated that the new government would proceed to enact the Crofters Commission's proposals regarding owner occupancy and added that the purchase price of holdings would relate to their crofting value only — a considerable advance on the Conservative measure. At the time of writing, the promised Bill is about to become law. Its provisions will enable many holdings, including the croft and other buildings, to be purchased by their tenants for not more than one or two hundred pounds. By its opponents the Bill has been castigated as a measure which will destroy the crofting community by exposing crofters to the full force of commercial development. Its supporters have portrayed it as a constructive and liberating influence. Its ultimate effects are difficult, if not impossible, to predict. But it certainly marks the end of an era. And as such it constitutes an appropriate stopping place.

In considering this and other aspects of the contemporary crofting situation the past may be deemed to be of little significance. But the past, in the Highlands at any rate, casts a long shadow. 'In order to make an appreciation of current crofting conditions,' observed the Taylor Commission in 1954,

> it is necessary to have regard to the historical background. This is important not only to enable the trend of events to be established but because the events of the past have a powerful influence on the minds of the crofting population. It was clear from the evidence put before us during our visits to the crofting areas that the history of the past remains vivid in the minds of the people and, in some measure, conditions their attitudes to current problems. (34)

The study of the past is not irrelevant, therefore, to a proper understanding of the Highland present; and in immediately preceding paragraphs, in fact, an attempt has been made to show that some knowledge of crofting history is a prerequisite to the effective tackling of contemporary crofting problems. The explanation of the present in historical terms is not, however, the historian's prime function. Historical investigation undertaken for such an entirely utilitarian end is apt to degenerate into propaganda, the task of uncovering and analysing the past being subsumed in that of reinforcing a preconceived view of the world. Absolute objectivity, in the sense of being quite uninfluenced by the circumstances of one's own time and place is, on the other hand, as unattainable a goal for the historian as for anyone else. The Highlander or Hebridean who can approach the history of the crofting community in a spirit of utter detachment has yet to be born. And I have no doubt that my own sympathy with crofters and their past and present predicament could be deduced from a casual reading of practically any page of this book. That sympathy, however, has not taken the form of uncritically reproducing crofters' understandably prejudiced view of their own history. Rather, as was indicated at the beginning, it has taken the form of explaining that view, of analysing the forces and events which have made the crofting community what it is. Myths have been treated as myths, not as facts. No space has been devoted to unprofitable speculation about what might have been; about how, for example, the catastrophe of the clearances might have been avoided. But in taking events as they happened I have tried to understand how crofters saw them, how they influenced crofters and what crofters did about them. The result, whatever its imper- fections, is the first full-length history of the crofting community. And its fundamental contention and conclusion is simply that the modern history of the Highlands, and certainly of crofters' part in it, can only be fully understood if it is considered in its entirety.

For example: while it became clear in the course of the research on which this book is based that the origins of the Highland land war of the 1880s are partially discernible in the economic and political circumstances of that decade, it became equally clear that crofters were then fighting to secure legal recognition of traditional rights in the land — rights of which they had been deprived, they believed, in the late eighteenth and early nineteenth centuries. The troubles of the 1880s, it was obvious too, were about lost lands as well as about lost rights. And even the men who returned from the Great War and set about seizing scores of Hebridean sheep farms knew, and said, that they were merely reoccupying the townships from which their great or great- great grandfathers had been evicted.

All this implied that the clearances at least would have to be taken into account — and described in starker terms than those employed by most recent historians. To landlords and economists, past and present, the Highland clearances, however regrett- able, were and are explicable in the jargon of historic necessity and economic inevit- ability. To crofters, past and present, they are explicable only as a brutal betrayal of traditional custom and belief, a reckless assertion of the interests of the few at the expense of those of the many. If that fact is not grasped the passions of the 1880s and indeed the entire legacy of bitterness bestowed by clearing landlords on succeeding generations of crofters are unintelligible. And without an understanding of these things a study of the crofting community's history would be meaningless and futile.

The clearances are not, however, the beginning of modern Highland history. The evictions of the nineteenth century had their origin in the events of the eighteenth century, in the transformation and modernisation of the traditional society of the Highlands and, above all, in the conversion of clan chieftains into commercial land- owners. From that extraordinarily successful absorption of the Gaelic aristocracy into the capitalist order all else followed. The rise of kelp and the coming of crofting; the clearance of inland glens and the settling of evicted tenantries on the coast; the initial proprietorial opposition to emigration as well as the subsequent conversion of estate managements to a pro-emigration stance when the kelp industry collapsed and crofters were seen to be of no more use to their landlords; the further extension and consolidation of the sheep farming system at crofters' expense: all these twists and turns of landlord policy can be seen to stem from the philosophy of commercial land management which was firmly implanted in the Highlands during the eighteenth century. That philosophy gave price of place to the pursuit of profit and was, as far as crofters were concerned, brutal, alien and wrong. But it was legitimised by a moral and economic code which sanctified self-interest, which derided the communal tradi- tions of the past, and which was supported by British governments in their role of guardians and representatives of the capitalist class whose creed it was.

That their chieftains frequently survived the turmoils of the eighteenth century —

albeit in new roles — made it immeasurably more difficult for the people of the Highlands to grasp the extent of the transformation which had occurred and to cope with the social and moral complexities of a situation in which the wellbeing of the kindred was subordinated to landlords' need to make more and more money from the land. In the summer of 1973, to give a modern example of the type of dilemma which inevitably arose, I talked to a Skye crofter who, while bitterly condemning lawyers, factors and other agents and representatives of the MacDonald estate management, told me that neither he nor his predecessors had ever had any quarrel with the MacDonalds of Sleat who, he assured me, had always been 'good landlords'. The MacLeods of Dunvegan, however, he damned to eternity as the proprietors responsible for some of the most brutal clearances in the Highlands. Had that old man been born in the north-west instead of in the east of Skye he would, I have no doubt, have reversed the roles he attributed to the island's principal families — between whom, incidentally, there is little to choose as far as numbers of evictions are concerned. Such was, and still is, the strength of a kin-based society allegedly destroyed more than two hundred years ago.

The persistence of such attitudes into the 1970s goes far to explain why effective popular resistance to Highland landlordism took so long to materialise. What was required was not just the courage to stand up to evictors who had the majesty of the law and the power of the state on their side, but a whole new way of looking at the world, of coming to terms with the reality of landlordism. The task of overthrowing the immense corpus of practice and belief inherited from a society with a continuous history of at least a thousand years was begun by the religious revivals of the first half of the nineteenth century — which gave a demoralised people a new confidence in themselves — and continued by the movement which eventually became known as the Highland Land League. But while the crofters of the 1880s owed a considerable debt to their predecessors of the Disruption era, their actions also mark the commencement of a new epoch in crofting history. The incipient conflict between the crofting community and the Highlands' landowning class broke into open warfare for the first time. An effective alliance was established between crofters and their sympathisers in the south. Landlordism was effectively challenged in the political arena while the social and economic foundations of landlords' power and authority were menaced by rent strikes and land raids. Highland landowners' consequent difficulties were compounded by the collapse of the sheep-farming economy established at the time of the clearances. And the outcome was that successive governments, prodded after 1900 by a new campaign of land seizures, conceded practically every one of the crofting community's demands. In 1886, 1911 and 1919 crofters gained security of tenure, judicially determined rents, compensation for improvements, more land and a steadily increasing amount of economic and financial assistance.

These were tremendous victories. Between 1881, when the land war began in Skye, and the 1920s, when a massive land settlement programme had been virtually completed, the whole trend of early nineteenth century crofting history was reversed. Insecurity of tenure was eliminated and the land given back to the people — developments which laid the basis for and were accompanied by a new prosperity symbolised by the rapid improvement in housing conditions. In more recent times, especially in the years since 1945, the prosperity of crofters has generally continued to increase. New and larger grants are available for housing. Wages have risen. Electricity, roads, and other services have been provided in all but the most remote localities. The welfare state has made its presence felt in the provision of old age pensions and other benefits. But still crofters and their families are worse off — and sometimes much worse off — than people in the south. All the attractions of crofting life — and there are not a few — cannot compensate for lack of employment opportunities, relatively low standards of living, high costs, remoteness and all the other disadvantages of life in crofting areas.

Thus it has come about that the crofting problem still remains — a problem now of how to halt depopulation and retain the crofting community on the land. And now, for the first time this century, many crofting areas are confronted with the problems, not of economic decline and decay, but of growth and expansion — especially the expansion of industries involved in the exploitation of North Sea oil. Oil-related industry provides great opportunities for the Highlands. But it also poses problems. And these, as the Crofters Commission has pointed out, could be considerable:

It would be ironic in the extreme if crofting townships, having lost a high proportion of their indigenous population over the past century through lack of employment opportunities, should be finally destroyed because of overwhelming and over-rapid development now. (35)

Unrestricted and uncontrolled industrialisation could thus prove to be an unmitigated disaster — especially in areas affected by essentially transient activities like the construction of the concrete production platforms needed to extract oil from the bed of the North Sea. And it is in this sense above all that oil-related industrial development can be seen as a continuation of the pattern of Highland exploitation established more than two hundred years ago. For the majority of the multinational corporations now involved in oil-related industry in the Highlands are interested, like sheep farmers and owners of kelping estates before them, only in the short-term exploitation of the region's natural resources. Then it was the seaweeds of the Atlantic seaboard and the pastures of the glens and straths. Now it is deep water and — if the Highlands' boundaries are extended seawards — oil itself. The combines and conglomerates of the 1970s, it might be said, bring prosperity to the localities in which they operate — thus demonstrating their superiority over the clearing landlords of the nineteenth century. But they will do so for a comparatively short period only. And the wages they pay are, in any-case, high only because they result from a 12-14 hour working day, a 6-7 day working week. Like the landlords of the previous century, moreover, these companies will not invest the profits of their exploitation in the Highlands. And even the bulk of the tax revenues derived from their activities and from oil itself seems likely, given Britain's ailing economy and a continuance of existing constitutional arrangements, to be appropriated by the British exchequer and set against the deficit on Britain's balance of payments account. The proportion of these revenues which will find its way back to the Highlands will consequently be small. And though it may be asserted that oil-related industry — on its eventual and inevitable withdrawal from the Highlands — will be replaced by other industries, the extent to which such replacement will actually occur is problematical. It is especially problematical in the area with which this book is concerned. And there is a real danger that, in the long run, oil-related industry will prove to be yet another downward spiral in the Highlands' long history of decline.

But if certain types of industry are likely to bring little benefit to the crofting community, this is not true of industry as such. And it is consequently arguable that the crofting community's survival is currently imperilled less by industrialisation than by those who are determined to preserve the existing social and economic situation in the Highlands. That there is much in the Highlands that ought to be conserved is undoubted. But to promote a policy of absolute and unwavering opposition to change, often in the name of preserving the Highland or crofting way of life, is implicitly or explicitly to condemn the indigenous population of the Highlands, repository of the way of life which is held to be at stake, to depressed, even declining, living standards. And from such a situation there would almost certainly ensue more migration, more depopulation.

For — as has already been remarked in this chapter — the modern crofter, particularly the younger crofter, knows all about the material benefits of urban civilisation and feels himself entitled to a share in these benefits. Thus while urban romanticists more than ever before tend to impose their own fantasies of primeval rustic bliss upon the crofter, the crofter himself, as the Crofters Commission has observed, is

> utterly bored with the romantic conception of his life and what the city dweller thinks good for him. He has long since rejected the role of the noble son of Nature who rejoices in homely fare and draws strength from stern privation. He now wants above all to be a citizen of this country as others are, not a curiosity or a 'character' or a being apart ... He prizes his Gaelic culture, but not to the extent of being treated as a museum piece on account of it; he will assuredly prize it still more highly when it is no longer the bedfellow of poverty and underprivilege. (36)

The key to the solution of the modern crofting problem lies, therefore, in giving crofters living standards and job opportunities equal to those elsewhere in Britain. And since sufficient income can never be won from the land, higher living standards can be achieved — to reiterate the vital fact about crofting life, past and present — only by the provision of adequate and remunerative employment opportunities outwith crofting agriculture itself.

Massive, temporary, uncontrolled oil-related industrialisation will not provide such opportunities. More permanent and more slowly developing oil-related industrialisation, such as is occurring in Lewis, may do so. Only time will tell. But throughout the crofting areas there is a need for more and better jobs — whether in new or traditional industries. There is a need also for a more imaginative Highland development policy — one that is concerned not merely with the provision of employment but with the regeneration of the social and cultural as well as the economic life of north-west Scotland. In this respect there is now some cause for optimism. For instance, in the newly created Western Isles Island Council or, to give its more manageable Gaelic designation, Comhairle nan Eilean, there exists, for the first time, an official body committed to the pursuit of economic development in conjunction with a vigorous policy of bilingual education and the fostering of Gaelic culture. To be successful, of course, such policies require money. And money can come only from central government which, as earlier chapters of this book have amply demonstrated, has traditionally taken a constructive interest in Highland affairs only when forced to do so.

The necessary funds could be made available from the tax revenues which will accrue from the exploitation of North Sea oil — exploitation which the deep, sheltered waters of the Highlands have made possible. And it is in this context that it is worth recalling the argument frequently heard at Highland Land League meetings in the 1880s: that the crofting problem would not be solved until self-government was restored to Scotland. (37) For it may be that only the creation of a fairly autonomous Scottish government will lead to North Sea oil wealth being made available in sufficient quantities to make possible the meaningful development of the Highlands or, for that matter, other parts of Scotland. It should be stressed, however, that even Scottish independence would not, in itself, do anything for the crofting community. There would still be a need for an imaginative and no doubt costly Highland development policy. And there would certainly still be a need for the reform of the Highlands' landholding structure. A recent and highly successful play which dealt with the same subject matter as this book concluded by declaring: 'The people do not own the land. The people do not control the land.' (38) And not until that situation is finally remedied will the crofting community be the master of its own destiny.

Hatton of Fintray.

References

Introduction

1. Based on data in Croft Comm., *Ann. Rep. for 1972*, 22.

2. *Report of the Commission of Enquiry into Crofting Conditions (Taylor Comm.)*, P.P. 1953-54, VIII, 9.

3. J. Bruce, *Letters on the Present Condition of the Highlands and Islands of Scotland*, Edinburgh, 1847, 15-17.

4. *Nap. Rep.*, 3.

5. Not surprisingly therefore the word *croitear* is a relatively recent importation into Gaelic from English. E. Dwelly, *The Illustrated Gaelic – English Dictionary*, Glasgow, 1971 edit.

6. The latter districts include the twelve parishes not designated crofting parishes under the 1886 Act: two in Easter Ross, two in the neighbourhood of Inverness and eight in south and mid-Argyll. Croft Comm., *Final Rep.*, 1912, xxiv. The common grazings which are a distinctive feature of the north-western crofting scene are seldom found elsewhere. The Scattalds of Shetland are an important exception – but they have a different historical origin. See J.R. Coull, 'Crofters Common Grazings in Scotland', *A.H.R.*, XVI, 143.

7. E.P. Thomson, *The Making of the English Working Class*, London, 1964, 8.

8. The works in question are those by M. Gray, E. Cregeen, P. Gaskell, E. Richards, and R.J. Adam. Details in Bibliography.

9. S. MacLean, 'The Poetry of the Clearances', *T.G.S.I.*, XXXVIII, 1939.

10. See, e.g., the works of J. Loch and the 8th Duke of Argyll cited in Bibliography.

11. The accounts in question are principally those by D. MacLeod, H. Miller, D. Ross, and A. MacKenzie. Details in Bibliography.

12. M. Gray, *The Highland Economy, 1750-1850*, Edinburgh, 1957, 246.

13. The authors I have in mind are I. Grimble and J. Prebble. Work cited in Bibliography.

14. P. Gaskell, *Morvern Transformed*, Cambridge, 1968, 25.

15. See inter al., Gray, *Highland Economy*, 246; Gaskell, *Morvern Transformed*, 25; E. Richards, *The Leviathan of Wealth*, London, 1973, 159 *et seq.*

Chapter 1

1. These paragraphs are based on a variety of secondary works, principally, E.J. Hobsbawm, *Industry and Empire*, London, 1968; H. Hamilton, *An Economic History of Scotland in the Eighteenth Century*, Oxford, 1963.

2. The feudal elements in the Highlands were largely legalistic, a result of medieval contacts with the south. Their existence in no way implies that the Highlands were

feudal in the generally accepted sociological sense of the term.

3. Quoted, J. Prebble, *Culloden,* London, 1961, 35.

4. A.R.B. Haldane, *The Drove Roads of Scotland,* (2nd edit.), Edinburgh, 1968, 7 *et seq.*

5. W. Matheson (ed.), *The Blind Harper,* Scottish Gaelic Texts Society, Edinburgh, 1970, 66-71. (The equivalent of seven collections are borrowed to pay for a shod, loud-snorting horse; a lordly saddle under the bottom; and he would of course be much the better of a golden bridle on his head... Five golden guineas – that is spent on a cord for the hat, and as much again for the hat itself... The price of a mart or more is paid for a pair of stockings of the best kind, and the change is not counted... He comes out of the shop with the latest fashion from France, and the fine clothes worn on his person yesterday with no little satisfaction are tossed into a corner... When he returns again to view his own country, though thousands of pounds have already been sent away, a cattle levy is imposed on the tenantry, and so the marts are exported, after being cured and sold at the market. Thus do the debts increase to be demanded from his son after him).

6. *Ibid.,* 132.

7. A. Cunningham, *The Loyal Clans,* Cambridge, 1932, 470.

8. I.F. Grant, *The MacLeods,* London, 1959, 404-409.

9. S. MacLean, 'Poetry of the Clearances', 1939, 298.

10. E.R. Cregeen, 'The Tacksmen and their Successors', *Scottish Studies,* XIII, 1969, 118.

11. R.H. Tawney, *The Agrarian Problem in the Sixteenth Century,* London, 1912, 188-189.

12. Cregeen, 'Tacksmen and their Successors', 1969, 126 *et seq.*

13. Tawney, *Agrarian Problem,* 1912, 188.

14. Prebble, *Culloden,* 1961, 42.

15. This account of the landholding system is largely based on, A. MacKerral, 'The Tacksman and his Holding in the South-West Highlands', *S.H.R.,* XXVI, 1947; E. Cregeen, 'The Changing Role of the House of Argyll in the Scottish Highlands', in N.T. Phillipson and R. Mitchison (eds.), *Scotland in the Age of Improvement,* Edinburgh, 1970, 5-23; Gray, *Highland Economy,* 1957, 3-54.

16. Thus the West African slave trade, though of immense importance to Britain, was carried on from coastal forts and hulks and the African peoples who produced and sold the slaves were left to their own devices. R. Oliver and J.D. Fage, *A Short History of Africa,* Harmondsworth, 1966, 120-121.

17. The one colonising venture in the north-west Highlands, that of the Fife Adventurers in Lewis, petered out about a dozen years after its commencement in 1598. See, W.C. MacKenzie, *History of the Outer Hebrides,* Paisley, 1903, 171-247.

18. Among all the vast literature on Jacobitism there is not one serious study of its social roots in the Highlands.

19. J.L. Campbell (ed.), *Highland Songs of the Forty-five,* Edinburgh, 1933, xxxiv.

20. A.J. Youngson, *After the Forty-five,* Edinburgh, 1973, 25 *et seq.*

21. MacL. P., Box 36(2), 'An Essay on the Late Emigration from the Highlands', 1774.

22. See, *e.g.,* the account of the activities of the fifth Duke of Argyll in the Introduction to, E. Cregeen (ed.), *Argyll Estate Instructions, 1771-1805,* Scottish History Society, Edinburgh, 1964.

23. Cregeen, 'Changing Role of the House of Argyll', 1970, 9.

24. Gray, *Highland Economy,* 1957, 86.

25. S. Johnson, *A Journey to the Western Islands of Scotland,* Oxford, 1924, 51.

26. Quoted, W.H. Murray, *The Islands of Western Scotland,* London, 1973, 212-213.

27. The importance of 'paternalism' in Highland affairs after 1746 has been wildly exaggerated. Usually such feelings were mere cloaks for economic self-interest. Occasionally, however, traces of a genuinely patriarchal attitude emerge, even in the nineteenth century. See, e.g., the account of MacLeod of Dunvegan's conduct during the famine of the 1840s, below, 58-9.

28. Earl of Selkirk, *Observations on the Present State of the Highlands of Scotland,* Edinburgh, 1805, 23.

29. A. Lang (ed.), *The Highlands of Scotland in 1750,* Edinburgh, 1898, 39.

30. T. Pennant, *A Tour in Scotland,* (3rd edit.), Warrington, (3 vols.), 1774, I, 208

31. J.E. Handley, *Scottish Farming in the Eighteenth Century,* London, 1953, 93-94.

32. M.I. Adam, 'The Highland Emigration of 1770', *S.H.R.,* XVI, 1919, 286-290. Also below, Chap. 9.

33. Pennant, *Tour,* 1774, II, 307.

34. See, e.g., T.C. Smout, *A History of the Scottish People, 1560-1830,* London, 1969, 358-359.

35. A. Carmichael, *Carmina Gadelica,* Edinburgh, (6 Vols.), 1928-1971, II, 244. (Bad is the tenancy but the evilness of the evil one is in the subtenancy).

36. W. Matheson (ed.), *The Songs of John MacCodrum,* Scottish Gaelic Texts Society, Edinburgh, 1938, 199-203, (The warrior chiefs are gone who had a yearning for the truth, who had regard for their faithful followers and had a yoke on their foe... Look around you and see the nobility without pity for poor folk, without kindness to friends; they are of the opinion that you do not belong to the soil, and though they have left you destitute they cannot see it as a loss; they have lost sight of every law and promise that was observed by those who took this land from the foe...)

37. Johnson, *Journey to the Western Islands,* 1924, 81.

38. J. Hall, *Travels in Scotland by an Unusual Route,* London, (2 vols.), 1807, II, 507.

Chapter 2

1. Gray, *Highland Economy,* 87-90. For a full account of the beginnings of sheep farming see, Gray, *op.cit.,* 86-104; Haldane, *Drove Roads,* 1968, 187-203.

2. J. Loch, *An Account of the Improvements on the Estates of the Marquess of Stafford,* London, 1820, xvii.

3. K. Marx, *Capital,* (3 vols.), London, 1887, II, 757.

4. R. Southey, *Journal of a Tour in Scotland in 1819,* London, 1929 edit., 136.

5, Marx, *Capital,* 1887, II, 757; D. MacLeod, *Gloomy Memories,* Glasgow, 1892 edit., XIV.

6. MacCulloch, *The Highlands and Western Isles,* 1824, IV, III.

7. Gray, *Highland Economy,* 86 *et seq.*

8. J. Walker, 'An Essay on Kelp', *Transactions of the Highland Society,* I, 1799, 1-4; R. Jamieson, 'Observations on Kelp', *loc. cit.,* 43.

9. Walker, 'Essay on Kelp', 2; Jamieson, 'Observations on Kelp', 44; Gray, *Highland Economy,* 130.

10. *Report on Home Industries in the Highlands and Islands,* P.P. 1914 XXXII, 24.

11. Gray, *Highland Economy,* 129-131.

12. Tods, Murray and Jamieson, P., GD 237/120/4, Memorial of The Kelp Proprietors, Feb. 1818.

13. J. MacDonald, *General View of the Agriculture of the Hebrides,* Edinburgh, 1811, 141.

14. Clan. P., GD 201/5/1228/2, Memorial of the Clanranald Trustees, n.d.; Clan. P., GD 201/5/1332/7a, Abstract of Clanranald's Kelp, n.d.

15. MacD. P., GD 211/36, Comparative View of Lord MacDonald's and Clanranald's Kelp Sales, 1806.

16. Walker, 'Essay on Kelp', 1799, 18.

17. Gray, *Highland Economy,* 18. The clear profit from N. Uist kelp amounted to £14,000 in 1812 alone. *N.S.A.,* XIV, 176.

18. Sea. P., GD 46/17/Vol. 36, Trustees Statement, July 1811, Sea. P., GD 46/17/Vol. 36.

19. Cregeen, *Argyll Estate Instructions,* 1964, xxxii, Gray, *Highland Economy,* 130.

20. Tods, Murray and Jamieson, P., GD 237/120/4, Memorial of the Kelp Proprietors, Feb. 1818.

21. A. Beaton, 'On the Art of Making Kelp', *Transactions of the Highland Society,* I, 1799, 33-39; J. Carr, *Caledonian Sketches,* London, 1799, 490; Walker, 'Essay on Kelp', 1799, 9. Details of seaweed types from Murray, *Western Isles,* 1973, 215.

22. Hall, *Travels in Scotland,* 1807, II, 548.

23. R. Brown, *Strictures and Remarks on the Earl of Selkirk's Observations,* Edinburgh, 1806, 93-97.

24. W. MacGillivray, 'Report on the Outer Hebrides', *Trans. of the Highland Soc.,* New Ser., II, 1831, 301.

25. Gray, *Highland Economy,* 128-129.

26. *Ibid.,* 132-133.

27. Grant, *The MacLeods,* 1959, 567.

28. The arguments in this paragraph are loosely based on Gray, *Highland Economy,* 131-134.

29. *N.C.,* Q. 11956.

30. RH 2/8/24, J. Blackadder, Survey and Valuation of Lord MacDonald's Estates, 1799, 4, 141.

31. *Ibid.,* 138; MacD. P., GD 221/15, Lord MacDonald's Commissioners, Minutes, 7 Nov. 1802.

32. Blackadder, Survey, 1799, 106.

33. *Ibid.,* 4.

34. *Ibid.,* 7-8; See also, MacD. P., GD221/116, Report on Lord MacDonald's Estate in Skye, 1811.

35. Blackadder, Survey, 1799, 137.

36. *Ibid.,* 131. According to the *N.S.A.,* N. Uist was not in fact lotted until 1814. (VIV, 174). But the 1799 survey was the basis of the allotment. See, H.A. Moisley, 'North Uist in 1799', *S.G.M.,* LXXVII, 1961, 89-92.

37. *Argyll Estate Instructions,* 48, Instructions to the Baillie of Tiree, 1799.

38. *Ibid.,* 51. For an account of improvement plans see, *Ibid.,* Introduction, *Passim.*

39. *Argyll Estate Instructions,* xxxii.

40. *N.C.,* Q. 13221.

41. *N.C.,* QQ. 3045-3046.

42. Blackadder, Survey, 1799, 106, 110.

43. MacD. P., GD 221/77, Chamberlain, N. Uist, to J. Campbell W.S., 9 May 1801.

44. See, *e.g.* MacD. P., GD 221/77, Petitions, Oct. 1801.

45. MacD. P., GD 221/51, List of Tenants Warned to Remove, 1801.

46. MacD. P., GD 221/77, Lord MacDonald's Commissioners, Minutes, 27 July 180

47. MacD. P., GD 221/58, Skye Chamberlain's Rep., 9 April 1803.

48. MacD. P., GD 221/53, Skye Chamberlain's Rep., 4 April 1803.

49. MacD. P., GD 221/15, Lord MacDonald's Commissioners, Memo., 3 April 1802

50. That particular remark was made by emigration agents in Benbecula in 1802. See Selkirk, *Observations,* (2nd edit.), Edinburgh, 1806, App. T, li.

51. MacD. P., GD 221/56, Resolutions of Lord MacDonald and his Commissioners, 18 April, 1803. For rentals see, Blackadder, Survey, 1799, 103; MacD. P., GD 221/15, Lord MacDonald's Commissioners, Minutes, 7 Jan. 1803.

52. MacD. P., GD 221/53, Skye Chamberlain's Reps., 11, 20 June 1803.

53. *Ibid.*

54. Selkirk, *Observations,* 1806, 32-33.

55. G.S. MacKenzie, *General View of the Agriculture of Ross and Cromarty,* London, 1813, 125.

56. MacCulloch, *Highlands and Western Isles,* 1824, IV, 111.

57. J. Walker, *Economical History of the Hebrides and Highlands of Scotland,* (2 vols.), London, 1812, II, 407.

58. MacDonald, *Agriculture of the Hebrides,* 1811, 674.

59. See *D.F.C.,* 1195.

60. S. MacMillan, *Bygone Lochaber,* Glasgow, 1971, 181-182; *D.F.C.,* Q. 48655; C. Fraser-MacIntosh, *Antiquarian Notes,* 2nd Ser., Inverness, 1897, 210 *et seq.*

61. Capt. Alex Cameron (son of Cameron of Invermallie) to Archibald MacMillan of Murlaggan, 30 Dec. 1804. Quoted MacMillan, *Bygone Lochaber,* 1971, 183.

62. *O.S.A.,* X, 265.

63. *O.S.A.,* XVI, 269.

64. *O.S.A.,* VI, 246; *N.S.A.,* XIV, 197.

65. *O.S.A.,* X, 470.

66. R.J. Adam, *Papers on Sutherland Estate Management,* 1802-1816, *S.H.S.,* Edinburgh, (2 vols.), 1972, I, xxvi-xxix.

67. Home Office Correspondence, Scotland, RH2/4/87, f. 151, Glengarry to Pelham, 21 March 1802.

68. *Trans. of the Highland Society,* II, 1803, vii.

69. *Ibid.,* x-xi; *Report on the Survey of the Coasts of Scotland,* P.P. 1803, 9-10; *Remarks on Selkirk's Observations,* 1806, 288-289.

70. *Trans. of the Highland Society,* II, 1803, vii-x; Sea. P., GD 46/17/Vol. 73, C. MacKenzie to Seaforth, 5 May 1803.

71. *Trans. of the Highland Society,* II, 1803, vii-x.

72. Highland Society, Committee on Emigration, 1st Rep., 1802. Quoted, Selkirk, *Observations,* 1805, 141. (The reports were not published).

73. A. Irvine, *Inquiry into the Causes and Effects of Emigration from the Highlands,* Edinburgh, 1802, 34, 36.

74. See, e.g., *O.S.A.,* III, 377; XIII, 317; XVI, 296; J. Girvin, *An Address to the Landholders, Factors, and Tenantry in the Highlands of Scotland for Preventing Emigration,* Edinburgh, 1803, 7-10.

75. *Mr. Telford's Survey and Report on the Coasts and Central Highlands of Scotland,* P.P. 1802-3, V, 15.

76. It is not without significance that Margaret Adam, whose contention it was that there was no connection between clearances and emigration in this period, does not mention the emigrations of 1801-1803 in her article, 'The Causes of the Highland Emigrations of 1783-1803', *S.H.R.,* XVII, 1920, 73-89.

77. A. MacMillan to E. Cameron, 1805. Quoted, MacMillan, *Bygone Lochaber,* 1971, 183.

78. *Sutherland Estate Management,* II, 64, C. Falconer to Marchioness of Stafford, 11 April 1807.

79. Among others, Selkirk makes this point. *Observations,* 1805, 131.

80. *Ibid.,* 131.

81. *Ibid.,* 131-134.

82. Brown, *Strictures and Remarks,* 1806, 93-97. Also, Selkirk, *Observations,* 1805, 135-136; *Select Committee on Emigration,* Scotland, P.P. 1841 VI, Q. 2377.

83. Home Office Correspondence, Scotland, R H 2/4/87, f. 151, Glengarry to Pelham, R H 2/4/87, f. 151.

84. *Trans. of the Highland Society,* II, 1803, vii-x; *Report on the Survey of the Coasts of Scotland,* P.P. 1803, 9-10; Sea. P., GD 46/17/Vol. 73, C. MacKenzie to Seaforth, 5 May 1803.

85. Telford, *Report,* 1803, 3.

86. See, K.A. Walpole, 'The Humanitarian Movement of the Early Nineteenth Century to Remedy Abuses on Emigrant Vessels to America', *T.R.H.S.,* 4th Ser., XIV, 1931, 198-201; O. MacDonagh, *A Pattern of Government Growth,* London, 1961, 54-65. Lacking a detailed knowledge of Highland affairs, Miss Walpole and Dr. MacDonagh tend to overemphasise the humanitarian motives of the Act's promulgators.

87. MacDonagh, *Pattern of Government Growth,* 1961, 61 *et seq.*

88. Home Office Correspondence, Scotland, R H 2/4/89, f. 140, Hope to Grant, 3 Sept. 1804.

89. *Select Committee on Emigration, 1st Rep.,* P.P. 1826 IV 1826-27 V, QQ, 329, 735. Also Selkirk, *Observations,* 1805, 154-157.

90. MacD. P., GD 221/53, Skye Chamberlain's Rep., 4 July 1803.

91. *Argyll Estate Instructions,* 201, Instructions to the Chamberlain of Mull, 20 Oct. 1803.

92. MacD. P., GD 221/53, Skye Chamberlain's Rep., 4 July 1803.

93. See, Telford, *Report*, 1803, 15.

94. MacD. P., GD 221/53, Skye Chamberlain's Rep., 7 Oct. 1803.

95. MacD. P., GD 221/53, 79, Skye Chamberlain's Reps., 2 March 1804, 17 April 1805; Home Office Correspondence, Scotland, R H 2/4/89, ff. 140-143, Hope to Grant, 3 Sept. 1804. Also *Argyll Estate Instructions*, 201 f.n., J. Maxwell to Argyll, 14 Aug. 1805.

96. A.R.B. Haldane, *New Ways Through the Glens*, London, 1962, vii.

97. As Selkirk warned at the time such projects gave only temporary relief to those employed on them. *Observations*, 1805, 58-59.

98. J. Headrick, *Report on the Island of Lewis*, n.d., 39; J. Browne, *A Critical Examination of Dr. MacCulloch's Work on the Highlands*, Edinburgh, 1825, 250-251.

99. MacKenzie, *Agriculture of Ross and Cromarty*, 1813, 83.

100. MacCulloch, *Highlands and Western Isles*, 1824, IV, 113.

101. Loch, *Account of Improvements*, 1820, 108-110; *Report from the Commissioners appointed for Inquiring into the Administration of the Poor Laws in Scotland* (afterwards *Poor Law Rep.*) P.P. 1884 XXVII-XXXVI, App. Pt. 2, 297.

102. The Most recent accounts are E. Richards, *The Leviathan of Wealth*, London, 1973; Adam, *Sutherland Estate Management*, 1972.

103. The name given to the events of 1813. *N.C.*, QQ. 38224-38225.

104. *N.C.*, Q. 27198.

105. *Sutherland Estate Management*, I, 156, P. Sellar to Lord Advocate Colquhoun, 24 May 1815.

106. Loch, *Account of Improvements*, 1820, 72-73.

107. *Ibid.*, 105.

108. J. Coull, 'Melness, A Crofting Community on the North Coast of Sutherland', *Scottish Studies*, VII, 1963, 184.

109. For these and other instances see, *N.S.A.*, XV, 73, 80, 95, 113, 125, 128.

110. See, Richards, *Leviathan of Wealth*, 1973, 205.

111. MacKenzie, *Agriculture of Ross and Cromarty*, 1813, 133-138, 248, 256-257, 323.

112. MacCulloch, *Highlands and Western Isles*, 1824, II, 271.

113. *N.S.A.*, XIV, 198.

114. *N.S.A.*, XIV, 136, 144; *Poor Law Rep.*, 1844, App. Pt. 2, 438.

115. *D.F.C.*, 1195; R. Somers, *Letters from the Highlands*, London, 1848, 55.

116. *Select Committee on Emigration, Scotland*, 1841, Q. 1067; *N.S.A.*, VII, 185-186. For a full account of removals in Morvern see, Gaskell, *Morvern Transformed*, 1968, 25-56.

117. MacD.P., GD 221/116, Report on Lord MacDonald's Estate in Skye, 1811.

118. MacD.P., GD 221/86, Lord MacDonald to his Skye Chamberlain, Aug. 1806.

119. Extract from letter, MacL. P., Box 35, J. MacPherson (Lord MacDonald's Skye Chamberlain) to J. Campbell W.S., 31 May, 1813.

120. *N.S.A.*, XIV, 322.

121. MacL. P., Box 61B, J. Nairne to MacLeod, 17 July 1810; Statement by MacLeod, *D.F.C.*, Q.5640.

122. MacL. P., Box 61B, Robertson to MacLeod, 9 March, 8 April, 10 June 1811.

123. See, Sea. P., GD 46/17/Vol. 37, W. Mackenzie W.S. to Seaforth, 2 April 1811.

124. Clan. P., GD 201/5/1233/64-73, Clanranald Trustees, Minutes, Feb. 1816 to March 1817.

125. Gray, *Highland Economy,* 67.

126. MacCulloch, *Highlands and Western Isles,* IV, 1824, 109.

127. Headrick, *Report on Lewis,* 29; *J.M.N. Rep.,* App. A, 91-97.

128. For these particular instances see, Clan. P. GD 201/5/1233/64-68, Clanranald Trustees, Minutes, 1816; *Argyll Estate Instruction,* 51, 55.

129. Developments in Sutherland and Skye are dealt with above, 19-21. For Lewis and Harris see below, 43-7.

130. F. Fraser Darling, *West Highland Survey,* Oxford, 1955, 282 *et seq;* A. Collier, *The Crofting Problem,* Cambridge, 1953, 31.

131. For a full account of the agrarian structure of crofting see, Fraser Darling, *West Highland Survey,* 197-211.

132. The divergence of the north-west's agrarian system from that of the rest of Scotland is a major theme of Gray, *Highland Economy.*

133. *Select Committee on Emigration, Scotland,* 1841, QQ. 4, 20, 32.

134. *Report on Home Industries,* 1914, 28. And statistics in Fraser Darling, *West Highland Survey,* 80-83.

135. R. Graham, Letter to Fox Maule, 28 June 1837: in *Select Committee on Emigration, Scotland,* 1841, App. 1, 213.

136. See below, 51.

137. Gray, *Highland Economy,* 136.

138. MacCulloch, *Highlands and Western Isles,* 1824, IV, 113. Early marriages are bemoaned by Highland and Hebridean ministers throughout the pages of the *N.S.A.*

139. Clan. P., GD 201/1/352, Factor's Rep., 21 April 1823.

140. Argyll, *Crofts and Farms in the Hebrides,* Edinburgh, 1883, 191.

141. MacDonald, *Agriculture of the Hebrides,* 1811, 119-120.

142. *O.S.A.,* X, 359-360.

143. MacDonald, *Agriculture of the Hebrides,* 1811, 113.

144. Pennant, *Tour,* I, 358. Cited, *Report on Home Industries,* 1914, 28.

145. Sea. P., GD 46/17/Vol. 43, W. MacKenzie W.S. to F. MacKenzie, 1 Jan. 1816.

146. Clan. P., GD 201/5/1233/61, Clanranald's Trustees, Minutes, 12 July 1815.

147. See above, 31.

148. MacDonald, *Agriculture of the Hebrides,* 1811, 5. Also, A. Fullarton and C.R. Baird, *Remarks on the Evils at Present Affecting the Highlands and Islands of Scotland,* Glasgow, 1838, 52-53.

149. Sea. P., GD 46/17/Vol. 44, Seaforth to P. Cockburn, 9 June 1823.

150. W. MacGillivray, 'Report on the Outer Hebrides', 1831, 263; *Select Committee on Emigration, Scotland,* 1841, Q. 868.

Chapter 3

1. *Report on Home Industries,* 1914, 28-29, 173-174. Also, Gray, *Highland Economy,* 155-156.

2. MacD. P., GD 221/33, Memorial of the Kelp Proprietors, 1813.

3. See, MacD. P., GD 221/33, Minutes of Meeting, 1 April 1813.

4. Tods, Murray and Jamieson, P., GD 237/120/4, Memorial of the Kelp Proprietors, Feb. 1818.

5. See, e.g., MacD. P., GD 221/47, Lord MacDonald's Commissioners, Draft Minutes, 2 April 1801.

6. *Report on Home Industries,* 1914, 26.

7. Sea. P., GD 46/17/Vol. 41, Seaforth to A. Mosman (his Liverpool kelp agent), 2 Oct. 1827.

8. Sea. P., GD 46/17/Vol. 41, Report on the State of Kelp, 12 Dec. 1827.

9. MacL. P., Box 39, Average Prices of Kelp at Liverpool, 1817-1828.

10. MacLaine of Lochbuie P., GD 174/47, J.L. Lindsay to MacLaine, 25 June 1827.

11. Sea. P., GD 46/17/Vol. 41, Report on the State of Kelp, 12 Dec. 1827.

12. See, Sea. P., GD 46/17/Vol. 41, Minutes of Meeting, 12 Dec. 1827.

13. Sea. P., GD 46/17/Vol. 41, Report on the State of Kelp, 12 Dec. 1827.

14. MacL. P., Box 39, Average Prices of Kelp at Liverpool, 1817-1828.

15. Clan. P., GD 201/5/1232/6/6, Report on Kelp by D. MacCrummen, 1830; Clan. P., GD 201/5/1232/6/10, D. Shaw to Hunter, Campbell & Co. W.S., 18 Aug. 1830.

16. MacL. P., Box 39, MacLeod to C. Grant, M.P., 18 April 1829. Also, MacL.P., Box 39, Petition of Proprietors of Land in the Hebrides, 1829; Sea. P., GD 46/17/ Vol. 41, Report on the State of Kelp, 12 Dec. 1827; Clan. P., D 201/1232/7/5b, J. Bowie to Hunter, Campbell & Co. W.S., 7 April 1831.

17. Highland Relief Board, Glasgow Section, *Final Rep.,* 1850, App. G, 46-47.

18. See below, 81-2.

19. Gray, *Highland Economy,* 156-157.

20. Clan. P., GD 201/5/1228/6, Goldie & Paton to Hunter, Campbell & Co. W.S., 12 March 1836; *N.C.,* Q. 44379.

21. Gray, *Highland Economy,* 157-158.

22. Clan. P., GD 201/4/97, D. Shaw to A. Hunter W.S., 25 Feb. 1827.

23. Clan. P., GD 201/1/352, 338, Factor's Reps., 21 April 1823, 25 Feb. 1827.

24. For a full analysis of the depression in the Highlands see, Gray, *Highland Economy,* 155-190.

25. MacD. P., GD 221/121, Report on Lord MacDonald's Estates, 1829.

26. See MacD. P., GD 221/39, 54, Factor's Reps., 14, 24 June 1816; Tods, Murray and Jamieson, P., GD 237/121/4, Memorial on Behalf of the Proprietors of the Hebrides, 26 March 1817.

27. See below, 108.

28. MacD. P., GD 221/121, Report on Lord MacDonald's Esatates, 1829; Sea. P., GD 46/17/Vol. 59, J. Adam (Lewis factor) to P. Cockburn, 23 Sept. 1823.

29. Clan. P., GD 201/1/352, Factor's Rep., 21 April 1823; Sea. P., GD 46/17/ Vol. 53, F. MacKenzie (Lewis factor) to Seaforth, 27 Sept. 1819.

30. *Book of Dunvegan,* II, 99.

31. Blackadder, Survey, 1799; MacD.P., GD 221/121, Report on Lord MacDonald' Estates, 1829.

32. Gray, *Highland Economy,* 146-147.

33. J. Hunter, 'Sheep and Deer: Highland Sheep Farming, 1850-1900', *Northern Scotland,* I, 1973, 200.

34. MacD. P., GD 221/40, MacDonald to J. Campbell, 25 Feb. 1817.

35. J. Anderson, 'Essay of the Present State of the Highlands', *Trans. of the Highland Society,* New Ser., II, 1831, 44; Gray, *Highland Economy,* 183.

36. Sea. P., GD 46/17/Vol. 44, Seaforth to P. Cockburn, 9 June 1823.

37. Fullarton and Baird, *Remarks,* 1838, 13.

38. Sea. P., GD 46/17/Vol. 44, Seaforth to P. Cockburn, 7 July 1823.

39. Such a confiscation was carried out in Barra in 1841. See above, 36.

40. Gray, *Highland Economy,* 183-184.

41. MacD. P., GD 221/54, Factor's Rep., 24 June 1816; MacD. P., GD 221/16, A. Murray to J. Campbell, 30 Aug. 1816; MacLaine of Lochbuie P., GD/174/28/1, Particulars of the Estate of Ulva, 1824.

42. Gray, *Highland Economy,* 183-184.

43. Clan. P., GD 201/1/352, Factor's Rep., 21 April 1823.

44. MacKenzie, *Agriculture of Ross and Cromarty,* 1813, 124.

45. Gray, *Highland Economy,* 184-185.

46. *The Witness,* 21 Oct. 1846.

47. See above, 2.

48. MacKenzie, *Outer Hebrides,* 1903, 493-496. Harris had originally belonged to MacLeod of Dunvegan who sold it in 1779 to Alexander MacLeod, a ship's captain and brother of and successor to MacLeod of Bernera. *Loc. cit.,* 485.

49. Gray, *Highland Economy,* 188.

50. *Book of Dunvegan,* II, 121.

51. Gray, *Highland Economy,* 157-158.

52. Clan. P., GD 201/1/338, Factor's Rep., 19 Nov. 1827.

53. See above, 29.

54. Clan. P., GD 201/5/1217/46, GD 201/4/97, Factor's Reps., 29 Jan., 26 Feb. 1827.

55. The population of S. Uist in 1831 was 6,890.

56. Clan. P., GD 201/5/1228/3, R. Brown to A. Swinton, 16 Feb. 1827.

57. Clan. P., GD 201/5/1217/46, GD 201/4/97, Factor's Reps., 29 Jan., 26 Feb., 1827.

58. *Select Committee on Emigration,* 1826-27, *1st Rep.,* 357; *3rd Rep.,* 500-508.

59. Clan. P., GD 201/1/338, Factor's Rep., 19 Nov. 1827; Clan. P., GD 201/5/1217/70, Note of Leases on Clanranald's Estate, 29 Jan. 1833.

60. Clan. P., GD 201/1/338, Factor's Rep., 19 Nov. 1827.

61. Stoneybridge, for example, survived to become a prominent centre of the land agitations of the late 19th and early 20th centuries.

62. Clan. P., GD 201/5/1217/70, Note of Leases on Clanranald's Estate, 29 Jan. 1833; Clan. P., GD 201/5/1235/16-17, Particulars of the Estate of Clanranald, 1836 and 1837. Also *D.F.C.,* QQ. 40472-40480.

63. *Select Committee on Emigration, Scotland,* 1841, Q. 1012.

64. See below, 81-2.

65. MacGillivray, 'Outer Hebrides', 1831, 301, 306. Also, *J.M.N. Rep.,* 1851, App. A, 115.

66. *Inverness Courier,* 16 July 1828; MacL. P., Box 39, A.N. MacLeod to C.Grant M.P., 18 April 1829.

67. Anderson, 'Present State of the Highlands', 1831 30; *N.S.A.,* XIV, 171, 208.

68. *Select Committee on Emigration, 1826, 1st Rep.,* QQ. 723-730.

69. See, e.g., Anderson, 'Present State of the Highlands', 1831, 30.

70. *Select Committee on Emigration,* 1827, *3rd Rep.,* QQ 2968-2971.

71. The phrase 'Shovelling out paupers' is the subtitle of H.J.M. Johnston, *British Emigration Policy, 1815-1830,* Oxford, 1972.

72. R.D.C. Black, *Economic Thought and the Irish Question,* Cambridge, 1960, 206-209; J.E. Pomfret, *The Struggle for Land in Ireland,* 1800-1923, Princeton, 1930, 10-15.

73. Sea. P., GD 46/17/Vol. 59, Seaforth to N. Vansittart, 13 Sept. 1822. Also, Sea. P., GD 46/17/Vol. 44, Seaforth to C. Grant M.P., 4 July 1823.

74. Sea. P., GD 46/17/Vol. 44, Seaforth to J. Gladstone, 11 June 1823.

75. *Select Committee on Emigration,* 1826-1827, *1st Rep.,* 356-357; *3rd Rep.,* 500-508. Also, H.I. Cowan, *British Emigration to British North America,* Toronto, 1961, 210-212.

76. Walpole, 'Abuses on Emigrant Vessels', 1931, 203-205.

77. See, e.g. Clan.P., GD 201/1/338, Factor's Rep., 19 Nov. 1827. Also, D.S. MacMillan, *Scotland and Australia, 1788-1850,* Oxford, 1967, 284.

78. 'Moladh Uibhist' ('In Praise of Uist'), M.F. Shaw, *Folksongs and Folklore of South Uist,* London, 1955, 79. (They come to us, deceitful and cunning, in order to entice us from our homes; they praise Manitoba to us, a cold country without coal or peat).

79. Sea. P., GD 46/17/Vol. 72, J. Adam to Seaforth, 31 March 1827.

80. See, *e.g.,* Riddell, P., AF 49/2B, Descriptive Survey of Ardnamurchan and Sunart, 1839.

81. *Select Committee on Emigration,* 1827, *3rd Rep.,* 14. The over-population of the Highlands is a theme that runs right through the relevant volumes of the *N.S.A.*

82. See, Clan. P., GD 201/5/1217/46, GD 201/4/97, Factor's Reps., 29 Jan., 26 Feb. 1827.

83. MacD. P., GD 221/85, Minutes Relative to Matters Submitted to Lord MacDonald, 29, 30 Oct. 1831.

84. *Select Committee on Emigration,* 1827, *3rd Rep.,* Q. 2984.

85. Riddell, P., AF 49/2B, Descriptive Survey of Ardnamurchan and Sunart, 1839.

86. *Select Committee on Emigration, Scotland,* 1841., QQ. 1765, 1767.

87. For an account of the Coigach clearances see, E. Richards, 'Problems on the Cromartie Estate, 1851-3', *S.H.R.,* L11, 1973, 149-164.

88. A. MacKenzie, *History of the MacKenzies,* Inverness, 1894, 345 *et seq.; Report by the Crofters Commission on the Social Condition of the People of Lewis in 1901 as Compared with Twenty Years Ago,* P.P. 1902, LXXXIII, xiii.

89. Sea. P., GD 46/17/Vol. 53, Seaforth to Coulburn, 27 July 1819.

90. Sea. P., GD 46/17/Vol. 53, Coulburn to Seaforth, 16 Aug. 1819.

91. Sea. P., GD 46/17/Vol. 55, Observations after examining the North Part of Lèwis, Oct. 1820.

92. Headrick, *Report on Lewis,* 1800, 27.

93. For his activities in Harris see below, this Chap.

94. H.A. Moisley *et al., Uig: A Hebridean Parish,* Glasgow, n.d., 11.

95. Sea. P., GD 46/17/Vol. 53, A. MacRae to Seaforth, 30 July 1819.

96. Some of his correspondence with Seaforth bears this address.

97. Sea. P., GD 46/1/315, A. MacRae to Seaforth, 9 Dec. 1833.

98. Sea. P., GD 46/17/Vol. 63, R. Brown to P. Cockburn, 29 Feb. 1823. Also,
Sea. P., GD 46/17/Vol. 53, J. Adam to Seaforth, 21 July 1823.

99. Sea. P., GD 46/17/Vol. 44, Seaforth to Cockburn, 9 June 1823.

100. *Report on the Condition of the Cottar Population of the Lews,* P.P. 1888
LXXX, 39-40.

101. *N.C.,* QQ. 17366-17393, 17407-17409, 17465-17474, 17556-17567, 17713-
17714.

102. See, Sea. P. GD 46/1/293-294, K. MacLeod *et al* to Seaforth, 11 Feb. 1823;
J. Smith *et al* to Seaforth, 12 Feb. 1823.

103. Sea. P., GD 46/17/Vol. 71, J. Adam to Seaforth, 15 May 1826. For Balallan
crofters' views of these events see *Scottish Highlander,* 29 Nov. 1888.

104. Statement by W. MacKay, Chamberlain to Lady Matheson, proprietrix of
Lewis, *Cottar Population,* 1888, 39-40. The statement was based on rentals in
MacKay's possession. See also, Sea. P. GD 46/17/Vol. 72, List of Townships Lotted,
Whitsun 1826.

105. Sea. P., GD 46/17/Vol. 44, Seaforth to Adam, 18 April 1823.

106. Sea. P., GD 46/17/Vol. 74, Adam to Seaforth, 6 March 1827.

107. Sea. P., GD 46/17/Vol. 76, A. Craig to Seaforth, 29 Feb. 1828.

108. Sea. P., GD 46/1/316, A. Stewart to Seaforth, 11 Dec. 1833.

109. Sea. P., GD 46/1/539, T. Knox, Memo., n.d.

110. See below, 47. Also *Cottar Population,* 1888, 39-40; *N.C.,* Q. 44863.

111. Sea. P., GD 46/17/Vol. 42, Seaforth to D. Stewart, 26 Feb. 1826.

112. Moisley *et al., Uig,* 11.

113. Sea. P., GD 46/17/Vol. 69, Seaforth to Cockburn, 20 Sept. 1825; Sea. P.,
GD 46/1/530, A. Stewart to Seaforth, n.d.

114. Sea. P., GD 46/17/Vol. 65, Adam to Seaforth, 15 March 1824; Sea. P.,
GD 46/17/Vol. 72, List of Townships Lotted, Whitsun 1826; Moisley *et al., Uig,* 11;
N.C., Q. 11470.

115. *Nap. Rep.,* App. A, 141; *N.C.,* QQ. 49986-49987.

116. Sea. P., GD 46/1/539, A. Stewart to Seaforth, n.d.

117. Sea. P., GD 46/1/323, T. Knox to Seaforth, 21 April 1836.

118. *N.C.,* QQ. 13850-13852.

119. *Report on the Applicability of Emigration to the Relief of the Distress in
the Highlands,* 1837, P.P. 1841 XXVII, 1.

120. See, MacMillan, *Scotland and Australia,* 1967, 278-288.

121. *Select Committee on Emigration,* 1827, *3rd Rep.,* QQ. 826, 2907, 2986.

122. *Ibid.*

123. MacD. P., GD 221/38, Report by N. Uist Factor as to Arrears, 14 Dec. 1839.

124. See above, 20.

125. *Poor Law Commission,* 1844, App. Pt. 2, 367.

126. *N.C.,* QQ. 12247-12262. Also, E. MacRury, *A Hebridean Parish,* Inverness, 1950, xi-xii; I.A. Crawford, 'Contributions to a History of Domestic Settlement in North Uist', *Scottish Studies,* IX, 1965, 40-41.

127. *N.C.,* Q. 17840; *D.F.C.,* QQ. 41889-42014.

128. See below, 43-4.

129. *N.C.,* QQ. 17723, 17805.

130. The quotation is part of a petition asking that the parish church of Harris be transferred from the west to the east of the island. CH 2/361/2, Presb. of Uist, Mins., 29 March 1837.

131. *Select Committee on Emigration, Scotland,* 1841, Q 2647; *Inverness Courier,* 24 July 1839.

132. *N.S.A.,* XIV, 157.

133. *D.F.C.,* QQ. 42283-42286. Also, J.B. Caird, 'The Isle of Harris', *S.G.M.,* LXVII, 1957, 89-95.

134. Fraser Darling, *West Highland Survey,* 1955, 44.

135. MacGillivray, 'Outer Hebrides', 1831, 306.

136. *Select Committee on Emigration, Scotland,* 1841, Q. 1012. Also, *Poor Law Commission,* 1844, App. Pt. 2, 369.

137. MacL. P., Box 51 C, E. Gibbons to MacLeod, 27 Dec. 1833.

138. *Ibid.*

139. *N.C.,* QQ. 5825-5938, etc. This evidence was of a particularly detailed kind. Lists of cleared townships were supplied along with the names of the sheep farmers who took them over. Many details were corroborated by several witnesses.

140. F. Fraser-Darling, *West Highland Survey,* 1955, 80-88.

141. *N.S.A.,* XIV, 296.

142. *Select Committee on Emigration,* 1826-27, *1st Rep.,* 356-357.

143. *N.S.A.,* XIV, 349.

144. The farm referred to was Rhu an Dunan in Bracadale, and the list of people on it, undated but probably drawn up about 1830, is to be found in MacL. P., Box 51 C.

145. MacL. P., Box 51 A, Rep. on Ebost by N. MacLean, 21 Jan. 1841.

146. *N.C.,* QQ. 4187-4191, 6169, 6231, 6822.

147. MacLeod's statement, *Nap. Rep.,* App. A, 25. Also, *N.C.,* QQ. 6056, 6822, 6954; *D.F.C.,* QQ. 4364, 4370-4371.

148. See below, 137-9.

149. *Reports of Commissioners for inquiring into the opportunities of Public Religious Worship afforded to the People of Scotland,* P.P. 1837 XXI - 1839 XXVI, *4th Rep.,* 1838, 198.

150. *N.S.A.,* VII, 187.

151. J.M. Gibbon, *Scots in Canada,* London, 1911, 133.

Chapter 4

1. J. Knox, *A Tour through the Highlands,* London, 1786, xci.

2. *Book of Dunvegan,* II, 10, Ullinish to MacLeod, 21 April 1772; S. Johnson, *Journey to the Western Isles,* Oxford, 1965 edit., 70.

3. J. Knox, *A View of the British Empire,* London, 1789, 615-617; *Documents Relative to the Distress in Scotland in 1783,* P.P. 1846 XXXVII; MacGregor, 'Destitution in the Highlands', *Celtic Magazine,* 1877, 436.

4. Gray, *Highland Economy,* 181.

5. Central Board of Management of the Fund for the Relief of the Destitute Inhabitants of the Highlands (afterwards, C.B.M.), *6th Rep.,* 1847, App. 3, 26.

6. W.P. Alison, *Letter to Sir John MacNeill,* Edinburgh, 1851, 6-7; Fullarton and Baird, *Remarks,* 1838, 69.

7. Fullarton and Baird, *Remarks,* 1838, 68; J.E. Handley, *The Irish in Scotland, 1798-1845,* Cork, 1943, 34-53.

8. See demographic statistics, Fraser Darling, *West Highland Survey,* 1955, 80-88.

9. MacL. P., Box 36(1), Sheriff-Sub. Fraser to MacLeod, 18 Feb. 1847.

10. The problem of congestion and land — hunger is more fully dealt with in Chaps. 5 and 7.

11. See *e.g.,* J. Bruce, *Letters,* 1847, 9.

12. E.R.R. Green, 'Agriculture', in R. Dudley Edwards and T. Desmond Williams, *The Great Famine,* Dublin, 1956, 122. And above, 18 *et seq.*

13. M. Martin, *A Description of the Western Isles of Scotland,* London (1884 edit.), 201.

14. MacKenzie, *Outer Isles,* 1903, 547. Also, *O.S.A.,* XIX, 249, 285.

15. R.N. Salaman, *History and Social Influence of the Potato,* Cambridge, 1949, pp.355-358. Salaman, after examining all the evidence, concludes that Martin was in error, but points out — somewhat paradoxically — that in view of the connections between the west Highlands, and Ireland, where the potato was in common use from the early 17th century, it is impossible that Highlanders can have been unaware of its existence before 1743.

16. MacCulloch, *Highlands and Western Isles,* 1824, III, 72; Gray, *Highland Economy,* 143, 207.

17. R. Somers, *Letters from the Highlands,* London, 1848, 72. Also, MacCulloch, *Highlands and Western Isles,* 1824, III, 217; W.P. Alison, *Observations on the Famine,* Edinburgh, 1847, 18; R.N. Salaman, *History of the Potato,* 1949, 367.

18. MacDonald, *Agriculture of the Hebrides,* 1811, 232.

19. C.B.M., *1st Rep.,* 1847, 10.

20. C.E. Trevelyan, *The Irish Crisis,* London, 1848, 9.

21. J.N. MacLeod, *Memorials of the Rev. Norman MacLeod,* Edinburgh, 1898, 219-220.

22. Tods, Murray and Jamieson, P., GD 237/121/4, Memorial on Behalf of the Proprietors in the Hebrides, Feb. 1817.

23. Tods, Murray and Jamieson, P., GD 237/121/4, W. Hik (Treasury Commissariat) to D. Shaw, 22 April 1817; Sea. P., GD 46/17/Vol. 48, Note of Payments due to Commissariat, n.d. Also, Sea, P., GD 46/13/178, Lady MacKenzie to Duke of Atholl, 27 Aug. 1817; and Sea. P., GD 46/13/170, vol. of correspondence relating to distress in Lewis.

24. MacD.P., GD 221/61, Factor's Rep., 23 May 1817.

25. MacD.P., GD 221/68, Factor's Rep., 5 June 1817.

26. Above, 35-6.

27. MacD.P., GD 221/38, List of Persons who got Seed Oats in 1837.

28. See, *e.g.*, Clan. P., GD 201/5/1223/61, Trustees Minutes, 12 July 1815.

29. *N.C.*, Q. 11975.

30. See, *e.g.*, Clan.P., GD 201/1/352, Factor's Rep., 21 April 1823.

31. Anderson, 'Present State of the Highlands', 1831, 33; *Inverness Courier*, 6 July 1831; *N.S.A.*, XIV, 77, 129-130.

32. Distress was greater in the spring of 1837 than at any other period before 1846. But as it was, in all its essentials, only a fairly brief foretaste of the much more serious crisis of the 1840s it has not been thought necessary to provide a full account. Information can be found in MacGregor, 'Destitution in the Highlands', 1877; *Select Committee on Emigration, Scotland*, 1841, Q. 135 *et seq.*

33. For a fairly full and comprehensible account of the nature of potato blight see, C. Woodham Smith, *The Great Hunger*, London, 1962, 94-102.

34. Reports of the Disease of the Potato Crop in Scotland in 1845, *THASS*, 1845-47, 460-469; *Correspondence Relating to the Measures Adopted for the Relief of the Distress in Scotland*, P.P. 1847 LIII, 60, Pole to Coffin, 6 Oct. 1846. (A second unpublished volume of this correspondence is available in the S.R.O. uncatalogued collection of material relating to Highland destitution. These volumes are afterwards referred to as *C.*, I and *C.*, II).

35. *J.M.N. Rep.*, xv, xvii.

36. Prebble, *Highland Clearances*, 172-173.

37. Reports of the Disease of the Potato Crop in Scotland in 1846, *THASS*, 1847-49, 94-123.

38. *The Witness*, 19 Sept. 1846.

39. *Inverness Courier*, 26 Aug. 1846.

40. J. Mitchell, *Reminiscences of My Life in the Highlands*, Chilworth (2 vols), 1883, II, 222.

41. *C.*, I, 65, Pole to Coffin, 6 Oct. 1846.

42. *C.*, I, 131, Coffin to Trevelyan, 22 Oct. 1846; *loc. cit.*, 132, Pole to Coffin, 19 Oct. 1846; *C.*, II, 246-247, Coffin to Trevelyan, 27 July 1847.

43. *C.*, I, 107, Coffin to Trevelyan, 17 Oct. 1846.

44. C.B.M., *1st Rep.*, 1847, 11.

45. *Inverness Courier*, 17 June 1846.

46. *C.*, I, II, N. MacLeod to Lord Advocate, 27 Aug. 1846.

47. *C.*, I, 52, Coffin to Trevelyan, 10 Oct. 1846.

48. *C.*, I, 144, Rev. A. MacGregor to Sir G. Grey, 27 Oct. 1846.

49. *Letters to the Rev. Dr. Norman MacLeod Regarding the Famine in the Highlands*, Glasgow, 1847, 8, Rev. N. MacKinnon to N. MacLeod, 29 Dec. 1846.

50. Prebble, *Highland Clearances*, 1963, 195.

51. Alison, *Observations*, 1847, 17.

52. Such was the fear of typhus that neighbours, friends and even the closest relatives suspected of having contracted it were frequently abandoned. For a much later example of the same practice see, T. Ferguson, *Scottish Social Welfare*, 1864-1914, Edinburgh, 1958, 398.

53. Free Church Destitution Committee, *2nd Statement*, 1847, 18-19.

54. *N.S.A.*, XIV, 345; Highland Relief Board, Glasgow Section (afterwards, Glas. Sect.), *Rep. on the Outer Hebrides*, 1849, 28.

55. *Select Committee Appointed to inquire into the refusal to grant Sites for Churches in Scotland,* P.P. 1847 XIII, QQ. 3594, 4495.

56. Coffin, Final Rep., 23 Sept. 1847, 59. Available in MacL. P., Box 36(1). Also, Somers, *Letters,* 1848, 161-3; Fullarton and Baird, *Remarks,* 1838, 19; Grey, *Highland Economy,* 158-70.

57. *C.,* I, 173, Coffin to Trevelyan, 14 Nov. 1846; *loc. cit.,* 107, Coffin to Trevelyan, 17 Oct. 1846.

58. See below, 78.

59. J.M.N. Rep., xii; *C.,* I, 107, Coffin to Trevelyan, 17 Oct. 1846; *Report on the State of Education in the Hebrides by Alexander Nicolson,* P.P. 1867 IV, 126-127.

60. *J.M.N. Rep.,* xii.

61. *Ibid.;* C.B.M., *1st Rep.,* 1847, 28 *et seq.*

62. *C.,* I, 1, Marquis of Lorne to Sir G. Grey, 25 July 1846.

63. *C.,* I, 3, Marquis of Lorne to Sir G. Grey, 20 Aug. 1846.

64. *C.,* I, 2, Baillie to Sir G. Grey, 20 Aug. 1846.

65. *C.,* I, 3-4.

66. CH 3/26/1, Free Synod of Argyll, Minutes, 3 Sept. 1846.

67. *C.,* I, 9, Lord Advocate to Sir G. Grey, 2 Sept. 1846.

68. Woodham - Smith, *Great Hunger,* 1962, 61.

69. *C.,* I, 6, Grey to Sir J. MacNeill, 2 Sept. 1846; *loc. cit.* 14, Treasury Minute, 8 Sept. 1846.

70. *D.N.B.,* IV, 672; Woodham - Smith, *Great Hunger,* 1962, 65-66.

71. *C.,* I, 107-109, Coffin to Trevelyan, 17 Oct. 1846; *loc. cit.,* 17, Traill to Chancellor of Exchequer, 14 Sept. 1846.

72. *C.,* I, 107-108, Coffin to Trevelyan, 17 Oct. 1846.

73. *C.,* I, 80, Trevelyan to MacNeill, 13 Oct. 1846; *loc. cit.* 109, Coffin to Trevelyan, 17 Oct. 1846.

74. *C.,* I, 115, Trevelyan to MacNeill, 16 Oct. 1846.

75. *C.,* I, 177, Treasury Minute, 20 Nov. 1846.

76. *C.,* II, 273, Coffin, Final Rep., 28 Sept. 1847.

77. *C.,* I, 195, Stewart to Trevelyan, 1 Dec. 1846.

78. *C.,* II, 273, Coffin, Final Rep., 28 Sept. 1847.

79. *Ibid.*

80. *C.,* I, 177, Treasury Minute, 20 Nov. 1846.

81. *C.,* II, 273, Coffin, Final Rep., 28 Sept. 1847.

82. *Ibid.*

83. S. Fairlie, 'The Corn Law Reconsidered', *E.H.R.,* XVIII, 1965, 568.

84. *C.,* I, 275, Coffin to Trevelyan, 9 Jan. 1847.

85. *C.,* I, 276, Trevelyan to Coffin, 13 Jan. 1847.

86. *C.,* I, 206, Coffin to Trevelyan, 9 Dec. 1846.

87. *C.,* I, 23, Trevelyan to Coffin, 11 Sept. 1846.

88. *Return of Applications for Advances under the Drainage Act,* P.P. 1847 XXXIV; *C.,* II, 276, Coffin, Final Rep., 28 Sept. 1847.

89. MacL. P., Box 36(2), MacLeod, Address to his Tenantry, Dec. 1846. Also, Grant, *The MacLeods,* 1959, 583.

90. *C.,* II, 186, MacLeod to Trevelyan, 17 April 1847; *loc. cit.,* 77, MacLeod to Coffin, 8 March 1847.

91. MacL. P., Box 36(2), MacLeod to his mother, 26 Jan. 1847.

92. MacL. P., Box 36(2), MacLeod to his mother, 26 Jan. 1847.

93. MacL. P., Box 36(2), MacLeod to Emily MacLeod, 10 Feb. 1847. Also, Grant, *The MacLeods,* 1959, 584-585. MacLeod's expenses did contribute to his being forced to sell part of his estate and take a job in London. But Miss Grant's contention that MacLeod ruined himself to save his people, while flattering to his family, is not entirely true. A series of injudicious investments, notably those surrounding the Glendale fishery station scheme (also the cause of widespread removals), had seriously weakened his finances before the famine. See, *Book of Dunvegan,* II, 142-144. Also above, 48.

94. See Richards, *Leviathan of Wealth,* 1973, 262-265.

95. *C.,* II, 246-248, Coffin to Trevelyan, 27 July 1847.

96. *Inverness Courier,* 11 July 1848; *J.M.N. Rep.,* xix-xx; *Social Condition of Lewis,* 1902, xv.

97. *C.,* II, 15, Fraser to Skene, 11 Feb. 1847. Also, *N.C.,* Q. 42561.

98. *C.,* II, 29, Coffin to Trevelyan, 26 Feb. 1847.

99. Somers, *Letters,* 1848, 148.

100. *C.,* II, 18, Trevelyan to Coffin, 26 Feb. 1847.

101. *Hansard,* 3rd Ser., LXXXIX, 608-609. Also, Home Office Domestic Entry Books, RH2/4/238, ff. 22-26, Sir G. Grey to Campbell of Islay, 21 Oct. 1846.

102. MacLaine of Lochbuie P., GD 174/28/2, Gregorson to MacLaine, 8 Jan. 1847.

103. *Book of Dunvegan,* II, 107.

104. *N.C.,* QQ. 4901, 5049, 5483, 5578, 5581, 33466.

105. *The Witness,* 19 Sept. 1846.

106. *C.,* I, 306-308, Coffin to Trevelyan, 4 Feb. 1847.

107. *C.,* I, 293-297, Pole to Coffin, 16 Jan. 1847.

108. J.L. Campbell (ed.), *Gaelic Words and Expressions from South Uist and Eriskay Collected by Rev. Fr. Allan MacDonald,* Dublin, 1958, 44. (They were dividing wild spinage at that time.)

109. *C.,* I, 293-297, Pole to Coffin, 16 Jan. 1847; *C.,* II, 234, Coffin to Trevelyan, 28 June 1847.

110. *C.,* II, 224, Sir J. MacNeill to Sir G. Grey, 3 May 1847.

111. *C.,* I, 297, Pole to Coffin, 16 Jan. 1847.

112. *C.,* I, 300, Coffin to Gordon, 19 Jan. 1847.

113. *C.,* II, 235, Coffin to Trevelyan, 28 June 1847.

114. Quoted, *Hansard,* 3rd Ser., XC, 311-313.

115. *C.,* I, 132, Pole to Coffin, 19 Oct. 1846.

116. See above, 22. Also, T.M. Murchison, 'Glenelg, Inverness-shire: Notes for a Parish History', *T.G.S.I.,* XL, 1957, 316-319.

117. Glas. Sect., *10th Rep.,* 1848, App. 1, 20.

118. Somers, *Letters,* 1848, 92.

119. *Ibid.* Also, *Hansard,* 3rd Ser., XC, 311-313.

120. *C.,* II, 261, Coffin to Trevelyan, 2 Sept. 1847.

121. *C.,* II, 15-16, Fraser to Skene, 11 Feb. 1847; Somers, *Letters,* 1848, 119.

122. C.B.M., *3rd Rep.,* 1847, App. 1, 17.

123. *C.,* II, 7, Fraser to Skene, 11 Feb. 1847.

124. *C.,* II, 42, Robertson to Coffin, 27 Feb. 1847.

125. *C.,* II, 33, Haliday to Pole, 2 March 1847.

126. *C.,* II, 187, Haliday to Trevelyan, 17 April 1847.

127. *C.,* I, 195, Stewart to Trevelyan, 28 Nov. 1846.

128. *C.,* II, 11, MacKinnon to Haliday, 19 Feb. 1847.

129. *C.,* I, 187, Haliday to Trevelyan, 17 April 1847.

130. *C.,* I, 177, Treasury Minute, 20 Nov. 1846; *C.,* II, 273-278, Coffin, Final Rep., 28 Sept. 1846.

131. *C.,* II, 277, Coffin, Final Rep., 28 Sept. 1847.

132. *Ibid.,* 274; *C.,* I, 297, Pole to Coffin, 16 Jan. 1847; *C.,* II, 15, Fraser to Skene, 11 Feb. 1847.

133. MacL. P., Box 36(2), Sir G. Grey to MacLeod, 5 March 1847; *C.,* II, 21-22, Coffin to Trevelyan, 23 Feb. 1847.

134. *C.,* II, 22, Coffin to Trevelyan, 23 Feb. 1847; *loc. cit.,* 23, Trevelyan to Coffin, 27 Feb. 1847.

135. C.B.M., *3rd Rep.,* 1847, 7.

136. *C.,* II, 48, Coffin to Trevelyan, 8 March 1847; C.B.M., *3rd Rep.,* 1847, 23.

137. MacL. P., Box 36(2), Account of the Operations of the Relief Board, n.d.

138. *C.,* II, 77, MacLeod to Coffin, 8 March 1847.

139. MacL. P., Box 36(2), MacLeod to [?], 10 Feb. 1847.

140. *C.,* II, 69, Trevelyan to Coffin, 11 March 1847; *loc. cit.,* 117, Haliday to Trevelyan, 21 March 1847; *loc. cit.,* 125-126. Coffin to Trevelyan, 22 March 1847; *loc. cit.,* 171, Coffin, Memo., 7 April 1847; MacL. P., Box 36(2), Trevelyan to Mrs. Perceval, 9 April 1847; C.B.M., *3rd Rep.,* 1847, 7-8.

141. CH 3/26/1, Free Synod of Argyll, Minutes, 2 Sept. 1847.

142. F.C. Dest Comm., *2nd Statement,* 1847, 4; *The Witness,* 21 Nov. 1846; Statement by the Free Church, *Nap. Rep.,* App. A, 398-399.

143. N.L. Walker, *Chapters from the History of the Free Church of Scotland,* Edinburgh, 1895, 138.

144. Bruce, *Letters,* 1847, 31.

145. C.B.M., *1st Rep.,* 1847, 1.

146. *C.,* I, 326, Coffin to Trevelyan, 4 Feb. 1847.

147. Trevelyan, *Irish Crisis,* 1848, 183.

148. *C.,* I, 276, Trevelyan to Coffin, 13 Jan. 1847; *loc. cit.,* 280, Trevelyan to Coffin, 21 Jan. 1847.

149. *C.,* I, 279-280, Trevelyan to Coffin, 21 Jan. 1847; *C.,* II, 105, Trevelyan to Baird, 19 March 1847; C.B.M., *1st Rep.,* 1847, 1.
1st Rep., 1847, 1.

150. C.B.M., *1st Rep.,* 1847, 4-5; Edin. Sect., *Final Rep.,* 1850, 9.

151. *C.,* II, 80, MacNeill to Trevelyan, 15 March 1847; Edin. Sect., *Final Rep.,* 1850, 10.

152. Sea. P., GD 46/13/199/4, T. Knox to Seaforth, 7 Feb. 1837.

153. Edin. Sect., *1st Rep.,* 1848, 70.

154. Lady MacCaskill, *Twelve Days in Skye,* (2nd edit.), London, 1852, 32.

155. *C.,* II, 274, Coffin, *Final Rep.,* 28 Sept. 1847; C.B.M., *1st Rep.,* 1847, 42; *2nd Rep.,* 1847, 10-11.

156. C.B.M., *1st Rep.*, 1847, 11; Glas. Sect., *Final Rep.*, 1850, 26; *Inverness Courier,* 1 Jan. 1852.

157. C.B.M., *4th Rep.*, 1847, 4-5; Glas. Sect., *5th Rep.*, 1847, 2; Edin. Sect., *7th Rep.*, 1847, 13.

158. *C.,* I, 256, Haliday to Trevelyan, 28 Dec. 1846; *C.,* II, 274, Coffin, *Final Rep.,* 28 Sept. 1847; MacL. P., Box 36(2), MacLeod to his mother, 21 Dec. 1846.

159. Edin. Sect., *6th Rep.*, 1847, 11; Glas. Sect., *5th Rep.*, 1847, 2.

160. C.B.M., *5th Rep.*, 1847, 1.

161. Glas. Sect., *5th Rep.*, 1847, 1.

162. C.B.M., *7th Rep.*, 1847, 8.

163. *C.,* II, 280, Coffin, *Final Rep.*, 28 Sept. 1847.

164. C.B.M., *7th Rep.*, 1847, 8.

165. Quoted, MacLeod, *Memorials,* 1898, 221-222.

166. Edin. Sect., *1st Rep.*, 1848, 28, 32, 35-36; Glas. Sect., *8th Rep.*, 1848, 5-7.

167. See, *C.,* II, 80, MacNeill to Trevelyan, 15 March 1847; *loc. cit.,* 250, Coffin, Memo., Aug. 1847; C.B.M., *3rd Rep.*, 1847, 5. Also, MacL. P., Box 36(2), MacLeod to his mother, 12 June 1847.

168. Somers, *Letters,* 1848, 67.

169. Edin. Sect., *1st Rep.*, 1848, 11.

170. *C.,* II, 105, Trevelyan to Baird, 19 March 1847.

171. C.B.M., *1st Rep.*, 1847, 3, 8.

172. Board of Supervision, 2nd Rep., 1847, 80.

173. Edin. Sect., *1st Rep.*, 1848, 4-12.

174. Edin. Sect., *1st Rep.*, 1848, 70; T. Mulock, *The Western Highlands and Islands of Scotland Socially Considered,* Edinburgh, 1850, 14.

175. MacL. P., Box 36(2), Account of the Operations of the Relief Board, n.d.

176. Edin. Sect., *1st Rep.*, 1848, 4-12; Final Rep., 1850, 15.

177. MacL. P., Box 36(2), E. MacLeod, undated and unaddressed letter.

178. Edin. Sect., *2nd Rep.*, 1848, 9-10.

179. CH 3/26/1, Free Synod of Argyll, Minutes, 2 Sept. 1847.

180. Edin. Sect., *1st Rep.*, 1848, 77.

181. Mulock, *Western Highlands,* 1850, 87.

182. MacL. P., Box 36(2), Rev. N. MacKinnon to Emily MacLeod, 11 July 1848.

183. Edin. Sect., *3rd Rep.*, 1848, 14-15.

184. *Ibid.,* 8, 19; Glas. Sect., *12th Rep.*, 1848, App. 3, 23.

185. Edin. Sect., *4th Rep.*, 1848, 64.

186. Edin. Sect., *4th Rep.*, 1848, 4; *2nd Rep.*, 1849, 122.

187. See, Richards, *Leviathan of Wealth,* 1973, 264; Glas. Sect., *10th Rep.*, 1848, App. 4, 9; Edin. Sect., *1st Rep.*, 1849, 19-20, 25;

188. Edin. Sect., *1st Rep.*, 1848, 50-52.

189. Mulock, *Western Highlands,* 1850, 97.

190. Edin. Sect., *3rd Rep.*, 1849, 261-262; *Final Rep.*, 1850, 26-27.

191. Edin. Sect., *3rd Rep.*, 1849, 261; *Final Rep.,* 1850, 26.

192. Edin. Sect., *3rd Rep.*, 1849, 271; *Final Rep.,* 1850, 33-35; Glas. Sect., *11th Rep.,* 1849, 7.

193. Agriculture and Fisheries Files, AF 7/85, Fishery Officer (W. Coast), Reps., 19 Nov. 1850, 8 April 1851.

194. Edin. Sect., *3rd Rep.,* 1849, 367; *Final Rep.,* 1850, 30-32.

195. MacCaskill, *Twelve Days in Skye,* 1852, 22, 29.

196. Edin. Sect., *2nd Rep.,* 1849, 78, 122; *Final Rep.,* 1850, 20.

197 Glas. Sect., *Rep. on the Outer Hebrides,* 1849, 9.

198. Home Office Domestic Entry Books, RH 2/4/238, f.23, Sir G. Grey to Campbell of Islay, 21 Oct. 1846.

199. C.B.M., *1st Rep.,* 1847, 4.

200. *J.M.N. Rep.,* xxxv.

201. *Inverness Courier,* 1 Jan. 1852.

202. See below, 132, 206.

203. This was eventually admitted by the Board itself. See, Edin. Sect., *Final Rep.,* 1850, 28-29.

204. E. MacIver (factor to the Duke of Sutherland), *D.F.C.,* Q. 29705.

205. W.A. Smith, *Lewsiana; or Life in the Outer Hebrides,* London, 1875, 282.

206. Mulock, *Western Highlands,* 1850, 87.

207. MacL. P., Box 36(2), Account of the Operations of the Relief Board, n.d.

208. MacL. P., Box 36(2), N. Ferguson to Emily MacLeod, 2 June 1848.

209. Edin. Sect., *1st Rep.,* 1848, 12.

210. MacGregor, 'Destitution in the Highlands', 1877, 440; Edin. Sect., *1st Rep.,* 1848, 68.

211. MacGregor, 'Destitution in the Highlands', 1877, 439.

212. MacL. P., Box 36(2), N. Ferguson to Emily MacLeod, 4 April 1848.

213. MacL. P., Box 36(2), Account of the Operations of the Relief Board, n.d.

214. MacL. P., Box 36(2), N. Ferguson to Emily MacLeod, 2 June 1848.

215. Peel to J. MacKenzie (factor, Gairloch estate), 28 Dec. 1849: quoted, J. MacKenzie, *Letter to Lord John Russell,* Edinburgh, 1851, 23.

216. Edin. Sect., *Final Rep.,* 1850, 49.

217. MacL. P., Box 36(1), Coffin, *Final Rep.,* Sept. 1847, 57. (Fuller version than that published in *Correspondence.*)

218. Edin. Sect., *3rd Rep.,* 1849, 387; G.P. Scrope, *Some Notes of a Tour in England, Scotland and Ireland,* London, 1849, 13.

219. Edin. Sect., *2nd Rep.,* 1849, 130-131.

220. Edin. Sect., *1st Rep.,* 1850, 2.

Chapter 5

1. MacL. P., Box 36(1), Coffin, *Final Rep.,* 28 Sept. 1849, 53-54.

2. *J.M.N. Rep.,* xxxvi.

3. MacL. P., Box 63, E. Gibbons to Emily MacLeod, 23 Nov. 1850.

4. See Fraser Darling, *West Highland Survey,* 1955, 80-88. Although some areas reached their population maxima before that date, 1851 is the demographic turning point for the north-west Highlands and islands as a while. The major exception, Lewis, where the maximum population was reached in 1911 is explained below, 125.

5. MacL. P., Box 36(1), Coffin, *Final Rep.,* 28 Sept. 1847, 53-54.

6. *Ibid.*

7. MacD. P., GD 221/160/4, State of Debts Due by Lord MacDonald, Nov. 1849.

8. MacD. P., GD 221/160/4, C.R. Souter to P. Cooper, 25 March 1850.

9. MacD. P., GD 221/148/4, Rep. on the MacDonald Estates, 1851.

10. 'Landed Tenure in the Highlands', *Westminster Review,* XXXIV, 1868, 289.

11. Hunter, 'Sheep and Deer', 1973, 200-202.

12. J. Campbell, *The Rev. Mr. Lachlan of Lochcarron, Additional Sermons, Lectures and Writings,* Inverness, 1930, 20.

13. T. MacLauchlan, *The Depopulation System in the Highlands,* Edinburgh, 1849, 15.

14. *C.,* II, 261, Coffin to Trevelyan, 2 Sept. 1847. Also, MacL. P., Box 36(1), Coffin, *Final Rep.,* 28 Sept. 1847, 57.

15. *N.C.,* QQ. 8283, 8449.

16. *Poor Law Commission,* 1844, v, xi, xv; *Social Condition of Lewis,* xxxviii.

17. Board of Supervision, *5th Rep.,* 1850, 62-74.

18. *J.M.N. Rep.,* xli. Also, *Select Committee on Emigration, Scotland,* 1841, *1st Re* Q. 1753; MacL. P., Box 36(1), Coffin, *Final Rep.,* 28 Sept. 1847, 57.

19. MacD. P., GD 221/148/4, Rep. on Lord MacDonald's Estates, 1851; MacD. P., GD 221/40, MacKinnon to Ranken, 13 Nov. 1847.

20. *Return of Population and Poor Rates, Scotland,* 1853, P.P. 1854-55 XLVII.

21. Home Office Domestic Entry Books, RH 2/4/240, ff. 1-2, H. Waddington to MacLeod of Dunvegan, 7 Dec. 1850.

22. J.P. Day, *Public Administration in the Highlands and Islands of Scotland,* London, 1918, 101-102.

23. Black, *Economic Thought and the Irish Question,* 1960, 129-130; Woodham - Smith, *Great Hunger,* 1962, 227.

24. Bruce, *Letters,* 1847, 74; MacLauchlan, *Depopulation System,* 1849, 16; Mulock, *Western Highlands,* 1850, 10.

25. Quoted, K. Marx, 'Forced Emigration', in *Marx and Engels on Britain,* Moscow, 1953, 372.

26. See below, 105.

27. Alison, *Letter to Sir John MacNeill,* 1851, *passim;* Scrope, *Notes of a Tour,* 1849, 8-18. As the ideas of economists and government officials about the Highlands tended to reflect their thinking about Ireland, a reading of Black, *Economic Thought and the Irish Question, 1960,* considerably clarifies the workings of the official mind on the Highland problem.

28. Home Office Domestic Entry Books, RH 2/4/238, f. 18, Grey to Marquess of Breadalbane, 20 Oct. 1846; *loc. cit., ff.* 90-93, Grey to MacLeod, 5 March 1847.

29. Glas. Sect., *12th Rep.,* 1849, 33; *13th Rep.,* 1850, 13; *Rep. on the Outer Hebrides,* 1849, 26.

30. Day, *Public Administration,* 1918, 102.

31. See e.g. *The Witness,* 22 Jan. 1851.

32. *The Witness,* 26 July 1851.

33. *J.M.N. Rep.,* xxxv-xxxvi; Alison, *Letter to Sir John MacNeill,* 1847, 11; *The Witness,* 2 Aug. 1851.

34. *Hansard,* 3rd Ser., CXVIII, 1303, 1842-1843, 1929.

35. *Nap. Rep.,* 104; Shepperson, *British Emigration to North America,* 1947, 48.

36. £15,545 was applied for and sanctioned under the Act. £5,250 was actually advanced to proprietors. *Nap. Rep.,* 104, f.n.

37. *Inverness Courier,* 18 Feb. 1848; MacL. P., Box 36(2), J. Loch to Trevelyan, 10 Jan. 1848.

38. The figure of 16,000 is arrived at by adding figures given in official and semi-official sources. Since about thirty separate references are involved they are not listed here (although many are cited in subsequent footnotes). And since all emigration statistics of this period are notoriously unreliable and incomplete, the fiture is merely provisional.

39. See above, 21.

40. *C.,* I, 63, Pole to Coffin, 6 Oct. 1846.

41. MacL. P., Box 36(2), N. Ferguson to Emily MacLeod, 2 June 1848.

42. *J.M.N. Rep.,* App. A, 142.

43. *Ibid.,* 7.

44. *J.M.N. Rep.,* xxxvi. But in view of Sir John's commitment to emigration such estimates should be treated with caution.

45. For its history see, F.H. Hitchins, *The Colonial Land and Emigration Commission,* Philadelphia, 1931.

46. MacL. P., Box 36(2), A. Allan to Emily MacLeod, 5 May 1849; Statement of the Skye Emigration Society, 18 Sept. 1851, in the *'Blue Book'* of the Highlands and Islands Emigration Society, 1853, 1-2. (Available in MacL. P. Box 36(1) and afterwards referred to as HIES, *'Blue Book'.*) Also, *loc. cit.,* 17, Statement of the Edinburgh Committee, March 1852.

47. MacL. P. Box 36(2), N. Ferguson to Emily MacLeod, 4 April, 2 June 1848; Letterbook IV of the HIES, Trevelyan to Dennison, 25 Oct. 1854. (Four HIES letterbooks are preserved in the SRO uncatalogued collection of material relating to Highland destitution. They are afterwards referred to as *HIES,* I-IV.)

48. MacCaskill, *Twelve Days in Skye,* 1852, 7.

49. Board of Supervision, *6th Rep.,* 1851, iv-v; Alison, *Letter to Sir John MacNeill,* 1847, 55. Also letters reproduced in D. Ross, *The Scottish Highlanders,* Glasgow, 1852, 9-13.

50. CH 3/26/1, Free Synod of Argyll, Minutes, 1 Sept. 1852.

51. MacL. P., Box 36(2), J. Ferguson to Emily MacLeod, 25 June 1852.

52. *Report of the Highland Emigration Society,* 1853, 12.

53. MacL. P., Box 36(2), Chant to Trevelyan, 8 Aug. 1852.

54. Quoted, *HIES,* II, Trevelyan to Cropper, 5 Aug. 1852.

55. HIES, *'Blue Book',* 1853, 1.

56. See, *inter al.,* MacL. P., Box 36(1), Coffin, *Final Rep.,* 28 Sept. 1847, 54-56; Fullarton and Baird, *Remarks,* 1838, 51.

57. See above, 76.

58. *The Witness,* 12 Sept. 1849.

59. Scrope, *Notes of a Tour,* 1849, 10-11.

60. T. MacLauchlan, 'The Influence of Emigration on the Social Condition of the Highlands', *Transactions of the National Association for the Promotion of Social Science,* 1863, 607.

61. See below, 122 *et seq.*

62. *Nap. Rep.,* App. A., 12.

63. *N.C.,* Q. 31163.

64. *N.C.*, QQ. 3772, 45065.

65. *Nap. Rep.*, 103.

66. J.M. MacKenzie (chamberlain, Lewis), *N.C.*, Q. 45993.

67. *Papers Relative to Emigration to the North American Colonies*, 1852, 7, A.C. Buchanan to J. Fleming, 26 Nov. 1851.

68. *J.M.N. Rep.*, App. A., 95.

69. *Nap. Rep.* App. A., 162; *N.C.*, QQ. 13741-13787, 13993-13999, 14440-14467. All facts and figures supplied by landowner's representatives who would not, presumably, be inclined to exaggerate. See also, Moisley, *et al., Uig*, n.d., 12.

70. *N.C.*, Q. 16216.

71. *HIES*, I, Trevelyan to Coffin, 13 July 1852. For figure see, *Papers Relative to Emigration to the British Provinces in North America*, 1849, 28; *Papers Relative to Emigration to the North American Colonies*, 1852, 7-8.

72. See *N.C.*, QQ. 11142-11151, etc.

73. Carmichael, *Carmina Gadelica*, 1928-1971, III, 351.

74. *The Witness*, 9 Aug. 1848. See also, *Papers Relative to Emigration to the British Provinces in North America*, 1849, 28.

75. *Papers Relative to Emigration to the North American Colonies*, 1852, 17, G.M. Douglas to A.C. Buchanan, 15 Dec. 1851; *loc.cit.*, Buchanan to J. Fleming, 26 Nov. 1851. Douglas was the medical superintendent at Grosse Isle. See, T. Coleman, *Passage to America*, London, 1972, 137-138.

76. *Dundas Warden*, 2 Oct. 1851: quoted, Gibbon, *Scots in Canada*, 191,132.

77. *Papers Relative to Emigration to the North American Colonies*, 1852, 8-10, Buchanan to J. Fleming, 26 Nov. 1851.

78. Gordon to Greig, 18 Dec. 1850: quoted, *The Witness*, 28 Dec. 1850. (Greig was raising funds for refugees from Barra).

79. *N.C.*, Q. 12112; C.F., AF 67/96, Pol. Rep., Barra, 10 Jan. 1888.

80. *The Witness*, 18, 21 Dec. 1850; *Inverness Courier*, 13 Feb. 1851.

81. *N.C.*, QQ. 11877-12113.

82. *Nap. Rep.*, App. A, 121; *N.C.*, Q 11170.

83. *N.C.*, QQ. 10318-10420; *D.F.C.*, QQ. 38333-38565.

84. See above, 74.

85. For emigration figures see, *The Witness*, 12 Sept. 1849; P. Cooper, *The So-Called Evictions from the MacDonald Estates in North Uist*, Aberdeen, 1881, 9-11; HIES, Lists of Emigrants (in S.R.O. collection of material on Highland destitutions). For details of N. Uist tenancies see, MacD.P., GD 22/51, Valuation of N. Uist, 1830; MacD.P., GD 221/111/1, View of the Rental of N. Uist. For information about the clearances on the island see, *Nap.Rep.*, App. A, 136; *D.F.C.*, QQ. 40621-40628, 40853-40944.

86. Above, 19.

87. MacD.P., GD 221/148/4, Rep. on the MacDonald Estates, 1851. 'Tacksman' was by this time used to describe tenant farmers — the traditional tacksman class being quite extinct by the mid-century.

88. *Nap. Rep.*, App. A, 42.

89. A. Geikie, *Scottish Reminiscences*, Glasgow, 1904, 226-227.

90. Board of Agriculture, Miscellaneous Files, AF 43/54, Rep. on Suishnish and Boreraig, 3 Dec. 1900.

91. See, *N.C.*, QQ. 5483, 5525, 5535; *Inverness Courier*, 3 Nov. 1853. Also, D. Ross, *Real Scottish Grievances*, Glasgow, 1854, 4-20.

92. MacD.P., GD 221/148/4, Rep. on Lord MacDonald's Estates, 1851; *N.C.*, QQ. 183, 426-442, 541-546, 593, 3625-3628; C.D.B., *3rd Rep.*, 1901, xi-xiii.

93. MacD.P., GD 221/148/4, Rep. on Lord MacDonald's Estates, 1851; *D.F.C.*, QQ. 2640, 2748-2775.

94. MacL. P., Box 51C, H. MacAskill to J. Smith, 22 June 1852.

95. Above, 29, 47-8.

96. Home Office Domestic Entry Books, RH 2/4/239, f. 442, G.C. Lewis to Lord Advocate, 18 June 1850; *loc. cit.*, f. 454, E.P. Bouverie to T. Mulock, 23 July 1850; *Inverness Courier*, 6 June 1850; *N.C.*, QQ. 3624-3626, 4225; *D.F.C.*, QQ. 1317-1333, 5899.

97. *D.F.C.*, Q. 51673. Information supplied by then factor of Raasay and based on rentals and other estate papers in his possession. See also, HIES, Lists of Emigrants.

98. *N.C.*, QQ. 7858, 7911; *D.F.C.*, QQ. 361-363.

99. *Nap. Rep.*, App. A, 62.

100. BoAS., *10th Rep.*, 1922, 22.

101. See below, Chaps. 6 and 7, *passim.*

102. Emigration figures: HIES, Lists of Emigrants. Clearances: *N.C.*, QQ. 13034-13036, 13281-13284.

103. For a detailed account, based on estate rentals, see, *D.F.C.*, QQ. 36600-36774.

104. Glas. Sect., *Rep. on Mull, Tiree and Coll*, 1849, 19-23; *The Witness*, 27 Oct. 1849.

105. Argyll, *Crofts and Farms in the Hebrides*, Edinburgh, 1883, 20, 26-27. Also, *N.C.*, QQ. 33430-33700, 34126-34170, 34252, 33979-33982.

106. *N.C.*, QQ. 34373-34390; *D.F.C.*, QQ. 36022-36031, 36199-36220.

107. Glas. Sect., *Rep. on Mull, Tiree and Coll*, 1849, 8.

108. T. Grierson, *Autumnal Rambles among the Scottish Mountains*, Edinburgh, 1850, 77; MacL. P., Box 36(2), Trevelyan, Memo., 16 Aug. 1852.

109. MacDonald, *Agriculture of the Hebrides*, 1811, 687-689; *N.S.A.*, VII, 348.

110. MacLaine of Lochbuie, P., GD 174/52, Rental of Ulva, May 1834.

111. *J.M.N. Rep.*, xvii.

112. Special Commissioner's Report, *Scotsman*, 12 Dec. 1877.

113. *J.M.N. Rep.*, xvii.

114. *N.C.*, QQ. 33552-33646. According to an 1834 rental (MacLaine of Lochbuie P., GD 174/52) there were 88 tenants in Ulva. According to Mull crofters' evidence to the *N.C.* (which referred to the 1840s) there were 73. And the figures given in the two sources for individual townships closely correspond. This is fairly striking evidence of the general accuracy of oral tradition about the clearances of the 1840s and 1850s as recorded in the four volumes of evidence to the Napier Commission.

115. *J.M.N. Rep.*, App. A. 11.

116. See *N.C.*, QQ. 26801-26810; *D.F.C.*, QQ. 29729-29749; Richards, *Leviathan of Wealth*, 1973, 270-273.

117. Riddell, P., AF 49/6, Rep. by T.G. Dickson on the Estates of Ardnamurchan and Sunart, 1852. For details of clearances in Ardnamurchan see, *N.C.*, QQ. 35981-36019; *D.F.C.*, QQ. 37061-37393, 37441-37454, 38158-38192.

118. See *N.C.*, QQ. 30056, 30261, 31296-31658, 32752-32767, 32858-32859, 32932. Also, C. MacDonald, *Moidart; or Among the Clanranalds,* Oban, 1889, 233, 26‹

119. See above, 61.

120. *J.M.N. Rep.,* App. A, 67. Also, *Inverness Courier,* 19 July 1849; *N.C.,* QQ. 31741-31755, 31960-31961.

121. Board of Supervision, *9th Rep.,* 1854, App. A, pp.1-9; *Papers Relative to Emigration to the North American Colonies,* 1854, 19; D. Ross, *The Glengarry Evictions,* Glasgow, 1853, 7-9.

122. E.O. Tregelles, *Hints on the Hebrides,* Newcastle, 1855, 5-6.

123. *N.C.,* QQ. 9256, 9298-9304; *D.F.C.,* QQ. 43824, 43455, 43500.

124. For an account of it see, D.A. MacMillan, 'Sir Charles Trevelyan and the Highlands and Islands Emigration Society', *Royal Australian History Society Journal,* LI, 1963. While excellent on the Society's operations, MacMillan's account of the Highland background is less than satisfactory.

125. HIES, *'Blue Book',* 1853, 1-2, Statement of the Skye Emigration Society, 18 Sept. 1851.

126. *Report of the Highlands and Islands Emigration Society,* 1853, 8; MacL.P., Box 62C, M. Ferguson to Emily MacLeod, 9 July 1853.

127. *Report of the Highlands and Islands Emigration Society,* 1853, 17; *HIES,* I, Trevelyan to Fraser, 3 April 1852.

128. *HIES,* I, Trevelyan to Cropper, 22 May 1852; *HIES,* III, MacNeill to Trevelyan, 21 Jan. 1853.

129. *Report of the Highlands and Islands Emigration Society,* 1853, 7-11.

130. HIES, *'Blue Book',* 1853, 9; *HIES,* II, Trevelyan to Cropper, 5 Aug. 1852.

131. HIES, *'Blue Book',* 29, Fraser to J. Smith, 8 Dec. 1851; *HIES, I,* MacLeod to Sutherland, 21 May 1852.

132. MacL. P., Box 36(2), Trevelyan to MacNeill, 13 Aug. 1852.

133. *HIES,* II, Trevelyan to MacNeill, 26 Aug. 1852. Also, MacMillan, 'Sir Charles Trevelyan and Highland Emigration', 1963, 181.

134. *HIES,* II, Trevelyan to R. Stewart, 13 Aug. 1852.

135. *HIES,* Lists of Emigrants.

136. MacL. P., Box 36(2), E. Gibbons to Emily MacLeod, 15 June 1853; *HIES,* III, MacNeill to Trevelyan, 21 Jan. 1853; *loc. cit.,* Trevelyan to L. MacKinnon, 19 Aug. 1853; *HIES,* Lists of Emigrants.

137. See e.g., Tregelles, *Hints on the Hebrides,* 1855, 9-10.

138. MacMillan, 'Sir Charles Trevelyan and Highland Emigration', 1963, 183.

139. *HIES,* IV, Trevelyan to MacNeill, 18 March 1856; *loc. cit.,* Trevelyan to Kinnaird, 13 May 1857; HIES, Lists of Emigrants.

140. Colonial Land and Emigration Commissioners, *18th Rep.,* 1858, 43-45.

141. *Report of Commissioners appointed to inquire into the state of Lunatic Asylums in Scotland,* P.P. 1857 V, 82.

Chapter 6

1. For this and several other points in this paragraph I am indebted to E. Richards, 'How Tame Were the Highlanders During the Clearances?', *Scottish Studies,* XVII, 1973, 35-50.

2. G. Broeker, *Rural Disorder and Police Reform in Ireland, 1812-36,* London, 1970, vii.

3. Quoted, W.M. MacKenzie, *Hugh Miller: A Critical Study,* London, 1905, 190-191.

4. Richards, 'How Tame Were the Highlanders?' 1973, *passim.*

5. Prebble, *Highland Clearances,* 1963, 270-283; Cooper, *The So-Called Evictions,* 1881, 9-11, etc., etc.

6. *Select Committee on Emigration, Scotland,* 1841, QQ. 2647-2650; *Inverness Courier,* 24 July, 7 Aug. 1839.

7. See, *inter al.,* Prebble, *Highland Clearances,* 1963; Richards, 'Problems on the Cromartie Estate', 1973, 149-164.

8. Richards, 'How Tame Were the Highlanders?', 1973, 47-48.

9. See below, Chaps. 8 and 9, *passim.*

10. See, *e.g., Sutherland Estate Management,* 1972, II, 4, C. MacKenzie to Countess of Sutherland, 14 Sept. 1799; Richards, *Leviathan of Wealth,* 1973, 210-216.

11. E.J. Hobsbawm and G. Rude, *Captain Swing,* London, 1969, 56.

12. See above, Chap. 1, *passim.*

13. See above, 9.

14. See, e.g., MacCulloch, *Highlands and Western Isles,* 1824, IV, 442-443.

15. For a possible parallel see, J.S. Saul and R. Woods, 'African Peasantries', in T. Shanin (ed.), *Peasants and Peasant Societies,* Harmondsworth, 1971, 103-114.

16. *Nap. Rep.,* 36. See also, *N.C.,* Q. 27011.

17. Carmichael, *Carmina Gadelica,* 1928-1971, VI, 72. (Though bad be the proprietor, it is the factor who is really bad).

18. MacLean, 'Poetry of the Clearances', 1939, 319.

19. *N.C.,* Q. 2683.

20. See above, 14; and below 216.

21. J. MacInnes, 'A Gaelic Song of the Sutherland Clearances', *Scottish Studies,* VIII, 1964, 104-106. (My curse on the big sheep./ Where are the children of the kindly folk?/ We parted when we were young/ Before MacKay's country had become a wilderness).

22. D. Thomson, *An Introduction to Gaelic Poetry,* London, 1974, 243-244.

23. There has been a tendency — not unconnected with the undue attention bestowed on events in Sutherland — to grossly underestimate the extent of the clearances. Even writers generally sympathetic to crofters have thought that only a small number of people were directly affected. (See, *e.g.,* Collier, *Crofting Problem,* 1953, 38). But while there is no way of even roughly estimating the number of people evicted or otherwise dispossessed, earlier chapters make clear that no part of the north-west was unaffected.

24. *N.C.,* QQ. 13850, 26098.

25. Selkirk, *Observations,* 1805, 119-120.

26. See, C. Hill, 'The Norman Yoke', in C. Hill, *Puritanism and Revolution,* (Panther edit.), London, 1968, 58.

27. Argyll, *Scotland as It Was and Is,* Edinburgh, (2 vols.), 1887, II, 1.

28. D. Stewart, *Sketches of the Character, Manners and Present State of the Highlanders of Scotland,* Edinburgh, (2 vols.), 1825, I, 155.

29. Carmichael, *Carmina Cadelica*, 1928-1971, III, 328-329.

30. Gearoid O Tuathaigh, *Ireland Before the Famine*, 1798-1848, Dublin, 1972, 1.

31. *N.C.*, Q. 33129. See also, QQ. 6085, 11471.

32. *Scotsman*, 4 Oct. 1884.

33. See, *e.g.*, Argyll, *Scotland as It Was*, 1887, II, 1 *et seq.*

34. *N.C.*, Q. 33129.

35. Below, 156-60.

36. *Nap. Rep.*, 4, 9.

37. See below, Chaps. 8-11, *passim.*

38. See V. Lanternari, *The Religions of the Oppressed*, London, 1963, *passim.*

39. W. Ferguson, 'The Problems of the Established Church in the West Highlands and Islands in the Eighteenth Century', *Records of the Scottish Church History Society*, XVII, 1969, 15-31; Smout, *History of the Scottish People*, 1969, 333.

40. J. MacInnes, *The Evangelical Movement in the Highlands of Scotland, 1688 to 1800*, Aberdeen, 1951, 14.

41. G. Grub, *Ecclesiastical History of Scotland*, Edinburgh, (4 vols.), 1861, IV, 43; Prebble, *Culloden*, 1961, 152, 163, 306.

42. J. MacKay, *The Church in the Highlands*, London, 1914, 205-207; *O.S.A.*, I, 491.

43. Church of Scotland Assembly Papers, CH 1/5/79, Report by those appointed to visit the Highlands and Islands, 1760.

44. *Ibid.*

45. For details see, *Reports of Commissioners for Building Churches in the Highlands and Islands of Scotland*, 1825-1835; *Specimens of the Ecclesiastical Destitution of Scotland*, Edinburgh, 1835, 35-50; *Commissioners of Religious Instruction*, Scotland, *4th Rep.*, P.P. 1837-38, XXXIII.

46. J.L. Buchanan, *Travels in the Western Hebrides from 1782 to 1790*, London, 1793, 218-251.

47. *Ibid.*, 36-7.

48. *An Account of the Present State of Religion Throughout the Highlands of Scotland*, Edinburgh, 1827, 2; Fullarton and Baird, *Remarks*, 1838, 26-30.

49. Roderick MacLeod of Bracadale is said to have 'declared that the first presbyterial act he performed after ordination was to assist his co-presbyters to bed. They were so helplessly intoxicated.' (A. MacRae, *Revivals in the Highlands in the Nineteenth Century*, Stirling, 1907, 68). Such allegations of loose living – and especially the equation of Moderatism with alcoholism – are common in Free Church sources.

50. *Present State of Religion*, 1827, 2.

51. See, *e.g.*, O. MacKenzie, *A Hundred Years in the Highlands*, London, 1921, 192.

52. D. Beaton, *Some Noted Ministers of the Northern Highlands*, Inverness, 1929, 81. J. Campbell, *The Rev. Mr. Lachlan of Lochcarron: Additional Lectures, Sermons and Writings*, Inverness, 1930, 19-20.

53. Quoted, Prebble, *Highland Clearances*, 1963, 75.

54. A. MacRae, *The Fire of God Among the Heather*, Inverness, 1929, 81.

55. The phrase is borrowed from the title of a recent study of independent church movements in Kenya: F.B. Welbourn and B.A. Ogot, *A Place to Feel at Home*, London, 1966.

56. MacInnes, *Evangelical Movement*, 1951, 13.

57. A. Haldane, *A Memoir of the Lives of Robert and James Haldane*, London, 1852, 181 *et seq.;* J. Campbell, *Missionary and Ministerial Life in the Highlands*, Edinburgh, 1853, 3.

58. MacKay, *Church in the Highlands*, 1914, 227.

59. W.H. Meikle, *Scotland and the French Revolution*, Edinburgh, 1912, 209 *et seq.*

60. Grub, *Ecclesiastical History*, 1861, IV, 170.

61. Haldane, *Memoir*, 1852, 248; N. Douglas, *Journal of a Mission to Part of the Highlands of Scotland in 1797*, Edinburgh, 1799.

62. Stewart, *Sketches*, 1825, I, 130-131.

63. *Ibid.*, 125.

64. *Ibid.*, 131.

65. MacDonald, *Agriculture of the Hebrides*, 1811, 109-110.

66. See above, Chaps. 2 and 3, *passim.*

67. 'The State of Religion in the Highlands', *Blackwood's Magazine*, V, 1814, 142-144.

68. Those whose traditional way of life has broken down have always been particularly attracted to such notions. See, *e.g.*, N. Cohn, *The Pursuit of the Millenium*, (Paladin edit.), London, 1970, *passim.*

69. *Remarks on the Earl of Selkirk's Observations on the Highlands*, Edinburgh, 1806, 39-40.

70. Adam, *Sutherland Estate Management*, 1972, I, 135.

71. *Present State of Religion*, 1827, 46.

72. MacKay, *Church in the Highlands*, 1914, 229.

73. See, H. Anderson, *The Life and Letters of Christopher Anderson*, Edinburgh, 1854, 125-128.

74. Gaelic School Society, *16th Rep.*, 1828, 28-29.

75. *Moral Statistics of the Highlands and Islands*, Inverness, 1821, 26.

76. *Report on the State of Education in the Hebrides by Alexander Nicholson*, P.P. 1867, XXV, 84-85, 130.

77. See below, 159-60.

78. It is perhaps noteworthy that a comparative study of independent church movements in Africa has demonstrated a close connection between the availability of the Bible in the vernacular and the appearance of religious independency in one form or another: D. Barrett, *Schism and Renewal in Africa*, Oxford, 1968, 127 *et seq.*

79. CH 2/273/3, Minutes of the Presbytery of Mull, 23 April 1829.

80. *Ibid.*, 10 March 1830.

81. N.C. MacFarlane, *The Men of the Lews*, Stornoway, 1924, iv.

82. CH 2/473/3, Minutes of the Presbytery of Lewis, 28 Nov. 1832.

83. CH 2/567/3, Minutes of the Presbytery of Lochcarron, 4 April 1820.

84. R. MacCowan, *The Men of Skye*, Glasgow, 1902, 1-30.

85. *Present State of Religion*, 1827, 62-63.

86. MacRae, *Revivals in the Highlands*, 1907, 80.

87. Sea.P., GD 46/17/Vol. 62, A. Simpson to J. Adam, 5 Feb. 1823; Sea.P., GD 46/17/Vol. 63, W. MacRae to Seaforth, 23 Dec. 1823.

88. MacFarlane, *Men of the Lews,* 1924, 245.

89. Sea.P., GD 46/17/Vols. 63 and 65, J. Adams to Seaforth, 31 Oct. 1823, 8 April 1824.

90. Sea.P., GD 46/17/Vol. 65, A. Kelly to Seaforth, 20 Dec. 1823.

91. *Present State of Religion,* 1827, 75-76.

92. CH 2/361/2, Minutes of the Presbytery of Uist, 7 Sept. 1829.

93. CH 2/361/2, Minutes of the Presbytery of Uist, 27 March 1839.

94. CH 2/273/4, Minutes of the Presbytery of Mull, 3 Dec. 1835.

95. CH 2/567/3, Minutes of the Presbytery of Lochcarron, 20 Nov. 1825.

96. CH 2/508/3, Minutes of the Presbytery of Tongue, 7 March 1827.

97. J. MacInnes, 'The Origins and Early Development of 'The Men' ', *Records of the Scottish Church History Society,* VIII, 1944, 16-41.

98. *Ibid.,* 16.

99. Several of 'the men' are referred to above. For short biographies of some of the best known see, MacCowan, *Men of Skye,* 1902; MacFarlane, *Men of the Lews,* 1924.

100. J. Kennedy, *The Days of the Fathers in Ross-shire,* Inverness, 1927, 86-88.

101. See, 'Investigator', *The Church and Her Accuser in the Far North,* Edinburgh, 1850, 36; 'Puritanism in the Highlands', *Quarterly Review,* LXXXVIII, 309.

102. For studies of these movements see, *Pursuit of the Millenium,* 1970; Lanternari, *Religions of the Oppressed,* 1963.

103. J. Browne, *A Critical Examination of Dr. MacCulloch's Work on the Highlands* Edinburgh, 1825, 142-143.

104. *Present State of Religion,* 1827, 63.

105. Sea.P., GD 46/17/Vol. 63, A. Simpson to J. Adams, 5 Feb. 1823.

106. MacKay, *Church in the Highlands,* 1914, 248-249.

107. MacInnes, 'Origins of 'The Men' ', 1944, 35, 41.

108. Kennedy, *Days of the Fathers,* 1927, 128.

109. MacInnes, 'Origins of 'The Men' ', 1944, 39-40. See also, A. MacRae, *Donald Sutherland: Saint and Seer,* Tongue, 1932.

110. J. Campbell (ed.), *The Rev. Mr. Lachlan of Lochcarron: Lectures, Sermons and Writings,* Inverness, 1928, 10.

111. See, *e.g.,* Carmichael, *Carmina Gadelica,* 1928-1971, I, xxv-xxxiii.

112. See, MacLean, 'Poetry of the Clearances', 1939.

113. L. MacBean, *Buchanan: The Sacred Bard of the Scottish Highlands,* London. 1920, 114; MacInnes, *Evangelical Movement,* 1951, 283.

114. 'Investigator', *Church and Her Accuser,* 1850, 78.

115. E. MacKenzie, *The Rev. Murdo MacKenzie: A Memoir,* Inverness, 1914, 86.

116. J. Sinclair, *The Christian Hero of the North,* Edinburgh, 1867, 61-62.

117. MacRae, *Revivals in the Highlands,* 1907, 82-83; Beaton, *Some Noted Ministers,* 1929, 188.

118. *Present State of Religion,* 1827, 67.

119. Sea.P., GD 46/17/Vol. 62, W. MacRae to Seaforth, 23 Dec. 1823.

120. MacCowan, *Men of Skye,* 1902, 18.

121. T. Brown, *Annals of the Disruption,* Edinburgh, 1890, 670.

122. *Committee on Sites,* 1847, Q. 5094 *et seq.*

123. *Present State of Religion,* 1827, 63.

124. See below, 105-6.

125. For details see, *The Witness,* 21 Dec. 1842, 25 Feb., 28 April 1843; Brown, *Annals,* 1890, 58-74; J. Kennedy, *The Apostle of the North,* Inverness, 1932, 242 *et seq.*

126. MacKay, *Church in the Highlands,* 1914, 266.

127. See, MacCowan, *Men of Skye,* 1902, 82; *Sutherland and the Sutherlanders: Their Religious and Social Condition,* Edinburgh, 9, 12-13; etc.

128. P.C. Simpson, *The Life of Principal Rainy,* London, (2 vols.), 1909, I, 433.

129. *Ibid.*

130. J. Barron, *The Northern Highlands in the Nineteenth Century,* Inverness, (3 vols.), 1903-1913, III, xxxix.

131. A. MacRae, *Kinlochbervie,* Tongue, 1932, 51.

132. *Committee on Sites,* 1847, *Rep.* iv.

133. Brown, *Annals,* 1890, 427-428, 655-657.

134. *Committee on Sites,* 1847, QQ. 4088-4094.

135. *Ibid.,* Q. 91.

136. *Ibid.,* QQ. 3684-3685, 4437-4462.

137. Somers, *Letters,* 1848, 65-66.

138. *Committee on Sites,* 1847, *1st Rep.,* 96; *2nd Rep.,* 92.

139. H. Miller, *Sutherland As It Was and Is,* Edinburgh, (3rd edit.), 1843, 35.

140. J.R. Fleming, *A History of the Church in Scotland,* 1843-1874, Edinburgh, 1927, 70.

141. See above, 63.

142. J.G. Kellas, 'The Liberal Party and the Scottish Church Disestablishment Crisis', *English History Review,* LXXIX, 31.

143. *Committee on Sites,* 1847, *3rd Rep., passim.*

144. See below, Chaps. 8 and 9, *passim.*

145. D. Thomson, 'Gaelic Scotland', in D. Glen (ed.), *Whither Scotland?,* London, 1971, 136.

146. See, J. MacInnes, Review of Sorley MacLean's poetry, *Scottish International,* Dec. 1973, 38-39.

Chapter 7

1. *Nap. Rep.,* 7.

2. *Ibid.* See also, J. MacDonald, 'The Agriculture of Ross and Cromarty', *T.H.A.S.S.,* 4th Ser., IX, 1877, 157.

3. See, Hunter, 'Sheep and Deer', 1973, 203 *et seq.*

4. The most extensive loss of pastures in the 1860s occurred on the Kilmuir estate in Skye. (*N.C.,* QQ. 1953, 1999-2000, 2204, 2305-2312, 2577-2582, 2650-2651, etc.) Although territorially insignificant compared to earlier clearances these losses were not unimportant. The first serious outbreak of the land war of the 1880s occurred because of a dispute about grazings taken from crofters in 1865. See below, 134.

5. Hunter, 'Sheep and Deer', 1973, 200-202.

6. *Nap. Rep.,* App. A., 20; *N.C.,* Q. 8283; *D.F.C.,* Q 53635; *Cottar Population,* 1888, 35, 39; Lothian, P., GD 40/16/32, M. MacNeill, Confidential Reports, 1886, 19; *Scotsman,* 5 July 1883.

7. *N.C.,* Q. 9752. Also below, 122 *et seq.*

8. *N.C.,* Q. 42648; *Cottar Population,* 1888, 39. The saying was a true one. Most croft rents were below £6 p.a.

9. G.J. Walker, 'Report on the Northern District of Scotland', *Royal Commission on the Depressed Condition of the Agricultural Interest,* P.P. 1881 XV – P.P. 1882 XIV, (P.P. 1881 XVI), 554.

10. *N.C.,* QQ. 4457-4458, 9754-9757. Also, Hunter, 'Sheep and Deer', 1973, 206-207.

11. See, e.g., J. MacDonald, 'The Agriculture of Sutherland', *T.H.A.S.S.,* 4th Ser., XII, 1880, 87.

12. It survived only here and there in the Outer Isles. *N.C.,* Q. 44379.

13. See, *Reports as to the Alleged Destitution in the Western Highlands and Islands,* P.P. 1883, LIX, 1-10. Also, contemporary *Valuation Rolls;* and Collier, *Crofting Problem,* 1953, 84.

14. *N.C.,* Q. 258; *Highlander,* 14 June 1873; *Nap. Rep.,* App. A, 6.

15. *D.F.C.,* Q. 5370. Also, *Nap. Rep.,* App. A, 6; *N.C.,* QQ. 26956; *D.F.C.,* QQ. 1584, 4522-4526.

16. Hunter, 'Sheep and Deer', 1973, 218.

17. W. MacDonald, 'The Agriculture of Inverness-shire', *T.H.A.S.S.,* 4th Ser., IV, 1872, 52.

18. *N.C.,* QQ. 4460, 6484; Board of Supervision, *40th Rep.,* 1885, 8; MacDonald, 'Agriculture of Sutherland', 1880, 88; MacDonald, 'Agriculture of Inverness-shire', 1872, 65; MacDonald, 'Agriculture of Ross and Cromarty', 1877, 208; *Royal Commission on Agricultural Depression,* P.P. 1894 XVI - P.P. 1897 XV, QQ, 52305-52306.

19. *Nap. Rep.,* 4, 53.

20. See below, 170-1.

21. *Cottar Population,* 1888, 35. Also, *Nap. Rep.,* App. A, 175-177; *N.C.,* QQ. 14394-14425.

22. This was partially remedied in the 1890s by the establishment of railheads at Mallaig and Kyle of Lochalsh.

23. For a recent account of the fishermen's difficulties see, M. Gray, 'Crofting and Fishing in the North-West Highlands, 1890-1914', *Northern Scotland,* 1, 1972, 89-114.

24. Smith, *Lewsiana,* 1875, 127.

25. *Nap. Rep.,* 53.

26. Fishery Board for Scotland, *2nd Rep.,* 1884, xlv; D. MacKinlay, *The Isle of Lewis and its Fishermen Crofters,* London, 1878, xxix.

27. *Nap. Rep.,* 53; *Cottar Population,* 1888, 36.

28. See, e.g., J.H. Dixon, *Gairloch in North-West Ross-shire,* Edinburgh, 1886, 143.

29. *Cottar Population,* 1888, 4.

30. *Poor Law Commission,* 1844, App. Pt. 2, 298, 303, 367, 423, 431, 434; *J.M.N. Rep.,* xix.

31. Smith, *Lewsiana,* 1875, 71.

32. *N.C.,* QQ. 588, 3528; *State of Education in the Hebrides,* 1867, 13.

33. See, MacDonald, 'Agriculture of Inverness-shire', 1872, 163; J. Tait, 'The Condition of the Scottish Peasantry', *T.H.A.S.S.,* 4th Ser., XV, 1883, 13; Dixon, *Gairloch,* 1886, 143; *Nap. Rep.,* App. A, 58; *Alleged Destitution,* 1883, 21-22;

Cottar Population, 35. For a glimpse of the effects on east coast communities see, C.R. Weld, *Two Months in The Highlands, Orcadia and Skye,* London, 1860; 52-59; E.J. March, *Sailing Drifters,* London, 1952, 241; W.G. Mowat, *The Story of Lybster,* Lybster, 1959, 8.

34. *Cottar Population,* 1888, 4, 36; Tait, 'Scottish Peasantry', 1883, 13.

35. *Cottar Population,* 1888, 35; Lothian P., GD 40/16/32, MacNeill, Confidential Reports, 1886, 9. The number of gutters greatly increased in the later nineteenth and early twentieth centuries. See, *e.g., Social Condition of Lewis,* 1902, xcvii.

36. See below.

37. This was not an indication of proprietorial generosity. Between 1815 and the 1850s rents had been far too high and all that happened in the 1860s and 1870s was that crofters were once more able to pay them. After 1886, having examined croft rents in relation to agricultural rents generally, the Crofters Commission enforced wholesale reductions. See below, 169-70, 179.

38. MacDonald, 'Agriculture of Inverness-shire', 1872, 21; Smith, *Lewsiana,* 1875, 33-35.

39. Smith, *Lewsiana,* 1875, 53-55; Tait, 'Scottish Peasantry', 1883, 13; *Alleged Destitution,* 1883, 22.

40. *Depressed Condition of Agriculture,* 1881, QQ. 30107-30108; *N.C.,* Q. 33478.

41. Smith, *Lewsiana,* 1875, 53-55; Tait, 'Scottish Peasantry', 1883, 13; *Depressed Condition of Agriculture,* 1881, Q. 30106; *N.C.,* QQ. 29148-29156.

42. By the 1880s the old custom of scouring the beaches for shellfish in bad seasons was only a memory. *Nap. Rep.,* App. A, 52; *N.C.,* Q. 9470.

43. *N.C.,* Q. 9470.

44. See, *Nap. Rep.,* App. A., 11; *N.C.,* QQ. 1076-1078, 1473, 2722, 3048, 4685, 29148-29156, *etc.;* Lothian P., GD 40/16/32, MacNeill, Confidential Reports, 1886, 25, 30.

45. 'Landed Tenure in the Highlands', *Westminster Review,* XXXIV, 1868, 297; *N.C.* QQ. 3105-3108; 'Transition in the Highlands of Scotland', *Scottish Review,* XII, 1888, 119-120.

46. *N.C.,* Q. 45993.

47. See above, Chaps. 4-5, *passim.*

48. *N.C.,* Q. 11474.

49. F.G. Rea, *A School in South Uist,* London, 1964, 7.

50. See, D. MacKay, *This Was My Glen,* Thurso, 1965, 44. The practice was given as a reason for clearances on the MacLeod estate in Skye in the 1840s. See, Rep. on Ebost by N. MacLean, 21 Jan. 1841, MacLean, 21 Jan. 1841, MacL. P., Box 51 A.

51. Board of Supervision, *40th Rep.,* 1885, 26; Dixon, *Gairloch,* 1886, 133; MacDonald, 'Agriculture of Inverness-shire, 1872, 13-14.

52. See MacGillivray, 'Present State of the Hebrides', 1831, 288-290; Johnson, *Journey to the Hebrides,* 1924, 91.

53. A practice enshrined in the remark made when something was mislaid: 'Gheibhear 'sa chartadh Chéitein e', it will be got at the May cleaning-out, Campbell, *Words and Expressions from South Uist,* 1958, 68.

54. *Scotsman,* 5 Jan. 1878.

55. *N.C.,* Q. 17032.

56. *Nap. Rep.,* 20-21, 62-63; *Education in the Hebrides,* 1867, 3-4, 26; *Report on the Sanitary Condition of the Lews,* P.P. 1905 XXXIV, 7. For contemporary descriptions of housing conditions see, *Nap. Rep.,* 48-49; Smith, *Lewsiana,* 17-22; Tait, 'Scottish Peasantry', 1883, 12-13; Walker, 'Northern District', 1881, 556; General Board of Commissioners in Lunacy for Scotland, *3rd Rep.,* 1861, 247-249; W.E. Carson, 'Through the Hebrides', Aberdeen University Library M.S. 897, 26-28. Also, J. Walton, 'The Skye House', *Antiquity,* 1957, 155-162.

57. A. Geddes, *The Isle of Lewis and Harris,* Edinburgh, 1955, 84.

58. Board of Supervision, *40th Rep.,* 1885, 26.

59. Ferguson, *Scottish Social Welfare, 1864-1914,* 1958, 386-387.

60. C.D.B. Files, AF 42/9702, Social and Economic Conditions in the Highlands, April 1924, 5.

61. See above, 54.

62. See, e.g., J.L. Campbell, Introduction, Rea, *School in South Uist,* 1964, xx-xxi.

63. *Scotsman,* 15 Dec. 1877.

64. *N.C.,* Q. 12420.

65. It is possible to argue that excessive scattering and divisibility of holdings is more difficult to correct under an individualistic as opposed to a communal tenure. (See the discussion of strip cultivation in L. Volin, *A Century of Russian Agriculture,* Harvard, 1970, 92). It is noteworthy, therefore, that in the few Outer Hebridean townships where runrig persisted the problem of continuous cropping was less serious than elsewhere as it was possible to let a number of rigs lie fallow each year — an effect impossible to achieve on a multitude of separate holdings. See, e.g., *N.C.,* QQ. 12654-12657.

66. *N.C.,* Q. 12490.

67. *N.C.* Q. 1987. See also, *N.C.,* QQ. 115-116, 1411, 2052, 2361, 13116, 15624, 26466, 30921, 33466, etc.

68. Crofters Commission, *1st Rep.,* 1888, ix.

69. See, e.g., *N.C.,* QQ. 6524-6529, 10275-10277.

70. *Nap. Rep.,* App. A. 11.

71. *Scotsman,* 19 Dec. 1877.

72. *N.C.,* Q. 41060; *D.F.C.,* Q. 2705.

73. *Scotsman,* 22 Dec. 1877.

74. See above, Chaps. 2-4, *passim.*

75. *Nap. Rep.,* App. A. 11.

76. See, *N.C.,* QQ. 7369, 10904, 12068, 25619, 25706, etc.

77. *N.C.,* Q. 10904. Also *N.C.,* Q. 891.

78. *N.C.,* QQ. 11175, 12319.

79. *Nap. Rep.,* App. A., 2. Also, *Nap. Rep.,* App. A, 58; *N.C.,* QQ. 1987, 2999-3000, 5039, 11704, 12490, etc.; Lothian P., GD 40/16/32, MacNeill, Confidential Reports, 1886, 5-6, 11, 16, etc.

80. *N.C.,* Q. 7263.

81. See above, 1.

82. *Nap. Rep.,* 110.

83. S. Laing, *Journal of a Residence in Norway,* London, (2nd edit.), 1837, 35-41, 287.

84. See e.g., N. Nicolson, *Lord of the Isles,* London, 1960, 32; A.A. MacGregor, *The Western Isles,* London, 1949, 231-245.

85. Fraser Darling, *West Highland Survey,* 1955, 304.

86. Specifically by the improvements which followed the Crofters Act of 1886.

87. Quoted, N.D. Palmer, *The Irish Land League Crisis,* New Haven, 1940, 17.

88. *N.S.A.,* XIV, 205.

89. Quoted, Cregeen, 'Changing Role of the House of Argyll', 1970, 18. (But for the fear of a double rent Tiree would yield a double crop).

90. *N.C.,* Q. 2052.

91. See, *N.C.,* QQ. 2054-2062.

92. *Royal Commission on Land in Wales and Monmouthshire, Minutes of Evidence,* P.P. 1896 XXV, p.409. For a particular instance of this practice see, *N.C.,* Q. 17386.

93. *N.C.,* Q. 14348.

94. *Land in Wales and Monmouthshire,* 1896, 407. See also, *N.C.,* QQ. 8538-8539.

95. *Nap. Rep.,* App. A. 77-79.

96. Quoted, Palmer, *Irish Land League,* 1940, 18.

97. Quoted, Brand, *Land in Wales and Monmouthshire,* 1896, 407.

98. G.G. MacKay, *On the Management of Highland Property,* Edinburgh, 1858, 10-17, 62.

99. See, e.g., 'Land Tenure in the Highlands', 1868, 280-291; R. Buchanan, *The Land of Lorne,* London, (2 vols.), 1871, I, 16-17; Smith, *Lewsiana,* 1875, 45.

100. See above, 71.

101. Hunter, 'Sheep and Deer', 1973, 200-202.

102. Smith, *Lewsiana,* 45 f.n. Also, Walker, 'Northern District', 1881, 557.

103. On the Sutherland estate, for example. *Nap. Rep.,* App. A. 302-303.

104. *N.C.,* QQ. 1524-1525. See also, *N.C.,* Q. 35977.

105. Somers, *Letters,* 1848, 55.

106. Blackadder, Survey, 1799.

107. Walker, 'Northern District', 1881, 556; *Scotsman* 22 Dec. 1877.

108. Smith, *Lewsiana,* 1875, 65. Also, *Nap. Rep.,* 113.

109. *Report of the Departmental Committee on the Work of the Congested Districts (Scotland) Commissioners,* P.P. 1910 XXI, 8. Also, Fraser Darling, *West Highland Survey,* 1955, 210.

110. *Scotsman,* 5 Jan. 1878.

111. See above 47. Also Walker, 'Northern District', 1881, 561; I.A. Crawford, 'Feannagan Taomaidh, Lazy Beds', *Scottish Studies,* VI, 1962, 244-245.

112. MacDonald, 'Agriculture of Inverness-shire', 1872, 40; MacDonald, 'Agriculture of Ross and Cromarty', 1877, 157.

113. F. Fraser Darling, *Crofting Agriculture,* Edinburgh, 1945, 7-8; I. Whitaker, 'Some Traditional Techniques in Modern Scottish Farming', *Scottish Studies,* III, 1959, 165-167.

114. *D.F.C. Rep.,* xi; Smith, *Lewsiana,* 1875, 66-68; MacDonald, 'Agriculture of Inverness-shire', 1872, 21, 164-165.

115. *D.F.C. Rep.,* xiii-xiv.

116. *Nap. Rep.,* App. A. 469.

117. Crofters Commission, *Final Rep.*, 1912, xxv.

118. Fraser Darling, *West Highland Survey*, 1955, 200-208; Coull, 'Crofters' Common Grazings', 1968, 152.

119. Walker, 'Northern District', 1881, 556; *D.F.C.* Rep., xiii-xiv.

120. *N.C.*, QQ. 9754-9757, 29041; *D.F.C.*, Q. 1101.

121. *D.F.C. Rep.*, xiv.

122. C.D.B., *Final Rep.*, 1912, xiii.

123. Walker, 'Northern District', 1881, 556.

124. *D.F.C. Rep.*, xiv. Crofters faced most competition in the sheep markets. But in the 1890s the few stirks raised by Skye farmers were worth twice as much as those reared by the island's crofters (*D.F.C.*, Q. 5525). The problem was not tackled until after 1900 when the Congested Districts Board and its successors provided bulls, advice, etc.

125. *Return of Owners of Lands and Heritages (Scotland), 1872-73*, P.P. 1874 LXXII. Subsequent statistics, unless otherwise indicated, are abstracted from the same source.

126. Walker, 'Northern District', 1881, 553-562.

127. *Celtic Magazine*, VII, 1882, 372.

128. *Ibid.*

129. *D.F.C.*, Q. 36228.

130. MacKenzie, *Agriculture of Ross and Cromarty*, 1813, 51. An identical view was expressed, seventy years later, by the Free Church minister of Assynt. See, *N.C.*, Q. 26956.

131. *Nap. Rep.*, 83. This was one consequence of the absence of a Highland middle class, an absence much regretted by many contemporary observers. See e.g., J.S. Blackie, *Gaelic Societies, Highland Depopulation and Land Law Reform*, Edinburgh, 1880, 15; *N.C.*, Q. 56883; An Old Highlander, 'Home Truths on the Crofter Agitation', *Blackwoods Magazine*, CXXXVIII, 1885, 99.

132. MacKinlay, *Isle of Lewis*, 1878, xix-xxvi; D.G.F. MacDonald, *The Highland Crofters Socially Considered*, London, 1878, 105-108; *Social Condition of Lewis*, 1902, lxxi.

133. *The Crofter*, June 1885; Balfour to R. Cecil, 4 Oct. 1886: quoted, E.C.B. Dugdale, *Arthur James Balfour*, London, (2 vols.), 1936, I, 114.

134. *N.C.*, QQ. 8291, 8394-8402. Donald Munro's list of offices was even more spectacular. *Social Condition of Lewis*, 1902, lxxi.

135. 'The Present Condition of the Highlands', *An Gaidheal*, V, 1876, 120.

136. Nicolson, *Lord of the Isles*, 1960, 43.

137. Carmichael, *Carmina Gadelica*, 1928-1971, VI, 17.

138. Collier, *Crofting Problem*, 1953, 53, f.n.

139. *Nap. Rep.*, App. A, 452; Fraser-Darling, *West Highland Survey*, 1955, 311-312.

140. M. MacInnes (ed.), *Gaelic Proverbs Collected by Alexander Nicolson*, Glasgow, 1951, 146. (May the day never come when you'll rise out of that!).

141. *Ibid.* (Heap on him! Heap on him! It's he that would put on us; And if he rise again, He'll just put more on us!).

142. Lothian P., GD 40/16/32, MacNeill, Confidential Reports, 1886, 9.

143. *N.C.*, Q. 9256, 9298-9304.

144. *D.F.C.,* Q. 4364.

145. *Nap. Rep.,* 15.

146. The interior of the mainland had, of course, been completely cleared.

147. These were the areas selected for detailed examination by the Napier Commission. Unless otherwise indicated the following details are abstracted from *Nap. Rep.,* 10-16, and refer to 1883.

148. *Nap. Rep.,* 10-11.

149. See above, 45-6, 80.

150. Hunter, Sheep and Deer', 1973, 214-219.

151. *Nap. Rep.,* 11.

152. Details are available in *Nap. Rep.,* 12-13.

153. See, Collier, *Crofting Problem,* 1953, 68; Fraser Darling, *West Highland Survey,* 1955, 198.

154. Moisley *et al., Uig,* n.d., 12.

155. *The Times,* 29 April 1884.

156. *Nap. Rep.,* 3. Also, Day, *Public Administration,* 1918, 21; A. Gailey, 'The Role of Sub-Letting in the Crofting Community', *Scottish Studies,* V, 1961, 60-61.

157. See above, Chaps. 2-5, *passim.*

158. *N.C.,* Q. 32793.

159. *N.C.* records, AF 50/8/1-7, Returns Respecting Cottars.

160. *Nap. Rep.,* 43-44.

161. C.F., AF 67/163, Memo. on Petition from Cottars in Tiree, 2 April 1906.

162. N.C. records, AF 50/8/4-6, Returns Respecting Cottars; *N.C.,* QQ. 42479, 42487.

163. Fraser-Darling, *West Highland Survey,* 1955, 69, 81.

164. N.C. records, AF 50/8/6, Returns Respecting Cottars; *D.F.C. Rep.,* xxiii.

165. For examples see, *D.F.C. Rep.,* xxiii; 'Present Condition of the Highlands', 1876, 123.

166. *Scotsman,* 5 Jan. 1878.

167. *C.,* II, 280, Coffin, Final Rep., 28 Sept. 1847. And below, 170-1.

168. See, *e.g., N.C.* Q. 34143; *D.F.C.,* Q. 674, 39697.

169. The 205 cottars of South Uist and Benbecula had in 1883 a grand total of 140 cows, 84 stirks and 518 sheep. N.C. records, AF 50/8/4, Returns Respecting Cottars.

170. *N.C.,* Q. 34252.

171. *N.C.,* Q. 346. For a similar case see, *N.C.,* Q. 11698.

172. See below, Chaps. 8-11, *passim.*

173. *Nap. Rep.,* 10.

174. *N.C.,* Q. 5535.

175. Napier, *Hansard,* 3rd Ser., CCXCIV, 108.

176. *N.C.,* Q. 2740.

177. *N.C.,* Q. 7425.

178. *N.C.,* Q. 10844. For an additional example see, *N.C.,* Q. 12961.

179. *N.C.,* Q. 11695.

180. Volin, *Century of Russian Agriculture,* 1970, 69.

181. *N.C.,* Q. 16110.

182. *N.C.,* Q. 888.

183. *N.C.*, QQ. 23, 12949.

184. *N.C.*, QQ. 13179, 13911. See also, *N.C.*, QQ. 40, 1315, 1435, 1771, 2399, 7263, etc., etc.

185. *D.F.C.*, Q. 7611.

186. Napier, *The Highland Crofters, Nineteenth Century*, XVII, 1885, 447.

187. Carmichael, *Carmina Gadelica*, 1928-1971, I, xxi. (The big beasts eating the little beasts, The little beasts doing as best as they can).

188. *Scotsman*, 6 May 1887.

189. *N.C.*, QQ. 14430, 14807.

190. For these and others see, *D.F.C.*, QQ. 84-110, 134-144, 360-364, 530, 736, 1317-1328, 1819, 1935, 3018-3020, 5072, 5899, 6469, 6803, 7611, 8024, 16405, 16490-16492, 17483 *et seq.*, 17809, 19652, 27519, 27829, 28638, 29117, 35977, 36228, 36903 *et seq.*, 37068 *et seq.*, 38327-38329, 40465-40566, 40712, 41900, 49862, 54716-54717, etc. etc.

191. See below, Chaps. 8-11, *passim.*

192. *D.F.C.*, Q. 29370; M.F. Shaw, *Folksongs and Folklore of South Uist*, London, 1930, 11.

193. Buchanan, *Land of Lorne*, 1871, I, 80. Crofters made the same point. See, *e.g.*, *D.F.C.*, QQ. 1935, 29370.

194. *Nap. Rep.*, 3.

195. This was the so-called Bernera Riot. See, *Highlander*, 23 May 1874; *Scotsman*, 21 July 1874; J.S. Blackie, *The Scottish Highlanders and the Land Laws*, London, 1885, 192-200; D. MacDonald, *Tales and Traditions of the Lews*, Stornoway, 1967, 147-152.

196. See above, Chap. 6, *passim.*

197. For the development of Highland educational facilities see, *State of Education in the Hebrides*, 1867, *passim; Nap. Rep.*, 67-81; Day, *Public Administration*, 1918, 143-176.

198. *Depressed Condition of Agriculture*, 1881, QQ. 30121, 30208-30210; 'Transition in the Highlands', 1888, 120.

199. For some account of Murdoch's life and ideas see, J.D. Young, 'John Murdoch: A Scottish Land and Labour Pioneer', *Society for the Study of Labour History Bulletin*, XIX, 1969, 22-24; W. O'Brien and D. Ryan (eds.), *Devoy's Post Bag*, Dublin, 1948, 332-333. Murdoch's partially completed M.S. autobiography is preserved in five notebooks in the Mitchell Library, Glasgow. It is referred to below as Murdoch, *Autobiography*, I-V.

200. Murdoch, *Autobiography*, III. For an account of Fintan Lalor's thought see, Palmer, *Irish Land League*, 1940, 108 *et seq.*

201. The political aspects of the struggle for Highland land reform are more fully examined in J. Hunter, 'The Politics of Highland Land Reform, 1873-1895', *S.H.R.* LIII, 1974, 45-68. That article deals almost exclusively with the extra-Highland leadership of the movement; this book with its crofter membership. But because the two are obviously related, some of the points made in the article are, for the sake of convenience and continuity, repeated here and in the following two chapters — though with a good deal of abbreviation and re-emphasis.

202. *Highlander*, 12 July 1873.

203. *Highlander,* 24 May 1873.

204. See, Murdoch, *Autobiography,* IV. For an account of the impression he made on his audiences see, N. MacLean, *The Former Days,* London, 1945, 81-83.

205. Murdoch, *Autobiography,* IV.

206. Murdoch, *Autobiography,* IV.

207. Murdoch, *Autobiography,* IV.

Chapter 8

1. The concept of a 'great depression' in British agriculture in this period has been challenged recently. See, e.g., T.W. Fletcher, 'The Great Depression in English Agriculture, 1873-1896', *EHR,* XIII, 1961, 417-432. For Highland agriculturalists, however, the period was one of undoubted crisis. Crofters' difficulties are dealt with in this Chapter and in Chapters 9-10. For sheep farmers' and landlords' difficulties see, Hunter, 'Sheep and Deer', 1973, *passim.*

2. 'Crop Report for 1881', *T.H.A.S.S.,* 4th Ser., XIV, 1882, 350-351.

3. 'Crop Report for 1882', *T.H.A.S.S.,* 4th Ser., XV, 1883, 294-295. Also, *Oban Times,* 15 July, 18 Nov. 1882; *The Times,* 9 March 1883; *Alleged Destitution,* 1883, 21.

4. *Alleged Destitution,* 1883, 2; *Oban Times,* 18 Nov. 1882; *Scotsman,* 6 Feb. 1883; *The Times,* 9 March 1883.

5. *Scotsman,* 4 Oct. 1882; *The Times,* 5 Oct. 1882; *Oban Times,* 7 Oct. 1882. Also, *N.C.,* Q. 46056; Fishery Board for Scotland, *1st Rep.,* 1883, xxii; *Alleged Destitution,* 1883, 2.

6. *Scotsman,* 15 Dec. 1882. Also, *Social Conditions in Lewis,* 1902, xvi.

7. For reports on the situation by local clergymen and others see, *Hansard,* 3rd Ser., CCLXXVII, 949-954. Also, *Oban Times,* 30 Dec. 1882; *The Times,* 30 Jan. 1883; *Scotsman,* 2 Feb. 1883.

8. See above, 54 *et seq.*

9. *Scotsman,* 15 Dec. 1882; *The Times,* 9 March 1883.

10. *Scotsman,* 26 Jan. 1883; *The Times,* 30 Jan., 24 July 1883; *N.C.,* Q. 46056.

11. Board of Supervision, *38th Rep.,* 1883, vii-viii.

12. *Hansard,* 3rd Ser., CCLXXVII, 2-3; *Oban Times,* 17 March 1883.

13. *Scotsman,* 22 March, 8 May 1883; *The Times,* 21 March, 3 April 1883.

14. The fullest account of the Irish Land League is Palmer, *Irish Land League,* 1940. See also, Pomfret, *Struggle for Land in Ireland,* 1930, 97-178; C.C. O'Brien, *Parnell and His Party,* Oxford, 1957, 36-79; and the relevant sections of recent general histories of modern Ireland, especially F.S.L. Lyons, *Ireland Since the Famine,* London, 1971. For Gladstone's role see, J.L. Hammond, *Gladstone and the Irish Nation,* London, 1938, a book whose Gladstonian bias is offset by L.P. Curtis, *Coercion and Conciliation in Ireland, 1880-1892,* Princeton, 1963.

15. Lothian, P., GD 40/16/32, MacNeill, Confidential Reports, 1886, 55.

16. *N.C.,* Q. 2804. Also, Q. 1461.

17. D.H. MacFarlane, *Hansard,* 3rd Ser., CCLXXXIX, 1608. Also, *N.C.,* Q. 45888.

18. *Highlander,* 23 March 1881.

19. *Owners of Lands and Heritages,* 1874; *Scottish Highlander,* 28 April 1887.

20. *N.C.,* QQ. 1556, 1782, 8562, etc. It was almost the only place where high rents were as much complained of as lack of land. *Nap. Rep.,* 50.

21. *Scotsman,* 22 Dec. 1877.

22. *Highlander,* 23, 30 March 1881.

23. *Highlander,* 4 May 1881; *Scotsman,* 22 April 1882; *N.C.,* QQ. 8549-8552.

24. *Scotsman,* 2 Dec. 1882.

25. *N.C.,* Q. 9385.

26. Described above, 19-21.

27. MacD.P., GD 221/148/1, Brodie to Lord MacDonald, 25 April 1882; Ivory, P., GD 1/36/1, J. MacLennan, Memo. as to Alleged Charges of Intimidation at Braes, 20 March 1882. Also, *N.C.,* Q. 9385.

28. A. Finlayson: statement at his trial, A. MacKenzie, *The Isle of Skye in 1882-1883,* Inverness, 1883, 74.

29. In 1887, on the basis of evidence presented by both sides in the dispute, the Crofters Commission conceded the justice of the crofters' case and restored Ben Lee to them. Crofters Commission, *1st Rep.,* 1888, 104; *Scottish Highlander,* 26 May 1887.

30. Home Office Miscellanea, HH 22/4, Memo on the Recent Disturbances in the Island of Skye, Feb. 1883.

31. *Oban Times,* 13 Jan. 1883.

32. *N.C.,* Q. 8552.

33. HH 22/4, Disturbances, Feb. 1883.

34. Lothian P., GD 40/16/32, MacNeill, Confidential Reports, 16.

35. For details of MacDonald's status see above, 121.

36. The manifesto was issued on 18 October 1881. Palmer, *Irish Land League,* 1940, 297.

37. MacD.P., GD 221/148/1, Brodie to Lord MacDonald, 23 April 1882; Ivory, P., GD 1/36/1, MacLennan, Memo as to Alleged Intimidation, 20 March 1882.

38. See above, 122 *et seq.*

39. For the proprietors' feelings as described by a relatively enlightened land-owner, Lachlan MacDonald of Skeabost, see, *Celtic Magazine,* VII, 1882, 396.

40. Home Office Miscellanea, HH 22/4, MacLennan to Crown Agent, 5 Jan. 1882; Ivory P., GD 1/36/1, A. MacDonald to J. MacLennan, 3 Jan. 1882; *loc. cit.,* MacLennan Alleged Intimidation, 20 March 1882; HH 22/4, Disturbances, Feb. 1883.

41. MacD.P., GD 221/148/1, Brodie to Lord MacDonald, 23 May 1882; *Scotsman,* 17 April 1882; *Hansard,* 3rd Ser., CCLXVIII, 1032.

42. Above, 89-90.

43. *Oban Times,* 22 April 1882. See also, MacLean, *Former Days,* 1945, 81-158. MacLean was a boy at Braes in 1882. His account of events is the only one written, as it were, from the inside and its accuracy is substantially borne out by contemporary evidence.

44. Ivory P., GD 1/36/1, Pol. Inspector (Portree) to Ivory, 31 March 1882. Also contemporary newspaper accounts – a particularly dramatic example of the latter, written by Alexander Gow of the *Dundee Advertiser* is reproduced in H.J. Hanham, 'The Problem of Highland Discontent, 1880-1885', *TRHS,* 4th Ser., XIX, 1969, 24-30.

45. Ivory P., GD 1/36/1, Ivory to Lord Advocate, 22 April 1882.

46. *Celtic Magazine,* VII, 1882, 344.

47. A point elaborated in Hanham, 'Highland Discontent', 1969, 24, 30.

48. Its development is examined in more detail in, Hunter, 'Politics of Land Reform', 1974.

49. *Hansard,* 3rd Ser., CCLXVIII, 1032; CCLXIX, 227.

50. Hunter, 'Politics of Land Reform', 1974, 49.

51. See, *inter al., N.C.,* QQ. 9470-9476, 9924; Argyll, *Hansard,* 3rd Ser., CCXCIV, 105; *Blackwood's Magazine,* CXXXVIII, 1885, 99.

52. For details of estate ownership see, *Owners of Lands and Heritages,* 1874; *Book of Dunvegan,* II, 99-100; *N.C.,* QQ. 7533-7534.

53. *N.C.,* QQ. 7263, 7425, 7474, *etc.* Also, Ivory P., GD 1/36/1, Spiers to Ivory, 27 April 1882.

54. MacKenzie, *Isle of Skye,* 1883, 16.

55. *Ibid.,* 17-18.

56. *Oban Times,* 22 April 1882.

57. *N.C.,* QQ. 7184-7187. Also, Lothian P., GD 40/16/3, J. MacLennan, Memo. to Sec. of State, 15 Aug, 1886; *Celtic Magazine,* VII, 1883, 343.

58. Ivory P., GD 1/36/1, cutting, *Northern Chronicle,* n.d.

59. Home Office Miscellanea, HH 22/4, Statement of D. MacDonald, 27 March 1882; Lothian P., GD 40/16/3, MacLennan, Memo. to Sec. of State, 15 Aug. 1886.

60. HH 22/4, Disturbances, Feb. 1883.

61. Ivory P., GD 1/36/1, N. MacPherson (Glendale trustee) to Lord Advocate, 20 March 1882; *loc. cit.,* GD 1/36/1, Spiers to Ivory, 26 March 1882.

62. *N.C.,* Q. 6571.

63. Ivory P., GD 1/36/1, Pol. Rep., Dunvegan, 30 May 1882.

64. Ivory P., GD 1/36/1, Pol. Reps., Dunvegan, 30 May, 14 Sept., 9 Nov. 1882; HH 22/4, Disturbances, Feb. 1883.

65. Ivory P., GD 1/36/1, Spiers to Ivory, 30 Nov. 1882.

66. Ivory P., GD 1/36/1, Spiers to Ivory, 30 Nov. 1882; *loc. cit.,* GD 1/36/1, Pol. Rep., Dunvegan, 26 Dec. 1882. Also, *Scotsman,* 2 Dec. 1882.

67. See, MacKenzie, *Isle of Skye,* 1883, 37-38.

68. HH 22/4, Disturbances, Feb. 1883.

69. Ivory P., GD 1/36/1, Statement of A. MacDonald (the deforced messenger), 13 Sept. 1882. Also, *loc. cit.,* GD 1/36/1, Spiers to Ivory, 3 Sept. 1882.

70. Ivory P., GD 1/36/1, Spiers to Ivory, 7 April, 5 May 1882.

71. Ivory P., GD 1/36/1, Spiers to Ivory, 8 Sept. 1882, Ivory P.

72. Home Office Miscellanea, HH 22/4, Ivory to Sir William Harcourt (Home Secretary), 21 Sept. 1882.

73. Ivory P., GD 1/36/1, Balfour to Ivory, 3 Nov. 1882. HH 22/4, Disturbances, Feb. 1883.

74. Ivory P., GD 1/36/1, Police Committee Minutes, 13 Nov. 1882; *Scotsman,* 21 Nov. 1882; *Hansard,* 3rd Ser., CCLXXIV, 1927.

75. C.F., AF 67/50, Sheriff Johnston, Rep. on Deforcement at Airdens, Sept. 1893.

76. Ivory, P., GD 1/36/1, Supt. Aitchison's Rep., 24 Oct. 1882; *Scotsman,* 25 Oct. 1882.

77. MacD. P., GD 221/148/1, Brodie to Crown Agent, 5 Sept. 1882.

78. MacD.P., GD 221/148/1, Brodie to Crown Agent, 27 Oct. 1882; *loc.cit.,* Brodie to Lord MacDonald, 20 Dec. 1882.

79. *N.C.,* Q. 93.

80. Ivory P., GD 1/36/1, Pol. Rep., Braes, 29 Dec. 1882.

81. Home Office Miscellanea, HH 22/4, Ivory to Balfour, 8 Jan. 1883; Ivory P., GD 1/36/1(2) Pol. Reps., Dunvegan, 9, 10 Jan. 1883.

82. Ivory P., GD 1/36/1(2), Pol. Rep. Dunvegan, 9 Jan. 1883.

83. Ivory P., GD 1/36/1(2), Precognitions, 26 Jan. 1883; *loc. cit.,* Medical Rep., 24 Jan. 1883; Lothian P., GD 40/16/3, MacDonald to MacHardy, 17 Jan. 1883; *The Times,* 18, 19 Jan. 1883.

84. HH 22/4, Disturbances, Feb. 1883.

85. Ivory P., GD 1/36/1(2), MacLennan to Crown Agent, 21 Jan. 1883; Lothian P., GD 40/16/3, MacHardy, Rep., 2 Feb. 1883.

86. Ivory P., GD 1/36/1, Ivory to Harcourt, 21 Sept. 1882; *loc. cit.,* Ivory to Balfour, 1 Oct. 1882; *Oban Times,* 4 Nov. 1882; *Scotsman,* 15 Dec. 1882.

87. See, *Highlander,* Oct. 1880 - Jan. 1881.

88. Above, 131-132.

89. *Scotsman,* 8 Aug., 7 Oct. 1882; *Celtic Magazine,* VII, 1882, 436-438; *Hansard,* 3rd Ser., CCLXX, 806-807.

90. *Oban Times,* 3 Feb. 1883; *N.C.,* QQ. 10354-10368; *Scotsman,* 26 March 1883.

91. *Scotsman,* 26 March 1883.

92. HH 22/4, Disturbances, Feb. 1883. Also, Ivory P., GD 1/36/1(2), MacLennan to Crown Agent, 21 Jan. 1883.

93. Home Office Miscellanea, HH 22/4, Balfour to Ivory, 17, 30 Jan. 1883.

94. HH 22/4, Disturbances, Feb. 1883. MacNeill was the nephew of Sir John MacNeill who figured largely in earlier chapters.

95. Home Office Miscellanea, HH 22/4, MacNeill, Rep. to Lord Advocate, 16 Feb. 1883.

96. *Scotsman,* 10, 12, 14, 17, 20 April 1883.

97. Cabinet Papers, RH 4/9/6, Balfour to Harcourt, 13 Jan. 1883.

98. See, e.g., W. Burns to James Patton, 10 May 1882 — reproduced, Hanham, 'Highland Discontent', 1969, 56-57.

99. *Celtic Magazine,* VIII, 1883, 284.

100. *Hansard,* 3rd Ser., CCLXXV. Also, Hanham, 'Highland Discontent', 1969, 55-56.

101. *Hansard,* 3rd Ser., CCLXXVI, 853.

102. For details of its inauguration see, Hunter, 'Politics of Land Reform', 1974, 60-61.

103. *Oban Times,* 7 April 1883, 29 March, 28 June 1884.

104. Hunter, 'Politics of Land Reform', 1974, 51.

105. *Celtic Magazine,* VIII, 1883, 317-319. Apart from Lord Napier, who was himself a landowner, the Commission consisted of Cameron of Locheil and Sir Kenneth MacKenzie of Gairloch, both of whom owned extensive Highland estates; Fraser-MacIntosh, who sympathised with crofters but was a landlord nevertheless; and two Gaelic scholars — Alexander Nicolson, sheriff of Kirkcudbright and son of a Skye proprietor; and Donald MacKinnon, the newly appointed Professor of Celtic at Edinburgh University, a Tory who had never shown any interest in crofting question

106. An official enquiry subsequently concluded that 'of all the means by which discontent has been fostered, none produced such baneful results as the Royal

Commission'. Lothian P., GD 40/16/32, MacNeill, Confidential Reports, 1886, 2.

107. *N.C.*, Q. 4443.

108. *Nap. Rep.*, App. A, 440-448.

109. *N.C.*, Q. 10.

110. See, e.g., *N.C.*, QQ. 13-21.

111. *N.C.*, Q. 44503. Also, *N.C.*, QQ. 41156-41159, 41192.

112. *The Times*, 2 April 1883; *Nap. Rep.*, 1.

113. *Oban Times*, 25 Aug. 1883.

114. Ivory P., GD 1/36/1(2), Pol. Rep., Skye, 4 Sept. 1883.

115. Hunter, 'Politics of Land Reform', 1974, 51.

116. *Oban Times*, 1 Dec. 1883.

117. Ivory P., GD 1/36/1(2), HLLRA tract, 'Shoulder to Shoulder'.

118. Ivory P., GD 1/36/1(2), HLLRA, 'Rules for Local Branches'.

119. Ivory P., GD 1/36/1(2), Pol. Rep. Colbost, 5 Dec. 1883; *Oban Times*, 29 Dec. 1883, 2 Feb. 1884. Also, Hunter, 'Politics of Land Reform', 1974, 52.

Chapter 9

1. Highland proverb and motto of the HLLRA. Translated by the Association as: 'The People are Mightier than a Lord'.

2. 'We are expecting much good as a result of the visit of the Commission,' a Glendale crofter had informed Lord Napier and his colleagues. *N.C.*, Q. 6597. Also *Nap. Rep.*, App. A. 7.

3. *Scotsman*, 5, 11 Jan. 1883; Ivory P., GD 1/36/1(2), Pol. Rep., Glendale, 4 June 1883.

4. *Scotsman*, 10 Dec. 1884; Cabinet Papers, RH 4/9/6, Lovat to J.B. Balfour, 2 Oct. 1885.

5. *Scotsman*, 3, 4 April 1884.

6. *Scotsman*, 5 April 1884; *Oban Times*, 26 April 1884.

7. *Scotsman*, 8 March 1884; *The Times*, 21 April 1884.

8. *Oban Times*, 23 Feb., 1 March 1884.

9. *Scotsman*, 24, 27 Nov. 1883; *Oban Times*, 1 Dec. 1883.

10. G.B. Clark, *The Highland Land Question*, London, 1885, 3.

11. *Nap. Rep.*, 16-53. Also, D.J. MacCuish, 'The Origin and Development of Crofting Law', *T.G.S.I.*, XLIII, 1962, 186-188.

12. *Oban Times*, May 1884. Also, Clark, *Highland Land Question*, 1885, 3.

13. *Hansard*, 3rd Ser., CCLXXXIX, 1607; CCXCIII, 539.

14. Ivory P., GD 1/36/1(2), Pol. Rep., Colbost, 24 May 1884.

15. Ivory P., GD 1/36/1(2), Pol. Reps., Colbost, 3 July, 28 Aug. 1884. Also, *Scotsman*, 10 Nov. 1884; *The Times*, 11 Nov. 1884.

16. *Oban Times*, 3 May, 28 June 1884; *The Times*, 14 June 1884.

17. Ivory P., GD 1/36/1(2), Pol. Reps., Dunvegan, 25 April, 3 May 1884; *Oban Times*, 17 May, 14 June, 6, 27 Sept. 1884.

18. *Oban Times*, 4 Oct. 1884.

19. Letter in *The Times*, 15 Oct. 1884. Also, *The Times*, 27 Sept. 1884.

20. *The Times*, 1 Sept. 1884.

21. *Scotsman,* 5 Sept. 1884; *The Times,* 8 Sept., 15 Oct. 1884.

22. *Nap. Rep.,* 50-51.

23. *The Times,* 5 Sept. 1884. Also, *Scotsman,* 7 Sept. 1884. The full Programme was printed in the *Oban Times,* 7 Feb. 1885.

24. Cabinet Papers, RH 4/9/6, J.B. Balfour to Harcourt, 13 Jan. 1885.

25. See, Hammond, *Gladstone and the Irish Nation,* 1938, 240 *et seq.*

26. *Oban Times,* 7 Feb. 1885.

27. *Oban Times,* 16 Aug. 1884; *Scotsman,* 1,3,4 Nov. 1884.

28. Wife of Sir Reginald Cathcart but proprietrix in her own right, having inherited the island from her father, Gordon of Cluny (who figured largely in earlier chaps.), in 1878.

29. *Scotsman,* 22 Nov. 1884.

30. *Scotsman,* 19 Dec. 1884.

31. *Scotsman,* 22 Nov. 1884.

32. Ivory P., GD 1/36/1(2), Chisholm (Proc. Fisc., Lochmaddy) to Ivory, 21 Feb. 1885; *loc. cit.,* Pol. Reps., Benbecula, 18 Dec. 1884, 18 Feb. 1885.

33. Ivory, P., GD 1/36/1(2), Chisholm to Ivory, 2, 8 Jan. 1885; *loc. cit.,* Pol. Rep., Howmore, 3 Jan. 1885; *Scotsman,* 9 March 1885.

34. Ivory P., GD 1/36/1(2), Chisholm to Ivory, 21 Nov. 1884, 21 Feb. 1885; *Scotsman,* 10 Nov., 11 Dec. 1884, 6 Jan. 1885; *Oban Times,* 3, 10 Jan. 1885.

35. *Oban Times,* 17 Jan. 1885.

36. *The Times,* 8, 13 Dec. 1885.

37. Ivory P., GD 1/36/1(2), Pol. Rep., Lochmaddy, 7 Aug. 1884; *Oban Times,* 16 Aug. 1884; *Scotsman,* 22 Jan. 1885. Also, *Hansard,* 3rd Ser., CCCIV, 86.

38. See Palmer, *Irish Land League,* 1940, 195 *et seq.*

39. *Oban Times,* 5 July 1884; *Scotsman,* 20 Oct., 15, 22 Nov. 1884.

40. Ivory P., GD 1/36/1(2), Pol. Rep., Portree, 6 Sept. 1885; *loc. cit.,* Ch. Cons. MacHardy, Rep. to Police Commissioners, 29 Dec. 1885.

41. *Scotsman,* 26, 27 Nov. 1884.

42. *Scotsman,* 15, 18 Oct. 1884.

43. See, *e.g., Scotsman,* 4 Nov. 1884.

44. Lothian P., GD 40/16/3, Statement by Sir Reginald and Lady Gordon Cathcart, Jan. 1886.

45. See, *Papers Relating to the Despatch of a Government Force to Skye,* P.P. 1884-85 LXIV, 3-5.

46. Ivory P., GD/1/36/1(2), MacHardy to Harcourt, 9 Nov. 1884; *Scotsman,* 31 Oct. 1884; *Despatch of a Government Force,* 1885, 8-9.

47. Ivory P., GD 1/36/1(2), MacHardy to Harcourt, 9 Nov. 1884. Also, *Scotsman,* 3 Nov. 1884; *The Times,* 4 Nov. 1884.

48. Ivory P., GD 1/36/1(2), Police Committee Minutes, 23 Sept. 1884; *loc. cit.,* MacHardy to Ivory, 27 Oct. 1884.

49. S.O. Misc. Files, HH 1/712, Pol. Committee to J.B. Balfour, 31 Oct. 1884. Also, Ivory P., GD 1/36/1(2), Anderson to Ivory, 8 Nov. 1884.

50. See, *e.g., The Times,* 10 Nov. 1884.

51. Ivory P., GD 1/36/1(2), J.B. Balfour to Ivory, 4, 13 Nov. 1884. Also, *Despatch of a Government Force,* 1885, *passim.*

52. Ivory P., GD 1/36/1(2), MacHardy to Ivory, 1 Nov. 1884; *Scotsman,* 12, 17 Nov. 1884; *The Times,* 13, 21 Nov. 1884.

53. Ivory P., GD 1/36/1(2), J.B. Balfour to J. MacLennan, 2 Dec. 1884. Detestation of the police was intensified by the knowledge that they kept the authorities informed of crofters' activities. See, Ivory P., GD 1/36/1(2), Spiers to Ivory, 19 Dec. 1884. Also, *Scotsman,* 3 Feb. 1885.

54. At a concert given by the marines in Portree, their commanding officer remarked that 'setting aside the question of why they were there, they should never forget the kindness with which they had been received in Skye'. *Scotsman,* 13 Dec. 1884.

55. *The Times,* 19 Nov. 1884.

56. S.O. Misc. Files, HH 1/712, J.B. Balfour to Ivory, 19 Nov. 1884.

57. Ivory P., GD 1/36/1(2), J.B. Balfour to Ivory, 4, 13 Nov. 1884.

58. Ivory P., GD 1/36/1(2), Police Committee Minutes, 7 April 1885; *loc. cit.,* Ivory, Rep. to Commissioners of Supply, 30 April 1885.

59. Ivory P., GD 1/36/1(2), Pol. Reps., Glendale and Portree, 30 Dec. 1884; *Scotsman,* 26, 30 Dec. 1884; *The Times,* 26 Dec. 1884.

60. Ivory P., GD 1/36/1(2), Ivory to J.B. Balfour, 10 Feb. 1885; *Scotsman,* 30, 31 Jan. 1885, *The Times,* 7 Feb. 1885.

61. Ivory P., GD 1/36/1(2), Spiers to Ivory, 11 Jan. 1885; *loc. cit.,* Martin to Ivory, 30 Jan. 1885.

62. See, *e.g., The Times,* 1 April 1885.

63. A.G. Gardiner, *The Life of Sir William Harcourt,* London, 1923, (2 vols.), 1, 531-534.

64. Ivory P., GD 1/36/1(4), Police Committee Minutes, 7 April 1885; Cabinet Papers, RH 4/9/6, Lovat to J.B. Balfour, 2 Oct. 1885.

65. See, *Scotsman,* 18, 22 Nov. 1884; *The Times,* 1 Dec. 1884.

66. The expedition's total cost to the government and the local authority was £12,636. S.O. Misc. Files, MacHardy to Under-Sec. of State, 18 Sept. 1886.

67. *Scotsman,* 25 Dec. 1884.

68. *Oban Times,* 24 Dec. 1884.

69. MacD. P., GD 221/148/1, Brodie to J.B. Balfour, 8 Dec. 1884.

70. *Oban Times,* 20 Dec. 1884; *Scotsman,* 10 Dec. 1884, 31 Jan. 1885.

71. *Scotsman,* 10 Feb. 1885. See also, *The Times,* 8, 26 Dec. 1884; *Scotsman,* 11 Dec. 1885.

72. See, E.H. Whetham, 'Livestock Prices in Britain, 1851-93', *A.H.R.,* XI, 1963, 29, 32.

73. *Cottar Population,* 1888, 35-36; *D.F.C.,* QQ. 30408-30412, 53635. Also, *Scottish Highlander,* 18 Aug. 1887.

74. See above, 108.

75. A point made frequently by crofters themselves. See, *e.g. Scottish Highlander,* 16 Sept., 14 Oct. 1886.

76. Lothian P., GD 40/16/32, MacNeill, Confidential Reports, 1886, *passim;* *Scottish Highlander,* 14 Oct. 1886, 4 Aug. 1887.

77. Lothian P., GD 40/16/32, MacNeill, Confidential Reports, 1886, 5.

78. *Oban Times,* 13 Dec. 1884.

79. Ivory P., GD 1/36/1(4), Ivory to Harcourt, 27 June 1885; *loc. cit.,* Pol. Rep., Portree, 27 June 1885.

80. Lothian P., GD 40/16/32, MacNeill, Confidential Reports, 1886, *passim.*

81. Ivory P., GD 1/36/1(4), A. Macdonald to Ivory, 31 Aug. 1885.

82. Cabinet Papers, RH 4/9/6, Lovat to J.B. Balfour, 2 Oct. 1885.

83. Ivory P., GD 1/36/1(4), A. MacDonald to Ivory, 19 Sept. 1885; *loc. cit.* MacHardy, Report to Police Committee, 29 Dec. 1885.

84. Lothian P., GD 40/16/32, MacNeill, Confidential Reports, 1886, 30.

85. *Ibid.* Also, Ivory P., GD 1/36/1(4), A. MacDonald to Ivory, 17 Sept. 1885.

86. See, Hunter, 'Sheep and Deer', 1973, 203 *et seq.*

87. Ivory, P., GD 1/36/1(4), A. MacDonald to Ivory, 17 Sept. 1885.

88. Hunter, 'Sheep and Deer', 1973, *passim.*

89. Cabinet Papers, RH4/9/6, Locheil to Harcourt, 20 Dec. 1884.

90. *The Times,* 10 Jan. 1995; *Scotsman,* 14 Jan. 1885.

91. *N.C.,* Q. 32166.

92. *Oban Times,* 24 Jan. 1885.

93. *Oban Times,* 31 Jan. 1885. See also, *Scotsman,* 20, 26 Jan., 3 Feb. 1885; *The Times,* 20, 23 Jan. 1885; *Celtic Magazine,* X, 1885, 228-229.

94. See, Hunter, 'Politics of Land Reform', 1974, 54.

95. *Oban Times,* 12 Dec. 1885.

96. *Ibid.*

97. *Scotsman,* 6 Oct. 1885.

98. *Scotsman,* 12 Dec..1885.

99. Lothian P., GD 40/16/32, MacNeill, Confidential Reports, 1886, 3 and *passim.*

100. See, D.W. Crowley, 'The Crofters' Party, 1885-1892', *S H.R.,* XXXV, 1956, 110; J.G. Kellas, 'The Crofters' War, 1882-1888', *History Today,* XII, 1962, 281.

101. *Scottish Highlander,* 30 Dec. 1886.

102. Ivory P., GD 1/36/1(2), MacPherson to Ivory, 4 Dec. 1884.

103. Below, 172.

104. Lothian P., GD 40/16/3, MacNeill, Confidential Reports, 1886, 7, 70-74.

105. *Oban Times,* 20 Dec. 1884.

106. *Oban Times,* 8 Oct. 1887.

107. *Oban Times,* 22 Aug. 1885. Also, 14 March, 26 Sept. 1885.

108. *Hansard,* 3rd Ser., CCCIII, 159.

109. *Nap. Rep.,* App. A, 10-11.

110. MacCallum's most eminent colleagues were his brother Malcolm, minister at Strontian, Argyll, in the 1880s, and the Rev. Angus MacIver, minister at Uig in Lewis. See, *Oban Times,* 27 Dec. 1884; *Scotsman,* 9 Jan. 1885.

111. *Oban Times,* 8 May 1886. The charge was eventually dropped.

112. *Scotsman,* 15 Nov. 1886. On this occasion he was not brought to trial. See also below, 169.

113. *Scottish Highlander,* 30 Sept. 1886. Also, Lothian P., GD 40/16/32, MacNeill, Confidential Reports, 1886, 3.

114. Above, 129-30.

115. *Scotsman,* 1 Dec. 1884.

116. See above, 100-3.

117. *Scotsman*, 15 Feb. 1883; W. MacKenzie, *Old Skye Tales*, Glasgow, 1934, 26-27; J. MacLeod, *Highland Heroes of the Land Reform Movement*, Inverness, 1917, 74-75. The latter work contains biographical sketches of a large number of HLLRA activists.

118. See above, Chap. 6, *passim.*

119. See, Hunter, 'Sheep and Deer', 1973, 214 *et seq.*

120. Irvine, *Inquiry into Emigration*, 1802, 56.

121. See, I.F. Grant, *Highland Folk Ways*, London, 1961, 7.

122. *Celtic Magazine*, IX, 1884, 337-338.

123. This notion, which appears to have its origins in the remote antiquity of the Celtic peoples, raises for the historian two separate problems. The first concerns the precise historical origins of the concept and falls outwith the scope of this book. The second, which falls firmly within it, concerns the nature and importance of the concept in nineteenth-century crofting life.

124. Argyll, *Scotland As It Was and Is*, Edinburgh, (2 vols.), 1887, I, 49.

125. MacL.P., Box 62A, MacLeod to Napier, 29 Oct. 1884.

126. *N.C.*, Q. 36138.

127. A.C. MacPherson, 'An Old Highland Genealogy and the Evolution of a Scottish Clan', *Scottish Studies*, X, 1966, 12. Also, Grant, *Highland Folk Ways*, 1961, 7.

128. Cunningham, *Loyal Clans*, 1932, 132-133.

129. Lang (ed.), *Highlands of Scotland*, 1898, 93.

130. *The Times*, 8 March 1886. Also, *N.C.*, QQ. 9127, 12293, 12295, *etc.*

131. The phrase in quotation marks appears in, E. Burt, *Letters from a Gentleman in the North of Scotland*, London, (2 vols.), 1754, II, 173; and in, Irvine, *Enquiry into Emigration*, 1802, 36.

132. Selkirk, *Observations*, 1805, 119-120.

133. MacCulloch, *Highlands and Western Isles*, 1824, IV, 122, 442.

134. *Sutherland Estate Management*, 1972, II, 177, Sellar to Marchioness of Stafford, 4 Feb. 1813.

135. *Nap. Rep.*, 8.

136. See, Palmer, *Irish Land League*, 1940, 2-3.

137. *Highlander*, 29 May 1875. For an analysis of the 1870 Act see, Palmer, *Irish Land League*, 1940, 34-63.

138. *Highlander*, 26 Feb. 1876.

139. *Oban Times*, 5 Sept. 1885.

140. Above, 92-4.

141. *Hansard*, 3rd Ser., CCLXXI, 770.

142. MacKenzie, *Isle of Skye*, 1883, xlix.

143. See above, Chap. 1, *passim.*

144. *The Times*, 25 April 1887.

145. See, *Social Condition of Lewis*, 1902, lxxxviii, f.n.

146. J.S. Mill, *Principles of Political Economy*, London, 5th edit., 1862, I, 400; *Highlander*, 26 July, 2 Aug. 1873, 25 May 1875.

147. Quoted, M. Davitt, *The Fall of Feudalism in Ireland*, London, 1904, 656-657.

148. *Oban Times*, 24 May 1884.

149. See, e.g., the quotation from Rousseau's *Discourse on the Origin of Inequality* which prefaces this book.

150. Above, 98.

151. They were neither the first nor the last to have done so. See Lanternari, *Religions of the Oppressed,* 1963, 306-307.

152. D. Campbell, *The Land Question in the Highlands and Islands,* Paisley, 1884, 11-12.

153. *Oban Times,* 28 Aug. 1886. For details of the raid in question see below, 165.

154. See, *inter al., Oban Times,* 29 Dec. 1883; *Scotsman,* 4 Sept. 1885.

155. MacL. P., Box 62 A, MacPherson to MacLeod, 11 Nov. 1884.

156. *Oban Times,* 21 Feb. 1885.

157. References to Irish events have already been provided. For rural unrest in Wales and England see, *inter al.,* P. Jones-Evans, 'Evan Pan Jones – Land Reformer', *Welsh History Review,* IV, 1968, 143-159; J.P.D. Dunbabin, 'The 'Revolt of the Field': The Agricultural Labourers' Movement in the 1870s', *Past and Present,* XXVI, 1963, 68-97.

158. F.M.L. Thomson, 'Land and Politics in England in the Nineteenth Century', *T.R.H.S.,* 5th Ser., XV, 1965, 39.

159. For an account of George's influence on British politics see, E.P. Lawrence, *Henry George in the British Isles,* Michigan, 1957.

160. George visited Skye in 1884 and 1885. *Oban Times,* 16, 23 Feb., 1 March 1884, 10, 17 Jan. 1885. Chamberlain toured the north-west in 1887. *The Times,* 19, 25, 27, 29 April 1887.

161. There was, in fact, little love lost between the Georgites and the HLLRA. See, Hunter, 'Politics of Land Reform', 1974, 67.

162. This was Mary MacPherson, the Skye bard referred to in a previous chapter. Above, Chap. 6. Also, MacLean, 'Poetry of the Clearances', 1939, 319-324; Thomson, *Introduction to Gaelic Poetry,* 1974, 245-248.

163. *Scotsman,* 4 Dec. 1885.

164. The phrase seems to have been first used in the *Oban Times,* 2 Jan. 1886.

165. Angus Sutherland had been defeated in Sutherland – but won the seat in 1886. For these and other details see, Hunter, 'Politics of Land Reform', 1974.

166. See, Cabinet Papers, RH 4/9/6, Locheil to Harcourt, 20 Dec. 1884.

167. Cabinet Papers, RH 4/9/6, J.B. Balfour to Harcourt, 13 Jan. 1885; *loc. cit.,* Harcourt to Gladstone, 17 Jan. 1885.

168. *Hansard,* 3rd Ser., CCLXXXIX, 1750; CCXCVIII, 845.

169. Cabinet Papers, RH 4/9/6, Locheil to Harcourt, 20 Dec. 1884.

170. Lord Colin Campbell: *Hansard,* 3rd Ser., CCLXXXIX, 1624.

171. Cabinet Papers, RH 4/9/6, Gladstone to Harcourt, 19 Jan. 1885. Also, Gardiner, *Sir William Harcourt,* 1923, I, 531-534; J. Chamberlain, *A Political Memoir, 1880-1892,* (ed. C.H.D. Howard), London, 1953, 123, 133, 270-271.

172. Cabinet Papers, RH 4/9/6, Gladstone to Harcourt, 19 Jan. 1885. Also, *Hansard,* 3rd Ser., CCLXCVIII, 556; *The Times,* 21 May 1885.

173. *Scotsman,* 21 July 1885.

174. *Scotsman,* 1 Feb. 1886.

175. *Hansard,* 3rd Ser., CCCII, 1305-1306; CCCV, 1468; *Scotsman,* 21 May 1886;

Blackwood's Magazine, CXXXIX, 1886, 560; *Annual Register,* 1886, 83.

176. *Hansard,* 3rd Ser., CCCV, 1481-1487. For the circumstances of the Duke's resignation see, Hammond, *Gladstone and the Irish Nation,* 1938, 216-217.

177. *Hansard,* 3rd Ser., CCCIII, 217-218. Also, Dugdale, *Balfour,* 1936, I, 108; S.H. Zebel, *Balfour,* Cambridge, 1973, 45, 56.

178. *Annual Register,* 1886, 82.

179. *Nap. Rep.,* 36.

180. For an account of the Act and subsequent legislation see, D.J. MacCuish, 'The Origin and Development of Crofting Law', *T.G.S.I.,* XLIII, 1962, 181-196. Also, Day, *Public Administration,* 1918, 190-196; G.C.H. Paton and J.G.S. Cameron, *The Law of Landlord and Tenant in Scotland,* Aberdeen, 1967, 387-495.

181. *Scotsman,* 4 March 1886; *The Times,* 13 March 1886.

182. See above, 147-8.

183. See above, 126-8.

184. It should be noted, however, that there was a strong parallel between the Highland situation and that prevailing in the extreme west of Ireland, the so-called 'congested districts', See below, 184.

185. Cabinet Papers, RH 4/9/6, J.B. Balfour to Harcourt, 13 Jan. 1885.

186. Below, Chap. 11, *passim.*

187. *Hansard,* 3rd Ser., CCLXCVIII, 859; CCCII, 1313; CCCIII, 172.

188. MacCuish, 'Crofting Law', 1962, 190.

189. *Hansard,* 3rd Ser., CCCII, 1338. Also, C.S. Orwin and E.H. Whetham, *History of British Agriculture, 1846-1914,* London, 1964, 296.

190. Croft. Comm., *Final Rep.,* 1913, xxv-xxvi.

191. *Hansard,* 3rd Ser., CCCII, 1324, 1332; CCCIII, 158, 195; CCCIV, 1747.

192. For Irish MPs' declarations of solidarity with crofters see, *Hansard,* 3rd Ser., CCCVIII, 930, 935, 977.

193. *Oban Times,* 19 June 1886.

194. *Oban Times,* 3 April 1886.

195. See, *Oban Times,* April-June 1886.

196. *Oban Times,* 20 Dec. 1884.

197. *Oban Times,* 10 April 1884.

198. Ivory P., GD 1/36/1(2), Pol. Rep., Benbecula, 14 May 1886.

199. *Oban Times,* 1 May 1886.

200. See below, 165.

201. Hunter, 'Politics of Land Reform', 1974, 57.

202. *Ibid.,* 58 *et seq.*

203. *Hansard,* 3rd Ser., CCCVIII, 995.

Chapter 10

1. Above, 163.

2. For the circumstances of that deprivation see above, 84.

3. *Oban Times,* 12 June, 31 July 1886.

4. Lothian, P., GD 40/16/3, Irvine to Dalhousie, 30 June 1886; *loc. cit.,* Dalhousie to Irvine, 6 July 1886.

5. *The Times,* 24 July 1886; *Scottish Highlander,* 29 July 1886.

6. *The Times,* 26 July 1886.

7. See, Dugdale, *Balfour,* 1936, I, 110.

8. *Scotsman,* 2-7 Aug. 1886; *Scottish Highlander,* 12 Aug. 1886; Dugdale, *Balfour,* 1936, I, 108-109.

9. *The Times,* 2 Aug. 1886; *Scottish Highlander,* 12 Aug. 1886; *Oban Times,* 30 Aug. 1886; *Return of Agrarian Offences, Scotland,* 1874-1888, P.P. 1888 LXXXII.

10. *Agrarian Offences,* 1888.

11. For petitions from Liberal Associations, Trades Councils, etc. see, S.O. Misc. Files, HH 1/284-306.

12. Ivory P., GD 1/36/12, Rep. to Commissioners of Supply, 27 April 1886.

13. Board of Supervision, *41st Rep.,* 1886, 16; S.O. Misc. Files, HH 1/1, Balfour, Memo., 10 Sept. 1886; Day, *Public Administration,* 1918, 120.

14. *Blackwood's Magazine,* CXXXIX, 1886, 559.

15. *Scotsman,* 4 May 1886.

16. Ivory P., GD 1/36/12, Rep. to Comms. of Supp., 27 April 1886.

17. S.O. Misc. Files, HH 1/711, Balfour, Memo., 15 Sept. 1886.

18. Ivory P., GD 1/36/12, W.C. Dunbar to Ivory, 6 Oct. 1886.

19. Quoted, Ivory P., GD 1/36/12, Balfour to Ivory, 3 Oct. 1886. See also, *loc. cit.,* Ivory to Balfour, 2 Oct. 1886.

20. L.P. Curtis, *Coercion and Conciliation in Ireland, 1880-1892,* Princeton, 1963, 217, 239.

21. Ivory, P., GD 1/36/12, telegram: Balfour to Ivory, 4 Oct. 1886.

22. Some of these agencies' roles are examined in the concluding chapter of this book.

23. Ivory P., GD 1/36/12, Ivory to Balfour, 4 Oct. 1886.

24. Ivory P., GD 1/36/12, Ivory to Sandford, 4 Aug. 1886.

25. Ivory P., GD 1/36/12, MacDonald to Ivory, 26 Oct. 1886.

26. Balfour to Cecil, 4 Oct. 1886: quoted, Dugdale, *Balfour,* 1936, I, 115.

27. S.O. Misc. Files, HH 1/96, Hamilton (sheriff-sub., Portree) to Balfour, 26 Oct. 1886; *loc. cit.,* HH 1/18, 152, Pol. Reps., Staffin, 3 Sept., 27 Nov. 1886.

28. Lothian P., GD 40/16/8, Balfour, Memo. on Bill to Amend the Crofters Act, 24 Jan. 1887.

29. S.O. Misc. Files, HH 1/141, telegram: Balfour to A. MacDonald, 30 Nov. 1886.

30. Ivory P., GD 1/36/12, Ivory to Balfour, 4 Dec. 1886.

31. Ivory P., GD 1/36/12, Ivory to Balfour, 7 Oct. 1886; *The Times,* 8 Oct. 1886.

32. *Scotsman,* 8 Oct. 1886.

33. Ivory P., GD 1/36/12, Ivory to Balfour, 17 Oct. 1886; *Scotsman,* 9-16, 21 Oct. 1886.

34. *The Times,* 13 Oct. 1886.

35. *Scotsman,* 23 Oct. 1886.

36. S.O. Misc. Files, HH 1/96, Hamilton (who was present when the incident occurred) to Balfour, 26 Oct. 1886.

37. *Ibid.* Also, S.O. Misc. Files, HH 1/112, Pol. Rep., Portree, 31 Oct. 1886.

38. *Scotsman,* 27 Oct. 1886. The contemporary correspondence about this incident places it at Gurilapin' — not on any map I have consulted. *The Return of Agrarian Offences,* 1888, however, places it at Woodend.

39. S.O. Misc. Files, HH 1/97, telegram: Ivory to Und.-Sec. of State, 27 Oct. 1886; *loc. cit.,* HH 1/127, Pol. Rep., Uig, 9 Nov. 1886; *Scotsman,* 28, 29 Oct. 1886.

40. S.O. Misc. Files, HH 1/152, 155, Pol. Reps., Portree, 29 Nov., 6 Dec. 1886.

41. S.O. Misc. Files, HH 1/99, telegram: Ivory to Balfour, 29 Oct. 1886.

42. Ivory P., GD 1/36/12, Ivory to Balfour, 7 Nov. 1886; S.O. Misc. Files, telegram: Ivory to Balfour, 10 Nov. 1886.

43. *Scotsman,* 10, 11 Nov. 1886.

44. *Scotsman,* 15 Nov. 1886; S.O. Misc. Files, HH 1/138, Pol. Rep., Portree, 14 Nov. 1886. Neither was brought to trial, *The Times,* 23 Nov. 1886.

45. For his own account see, J. Cameron, *The Old and the New Highlands and Hebrides,* Kirkcaldy, 1912, 109-112. Also, N. MacLean, *Set Free,* London, 1949, 52-67.

46. *Scottish Highlander,* 18 Nov. 1886; *Hansard,* 3rd Ser., CCCX, 1630.

47. MacLeod: *The Times,* 14 Dec. 1886.

48. *Hansard,* 3rd Ser., CCCX, 1688-1699.

49. Curtis, *Coercion and Conciliation,* 1963, 178-179; Dugdale, *Balfour,* 1936, I, 112.

50. *Oban Times,* 16 April 1887. Balfour's popularity was not enhanced by the fact that his father had been responsible for some fairly notorious evictions in Strathconon, Ross-shire, in the 1840s. *Oban Times,* 11 Sept. 1886; *Scottish Highlander,* 5 Dec. 1889.

51. Ivory P., GD 1/36/12, Ivory to Balfour, 22 Dec. 1886.

52. Ivory P., GD 1/36/12, Ivory to Balfour, 4 Dec. 1886; *Agrarian Offences,* 1888. Also, S.O. Misc. Files, HH 1/165, Pol. Rep. Portree, 18 Dec. 1886; and further reports in same series.

53. Croft. Comm. *1st Rep.,* 1888, 96-98.

54. Hunter, 'Sheep and Deer', 1973, *passim.*

55. *Oban Times,* 8 Jan. 1887. Also, *Scottish Highlander,* 13 Jan. 1887.

56. Croft. Comm., *1st Rep.,* 1888, 88-98.

57. *Oban Times,* 2 Jan. 1886.

58. S.O. Misc. Files, HH 1/200, A. MacDonald to Balfour, 31 Jan. 1887.

59. *Ibid.*

60. Above, 133.

61. S.O. Misc. Files, HH 1/188, Pol. Rep., Staffin, 19 Jan. 1887; *Scotsman,* 20 Jan. 1887.

62. S.O. Misc. Files, HH 1/187, Und.-Sec. to Ivory, 22 Jan. 1887; *loc. cit.,* HH 1/197, Balfour to Lord Advocate, 29 Jan. 1887; *loc. cit.,* HH 1/209, S.O. Memo., 16 Feb. 1887; Ivory P., GD 1/36/1(5), Sandford to Ivory, 28 Feb. 1887.

63. Lothian P., GD 40/16/8, Lothian, Memo., 25 April 1887.

64. The Amendment Act was prepared by Balfour but enacted by his successor, Lothian. *Hansard,* 3rd Ser., CCCXV, 238. Also, *The Times,* 14 April 1887.

65. Above, 163.

66. S.O. Misc. Files, HH 1/222, Webster to Ivory, 2 March 1887; *loc. cit.,* HH 1/233, Pol. Rep., Lochmaddy, 30 April 1887.

67. S.O. Misc. Files, HH 1/241, Webster to Ivory, 9 July 1887.

68. Above, 152.

69. Above, 110-1.

70. *Cottar Population*, 1888, 4-5; Fishery Board for Scotland. *5th Rep.*, 1887, xviii; *6th Rep.*, 1888, xx-xxi, xlvi.

71. Above, 125.

72. *Cottar Population*, 1888, 5, 7, 40.

73. *Ibid.*, 5.

74. C.F., AF 67/36, Cheyne to Lothian, 3 Dec. 1887.

75. *Scottish Highlander*, 28 April 1887. (Garrabost is situated near Aignish, the significance of which will soon become apparent).

76. Above, 44-5.

77. *N.C.*, QQ. 17449-17458; *Cottar Population*, 1888, 39-40. For an account of the growth of deer forests generally, see Hunter, 'Sheep and Deer', 1973, 214-222.

78. *Scotsman*, 24 Nov. 1887; R. Hall, *The Highland Sportsman*, London, (2nd edit.), 1883, 216.

79. Lothian P., GD 40/16/32, MacNeill, Confidential Reports, 1886, 7; *Scotsman*, 29 Sept. 1885; *The Times*, 8 March 1887. Also, Hunter, 'Sheep and Deer', 1973, 220-221.

80. *Scottish Highlander*, 24 Nov. 1887.

81. See, D. MacDonald, *Tales and Traditions of the Lews*, Stornoway, 1967, 201-202 MacRae was dismissed from a previous teaching post at Alness because of his Land League connections. *Scottish Highlander*, 20 Jan. 1887.

82. *Scotsman*, 23 Nov. 1887.

83. *Scottish Highlander*, 24 Nov. 1887.

84. These details from *The Times*, 23 Nov. 1887; *Scotsman*, 23, 24 Nov. 1887; *Glasgow Herald*, 23 Nov. 1887; *Scottish Highlander*, 24 Nov., 1 Dec. 1887. According to Michael Davitt some of the rifles used in the raid came from Ireland. But this is nowhere corroborated. Davitt, *Fall of Feudalism*, 1903, 228.

85. Lothian P., GD 40/16/34, Cheyne, Rep., 27 Nov. 1887.

86. Contemporary estimates ranged from a mere handful to 200, the lower figures emanating from those anxious to play down the raid's significance. Given the number of men and guns involved, the fact that the forest contained several hundred deer and the probability that some raiders were skilled poachers — in January 1887, for example, two Lochs cottars were jailed for poaching in Park (*Scottish Highlander*, 27 Jan. 1887) — a figure of around 100 seems a fair estimate.

87. *The Times*, 25 Nov. 1887.

88. *Scotsman*, 26 Nov. 1887.

89. Lothian P., GD 40/16/34, Cheyne, Rep., 27 Nov. 1887.

90. *Scotsman*, 25 Nov. 1887.

91. For land settlement in Lewis see below, Chap. 11, *passim.*

92. *The Times*, 25, 26, 28, 29 Nov., 3 Dec. 1887; *Scotsman*, 25, 26, Nov. 1887.

93. C.F., AF 67/68, Treasury to Lothian, 20 Dec. 1887.

94. *The Times*, 23 Jan. 1888.

95. *Cottar Population*, 1888, *passim.*

96. C.F., AF 67/70, W.A. Peterkin, Confidential Memo., 14 April 1888.

97. Lothian's minutes on above Memo. Also below, 178-9.

98. *Oban Times*, 17 Dec. 1887.

99. C.F., AF 67/35, Cheyne to Lothian, 26 Nov. 1887; *Glasgow Herald,* 9 Dec. 1887.

100. C.F. AF 67/37, Pol. Rep., Ness, 21 Dec. 1887.

101. *Glasgow Herald,* 26 Dec. 1887; *Scotsman,* 26 Dec. 1887.

102. *Scotsman,* 30 Dec. 1887.

103. C.F., AF 67/38, Pol. Rep., Stornoway, 6 Jan. 1888.

104. *Ibid.*

105. C.F., AF 67/38, telegram: Fraser to Und.-Sec., 9 Jan. 1888.

106. C.F., AF 67/38, Fraser to Und.-Sec., 9 Jan. 1888; *Scotsman,* 10, 11 Jan. 1888; *Glasgow Herald,* 10 Jan. 1888; *Scottish Highlander,* 12 Jan. 1888.

107. *Oban Times,* 15 Jan. 1888.

108. C.F., AF 67/39, Cheyne to Lothian, 15 Jan. 1888.

109. C.F., AF 67/38, Pol. Rep., Stornoway, 6 Jan. 1888; *Scotsman,* 6 Jan. 1888; *The Times,* 9 Jan. 1888; *Scottish Highlander,* 12 Jan. 1888.

110. C.F., AF 67/39, Cheyne to Lothian, 15 Jan. 1888; *The Times,* 13 Jan. 1888.

111. C.F., AF 67/39, Cheyne to Lothian, 19 Jan. 1888.

112. *The Times,* 14, 19 Jan. 1888.

113. C.F., AF 67/39, Cheyne to Lothian, 19 Jan. 1888. Also, *The Times,* 23 Jan. 1888.

114. C.F., AF 67/40, Cheyne to Und.-Sec. for Scotland, 31 Jan. 1888.

115. *N.C.,* Q. 15989.

116. Lothian P., GD 40/16/32, MacNeill, Confidential Reports, 1886, 13.

117. *Ibid.; N.C.,* Q. 45040.

118. C.F., AF 67/37, Pol. Rep., Ness, 21 Dec. 1887; *loc. cit.,* AF 67/39, Pol. Rep., Stornoway, 14 Jan. 1888; *Glasgow Herald,* 26 Dec. 1887.

119. C.F., AF 67/38, Pol. Rep., Ness, 2 Jan. 1888; *loc. cit.,* AF 67/40, Cheyne to Und.-Sec., 31 Jan. 1888.

120. S.O. Misc. Files, HH 1/917, MacKenzie to Lothian, 28 Nov. 1887; *loc. cit.,* Lord Advocate to Cheyne, 30 Nov. 1887; *loc. cit.,* Cheyne to Lothian, 29 Nov. 1887; *Scotsman,* 23 Nov., 26 Dec. 1887; *The Times,* 31 Dec. 1887.

121. *Scottish Highlander,* 22 Dec. 1887; C.F., AF 67/98, Pol. Rep., Glenelg, 19 April 1888.

122. S.O. Misc. Files, Hamilton to Ivory, 5 Sept. 1887.

123. C.F., AF 67/95, Pol. Rep., Dunvegan, 9 Jan. 1888; *Scotsman,* 12 Jan. 1888. Also, *Scottish Highlander,* 15 March 1888.

124. C.F., AF 67/95, Pol. Reps., Uig, 16, 19 Jan. 1888; *Scottish Highlander,* 9 Feb. 1888.

125. C.F., AF 67/96, Pol. Rep., Lochmaddy, 3 Feb. 1888; *loc. cit.,* Pol. Reps., Obbe, 4, 11 Feb. 1888; *loc. cit.* Pol. Rep., Tarbert, 10 Feb. 1888.

126. C.F., AF 67/96, Rep. by Medical Officer for North Harris, 25 Jan. 1888; *loc. cit.,* AF 67/97, Webster to Ivory, 1 March 1888.

127. *Oban Times,* 25 Feb. 1888; C.F., AF 67/96, Pol. Rep., Lochboisdale, 1 Feb. 1888; S.O. Misc. Files, HH 1/713, Webster to Ivory, 2 Feb. 1888.

128. C.F., AF 67/97, Pol. Rep., Barra, 1 March 1888. See also, *Oban Times* and *Scottish Highlander,* Jan. – March 1888.

129. *Scottish Highlander,* 9 Feb. 1888; *Agrarian Offences,* 1888.

130. C.F., AF 67/95, 97, Webster to Ivory, 2, 25 Feb., 1 March 1888.

131. *Scottish Highlander,* 8 March 1888; C.F., AF 67/97, 99, Pol. Reps., Staffin, 23 March, 28 June 1888; *loc. cit.,* AF 67/98, Pol. Rep., Lochmaddy, 2 April 1888; *loc. cit.,* AF 67/98, Pol. Rep., Portree, 2 May 1888; *loc. cit.,* AF 67/99, Hamilton to Ivory, 8 June 1888.

132. C.F., AF 67/44, Pol. Rep., Stornoway, 6 May 1888; *The Times,* 7, 28 May 1884.

133. *The Times,* 8 May 1888; *Oban Times,* 12 May 1888.

134. C.F., AF 67/44, S.O. Minute, 3 Sept. 1888; *Scottish Highlander,* 6 Sept. 1888.

135. Ivory P., GD 1/36/1(5), Und.-Sec. to Ivory, 15, 17 Dec. 1890; C.F., AF 67/112 Ivory to Und.-Sec., 24 April 1891. Also relevant Pol. Reps. in C.F.

136. Michael Buchanan: *Scottish Highlander,* 25 Feb. 1892. The Land League's political decline is examined in Hunter, 'Politics of Land Reform', 58-68.

137. C.F., AF 67/73, Insp. of Poor, Stornoway, to Board of Supervision, 6 Sept. 1889; *Glasgow Herald,* 22 Aug. 1889.

138. *Reports on the Burden of the Existing Rates and the General Financial Position of the Outer Hebrides,* P.P. 1906 CIV, xxviii-xxix. For fishermen's fortunes see Gray, 'Crofting and Fishing, 1890-1914', 1972, 89-114.

139. Collier, *Crofting Problem,* 1953, 69.

140. Lothian P., GD 40/16/27, Memo., 10 May 1887. Balfour was of the same opinion. B. Alderson, *Arthur James Balfour,* London, 1903, 56.

141. *Nap. Rep.,* 97-108; C.F., AF 67/42, West Highland Proprietors' Memorial, April 1888. Signed by almost all west coast and Hebridean landlords.

142. *N.C.,* Q. 15649.

143. Under this scheme 465 people (79 families) were settled in Manitoba and Saskatchewan. The experiment was not very successful. See, Crofters and Cottars Colonisation Commission, *Ann. Reps.,* 1890-1906; Day, *Public Administration,* 1918, 122-125.

144. From resolutions adopted in Tiree and Barra. *Oban Times,* 4, 25 Feb. 1888. For others see, *Oban Times,* Jan.-April 1888.

145. *Scottish Highlander,* 24 Jan. 1889.

146. For Chamberlain's pronouncements on the subject see, *inter al., The Times,* 19, 15, 17, 19 April 1887; *Oban Times,* 30 April, 23 July, 20 Aug. 1887.

147. *Oban Times,* 15 June 1889.

148. Lothian P., GD 40/16/45, Lothian to Goschen, 10 Aug. 1888.

149. *Reports of the Royal Commission on Certain Matters affecting the Interests of the Population of the Western Highlands and Islands,* P.P. 1890 XXVII, 1890-91 XIIV.

150. Lothian P., GD 40/16/53, Treasury Statement, 1892.

151. See, *e.g., Scottish Highlander,* 16 May, 13 June, 18, 25 July, 8 Sept. 1889. Telegraph and Steamer services were improved and the west coast railways extended from Fort William to Mallaig and from Strome Ferry to Kyle of Lochalsh.

152. *Commission on Land in Wales and Monmouthshire,* 1896, 294.

153. See, e.g., Sheriff Brand's evidence to the same Commission. *Ibid.,* 407.

154. *Scottish Highlander,* 3 Feb. 1887.

155. See above, 157-60.

156. *D.F.C. Rep.*, xii.

157. *Report of the Scottish Land Enquiry Commission*, 1914, 76.

158. Croft. Comm., *Final Rep.*, 1913, xxv-xxvi.

159. *Report on Land Settlement in Scotland*, P.P. 1944-45 V, App. 3, 81. Unless otherwise indicated, subsequent land settlement statistics are abstracted from the same source. See also, Croft. Comm., *Final Rep.*, 1913, xxv-xxvi; Day, *Public Administration*, 1918, 194.

160. Above, 163-4.

161. *Oban Times*, 4 May 1901.

162. C.F., AF 67/49, Sheriff Johnson, Rep., 4 Nov. 1892.

163. C.F., AF 67/48, Rep. as to Seizure of Land at Ornsay, 26 March 1891; *Scottish Highlander*, 26 March, 2, 9, 16 April, 29 May 1891.

164. C.F., AF 67/48, Pol. Reps., Trumisgarry and Bernera, 2, 3, 29 Oct. 1890; *Scottish Highlander*, 13 July 1892.

165. C.F., AF 67/49, Chief Constable of Sutherland to Und.-Sec., 4 April 1892; *loc. cit.*, AF 67/53, S.O., Minute, 30 Nov. 1895.

166. *Scottish Highlander*, 22 June 1893; C.F., AF 67/50, Pol. Reps., Uig and Staffin, 3, 6 June 1893.

167. C.F., AF 67/49, Johnson to Und.-Sec., 28 April 1891.

168. Above, Chaps. 8-9, *passim.*

169. *Oban Times*, 8 June 1889.

170. For the deer forest boom see, Hunter, 'Sheep and Deer', 1974. 214-222.

171. S.O., Misc. Files, HH 1/235, S.O., Minute, 10 May 1887; *loc. cit.*, Lord MacDonald *et al* to Lothian, 7 May 1887.

172. Curtis, *Coercion and Conciliation*, 1963, 343-355.

173. S.O. Misc. Files, HH 1/235, Lord MacDonald *et al.* to Lothian, 7 May 1887.

174. Below, Chap. 11, *passim.*

175. Day, *Public Administration*, 1918, 227.

176. Hunter, 'Politics of Land Reform', 1974, 61-62.

177. *D.F.C. Rep.*, v.

178. *Ibid.*, x.

179. *Ibid.*, xxii.

180. *Scotsman*, 3 June 1895. The manifesto quoted was in fact issued for a bye-election in Inverness-shire a few weeks before the general election. For a full account of the complex politics of the time see, Hunter, 'Politics of Land Reform', 1974, 63-66.

181. *Scotsman*, 3 June 1895.

182. C.D.B., *7th Rep.*, 1905, App., 15-22.

Chapter 11

1. Curtis, *Coercion and Conciliation*, 1963, 355.

2. William O'Brien: quoted, F.S.L. Lyons, *John Dillon*, London, 1968, 180.

3. For an account of the Board's activities see, W.L. Micks, *An Account of the Congested Districts Board*, Dublin, 1925; Curtis, *Coercion and Conciliation*, 1963, 355-362.

4. Curtis, *Coercion and Conciliation*, 1963, 361.

5. CDB, *1st Rep.*, 1899, vi-vii. This area is — not coincidentally — practically the same as that defined in the Introduction as 'the heartland of the crofting community'.

6. *Hansard*, 4th Ser., L, 1897, 924.

7. CDB, *1st Rep.*, 1899, v.

8. Details in, *Report of the Departmental Committee on the Work of the Congested Districts (Scotland) Commissioners*, P.P. 1910, XXI; CDB, *Final Rep.*, 1912, xii-xxix.

9. CDB, *1st Rep.*, 1899, ix; Day, *Public Administration*, 1918, 208.

10. See, CDB, *Final Rep.*, vi.

11. See, CDB, *7th Rep.*, 1905, viii; *8th Rep.*, 1906, viii, xii; Day, *Public Administration*, 1918, 209.

12. *Oban Times*, 20 Aug., 1887.

13. CDB, *8th Rep.*, 1906, x-xi. Also, *Oban Times*, 13 March 1909.

14. BoAS, *1st Rep.*, 1913, xviii. Glendale crofters paid their last annuities in 1955 and are now the owners of the Glendale estate. (In this context, it is noteworthy that Lewis crofters refused Lord Leverhulme's 1923 offer to become owners of the island for reasons identical to those outlined above. See, Nicolson, *Lord of the Isles*, 1960, 200-20

15. E.g., *Hansard*, 4th Ser., L, 473.

16. *Highland News*, 20 April 1901.

17. For Liberal policy see, J. Brown, 'Scottish and English Land Legislation, 1905-1911', *SHR*, XLVII, 1968, 72-85.

18. Above, Chaps. 8-10, *passim*.

19. Sources for these statements can be found in the pages of publications like *Forward* and *Guth na Bliadhna*. See, J. Hunter, 'The Gaelic Connection: the Highlands, Ireland and Nationalism', *SHR*, LIV, 1975, 178-204.

20. MacD. P., GD 221/148/4, Report on the MacDonald Estates in Skye, 1851. Also above, 82-3.

21. C.F., AF 67/124, Pol. Rep., Portree, 30 Oct. 1900; *Scotsman*, 15 Nov. 1900.

22. C.F., AF 67/124, S.O. Minute, 13 Nov. 1900; CDB, *3rd Rep.*, 1901, xi-xiii; *Oban Times*, 22 Dec. 1900, 31 Jan. 1901; *Scotsman*, 31 Dec. 1900.

23. CDB, *Final Rep.*, 1912, x.

24. See, CDB, *3rd Rep.*, 1901, x, and App. IV, 12-19. Also, A. Goodrich-Freer, *Outer Isles*, London, 1902, 119 *et seq.*

25. *Oban Times*, 4 May 1901. Also, *Highland News*, 15 Sept. 1900; *Report of a Special Committee of the County Council of Inverness upon Applications for Allotments in North Uist and Barra*, P.P. 1908, LXXXVIII, 2-3.

26. CDB, *3rd Rep.*, 1901, x.

27. C.F., AF 67/120, Pol. Rep., Barra, 10 Sept. 1900; *Highland News*, 15 Sept. 1900

28. C.F., 67/120, Petition to Lady Gordon Cathcart, n.d.

29. *Highland News*, 29 Sept. 1900.

30. C.F., AF 67/120, Skene, Edwards and Garson to W.C. Dunbar, 2 Oct. 1900.

31. C.F., AF 67/121, Scottish Office Minute, 12 March 1901; *Oban Times*, 19 Oct. 1901; CDB, *Final Rep.*, 1912, viii.

32. C.F., AF 67/121, Pol. Rep., Barra, 20 Feb. 1901; *Highland News*, 6 April 1901.

33. C.F., AF 67/126, Pol. Rep., Lochboisdale, 17 May 1901; *loc. cit.* Pol. Rep., Stoneybridge, 30 Nov. 1901; *Oban Times*, 25 May, 9 Nov. 1901. Also, C.F., AF 67/126 H. MacEachen to CDB, 11 Jan. 1902.

34. C.F., AF 67/126, Pol. Rep., Lochboisdale, 17 May 1901; *loc. cit.* Pol. Rep., Stoneybridge, 30 Nov. 1901; *Oban Times,* 25 May, 9 Nov. 1901. Also, C.F., AF 67/126, H. MacEachen to CDB, 11 Jan. 1902.

35. *Highland News,* 25 May 1901.

36. C.F., AF 67/125, Pol. Rep., Sollas, 1 April 1901; *Highland News,* 20 April 1901.

37. C.F., AF 67/53, M. MacDonald *et al.* to Maj. Matheson, 10 April 1901.

38. C.F., AF 67/53, Und.-Sec. to Chief Constable, Ross-shire, 17 April 1901.

39. C.F., AF 67/53, Petition to CDB, 14 April 1901.

40. C.F., AF 67/53, Pol. Rep., Callanish, 18 April 1901; *loc. cit.,* AF 67/54, Pol. Rep., Tobson, 24 May 1901.

41. C.F., AF 67/54, Chief Constable, Ross-shire, to Und.-Sec., 10 June 1901; *Highland News,* 15 June 1901.

42. For earlier 'assisted' emigrations from the island see above, 84.

43. CDB, *3rd Rep.,* 1901, App. IV, 10; C.F., AF 67/162, Argyll, Circular to Tiree Cottars, May 1901; *loc. cit.,* R. MacLennan, Memo. on Tiree Cottars, 5 Aug. 1903.

44. C.F., AF 67/129, J. MacKinnon *et al.* to CDB, 10 Feb. 1902.

45. C.F., AF 67/127, Pol. Rep., Lochboisdale, 21 Feb. 1903; *loc. cit.,* Pol. Reps., Stoneybridge, 24 Feb., 13 March 1903.

46. See, *inter al., Highland Times,* 22 Feb. 1906; cutting, C.F., AF 67/132.

47. C.F., AF 67/130, Pol. Rep., Barra, 19 Sept. 1902.

48. C.F., AF 67/130, Pol. Rep., Lochmaddy, 25 March 1902.

49. C.F., AF 67/134, Und.-Sec. to J. Wilson (Sheriff of Inverness-shire), 7 May 1907; CDB, *Final Rep.,* 1912, viii; *Correspondence with Reference to the Occupation of the Island of Vatersay,* P.P. 1908 LXXXVIII, 5-6.

50. C.F., AF 67/132, Pol. Rep., Barra, 9 Feb. 1906.

51. C.F., AF 67/134, Pol. Reps., Barra, 23 June, 30 July, 9 Aug., 30 Oct., 13 Nov., 1906.

52. C.F., AF 67/163, H. MacDonald *et al.* to Sinclair, 10 March 1906.

53. C.F., AF 67/139, Pol. Rep., Staffin, 21 Feb. 1906.

54. C.F., AF 67/363, S.O. Minute, 19 Feb. 1906.

55. C.F., AF 67/132, Pol. Rep., Lochboisdale, 23 Feb. 1906; *Highland News,* 3 March 1906; *Oban Times,* 10 March 1906.

56. C.F., AF 67/133, Pol. Rep., Stoneybridge, 6 March 1906.

57. C.F., AF 67/133, J. Wilson to Und.-Sec., 28 May 1906.

58. The opposition in this quarter being led by the eminent Liberal Imperialist and former electoral victim of the HLLRA, Munro-Ferguson of Novar.

59. See, *inter al.,* Brown, 'Scottish and English Land Legislation', 1968, 73 *et seq.;* Lady Pentland, *The Right Honourable John Sinclair, Lord Pentland: A Memoir,* London, 1928, 69-73.

60. Brown, 'Scottish and English Land Legislation', 1968, 75 *et seq.;* P. Rowland, *The Last Liberal Governments: The Promised Land, 1905-1910,* London, 1968, 121-122.

61. *Highland News,* 18 April 1908. Also, *Highland News,* 11 Aug. 1906, 31 Aug., 5 Oct. 1907, 8 Feb., 14 March 1908.

62. C.F., AF 67/139, R. Gillies to J. Sinclair, 14 April 1908. Also, *Highland News,* 11 April 1908; *Oban Times,* 18 June 1910.

63. C.F., AF 67/34, List of People on Vatersay, Sept. 1907.

64. C.F., AF 67/134, J. Wilson, Report on the Proceedings of the Cottars at Castlebay, 23 May 1907.

65. C.F., AF 67/138, Sinclair, Minute on Vatersay, 19 Feb. 1909.

66. *Scotsman,* 3 June 1908.

67. See representations from Trades Councils, Liberal Associations, etc., C.F., AF 67/136-137.

68. C.F., AF 67/138, Sinclair, Minute on Vatersay, 19 Feb. 1909.

69. C.F., AF 67/142, D. Campbell *et al.* to Sinclair, 14 May 1909; *loc. cit.,* AF 67/370, A. MacIntosh to Pentland, 5 Oct. 1909. Also, *Scotsman,* 29, 30 April 1909.

70. *Scotsman,* 18 March 1909.

71. See correspondence on this subject, C.F., AF 67/142.

72. C.F., AF 67/137, Cottars of Bruernish to CDB, 11 Aug. 1908; *loc. cit.,* S.O. Memo, 19 Oct. 1908; *loc. cit.,* AF 67/141, Pol. Rep., Barra, 6 March 1909; *Oban Times,* 13 March 1909.

73. C.F., AF 67/138, Pol. Reps., Lochboisdale, 9 Feb., 29 April 1909; *Oban Times,* 13 March 1909; *Glasgow Herald,* 1 May 1909.

74. C.F., AF 67/59, Minutes of cottars' meeting, 18 Dec. 1908; *loc. cit.,* AF 67/140 Pol. Rep., Stornoway, 30 April 1909.

75. *Scotsman,* 3 June 1909.

76. *Scotsman,* 29 July 1909; *Highland News,* 31 July 1909.

77. Pentland, *John Sinclair,* 1928, 95; *Highland News,* 30 Dec. 1911.

78. BoAS, *1st Rep.,* 1913, xi; Allotments and Smallholdings Files, AF 67/54, Land Settlement in Scotland, Feb. 1924.

79. See, *e.g., Highland News,* 24 Feb., 9 March 1912.

80. BoAS, *1st Rep.,* 1913, xi.

81. *Report of the Committee on Land Settlement in Scotland,* P.P. 1928 XI, 9-10; BoAS, *3rd Rep.,* 1915, xvii.

82. As a radical Highland newspaper had warned when it passed through Parliament. *Highland News,* 30 Dec. 1911.

83. Hunter, 'Sheep and Deer', 1973, *passim.*

84. R.C. MacLeod, *Book of Dunvegan,* II, 100.

85. C.F., AF 67/142, J. Coull to CDB, 3 May 1909.

86. Allotments and Smallholdings Files, AF 66/57, Memo., 1 Feb. 1926.

87. *Taylor Comm.,* 1954, 15.

88. *Scottish Jour. of Agric.,* I, 1918, 491-492.

89. *Committee on Land Settlement,* 1928, 9-10; BoAS, *3rd Rep.,* 1915, xii-xvii; *4th Rep.,* 1916, vi-vii; C.F., AF 67/61, Memo. on Reef, 4 Dec. 1913.

90. *Highland News,* 15 March 1913.

91. Nicolson, *Lord of the Isles,* 1960, 129; C.F., AF 67/61, Statement of Schemes in Lewis, 2 Dec. 1913.

92. *Oban Times,* 21 June 1913. Also, C.F., AF 67/142, Pol. Rep., Lochboisdale, 25 June 1913.

93. *Highland News,* 2 Aug. 1913. Also, *Highland News,* June-Aug. 1913.

94. C.F., AF 67/61, Pol. Reps., Miaveg, 5, 19 Dec. 1913.

95. C.F., AF 67/62, – to Und.-Sec., 3 Feb. 1914. For the protection of persons still living the Crofting Files are closed to the public from c.1913 onwards. I am

grateful to the Dept. of Agriculture and Fisheries for Scotland for permission to consult these files and have readily agreed to protect the privacy of individuals (other than public personages whose identity is, in any case, well known) mentioned in them. Hence the blanks in this and subsequent footnotes.

96. *Scotsman,* 31 Dec. 1913. Also, C.F., AF 67/61, Pol. Rep., Miaveg, 1 Dec. 1913.

97. *Scotsman,* 20 March 1914.

98. C.F., AF 67/61, Memo. on Reef, 4 Dec. 1913.

99. C.F., AF 67/142, Pol. Rep., Lochboisdale, 17 Nov. 1913; *loc.cit.,* AF 67/143, Pol. Rep., Barra, 11 Jan. 1914; *loc. cit.,* AF 67/145, Pol. Rep., Obbe, 7 Feb. 1914; *Highland News,* 16 May, 1 Aug. 1914; *Oban Times,* 18 July 1914.

100. See, BoAS, *4th Rep.,* 1916, x-xi; *5th Rep.,* 1915, vii-ix; etc.

101. *Glasgow Herald,* 5 Oct. 1917.

102. See, eg. *Glasgow Herald,* 6 Dec. 1917, 26 May 1919.

103. Allotments and Smallholdings Files, AF 66/57, Memo. on Land Settlement, n.d.

104. Additions represented by the Small Holdings Colonies Act and the Sailors and Soldiers (Gifts for Land Settlements) Act.

105. A.F., AF 67/299, S.O., Memo., 10 July 1917; *loc. cit.,* AF 67/143, Pol. Rep., Barra, 26 March 1917.

106. C.F., AF 67/143, Rep. on Eoligarry, 7 Nov. 1917.

107. See, *Glasgow Herald,* 8, 9, 23 April 1918; *Oban Times,* 16 Feb., 30 March, 13, 20 April 1918.

108. *Glasgow Herald,* 20 July 1918.

109. BoAS, *6th Rep.,* 1919, x-xi. Also, *Oban Times,* 26 Oct. 1918.

110. *Stornoway Gazette,* 28 Nov. 1919.

111. *Glasgow Herald,* 18 Aug. 1920.

112. BoAS, *7th Rep.,* 1919, xii-xiii. Also, C.F., AF 67/159, Note on Raiding, 24 Feb. 1923.

113. See, *inter al., Nap. Rep.,* 101; *DFC Rep.,* xxiv; *Social Condition of Lewis,* 1902, civ; CDB, *Final Rep.,* vii-viii.

114. *Stornoway Gazette,* 30 March 1917.

115. C.F., AF 67/252, Memo. on Lewis, 28 Oct. 1920; *Stornoway Gazette,* 9 Nov. 1917.

116. The controversy aroused by Leverhulme's activities continues still. For a full, though distinctly pro-Leverhulme account of them, see, Nicolson, *Lord of the Isles,* 1960, *passim.*

117. C.F., AF 67/248, H. MacGregor and Co. to BoAS, 9 Oct. 1919. Also, BoAS, *7th Rep.,* 1919, xi.

118. CDB Files, AF 42/9702, Social and Economic Conditions of the Highlands, April 1924, 23.

119. *Ibid.,* 12.

120. *Stornoway Gazette,* 24 Sept. 1920.

121. Collier, *Crofting Problem,* 1953, 82-85; Fraser-Darling, *West Highland Survey,* 1955, 347-348.

122. See, *Scotsman,* 1 July 1919; Nicolson, *Lord of the Isles,* 1960, 140; A. Geddes, *The Isle of Lewis and Harris,* Edinburgh, 1955, 265-267.

123. C. MacDonald, *Highland Journey,* Edinburgh, 1943, 143-144.

124. Nicolson, *Lord of the Isles,* 1960, 158.

125. C.F., AF 67/251, Leverhulme to D. Murray MP, 11 Aug. 1919.

126. *Ibid.*

127. Nicolson, *Lord of the Isles,* 1960, 129-130, 179-182.

128. *Ibid.,* 133, 148. Also, VoAS, *7th Rep.,* 1919, xi.

129. C.F., AF 67/252, Memo. on Lewis, 28 Oct. 1920.

130. *Stornoway Gazette,* 14, 28 March 1919; C.F., AF 67/251, – to BoAS, 27 April 1919; *loc.cit.,* AF 67/234, Pol. Rep., Stornoway, 8 April 1919.

131. Several of the raiders had been decorated for gallantry. C.F., AF 67/326, S.O. Memo., 23 April 1920.

132. *Scotsman,* 26 May 1919.

133. C.F., AF 67/254, – to Munro, 16 Oct. 1920.

134. *Ibid.*

135. *Stornoway Gazette,* 24 Oct. 1919.

136. *Scotsman,* 23 May 1919.

137. Above, 174-5.

138. *Stornoway Gazette,* 2, 9 May 1919.

139. C.F., AF 67/145, Land Seizure at Miaveg, 18 July 1919; *loc. cit.,* AF 67/152, S.O. Memo., 20 Nov. 1919; *loc. cit.,* AF 67/142, Memo. on Askernish, 10 March 1920; *loc. cit.,* Af 67/152, BoAS to Und.-Sec., 9 Dec. 1920.

140. Scottish Office Memos., 19 Aug. 1919, 21 Nov. 1919, 11 Feb. 1920, Crofting Files, AF 67/65, 165.

141. BoAS, *8th Rep.,* 1920, xi.

142. *Highland News,* 3 Jan. 1920.

143. *Hansard,* 5th Ser., (Lords), XXXVIII, 920.

144. *Committee on Land Settlement,* 1928, 11-13; BoAS, *8th Rep.,* 1920, xi; C.F., AF 67/159, Note on Raiding, 24 Feb. 1923; DoAS, 27th Rep., 1929, 36.

145. *Committee on Land Settlement,* 1928, 33.

146. BoAS, *9th Rep.,* 1921, xiv.

148. C.F., AF 67/147, – to BoAS, 15 March 1920.

149. *Glasgow Herald,* 3, 23, 28 Jan., 4, 5 Feb. 1920; *Stornoway Gazette,* 20 Feb. 1920.

150. *Glasgow Herald,* 10-13 Feb. 1920.

151. C.F., AF 67/252, Memo. on Lewis, 28 Oct. 1920.

152. C.F., AF 67/239, Pol. Rep., Uig, 14 April 1920. Also, *loc. cit.,* AF 67/65, S.O. Memo., 14 Feb. 1920.

153. *Glasgow Herald,* 13, 21 April 1920. The latter was also unwelcome to crofters who had no wish to lose any of their none too adequate pastures. *Glasgow Herald,* 4 Dec. 1920.

154. *Glasgow Herald,* 8, 10 May, 9 June 1920.

155. C.F., AF 67/254, Munro to Leverhulme, 11 June 1920.

156. C.F., AF 67/254, Leverhulme to Munro, 21 June, 8 July, 10 Aug. 1920. And reports of meetings, *Glasgow Herald,* 10, 20 Sept. 1920.

157. C.F., AF 67/254, BoAS, Confidential Memo on Lewis, 22 Oct. 1920.

158. *Glasgow Herald,* 4 Dec. 1920.

159. C.F., AF 67/254, J.B. Morrison, Rep. on Lewis, 12 Oct. 1920.

160. C.F., AF 67/254, – to Munro, 16 Oct. 1920; *loc. cit.,* AF 67/238, – to Munro, 20 Dec. 1920. Also, *Glasgow Herald,* 19, 29 Nov., 1, 4 Dec. 1920.

161. *Glasgow Herald,* 16 Feb., 29 March, 13 April 1920; *Oban Times,* 21 Feb., 27 March 1920; C.F., AF 67/49, Pol. Rep., Portree, 13 April 1920.

162. *Glasgow Herald,* 23 June, 3 July, 11 Oct. 1920.

163. BoAS, *9th Rep.,* 1921, xviii-xix. Also, the relevant papers in, C.F., AF 67/147-148.

164. *Oban Times,* 7 Aug. 1920.

165. *Oban Times,* 18 Dec. 1920.

166. *Glasgow Herald,* 9, 10 Dec. 1920; *Oban Times,* 18, 25 Dec. 1920.

167. C.F., AF 67/152, Pol. Rep., Clachan, 14 Feb. 1921.

168. C.F., AF 67/152, Memo. on Land Seizures on Balranald Estate, 16 Aug. 1921.

169. C.F., AF 67/148, – to BoAS, 7 Dec. 1921.

170. C.F., AF 67/148, – to BoAS, 3 Aug. 1920; *loc. cit.,* Pol. Rep., Stoneybridge, 19 Jan. 1921.

171. *Oban Times,* 18 Dec. 1920. Also, C.F., AF 67/151, – to BoAS, 25 Oct. 1922.

172. C.F., AF 67/159, Note on Raiding, 24 Feb. 1923. Also, BoAS, *9th Rep.,* 1921, xix.

173. As the Board itself admitted. BoAS, *10th Rep.,* 1922, 23.

174. BoAS, *10th Rep.,* 1922, 21-22; *Oban Times,* 19 March 1921.

175. C.F., AF 67/146, Pol. Rep., Leverburgh, 13 July 1921; *loc. cit.,* AF 67/159, Note on Raiding, 24 Feb. 1923.

176. C.F., AF 67/149, Pol. Rep., Portree, 9 April 1921; *Glasgow Herald,* 5 May 1921; BoAS, *10th Rep.,* 1922, 22.

177. *Oban Times,* 15 Jan. 1921.

178. C.F., AF 67/149, – to BoAS, 19 Feb. 1920.

179. The ironstone works closed in early 1919 and the consequent unemployment did nothing to mitigate the troubles in the island. *Oban Times,* 29 March, 3 April 1919.

180. C.F., AF 67/149, Pol. Reps., Portree, 2, 9 April 1921.

181. C.F., 67/175, Note of cases in which raiders have been sentenced for Breach of Interdict, 16 July 1923; *Glasgow Herald,* 21 Sept., 7 Oct., 23 Nov. 1921.

182. *Oban Times,* 3 Dec. 1921.

183. BoAS, *11th Rep.,* 1923, 15.

184. C.F., AF 67/149, S.O. Memo., 10 Dec. 1921. Also, *Stornoway Gazette,* 22 Dec. 1921; BoAS, *10th Rep.,* 1922, 22.

185. *Stornoway Gazette,* 24, 31 Dec. 1920.

186. C.F., AF 67/254, Munro to Leverhulme, 22 Jan. 1921.

187. C.F., AF 67/329, – to Munro, 6 Sept. 1921.

188. Above, 201.

189. *Glasgow Herald,* 10 Feb. 1921; BoAS, *10th Rep.,* 1922, 21.

190. C.F., AF 67/331, Rep. on Raid on Coll Farm, 2 May 1921; *Glasgow Herald,* 30 April, 7 May 1921.

191. Nicolson, *Lord of the Isles,* 1960, 164-169.

192. *Ibid.,* 173-175; *Glasgow Herald,* 2 Sept. 1921.

193. *Stornoway Gazette,* 8 Sept. 1921.

194. C.F., AF 67/329, – to Munro, 6 Sept. 1921, Crofting Files, AF 67/329.

195. C.F., AF 67/331, Munro to Leverhulme, 6 Sept. 1921.

196. BoAS, *10th Rep.*, 1922, 21.

197. C.F., AF 67/151, – to BoAS, 25 Oct. 1922. Also, *loc. cit.*, – to BoAS, 14 Jan. 1922.

198. C.F., AF 67/151, Pol. Reps., Lochmaddy, 23 Jan., 14 May 1923.

199. C.F., AF 67/159, Note on Raiding, 24 Feb. 1923; *loc. cit.*, AF 67/156, Pol. Rep., Leverburgh, 27 March 1923; *loc. cit.*, AF 67/154, Memo. on Nunton, 7 June 192 BoAS, *12th Rep.*, 1924, 17; *Oban Times*, 7 April, 2 June 1923; *Glasgow Herald*, 8, 26, 28, 31 March 1923.

200. BoAS, *13th Rep.*, 1925, 23.

201. *Ibid.*, 20-22. Also, C.F., AF 67/387, Economic Conditions of the Crofting Counties, 1924.

202. Above, 124-5.

203. C.F., AF 67/387, Economic Conditions of the Crofting Counties, 1924.

204. *Ibid.* Also, BoAS, *13th Rep.*, 1925, 22-23; *14th Rep.*, 1926, 15.

205. Below, 211.

206. C.F., AF 67/272, Memo. on Existing and Prospective Distress, 13 Nov. 1923; BoAS, *13th Rep.*, 1925, 70, 84; *Glasgow Herald*, Nov. 1923-Jan.1924, especially 17-19 Dec. 1923.

207. *Taylor Comm.*, 1954, 14-16.

208. *Report of the Committee on Land Settlement*, 1928, 25-26; DoAS, *27th Rep.*, 1939, 41-43.

209. DoAS, *19th Rep.*, 1931, 22–23.

Chapter 12

1. Croft. Comm., *Ann. Rep. for 1972*, 4.

2. *A Programme of Highland Development*, P.P. 1950 XIX, 5; HIDB, *1st Rep.*, 1966, 2.

3. *Taylor Commission*, 1954, 35-36.

4. *Ibid.*, 31.

5. For a recent consideration of these questions see, J. Sewel *et al.*, *Education and Migration: A study of the migration and job expectations of young people and their parents in the Highlands and Islands of Scotland*, University of Aberdeen, 1975. See also, J.L. Williams, 'Social Consequences of Grammar School Education in a Rural Area of Wales', *British Journal of Sociology*, X, 1959, 125-128.

6. D.J. MacCuish, 'Reform of Crofting Tenure', (an as yet unpublished paper read to the Gaelic Society of Inverness, 29th March, 1974), 2.

7. *Taylor Comm.*, 1954, 9, 37-46.

8. *Ibid.*, 13.

9. F. Gillanders, 'The Economic Life of Gaelic Scotland Today', in D.C. Thomson and I. Grimble (eds.), *The Future of the Highlands*, London, 1968, 97.

10. *Nap. Rep.*, 39.

11. E.g., compare Gillanders with Argyll: *Hansard*, 3rd Ser., CCCV, 1480-1485.

12. *Report of the Committee on Land Settlement*, 1928, 25.

13. Croft. Comm., *Ann. Rep. for 1963*, 26.

14. Collier, *Crofting Problem,* 1953, 61-64.

15. Croft. Comm., *Ann. Rep. for 1963,* 26.

16. Croft. Comm., *Ann. Rep. for 1964,* 30-31.

17. Croft. Comm., *Ann. Rep. for 1968,* 13.

18. Croft. Comm., *Ann. Rep. for 1968,* 12-13; *Ann. Rep. for 1972,* 4.

19. HIDB, *Island of Mull,* 1973, 7-9; Murray, *Islands of Western Scotland,* 1973, 258-259.

20. HIDB, *Island of Mull,* 1973, 28; HIDB, *1st Rep.,* 1966, 4.

21. The Crofters (Scotland) Act, 1955 — based on the Taylor Commission's recommendations.

22. Croft. Comm., *Ann. Rep. for 1966,* 11.

23. HIDB, *1st Rep.,* 1966, 5.

24. For a critical analysis of the Board's performance see I.R. Carter, 'Six Years On', *Aberdeen University Review,* XLV, 1973, 55-78.

25. HIDB, *1st Rep.,* 1966, 28.

26. HIDB, *1st Rep.,* 1966, 1; Carter, 'Six Years On', 1973, 75-76. Also, *inter al.,* E.H. Jacoby, *Man and Land: The Fundamental Issue in Development,* London, 1971.

27. HIDB, *Occasional Bulletin No. 2: Agriculture,* 1968. My italics.

28. HIDB, *Strath of Kildonan — Proposals for Development,* 1970, 24, 29. My italics.

29. *See West Highland Free Press,* 16 Nov. 1973 for a photograph of one of the crofters concerned burning his compensation cheque.

30. Above, 185-6.

31. Croft. Comm., *Ann. Rep. for 1968,* 7. For the Commission's proposals and reasons for them see their *Ann. Rep. for 1968,* 27-38; *Ann. Rep. for 1969,* 27-28. Also, D.J. MacCuish, 'The Case for Converting Crofting Tenure to Ownership', *TGSI,* XLVI, 1969-70, 89-113. Mr. MacCuish is secretary to the Commission.

32. See, *inter al.,* Croft. Comm., *Ann. Rep. for 1968,* 30-32; *Oban Times,* 24 Oct., 12 Dec. 1968.

33. *The Crofting Reform (Scotland) Bill,* 1973.

34. *Taylor Comm.,* 1954, 35-36.

35. Croft. Comm., *North Sea Oil Developments and their Possible Effects on Crofting,* 23 Oct. 1973, para. 6.

36. Croft. Comm., *Ann. Rep. for 1937,* 15.

37. *E.g., Oban Times,* 19, 26 June 1886, 19 Nov. 1887.

38. J. McGrath, *The Cheviot, the Stag and the Black, Black Oil,* Kyleakin, 1974, 32.

Bibliography

THE material on which this book is based can be divided into the following categories:

1. **Unpublished collections of estate papers and official records.** The former are heavily relied upon in those chapters which deal with events before c.1860, while the latter become of overwhelming importance in later chapters – a fact which is in itself indicative of the course of modern Highland history. Hardly any of this material was written by people sympathetic to crofters. But from it, it is possible to reconstruct the events, if not the emotions, of crofting history. Estate papers give valuable insight into the nature of and motives for the policies of landlords. Official records perform the same service for government. And in both, especially in the numerous police reports that are to be found in the official records, c.1880-c.1930, there are indications of what crofters felt and said about what was being done to them. The papers of Sheriff Ivory and Lord Lothian complement the official records of the 1880s and 1890s while those of Prof. J.S. Blackie contain some information on the setting up of the HLLRA.

2. **Ecclesiastical records.** Consisting for the most part of the minute books of Highland presbyteries, these are important sources for the study of religious dissent included in Chapter 6.

3. **Official publications.** These largely consist of the reports of and evidence submitted to the legions of commissions and committees which have enquired into Highland problems during the last 170 years – as well as the annual reports of bodies set up to do something about these problems. In this category the Napier Commission of 1883 deserves special mention. Without its five bulky volumes to draw on this book would have been considerably more difficult to write.

4. **Newspapers and periodicals.** The press, and especially local and radically minded Highland newspapers like the *Highlander, Oban Times,* etc., provide information about the late nineteenth and early twentieth century land agitations not recorded elsewhere. And in their long and detailed reports of crofters' meetings are to be found uniquely valuable insights into the crofting community's opinions, beliefs and aspirations.

5. **Unpublished theses.**

6. **Books pamphlets and articles.** This category is subdivided into (a) primary and (b) secondary works. The subdivision is in some ways artificial, a book like J.S. Blackie's *Scottish Highlanders and the Land Laws* being 'secondary' insofar as it includes its author's interpretation of Highland history and 'primary' insofar as it is the personal manifesto of a land reformer and HLLRA member. Throughout, however all works which are in any way 'primary' are included in subdivision (a). These include

published collections of Gaelic poetry and estate papers as well as the many books and pamphlets written on Highland affairs during the period in question. Not every work mentioned is cited in the text, but all have been usefully consulted. Sub-division (b) includes modern accounts and analyses of Highland history and society as well as a few of the more serious of the hundreds of 'travelogues' which, for better or worse, constitute the greater part of recent writing on the Highlands. And in this category, too, are included the works dealing with non-Highland history and sociology which I have found most useful. Of these, the most important are studies of Irish history, for the parallels and connections between the recent past of Ireland and the Highlands are numerous and instructive.

1. Estate papers, official records, etc.

A. *In the Scottish Record Office, Edinburgh.*

Sheriff Ivory Papers.	GD1/36
Riddell Papers.	GD1/395. And AF 49.
Lothian Papers.	GD 40.
Seaforth Papers.	GD 46.
Reay Papers.	GD 84.
MacLaine of Lochbuie Papers.	GD 174.
Clanranald Papers.	GD 201. (And the material relating to the

Clanranald estates in Tods, Murray and Jameson Papers. GD 237/120-122).

Lord MacDonald Papers.	GD 221.

Material on Highland Destitution. (Uncatalogued and unsorted collection. Principal items consulted were the printed volume of 'Correspondence Relating to the Relief of Distress', referred to in Chap. 4, and the Minute Books and Lists of Emigrants of the Highlands and Islands Emigration Society).

Scottish Office Miscellaneous Files. HH 1.

Official Reports and Papers relating to the Recent Disturbances in the Island of Skye, 1882-83. (Home Office Miscellanea). HH 22/4.

Fishery Officer (West Coast). Reports for 1850-51. AF 7/85.

Congested Districts Board Files. AF 42.

Confidential Report by Scottish Education Dept., Scottish Board of Health, Board of Agriculture for Scotland, and Fishery Board for Scotland on the Social and Economic Conditions in the Highlands, 1924. AF 42/9702.

Board of Agriculture, Miscellaneous Files. AF 43.

Royal Commission on the Highlands and Islands, 1883. (Napier Commission records). AF 50.

Emigration Files, (Scottish Office Series). AF 51.

Allotments and Smallholdings Files. AF 66.

Crofting Files. AF67.

Home Office Correspondence, Scotland, 1802-1804. RH 2/4/87-89.

Home Office Domestic Entry Books, 1846-1850. RH 2/4/238-240.

J. Blackadder, Survey and Valuation of Lord MacDonald's Estates, 1799. RH 2/8/24.

Cabinet Papers, 1885. RH 4/9/7.

(All 'RH' series are microfilm or photostat copies of records held elsewhere).

B. *At the National Library of Scotland, Edinburgh.*

John Stuart Blackie Papers.

C. *At Dunvegan Castle, Skye.*

MacLeod of Dunvegan Papers.

D. *At the Mitchell Library, Glasgow.*

The Autobiography of John Murdoch.

E. *At Aberdeen University Library.*

Through the Hebrides: The Journal of a Tour to the Western Isles of Scotland in 1897 by William S. Carson.

2. Ecclesiastical Records in the Scottish Record Office, Edinburgh.

S.S.P.C.K. Records.   GD 95.

Report by those appointed to visit the Highlands and Islands, 1760. (Church of Scotland Assembly Papers). CH 1/5/79.

Minutes of the Synods of Sutherland and Caithness, Argyll, and Glenelg. CH 2/345, 557, 568.

Minutes of the Presbyteries of Mull, Skye, Uist, Lewis, Tongue and Lochcarron. CH 2/273, 330, 361, 473, 508, 567.

Minutes of the Free Synod of Argyll. CH 3/26/1.

3. Official publications.

(Includes sessional volume numbers of Parliamentary Papers).

Hansard's Parliamentary Debates.
Mr. Telford's Survey and Report on the Coasts and Central Highlands of Scotland, 1802-03 IV.
Reports from the Select Committee to whom the Survey and Report of the Coasts and Central Highlands was referred, 1802-03 IV.
Reports from the Select Committee appointed to inquire into the expediency of encouraging Emigration from the United Kingdom, 1826 IV; 1826-27 V.
Comparative Account of the Population of Great Britain in the Years 1801, 1811, 1821 and 1831, 1831 XVIII.
Letter addressed to Mr. F. Maule by R. Graham relative to the Distress of the Highlands of Scotland, 1837, LI.

Reports of Commissioners for inquiring into the opportunities of Public Religious Worship afforded to the People of Scotland, 1837 XXI - 1839 XXVI.
Report from the Select Committee appointed to inquire into the condition of the Population of the Highlands and Islands of Scotland, and into the practicability of affording the People relief by means of Emigration, 1841 VI.
Report of the Agent General for Emigration on the Applicability of Emigration to relieve Distress in the Highlands, (1837), 1841 XXVII.
Colonial Land and Emigration Commissioners, *Annual Reports*, 1842-1873.
Report from the Commissioners appointed for inquiring into the Administration and Practical Operation of the Poor Laws in Scotland, 1844 XXVII-XXXVI.
Documents Relative to the Distress in Scotland in 1783, 1846 XXXVII.
Board of Supervision for the Relief of the Poor in Scotland, *Annual Reports*, 1847-1894.
Correspondence relating to the measures adopted for the Relief of Distress in Ireland and Scotland, 1847 LIII.
Papers Relative to Emigration to the British Provinces in North America, 1847. (And annually under various titles until 1862).
Return of Applications for Advances under the Drainage Act, 1847 XXXIV.
Report of the Select Committee appointed to inquire into the Refusal to grant Sites for Churches in Scotland, 1847 XIII.
Report to the Board of Supervision by Sir John MacNeill on the Western Highlands and Islands, 1851 XXVI.
Return of Population and Poor Rates, Scotland, (1853), 1854-55 XLVII.
Report of the Commissioners appointed to inquire into the state of Lunatic Asylums in Scotland, 1857 V.
Report on the State of Education in the Hebrides by Alexander Nicolson, 1867 XXV.
Return of Owners of Lands and Heritages, Scotland, (1872-73), 1874 LXXII.
Reports of the Royal Commission on the Depressed Condition of the Agricultural Interest, 1881 XIV – 1882 XV.
Letter, dated 3rd November 1882, from the Lord Advocate to the Sheriff of Inverness-shire relative to the disturbances among the Skye crofters, 1882 LIV.
Reports as to the Alleged Destitution in the Western Highlands and Islands, 1883 LIX.
Report of the Commissioners of Inquiry into the condition of the Crofters and Cottars in the Highlands and Islands of Scotland, 1884 XXXII - XXXVI.
Papers relating to the Despatch of a Government Force to Skye, 1884-85 LXIV.
Crofters Commission, *Annual Reports*, 1888-1912.
Memorandum of arrangements for starting a Colonisation Scheme for the Crofters and Cottars of the Western Highlands and Islands, and relative correspondence, 1888 LXXX.
Report on the Condition of the Cottar Population of the Lews, 1888 LXXX.
Return of Agrarian Offences Committed in Crofting Parishes, Scotland (1874-88), 1888 LXXXII.
Reports of the Committee appointed to Inquire into Certain Matters affecting the Interests of the Population of the Western Highlands and Islands of Scotland, 1890 XXVII, 1890-91 XLIV.

Crofters and Cottars Colonisation Commission, *Annual Reports*, 1890-1906.
Royal Commission on Agricultural Depression, 1894 XVI - 1897 XV.
Royal Commission (Highlands and Islands, 1892), Report and Minutes of Evidence, 1895 XXXVIII – XXXIX.
Royal Commission on Land in Wales and Monmouthshire, Minutes of Evidence, 1896, XXXV.
Congested Districts Board for Scotland, *Annual Reports*, 1899-1912.
Report to the Secretary for Scotland by the Crofters Commission on the Social Condition of the People of Lewis in 1901 as compared with Twenty Years Ago, 1902 LXXXIII.
Report on the Sanitary Condition of the Lews, 1905 XXXIV.
Reports on the Burden of the Existing Rates and the General Financial Position of the Outer Hebrides, 1906 CIV.
Correspondence with reference to the Seizure and Occupation of the Island of Vatersay, 1908 LXXXVIII.
Report of a Special Committee of the County Council of Inverness upon Applications for Allotments in North Uist and Barra made in September 1897, with relevant papers, 1908 LXXXVIII.
Report of the Departmental Committee on Poultry Breeding in Scotland with special reference to the efforts of the Congested Districts Board to promote the Industry, 1909 XXXVI.
Reports of the Departmental Committee on the Work of the Congested Districts (Scotland) Commissioners, 1910 XXI; 1911 XXII.
Board (since 1929, Department) of Agriculture for Scotland, *Annual Reports*, 1913 –
Report of the Scottish Land Enquiry Commission, 1914.
Report on Home Industries in the Highlands and Islands, 1914 XXXII.
Report of the Departmental Committee appointed to enquire and report with regard to Lands in Scotland used as Deer Forests, 1922 VII.
Report of the Committee on Land Settlement in Scotland, 1928 XI.
Scottish Economic Committee, *The Highlands and Islands of Scotland: A Review of the Economic Conditions with Recommendations for Improvement*, 1938.
Report by the Scottish Lànd Settlement Committee on Land Settlement in Scotland, 1944-45 V.
A Programme of Highland Development, 1950 XIX.
Report of the Commission of Enquiry into Crofting Conditions, 1953-54 VIII.
Crofters Commission, *Annual Reports*, 1956 –
Review of Highland Policy, 1958-59 XXV.
Advisory Panel on the Highlands and Islands, *Land Use in the Highlands and Islands*, 1964.
Highlands and Islands Development Board, *Annual Reports*, 1966 –
Place Names and Population, Scotland. (General Register Office, Edinburgh), 1967.
HIDB, *Occasional Bulletin No.2: Agriculture*, 1968.
HIDB, *Strath of Kildonan: Proposals for Development*, 1970.

HIDB, *Explore the Highlands and Islands,* 1972.
Crofters Commission, *North Sea Oil Developments and their Possible Effects on Crofting,* 1973.
Crofting Reform (Scotland) Bill, 1973.
HIDB, *Island of Mull: Survey and Proposals for Development,* 1973.

4. Newspapers and periodicals.

Glasgow Herald.	*An Gaidheal.*
Highlander.	*Annual Register.*
Highland News.	*Blackwood's Magazine.*
Oban Times.	*Celtic Magazine.*
Scotsman.	*Celtic Monthly*
Scottish Highlander.	*The Crofter.*
Stornoway Gazette.	*Highland Magazine.*
Times.	*Scots Magazine.*
West Highland Free Press.	*Scottish Journal of Agriculture.*
Witness.	

(Individual articles in these and other periodicals are listed below.)

5. Unpublished theses in Edinburgh University Library.

R.A.C.S. Balfour, 'Emigration from the Highlands and Western Isles of Scotland to Australia during the Nineteenth Century', (M. Litt.), 1973.
R.D. Lobban, 'The Migration of Highlanders into Lowland Scotland (c.1750-1890), with particular reference to Greenock', (Ph.D.), 1970.

6. Books, pamphlets and articles.

a) *Primary.*

An Account of the Present State of Religion throughout the Highlands of Scotland by a Lay Member of the Established Church, Edinburgh, 1827.
R.J. Adam (ed.), John Home's Survey of Assynt, *SHS,* Edinburgh, 1960.
R.J. Adam (ed.), Papers on Sutherland Estate Management, 1802-1816, (2 vols.), *SHS,* Edinburgh, 1972.
W.P. Alison, *Observations on the Famine of 1846-7 in the Highlands of Scotland and in Ireland,* Edinburgh, 1847.
W.P. Alison, *Letter to Sir John MacNeill on Highland Destitution,* Edinburgh, 1851.
H. Anderson, *The Life and Letters of Christopher Anderson,* Edinburgh, 1854.
J. Anderson, *On the State of Society and Knowledge in the Highlands,* Edinburgh, 1827.
J. Anderson, 'Essay on the Present State of the Highlands', *THASS,* New Ser., II, 1831.
Argyll, Duke of (G.D. Campbell), *Crofts and Farms in the Hebrides,* Edinburgh, 1883.
Argyll, 'A Corrected Picture of the Highlands', *Nineteenth Century Review,* XVI, 1884.

Argyll, *Scotland As It Was and Is,* (2 vols.), Edinburgh, 1887.

Argyll, 'Isolation, or Survival of the Unfittest', *Nineteenth Century,* XXV, 1889.

A. Auld, *Memorial of David Stephen,* Wick, 1874.

A. Auld, *Ministers and Men in the Far North,* Edinburgh, 1891.

J. Barron, *The Northern Highlands in the Nineteenth Century,* (3 vols.), Inverness, 1907-1913.

J. Bateman, *The Great Landowners of Great Britain and Ireland,* London, (4th edit.), 1883.

A. Beaton, 'On the Art of Making Kelp', *Trans. of the Highland Soc.,* I, 1799.

J. Begg, *How Every Man may become his own Landlord,* Edinburgh, 1851.

A. Beith, *A Highland Tour,* Edinburgh, 1874.

J.S. Blackie, *Gaelic Societies, Highland Depopulation and Land Law Reform,* Edinburgh, 1880.

J.S. Blackie, *Altavona: Fact and Fiction from my Life in the Highlands,* Edinburgh, 1882.

J.S. Blackie, 'The Highland Crofters', *Nineteenth Century Review,* XIII, 1883.

J.S. Blackie, *The Scottish Highlanders and the Land Laws,* London, 1885.

B. Botfield, *Journal of a Tour through the Highlands of Scotland,* Norton Hall, 1830.

R. Brown, *Remarks on the Earl of Selkirk's Observations on the Present State of the Highlands,* Edinburgh, 1806.

T. Brown, *Annals of the Disruption,* Edinburgh, 1890.

J. Browne, *A Critical Examination of Dr. MacCulloch's Work on the Highlands,* Edinburgh, 1825.

J. Bruce, *Letters on the Present Condition of the Highlands and Islands of Scotland,* Edinburgh, 1847.

J.L. Buchanan, *Travels in the Western Hebrides, from 1782 to 1790,* London, 1793.

R. Buchanan, *The Land of Lorne,* (2 vols.), London, 1871.

E. Burt, *Letters from a Gentleman in the North of Scotland,* (2 vols.), London, 1815.

A. Cameron, *History and Traditions of the Isle of Skye,* Inverness, 1871.

C. Cameron, *The Skye Expedition of 1886,* Glasgow, 1886.

J.A. Cameron, 'Storm Clouds in the Highlands', *Nineteenth Century Review,* XVI, 1884.

A. Campbell, *The Grampians Desolate: a Poem,* Edinburgh, 1804.

C. Campbell, *The Crofter in History,* Edinburgh, 1885.

D. Campbell, *The Land Question in the Highlands and Islands,* Paisley, 1884.

J. Campbell, *Missionary and Ministerial Life in the Highlands,* Edinburgh, 1853.

J. Campbell (ed.), *The Rev. Mr. Lachlan of Lochcarron: Lectures, Sermons and Writings,* Inverness, 1928.

J. Campbell (ed.), *The Rev. Mr. Lachlan of Lochcarron: Additional Lectures, Sermons and Writings,* Inverness, 1930.

J.L. Campbell (ed.), *Highland Songs of the Forty-five,* Edinburgh, 1933.

J.L. Campbell (ed.), *The Book of Barra*, London, 1936.

J.L. Campbell (ed.), *Gaelic Words and Expressions from South Uist and Eriskay collected by Rev. Fr. Allan MacDonald*, Dublin, 1958.

A. Carmichael, *Carmina Gadelica*, (6 vols.), Edinburgh, 1928-1971.

J. Carr, *Caledonian Sketches*, London, 1809.

Central Board of Management of the Fund for the Relief of the Destitute Inhabitants of the Highlands (and Highland Relief Committees, Edinburgh and Glasgow), *Reports*, 1847-1850.

J. Chamberlain, *A Political Memoir*, (ed. C.H.D. Howard), London, 1953.

J.M. Cherrie, *On the Economic Conditions of Land Occupancy and the Depopulation of the Highlands*, London, 1884.

J.M. Cherrie, *The Restoration of the Land to the State*, London, 1884.

G.B. Clark, *A Plea for the Nationalisation of the Land*, London, 1882.

G.B. Clark, *The Highland Land Question*, London, 1885.

D. Clerk, 'On the Agriculture of Argyll', *THASS*, 4th Ser., X, 1878.

H.M. Conacher, 'Land Settlement in Scotland', *Scottish Journal of Agriculture*, IV, 1921.

P. Cooper, *The So-Called Evictions from the MacDonald Estates in North Uist in 1849*, Aberdeen, 1881.

J.B. Craven (ed.), *Journals of the Episcopal Visitations of Robert Forbes*, London, 1886.

E. Cregeen (ed.), *Argyll Estate Instructions, 1771-1805*, *SHS*, Edinburgh, 1964.

'The Crofters of the Highlands', *Westminster Review*, CXXIX, 1888.

M. Davitt, *The Fall of Feudalism in Ireland*, London, 1904.

N. Douglas, *Journal of a Mission to Part of the Highlands of Scotland*, Edinburgh, 1799.

T. Douglas, (Earl of Selkirk), *Observations on the Present State of the Highlands of Scotland*, London, 1805.

A. Duff *et al.*, *Disruption Worthies of the Highlands*, Edinburgh, 1877.

B.E.C. Dugdale, *Arthur James Balfour*, (2 vols.), London, 1936.

E. Ellice, *A Letter to Sir George Gray on the Administration of the Poor Law in the Highlands*, London, 1855.

W. Ewing, *Annals of the Free Church of Scotland*, (2 vols.), Edinburgh, 1914.

Fasti Ecclesiae Scoticanae, (9 vols.), Edinburgh, 1915-1961.

M. Ferguson, *Rambles in Skye*, Irvine, 1885.

C. Fraser-MacIntosh, *Antiquarian Notes* (first and second series), Inverness, 1865, 1897.

C. Fraser-MacIntosh, *Letters of Two Centuries*, Inverness, 1890.

Free Church Destitution Committee, *Statements*, Edinburgh, 1847.

A. Fullarton and C.R. Baird, *Remarks on the Evils at Present Affecting the Highlands and Islands of Scotland*, Glasgow, 1838.

Gaelic School Society, *Annual Reports*, Edinburgh, 1825-1845.

A.G. Gardiner, *The Life of Sir William Harcourt*, (2 vols.), London, 1923.

A. Geikie, *Scottish Reminiscences*, Glasgow, 1904.

J. Girvin, *An Address to the Landholders, Factors and Tenantry in the Highlands of Scotland for Preventing Emigration*, Edinburgh, 1803.

A. Goodrich-Freer, *Outer Isles,* London, 1902.

A. Grant, *Letters from the Mountains,* (3 vols.), London, 1807.

E. Grant, *Memoirs of a Highland Lady,* London, 1898.

R. Greig, 'Agricultural Administration in Scotland during the present Reign', *Scottish Journal of Agriculture,* XVIII, 1935.

T. Grierson, *Autumnal Rambles among the Scottish Mountains,* Edinburgh, 1850.

A. Haldane, *Memoirs of the Lives of Robert Haldane and James Haldane,* London, 1852.

J. Hall, *Travels in Scotland by an Unusual Route,* (2 vols.), London, 1807.

R. Hall, *The Highland Sportsman,* London, 1883.

W.N. Hancock, *What are the Causes of the Distressed State of the Highlands of Scotland?,* Belfast, 1852.

J. Headrick, *Report on the Island of Lewis,* London, 1800.

Highland Emigration Society, *Report,* London, 1853.

'The Highlands: Men, Sheep and Deer', *Edinburgh Review,* CVI, 1857.

P.B. Homer, *Observations on a Short Tour to the Western Highlands of Scotland,* London, 1804.

Inverness Society for the Education of the Poor, *Moral Statistics of the Highlands and Islands,* Inverness, 1826.

'Investigator', *The Church and Her Accuser in the Far North,* Glasgow, 1850.

'Investigator', *Fanaticism in the North,* Edinburgh, 1852.

A. Irvine, *An Inquiry into the Causes and Effects of Emigration from the Highlands and Western Islands of Scotland,* Edinburgh, 1802.

E. Jameson, 'Observations on Kelp', *Trans. of the Highland Soc.,* I, 1799.

S. Johnson, *Journey to the Western Islands of Scotland,* Oxford, 1924.

J.S. Keltie, *A History of the Scottish Highlands,* (2 vols.), Edinburgh, 1875.

J. Kennedy, *The Days of the Fathers in Ross-shire,* Inverness, 1927.

J. Kennedy, *The Apostle of the North,* Inverness, 1932.

J. Knox, *A Tour through the Highlands of Scotland,* London, 1786.

J. Knox, *A View of the British Empire, more especially Scotland,* London, 1789.

S. Laing, *Journal of a Residence in Norway,* London, 1837.

'Land in the Highlands. Should the Government Legislate?', *Blackwood's Mag.,* CLVIII,.1895.

'Land Settlement in Scotland', *Scottish Journal of Agriculture,* XV, 1932.

'Landed Tenure in the Highlands', *Westminster Review,* XXIV, 1868.

A. Lang (ed.), *The Highlands of Scotland in 1750,* Edinburgh, 1908.

J. Leyden, *Journal of a Tour in the Highlands and Western Islands of Scotland in 1800,* Edinburgh, 1903.

J. Loch, *An Account of the Improvements on the Estates of the Marquess of Stafford,* London, 1820.

L. MacBean, *Buchanan: The Sacred Bard of the Scottish Highlands,* London, 1920.

Lady MacCaskill, *Twelve Days in Skye,* London, 1852.

R. MacCowan, *The Men of Skye,* Glasgow, 1902.

J. MacCulloch, *A Description of the Western Islands of Scotland,* (3 vols.),
  London, 1819.
J. MacCulloch, *The Highlands and Western Isles of Scotland,* (4 vols.),
  London, 1824.
C. MacDonald, *Moidart; or Among the Clanranalds,* Oban, 1889.
C. MacDonald, *Highland Journey,* Edinburgh, 1943.
D.G.F. MacDonald, *Cattle, Sheep and Deer,* London, 1872.
D.G.F. MacDonald, *The Highland Crofters of Scotland Socially Considered,*
  London, 1878.
J. MacDonald, *General View of the Agriculture of the Hebrides,* Edinburgh,
  1811.
J. MacDonald, 'The Agriculture of Caithness', *THASS,* 4th Ser., VII, 1875.
J. MacDonald, 'On the Agriculture of Ross and Cromarty', *THASS,* 4th Ser.,
  IX, 1877.
J. MacDonald, 'On the Agriculture of Sutherland', *THASS,* 4th Ser., XII, 1880.
R.H. MacDonald, *The Emigration of Highland Crofters,* Edinburgh, 1885.
W. MacDonald, 'On the Agriculture of Inverness-shire', *THASS,* 4th Ser., IV,
  1872.
D.H. MacFarlane, *Depopulation of Rural Scotland,* London, 1882.
D.H. MacFarlane, *The Highland Crofters versus Large Farms,* London, 1884.
N.C. MacFarlane, *The Men of the Lews,* Stornoway, 1924.
A. MacGillivray, *Sketches of Religion and Revivals in the North Highlands,*
  Edinburgh, 1859.
W. MacGillivray, 'Report on the Present State of the Outer Hebrides', *THASS,*
  New Ser., II, 1831.
A. MacGregor, 'Destitution in the Highlands and Islands', *Celtic Magazine,*
  II, 1877.
D. MacKay, *This Was My Glen,* Thurso, 1965.
G.G. MacKay, *On the Management of Landed Property in the Highlands,*
  Edinburgh, 1858.
G.G. MacKay, *The Land and the Land Laws,* Inverness, 1882.
A. MacKenzie, *The Highland Clearances,* Inverness, 1883.
A. MacKenzie, *The Isle of Skye, 1882-1883,* Inverness, 1883.
A. MacKenzie, *The Trial of Patrick Sellar,* Inverness, 1883.
A. MacKenzie, *The Military Expedition to the Isle of Skye,* Inverness, 1884.
A. MacKenzie, *John MacKay: Highland Evangelist,* Paisley, 1921.
E. MacKenzie, *Rev. Murdo MacKenzie: A Memory,* Inverness, 1914.
G.S. MacKenzie, *Letter to the Proprietors of Land in Ross-shire,* Inverness,
  1803.
G.S. MacKenzie, *General View of the Agriculture of the Counties of Ross
  and Cromarty,* London, 1813.
H.R. MacKenzie, *Yachting and Electioneering in the Hebrides,* Inverness, 1887.
J. MacKenzie, *Letter to Lord John Russell on Sir John MacNeill's Report,*
  Edinburgh, 1851.
O. MacKenzie, *A Hundred Years in the Highlands,* London, 1921.
W. MacKenzie, *Old Skye Tales,* Glasgow, 1934.

W.C. MacKenzie, 'The Highland Crofters and their Needs', *Progressive Review,* London, II, 1897.

D. MacKinlay, *The Island of Lewis and its Fishermen Crofters,* London, 1878.

T. MacLauchlan, 'The Influence of Emigration on the Social Conditions of the Highlands', *Trans. of the National Assoc. for the Promotion of Social Science,* 1863.

N. MacLean, *The Life of James Cameron Lees,* Glasgow, 1922.

N. MacLean, *The Former Days,* London, 1945.

N. MacLean, *Set Free,* London, 1949.

A. MacLellan, *The Furrow Behind Me,* London, 1962.

D. MacLeod, *The Sutherlandshire Clearances,* Glasgow, 1856.

D. MacLeod, *Gloomy Memories,* Glasgow, 1892.

J. MacLeod, *Highland Heroes of the Land Reform Movement,* Inverness, 1917.

J.N. MacLeod, *Memorials of the Rev. Norman MacLeod,* Edinburgh, 1898.

N. MacLeod, *Reminiscences of a Highland Parish,* London, 1867.

(N. MacLeod), *Letters to the Rev. Dr. MacLeod regarding the Famine and Destitution in the Highlands and Islands,* Glasgow, 1847.

R. MacLeod, 'The Crofter Commission', *Blackwood's Mag.,* CXLVI, 1889.

R.C. MacLeod, (ed.), *The Book of Dunvegan,* (2 vols.), *Third Spalding Club,* Aberdeen, 1938-1939.

C. MacNaughton, *Church Life in Ross and Sutherland, 1688-1914,* Inverness, 1915.

J. MacNeill, 'Emigration from the Isle of Skye', *Illustrated London News,* 15 Jan. 1853.

M. MacPherson, *Dain agus Orain Ghaidhlig,* Inverness, 1891.

A. Macrae, *Donald Sutherland, Saint and Seer,* Tongue, 1932.

M. Martin, *A Description of the Western Isles of Scotland,* London, 1884.

K. Marx, 'Forced Emigration', in, *K. Marx and F. Engels on Britain,* Moscow, 1953.

K. Marx, *Capital,* (3 vols.), London, 1886.

W. Matheson (ed.), *The Songs of John MacCodrum, Scottish Gaelic Texts Society,* Edinburgh, 1938.

W. Matheson (ed.), *The Blind Harper; the songs of Roderick Morrison and his music, Scottish Gaelic Texts Soc.,* Edinburgh, 1970.

W.L. Micks, *An Account of the Congested Districts Board,* Dublin, 1925.

H. Miller, *Sutherland as It Was and Is,* Edinburgh, 1843.

H. Miller, *The Cruise of the Betsy,* Edinburgh, 1858.

J. Mitchell, *Reminiscences of My Life in the Highlands,* (2 vols.), London, 1883-1884.

T. Mulock, *The Western Highlands and Islands of Scotland Socially Considered,* Edinburgh, 1850.

D. Nairne, *Memorable Floods in the Highlands during the Nineteenth Century,* Inverness, 1895.

Lord Napier, 'The Highland Crofters', *Nineteenth Century Review,* XVII, 1885.

New Statistical Account of Scotland, (15 vols.), Edinburgh, 1835-1845.

G. Nicholls, *A History of the Scotch Poor Law,* London, 1856.

'An Old Highlander', 'Home Truths on the Crofter Agitation', *Blackwood's Mag.,* CXXXVIII, 1885.

T. Pennant, *A Tour in Scotland and a Voyage to the Hebrides,* (3 vols.), Warrington, 1774.

Lady Pentland, *The Right Honourable John Sinclair, Lord Pentland: A Memoir,* London, 1928.

'Puritanism in the Highlands', *Quarterly Review,* LXXXIX, 1851.

J. Rae, 'The Highland Crofters', *Contemporary Review,* XLIII, 1883.

J. Rae, 'The Crofter Problem', *Contemporary Review,* XLVII, 1885.

F.G. Rea, *A School in South Uist,* London, 1964.

Remarks on the Earl of Selkirk's Observations on the Highlands, Edinburgh, 1806.

Report on Mull, Tiree, Coll and Morvern by a Deputation of the Glasgow Section of the Highland Relief Board, Glasgow, 1849.

Report on the Outer Hebrides by a Deputation of the Glasgow Section of the Highland Relief Board, Glasgow, 1849.

P. Robertson, *Report of the Trial of Patrick Sellar,* Edinburgh, 1816.

D. Ross, *The Scottish Highlanders: Their Present Sufferings and Future Prospects,* Glasgow, 1852.

D. Ross, *The Glengarry Evictions,* Glasgow, 1853.

D. Ross, *Real Scottish Grievances,* Glasgow, 1854.

D. Ross, *The Russians of Ross-shire, or Massacre of the Rosses in Strath-carron,* Glasgow, 1854.

J. Ross, *Brief Sketch of the Life of Donald MacQueen,* London, 1891.

D. Sage, *Memorabilia Domestica,* Edinburgh, 1889.

G.P. Scrope, *Some Notes of a Tour in England, Scotland and Ireland,* London, 1849.

T. Sellar, *The Sutherland Evictions of 1814,* London, 1883.

P.C. Simpson, *The Life of Principal Rainy,* (2 vols.), London, 1909.

G. Sinclair, *Six Letters on the Position and Prospects of the Established Church in Scotland, especially in the Northern Counties,* Edinburgh, 1850.

J. Sinclair, *The Christian Hero of the North,* Edinburgh, 1867.

J. Sinclair, *Analysis of the Statistical Account of Scotland,* London, 1826.

W. Singer, 'On the Introduction of Sheep Farming into the Highlands', *Trans. of the Highland Soc.,* III, 1807.

W.F. Skene, *Celtic Scotland,* (3 vols.), Edinburgh, 1880.

W.A. Smith, *Lewsiana, or Life in the Outer Hebrides,* London, 1875.

W. Smith, *Men or Deer in the Scottish Glens,* Inverness, 1893.

R. Somers, *Letters from the Highlands; or the Famine of 1847,* London, 1848.

R. Southey, *Journal of a Tour in Scotland in 1819,* London, 1929.

Specimens of the Ecclesiastical Destitution of Scotland, Edinburgh, 1835.

'The State of Religion in the Highlands', *Blackwood's Mag.,* V, 1814.

Statistical Account of Scotland, (21 vols.), Edinburgh, 1791-1799.

D. Stewart, *Sketches of the Character, Manners and Present State of the Highlanders of Scotland,* (2 vols.), Edinburgh, 1822.

Sutherland and the Sutherlanders: Their Religious and Social Condition, Edinburgh, 1844.

J. Tait, 'The Condition of the Scottish Peasantry', *THASS*, 4th Ser., XV, 1883.

Lord Teignmouth, *Sketches of the Coasts and Islands of Scotland and of the Isle of Man*, (2 vols.), London, 1836.

'Transition in the Highlands of Scotland', *Scottish Review*. XII, 1888.

E.O. Tregelles, *Hints on the Hebrides*, Newcastle, 1855.

C.E. Trevelyan, *The Irish Crisis*, London, 1848.

J. Walker, 'An Essay on Kelp', *Trans. of the Highland Soc.*, I, 1799.

J. Walker, *An Economical History of the Hebrides and Highlands of Scotland*, (2 vols.), London, 1812.

A.R. Wallace, *Land Nationalisation*, London, 1883.

C.R. Weld, *Two Months in the Highlands, Orcadia and Skye*, London, 1860.

b) *Secondary.*

M.I. Adam, 'The Highland Emigration of 1770', *SHR*, XVI, 1919.

M.I. Adam, 'The Causes of the Highland Emigrations of 1783-1803', *SHR*, XVII, 1920.

M.I. Adam, 'Eighteenth Century Highland Landlords and the Poverty Problem', *SHR*, XIX, 1921-1922.

C.M. Arensberg, *The Irish Countryman*, London, 1937.

D. Barrett, *Schism and Renewal in Africa*, Oxford, 1968.

D. Beaton, 'Fast-Day and Friday Fellowship Meeting Controversy in the Synod of Sutherland and Caithness, 1737-1758', *TGSI*, XXIX, 1917.

D. Beaton, *Some Noted Ministers of the Northern Highlands*, Inverness, 1929.

R.D.C. Black, *Economic Thought and the Irish Question*, Cambridge, 1960.

J. Blum, *Lord and Peasant in Russia – from the Ninth to the Nineteenth Century*, Princeton, 1961.

O. Blundell, *The Catholic Highlands of Scotland*, (2 vols.), Edinburgh, 1909, 1917.

C.C..O'Brien, *Parnell and His Party*, Oxford, 1957.

M. Brody, *Inishkillane: Change and Decline in the West of Ireland*, London, 1973.

G. Broeker, *Rural Disorder and Police Reform in Ireland*, 1812-1836, London, 19

J. Brown, 'Scottish and English Land Legislation, 1905-1911', *SHR*, XLVII, 1968

D. Buchanan, *Reflections on the Isle of Barra*, London, 1942.

J.B. Caird, 'The Isle of Harris', *SGM*, LXVII, 1951.

J.B. Caird and H.A. Moisley, 'Leadership and Innovation in the Crofting Communities of the Outer Hebrides', *Sociological Review*, IX, 1961.

J. Cameron, *The Old and the New Highlands and Hebrides*, Kirkcaldy, 1912.

J. Cameron, *Celtic Law*, London, 1937.

A.J. Campbell, *Two Centuries of the Church of Scotland*, Paisley, 1930.

H.F. Campbell, 'Donald Matheson and other Gaelic Poets in Kildonan and Reay', *TGSI*, XXIX, 1917.

J.L. Campbell, *Gaelic in Scottish Education and Life*, Edinburgh, 1950.

J.L. Campbell, *Fr. Allan MacDonald of Eriskay*, Edinburgh, 1954.

R.H. Campbell, *Scotland Since 1707*, Oxford, 1965.

I. Carter, 'Economic Models and the Recent History of the Highlands', *Scottish Studies*, XV, 1971.

I.R. Carter, 'Six Years On, an evaluative study of the Highlands and Islands Development Board', *Aberdeen University Review*, XLV, 1973.

N. Cohn, *The Pursuit of the Millenium*, London, 1970.

A. Collier, *The Crofting Problem*, Cambridge, 1953.

J.R. Coull, 'The Island of Tiree', *SGM*, LXXVIII, 1962.

J.R. Coull, 'Melness, a Crofting Community on the North Coast of Sutherland', *Scottish Studies*, VII, 1963.

J.R. Coull, 'Crofters' Common Grazings in Scotland', *AHR*, XVI, 1968.

D. Cooper, *Skye*, London, 1970.

H.L. Cowan, *British Emigration to British North America*, Toronto, 1961.

I.A. Crawford, 'Feannagan Taomaidh (Lazy Beds)', *Scottish Studies*, VI, 1962.

I.A. Crawford, 'Kelp Burning', *Scottish Studies*, VI, 1962.

I.A. Crawford, 'Contributions to a History of Domestic Settlement in North Uist', *Scottish Studies*, IX, 1965.

E. Cregeen, 'The Tacksmen and their Successors', *Scottish Studies*, XIII, 1969.

E. Cregeen, 'The Changing Role of the House of Argyll in the Scottish Highlands', in N.T. Phillipson and R. Mitchison (eds.), *Scotland in the Age of Improvement*, Edinburgh, 1970.

D.W. Crowley, 'The 'Crofters' Party', 1885-1892', *SHR*, XXXV, 1956.

A. Cunningham, *The Loyal Clans*, Cambridge, 1932.

L.P. Curtis, *Coercion and Conciliation in Ireland, 1880-1892*, Princeton, 1963.

F. Fraser Darling, *Crofting Agriculture*, Edinburgh, 1945.

F. Fraser Darling, *West Highland Survey*, Oxford, 1955.

G.L. Davies, 'The Parish of North Uist', *SGM*, LXXII, 1956.

J.P. Day, *Public Administration in the Highlands and Islands of Scotland*, London, 1918.

G. Donaldson, *The Scots Overseas*, London, 1966.

I.D. Duff, 'The Human Geography of South-Western Ross-shire, 1800-1929', *SGM*, XLV, 1929.

C.W. Dunn, *Highland Settler*, Toronto, 1953.

E. Dwelly, *The Illustrated Gaelic-English Dictionary*, Glasgow, 1971.

R. Dudley Edwards and T. Desmond Williams (eds.), *The Great Famine*, Dublin, 1956.

H. Fairhurst, 'The Surveys for the Sutherland Clearances, 1813-1820', *Scottish Studies*, VIII, 1964.

S. Fairlie, 'The Corn Law Reconsidered', *EHR*, XVIII, 1965.

T. Ferguson, *The Dawn of Scottish Social Welfare*, London, 1947.

T. Ferguson, *Scottish Social Welfare, 1864-1914*, Edinburgh, 1958.

W. Ferguson, *Scotland, 1689 to the Present*, Edinburgh, 1968.

W. Ferguson, 'The Problems of the Established Church in the West Highlands in the Eighteenth Century', *Records of the Scottish Church History Society*, XVII, 1969.

J.R. Fleming, *A History of the Church in Scotland, 1843-1874*, Edinburgh, 1927.

T.B. Franklin, *A History of Scottish Farming*, Edinburgh, 1952.

Gaelic Society of Glasgow, *The Old Highlands*, Glasgow, 1908.

V. Gaffney, 'Summer Shealings', *SHR,* XXXVIII, 1959.

V. Gaffney, *The Lordship of Strathavon, Third Spalding Club,* Aberdeen, 1960.

R.A. Gailey, 'Mobility of Tenants on a Highland Eatate in the early Nineteenth Century', *SHR,* XL, 1961.

R.A. Gailey, 'The Role of Sub-Letting in the Crofting Community', *Scottish Studies,* V, 1961.

R.A. Gailey, 'The Evolution of Highland Rural Settlement with particular reference to Argyllshire', *Scottish Studies,* VI, 1962.

P. Gaskell, *Morvern Transformed,* Cambridge, 1968.

A. Geddes, 'Conjoint Tenants and Tacksmen in the Isle of Lewis, 1715-26', *EHR,* I, 1948.

A. Geddes, *The Isle of Lewis and Harris,* Edinburgh, 1955.

J.M. Gibbon, *Scots in Canada,* London, 1911.

F. Gillanders, 'The West Highland Economy', *TGSI,* XLIII, 1962.

D.V. Glass and D.E.C. Eversley (eds.), *Population in History,* London, 1965.

H.C. Graham, *The Social Life of Scotland in the Eighteenth Century,* (2 vols.), London, 1899.

I.F. Grant, *Everyday Life on an Old Highland Farm,* London, 1924.

I.F. Grant, *The MacLeods; the history of a clan, 1200-1956,* London, 1959.

I.F. Grant, *Highland Folk Ways,* London, 1961.

M. Gray, 'The Abolition of Runrig in the Highlands of Scotland', *EHR,* V, 1952.

M. Gray, 'Economic Welfare and Money Income in the Highlands, 1750-1850', *Scottish Journal of Political Economy,* II, 1955.

M. Gray, 'The Highland Potato Famine of the 1840s', *EHR,* VII, 1955.

M. Gray, 'The Consolidation of the Crofting System', *AHR,* V, 1957.

M. Gray, *The Highland Economy,* Edinburgh, 1957.

M. Gray, 'The Place of Fishing in the Economy of the North-West, 1886-1914', in L.D. Stamp (ed.), *Land Use in the Scottish Highlands, The Advancement of Science,* XXI, 1964.

M. Gray, 'Settlement in the Highlands, 1750-1950: The Documentary and the Written Record', *Scottish Studies,* VI, 1962.

M. Gray, 'Crofting and Fishing in the North-West Highlands, 1890-1914', *Northern Scotland,* I, 1972.

I. Grimble, *The Trial of Patrick Sellar,* London, 1962.

I. Grimble, 'Emigration in the Time of Robb Donn, 1714-1778', *Scottish Studies,* VII, 1963.

A.R.B. Haldane, *New Ways Through the Glens,* Edinburgh, 1962.

A.R.B. Haldane, *The Drove Roads of Scotland,* Edinburgh, 1968.

H. Hamilton, *The Industrial Revolution in Scotland,* Oxford, 1932.

H. Hamilton, *An Economic History of Scotland in the Eighteenth Century,* Oxford, 1963.

J.L. Hammond, *Gladstone and the Irish Nation,* London, 1938.

J.E. Handley, *The Irish in Scotland, 1798-1845,* Cork, 1943.

J.E. Handley, *Scottish Farming in the Eighteenth Century,* London, 1953.

H.J. Hanham, 'The Problem of Highland Discontent, 1880-1885', *TRHS,*

H.J. Hanham, *Scottish Nationalism,* London, 1969.

G.D. Henderson, *Heritage: A Study of the Disruption,* Edinburgh, 1943.

I. Henderson, *Scotland: Kirk and People,* London, 1969.

Highland Village Association, *Home Life of the Highlanders. 1400-1746,* Glasgow, 1911.

F.H. Hitchins, *The Colonial Land and Emigration Commission,* Philadelphia, 1931.

E.J. Hobsbawm, *Primitive Rebels,* Manchester, 1959.

E.J. Hobsbawm, *Industry and Empire,* London, 1968.

E.J. Hobsbawm and G. Rude, *Captain Swing,* London, 1969.

P.M. Hobson, 'Assynt Parish', *SGM,* LXV, 1949.

P.M. Hobson, 'The Parish of Barra', *SGM,* LXV, 1949.

J. Hunter, 'Sheep and Deer: Highland Sheep Farming, 1850-1900', *Northern Scotland,* I, 1973.

J. Hunter, 'The Politics of Highland Land Reform, 1873-1895', *SHR,* LIII, 1974.

E.H. Jacoby, *Man and Land: The Fundamental Issue in Development,* London, 1971.

H.J.M. Johnston, *British Emigration Policy, 1815-1830,* Oxford, 1972.

T. Johnston, *The History of the Working Classes in Scotland,* Glasgow, 1922.

J.G. Kellas, 'The Liberal Party and the Scottish Church Disestablishment Crisis', *English Historical Review,* LXXIX, 1964.

J.G. Kellas, 'The Liberal Party in Scotland, 1876-1895', *SHR,* XLIV, 1965.

V. Lanternari, *The Religions of the Oppressed,* London, 1963.

E.P. Lawrence, *Henry George in the British Isles,* Michigan, 1957.

A.T.A. Learmonth, 'The Population of Skye', *SGM,* LXVI, 1950.

J.C. Lees, *A History of the County of Inverness,* Edinburgh, 1847.

M.M. Leigh, 'The Crofting Problem, 1790-1883', *Scottish Journal of Agriculture,* XI-XII, 1928-1929.

Lewis Association, *Reports,* Stornoway, 1944-1954.

F.S.L. Lyons, *John Dillon,* London, 1968.

F.S.L. Lyons, *Ireland Since the Famine,* London, 1971.

D.J. MacCuish, 'The Origin and Development of Crofting Law', *TGSI,* XLIII, 1962.

D.J. MacCuish, 'The Case for Converting Crofting Tenure to Ownership', *TGSI,* XLVI, 1969-70.

C. MacDonald, *Crofts and Crofters,* Edinburgh, 1955.

C.M. MacDonald (ed.), *The County of Argyll,* Glasgow, 1961.

D.F. MacDonald, *Scotland's Shifting Population,* Glasgow, 1937.

D. MacDonald, *Tales and Traditions of the Lews,* Stornoway, 1967.

N. MacDonald, *Canada, 1763-1841: Immigration and Land Settlement,* London, 1939.

N. MacDonald, *Canada: Immigration and Colonisation, 1841-1903,* Aberdeen, 1966.

J. McGrath, *The Cheviot, the Stag and the Black, Black, Oil,* Kyleakin, 1974.

A.A. MacGregor, *The Western Isles,* London, 1949.

J. MacInnes, 'The Origin and Early Development of 'The Men' ', *Scottish Church History Society Records,* VIII, 1944.

J. MacInnes, *The Evangelical Movement in the Highlands of Scotland, 1688 to 1800,* Aberdeen, 1951.

J. MacInnes, 'A Gaelic Song of the Sutherland Clearances', *Scottish Studies,* VIII, 1964.

J. MacInnes, Review of Sorley MacLean's Poetry, *Scottish International,* Dec. 1973.

D.I. MacKay, 'Regional Planning for the North of Scotland', *Aberdeen University Review,* XLI, 1965.

J. MacKay, *The Church in the Highlands, 563-1843,* London, 1914.

W.C. MacKenzie, *History of the Outer Hebrides,* Paisley, 1903.

W.C. MacKenzie, *The Book of the Lews,* London, 1919.

W.C. MacKenzie, *The Western Isles,* Paisley, 1932.

W.M. MacKenzie, *Hugh Miller: A Critical Study,* London, 1905.

A. MacKerral, 'The Tacksman and his Holding in the South-West Highlands', *SHR,* XXVI, 1947.

A. MacKerral, *Kintyre in the Seventeenth Century,* Edinburgh, 1948.

D. MacKinnon, *The Gaelic Bible and Psalter,* Dingwall, 1930.

N.B. MacKinnon, 'The Effect of the Highland Clearances on Gaelic Life and Letters', *An Gaidheal,* V, 1964.

C.I. MacLean, *The Highlands,* London, 1959.

J.P. MacLean, *History of the Island of Mull,* (2 vols.), San Mateo, 1925.

S. MacLean, 'Realism in Gaelic Poetry', *TGSI,* XXXVII, 1938.

S. MacLean, 'The Poetry of the Clearances', *TGSI,* XXXVIII, 1939.

S. MacLean, 'The Poetry of William Livingstone', *TGSI,* XXXIX, 1940.

J. MacLeod, *The North Country Separatists,* Inverness, 1930.

R.C. MacLeod, 'A West Highland Estate During Three Centuries', *SHR,* XXII, 1925.

D.S. MacMillan, 'Sir Charles Trevelyan and the Highland and Island Emigration Society, 1849-1859', *Royal Australian Historical Society Journal,* XLIX, 1963.

D.S. MacMillan, *Scotland and Australia, 1788-1850,* Oxford, 1967.

S. MacMillan, *Bygone Lochaber,* Glasgow, 1971.

P.A. MacNab, *The Island of Mull,* Newton Abbott, 1970.

A.G. MacPherson, 'An Old Highland Genealogy and the Evolution of a Scottish Clan', *Scottish Studies,* X, 1966.

A.G. MacPherson, 'An Old Highland Parish Register: Survivals of Clanship and Social Change in Laggan, Inverness-shire, 1775-1854', *Scottish Studies,* XI-XII, 1967-1968.

A. MacRae, *Revivals in the Highlands and Islands in the Nineteenth Century,* Stirling, 1907.

A. MacRae, *The Fire of God Among the Heather,* Inverness, 1929.

A. MacRae, *Kinlochbervie,* Tongue, 1932.

E. MacRury, *A Hebridean Parish,* Inverness, 1950.

M.D. MacSween, 'Transhumance in North Skye', *SGM,* LXXV, 1959.

M.D. MacSween and A. Gailey, 'Some Shielings in North Skye', *Scottish Studies,* V, 1961.

E.J. March, *Sailing Drifters,* London, 1952.

W.H. Marwick, *Labour in Scotland,* Glasgow, 1948.

P. Mathias, *The First Industrial Nation,* London, 1969.

S. Mechie, *The Church and Scottish Social Development, 1780-1870,* London, 1960.

H.W. Meikle, *Scotland and the French Revolution,* Edinburgh, 1912.

R. Mitchison, 'The Government and the Highlands, 1707-1745', in N.T. Phillipson and R. Mitchison (eds.), *Scotland in the Age of Improvement,* Edinburgh, 1970.

D. Mitrany, *Marx Against the Peasant,* London, 1951.

H.A. Moisley, 'North Uist in 1799', *SGM,* LXXVII, 1961.

H.A. Moisley, 'Population Changes and the Highland Problem, 1951-1961', *Scottish Studies,* VI, 1962.

H.A. Moisley, 'The Highlands and Islands — a Crofting Region?', *Transactions of the Institute of British Geographers,* XXI, 1962.

H.A. Moisley, 'The Deserted Hebrides', *Scottish Studies,* X, 1966.

B. Moore, *The Social Origins of Dictatorship and Democracy,* London, 1967.

W.G. Mowat, *The Story of Lybster,* Lybster, 1959.

T.M. Murchison, 'Highland Life as Reflected in Gaelic Literature', *TGSI,* XXXVIII, 1938.

T.M. Murchison, 'Glenelg, Inverness-shire: Some Notes for a Parish History', *TGSI,* XL, 1957.

W.H. Murray, *The Islands of Western Scotland,* London, 1973.

A. Nicolson, *History of Skye,* Glasgow, 1930.

N. Nicolson, *Lord of the Isles; Lord Leverhulme in the Hebrides,* London, 1960.

T.A.F. Noble, 'The Economic Development of the Highlands', *Manchester School,* XIX, 1951.

T.A.F. Noble, 'The Future of Crofting', *Scottish Journal of Political Economy,* I, 1954.

A.C.O'Dell and K. Walton, *The Highlands and Islands of Scotland,* London, 1962.

R. Oliver and J.D. Fage, *A Short History of Africa,* Harmondsworth, 1962.

R.H. Osborne, 'The Movements of People in Scotland, 1851-1951', *Scottish Studies,* II, 1958.

N.D. Palmer, *The Irish Land League Crisis,* New Haven, 1940.

G.C.H. Paton and J.G.S. Cameron, *The Law of Landlord and Tenant in Scotland,* Aberdeen, 1967.

J.E. Pomfret, *The Struggle for Land in Ireland, 1800-1923,* Princeton, 1930.

J. Prebble, *Culloden,* London, 1961.

J. Prebble, *The Highland Clearances,* London, 1963.

E. Richards, 'The Mind of Patrick Sellar', *Scottish Studies,* XV, 1971.

E. Richards, 'How Tame Were the Highlanders During the Clearances?' *Scottish Studies,* XVII, 1973.

E. Richards, *The Leviathan of Wealth,* London, 1973.

P. Rowland, *The Last Liberal Governments: The Promised Land, 1905-1910,* London, 1968.

R.N. Salaman, *The History and Social Influence of the Potato,* Cambridge, 1949.

D.C. Savage, 'Scottish Politics, 1885-6', *SHR,* XL, 1961.

J. Sewel *et al., Education and Migration: A Study of the Migration and Job Expectations of Young People and their Parents in the Highlands and Islands of Scotland,* University of Aberdeen, 1975.

T. Shanin (ed.), *Peasants and Peasant Societies,* Harmondsworth, 1971.

M.F. Shaw, *Folksongs and Folklore of South Uist,* London, 1955.

W.S. Shepperson, *British Emigration to North America,* Oxford, 1957.

F.C. Sillar and R. Meyer, *Skye,* Newton Abbott, 1973.

T.C. Smout, *A History of the Scottish People, 1960-1830,* London, 1969.

T.C. Smout, 'The Highland Clearances', *Scottish International,* Feb. 1972.

L.D. Stamp (ed.), *The Report of the Land Utilisation Survey of Britain, Parts 3, 9-12,* London, 1939, 1944.

M.C. Storrie, 'A Note on William Bald's Plan of Ardnamurchan and Sunart', *Scottish Studies,* V, 1961.

M.C. Storrie, 'Two Early Resettlement Schemes in Barra', *Scottish Studies,* VI, 1962.

R.H. Tawney, *The Agrarian Problem in the Sixteenth Century,* London, 1912.

D.C. Thomson, 'Gaelic Scotland', in D. Glen (ed.), *Whither Scotland?* London, 1971.

D.C. Thomson, *An Introduction to Gaelic Poetry,* London, 1974.

D.C. Thomson and I. Grimble (eds.), *The Future of the Highlands,* London, 1968.

E.P. Thomson, *The Making of the English Working Class,* London, 1964.

F. Thomson, *Harris and Lewis: Outer Hebrides,* Newton Abbott, 1968.

F. Thomson, *Harris Tweed: The Story of a Hebridean Industry,* Newton Abbott, 1969.

M. Tracy, *Agriculture in Western Europe: Crisis and Adaptation since 1880,* London, 1964.

D. Turnock, 'North Morar – The Improvement Movement on a West Highland Estate', *SGM,* LXXXV, 1969.

D. Turnock, 'Some Geographical Aspects of Crofting in Lochaber', *Scottish Studies,* XIII, 1969.

D. Turnock, *Patterns of Highland Development,* London, 1970.

L. Volin, *A Century of Russian Agriculture,* Harvard, 1970.

N. Walker, *Chapters in the History of the Free Church of Scotland,* Edinburgh, 1895.

K.A. Walpole, 'The Humanitarian Movement of the Early Nineteenth Century to Remedy Abuses on Emigrant Vessels to America', *TRHS,* 4th Ser., XIV, 1931.

J. Walton, 'The Skye House', *Antiquity,* XXXI, 1957.

J.A.S. Watson, 'The Rise and Development of the Sheep Industry in the Highlands', *THASS,* 5th Ser., XLIV, 1932.

P.T. Wheeler, 'The Sutherland Crofting System', *Scottish Studies,* VIII, 1964.

P.T. Wheeler, 'Landownership and the Crofting System in Sutherland since 1800', *AHR,* XIV, 1966.

E.H. Whetham, 'Livestock Prices in Britain, 1851-93', *AHR,* XI, 1963.

I. Whitaker, 'Some Traditional Techniques in Modern Scottish Farming', *Scottish Studies,* III, 1959.

G. Whittington, 'Field Systems in Scotland', in R.H. Baker and R.A. Butlin (eds.), *Studies of Field Systems in the British Isles,* Cambridge, 1973.

J.L. Williams, 'Social Consequences of Grammar School Education in a Rural Area of Wales', *British Journal of Sociology,* X, 1959.

D.J. Withrington, 'The SSPCK and Highland Schools in the Mid-Eighteenth Century', *SHR,* XLI, 1962.

A.J. Youngson, *After the Forty Five,* Edinburgh, 1973.

S.H. Zebel, Balfour, *A Political Biography,* Cambridge, 1973.

Index